Palgrave Advances in Luxury

Series Editors
Paurav Shukla
Southampton Business School
University of Southampton
Southampton, UK

Jaywant Singh
Kingston Business School
Kingston University
Kingston Upon Thames, UK

The field of luxury studies increasingly encompasses a variety of perspectives not just limited to marketing and brand management. In recent times, a host of novel and topical issues on luxury such as sustainability, counterfeiting, emulation and consumption trends have gained prominence which draw on the fields of entrepreneurship, sociology, psychology and operations.

Examining international trends from China, Asia, Europe, North America and the MENA region, *Palgrave Advances in Luxury* is the first series dedicated to this complex issue. Including multiple perspectives whilst being very much grounded in business, its aim is to offer an integrated picture of the management environment in which luxury operates. It explores the newer debates relating to luxury consumption such as the signals used in expressing luxury, the socially divisive nature of luxury and the socio-economic segmentation that it brings. Filling a significant gap in our knowledge of this field, the series will help readers comprehend the significant management challenges unique to this construct.

All submissions are single blind peer reviewed. For more information on our peer review process please visit our website: https://www.palgrave.com/gp/book-authors/your-career/early-career-researcher-hub/peer-review-process.

For information on how to submit a book proposal for inclusion in this series please contact Liz Barlow: liz.barlow@palgrave.com. For further information on the book proposal process please visit our website: https://www.palgrave.com/gp/book-authors/publishing-guidelines/submit-a-proposal.

More information about this series at
http://www.palgrave.com/gp/series/15396

Beata Stępień

The Value of Luxury

An Emerging Perspective

palgrave
macmillan

Beata Stępień
Poznań University of Economics and Business
Poznań, Poland

ISSN 2662-1061 ISSN 2662-107X (electronic)
Palgrave Advances in Luxury
ISBN 978-3-030-51217-0 ISBN 978-3-030-51218-7 (eBook)
https://doi.org/10.1007/978-3-030-51218-7

Cover illustration: MirageC/Moment/Getty Images

This Palgrave Macmillan imprint is published by the registered company Springer Nature Switzerland AG
The registered company address is: Gewerbestrasse 11, 6330 Cham, Switzerland

Acknowledgements

This book is the result of a project financed by the Polish National Centre of Science (DEC-2013/11/B/HS4/01484).

Introduction

Since the early 1990s the production and sale of luxury goods in the world has been growing rapidly. The main force behind this impressive growth has been the so-called new, fast-growing luxury markets: a group of aspiring consumers from emerging economies led by China (see e.g. Delloite 2019; KPMG 2019; Bain 2020). Chinese consumers' purchases have already exceeded the annual sales value of the USA, a country that for decades has been the leading market for luxury consumption. Today when the luxury business has been suffering from the COVID-19 pandemic with more than 30 percent drop in sales in comparison with the first quarter of 2019 (see Bain 2020) everybody's eyes are set on China and new luxury markets as these can help to speedily make up losses.

The increase in demand from aspiring consumers mainly from generation Y (the so-called Millennials) is leading to the extension of the production of goods and services to the lowest level of the luxury pyramid. It is goods produced within supply chains dispersed worldwide and offered on a large scale, at relatively low (for luxury goods) prices that drive the luxury market today. Strategies to expand segments and extend brands are aimed at maintaining a global group of consumers who, as wealth increases, buy more expensive products from the higher levels of the luxury pyramid (Vigneron and Johnson 2004; Okonkwo 2007; Kastanakis and Balabanis 2014).

We are therefore faced with a global wave of the democratization of luxury and new target groups. Their expectations may be high (due to high professional and social aspirations) but different from the expectations of the previous, traditional group of luxury consumers living in mature economies. New aspiring consumers are younger and less wealthy than those from Western Europe or the USA and live in countries that are economically, institutionally and culturally diverse (Shukla and Purani 2012). Empirical research focusing on the perception of luxury or attitudes towards luxury brands in relation to the group of so-called aspiring consumers, focuses primarily on the analysis of the behaviour of Chinese consumers, which is understandable because of their importance for the growth of this market. Nevertheless China is not the only country where demand for luxury is growing rapidly and research findings so far clearly show that the new global consumer group is heterogeneous in the perception of luxury. This book attempts to empirically examine what is the perception of luxury goods by consumers in emerging luxury markets (Poland, Turkey, Saudi Arabia, India and Portugal) and what factors (market, socio-demographic, economic, psychographic) differentiate this perception in terms of the values they symbolize in comparison with consumers in the so-called old cradles of luxury (Germany, France, USA, etc.).

However the luxury business is still universal and global. Standardized goods are sold with the use of globally selective distribution chains, mainly situated in first-order cities around the world (Liu et al. 2016; Moore et al. 2000; Kapferer et Bastien 2009b). The high mobility of luxury consumers additionally legitimizes universal marketing strategies. The demographic, economic and market diversity of new consumers in relation to existing groups of buyers from the "old luxury base", combined with the observed democratization of luxury, raises the following questions:

1. What is the hierarchy of luxury value components for consumers in luxury rising markets and what are the most influential factors shaping this perception?
2. How creation, communication, distribution and monetization of the value proposition by companies influences the consumers' perception of luxury?
3. Who creates the value of luxury according to consumers and companies from within the luxury business segment?
4. What are the marketing and business consequences of the transformation of luxury business models and the growing discrepancy between what is proposed, communicated/expected and then received by consumers?

The book reviews first and foremost the perspective of aspiring consumers from new luxury markets: their perception of the value of luxury is examined. However the analysis from a consumer perspective would be incomplete and flawed if it were not contrasted with a description of luxury as a global business and a demonstration of how companies create, communicate, distribute and monetize a value proposition for consumers within a value system.

As both value and luxury are individually and socially constructed terms the book utilizes the achievements of philosophy, sociology, social psychology and economic sciences to describe these constructs as fully as possible. In order to provide a comprehensive presentation of how consumers perceive luxury (from the point of view of the value it provides) and the premises, manifestations and consequences of this valuation, the book recalls and discusses the results of research published elsewhere and the author's own empirical research on the perception of the value of luxury.

The author's own research was conducted using a mixed research methodology combining the quantitative (an international survey conducted with the use of an electronic questionnaire addressed to luxury consumers in twenty countries with more than 1400 responses) as well as qualitative research: interviews with consumers (individual and focus group interviews), representatives of companies offering luxury goods and research in the form of so-called mystery shopping aimed at luxury fashion retailers.

The book consists of three parts and eight chapters. Figure 1 shows the connections between the parts, the relevance of the individual chapters to specific parts and the logic of the argument.

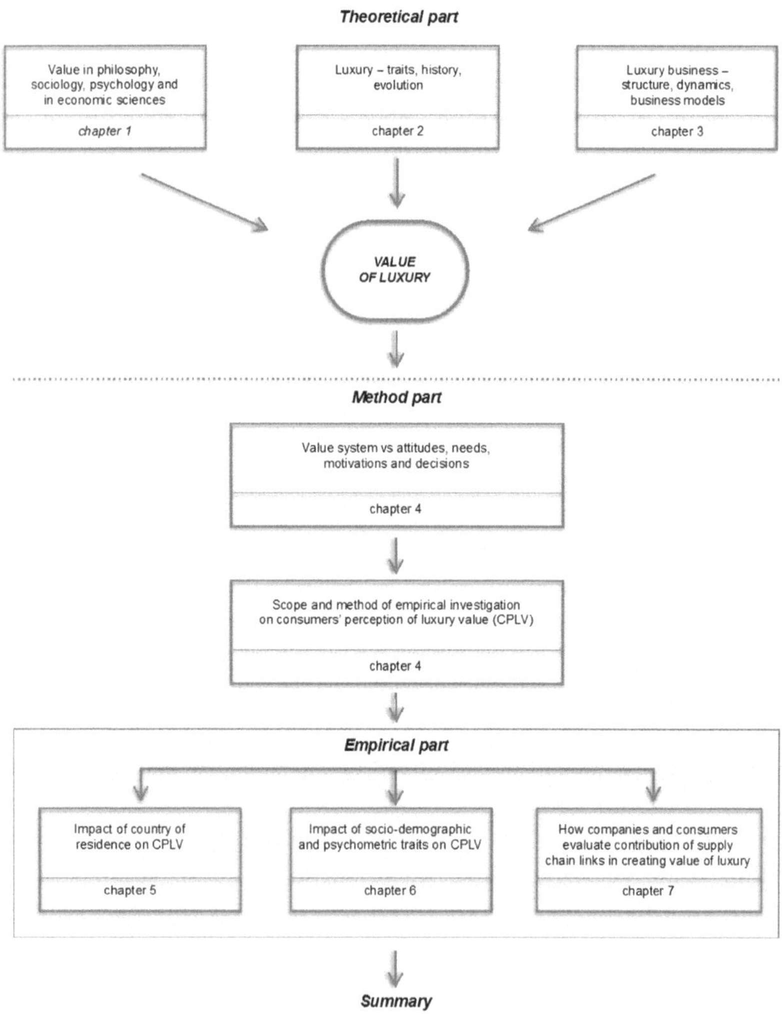

Fig. 1 Book structure. (*Source* Own calculations)

The theoretical part consisting of three chapters is devoted to the analysis of the notions of value and luxury. Chapter 1 describes the evolution of the understanding of values in philosophy, sociology, social psychology and economic sciences.

Chapters 2 and 3 discuss the characteristics of luxury and its evolution (Chapter 2) and analyze luxury as a global business (Chapter 3). Chapter 2 defines the concept of luxury by presenting its features and describes the past, present and probable future of the global shape and development of luxury as a specific category of goods and services. Chapter 3 focuses on luxury business: types of goods and services considered as part of the luxury market as well as the structure and dynamics of this business. It also describes which business models and strategies are used in modern luxury business. The so-called DNA of the business model in luxury is critically examined by describing in which areas it becomes more of a set of guidelines than applied rules.

Chapter 4 is methodological and consists of two parts. The first part shows the relationship between the value system and consumer behaviour in the luxury business and the research methodology used to study this area. The second part presents in detail the methodology of the author's own research together with the justification of the chosen approach.

The third, empirical part of the book (Chapters 5, 6 and 7) summarizes and discusses the research results of others and the author's own research on the perception of luxury by consumers. Chapter 5 presents a study on the market perception of luxury value. The chapter justifies why the differences in the perception of luxury values in individual markets may have not only cultural but also institutional and economic grounds.

Chapter 6 illustrates the convergence or diversity of the perception of luxury among consumers differing in age, gender, income or education and proves that psychographic factors differentiate the perception of luxury value to the greatest extent.

Chapter 7 is a presentation of the author's own research on the perception of the contribution of enterprises (links in the value system) to the creation and communication of value propositions for luxury consumers. A compilation of the results of consumer surveys and the opinions of business representatives reveals significant discrepancies in the assessment of this contribution and the role of the different links in creating and communicating value propositions.

The summary provides answers to the questions posed in the introduction. The analysis of the components of the value of luxury goods and the causes of the convergence/diversification of its perception among consumers (originating mainly from new luxury markets) is enriched with possible business and social consequences of the phenomena observed and the relationships discovered.

Contents

List of Figures

List of Tables

1
Value

Value, embodied in goods, services and in the process of offering them to customers, is today considered to be the core of business logic. The correct definition, measurement and analysis of value and the subsequent translation of its outcomes into action is essential for companies to be able to achieve competitive advantage (Gale et al. 1994; Woodruff and Gardial 1996, Holbrook 1996; Woodruff 1997; Payne and Holt 2001; Eggert and Ulaga 2002; Vargo and Lusch 2004).

The considered preparation of a value proposition depends first of all on recognizing what the value is and in what areas, activities consumers see it. However finding an answer to this question is one of the most difficult business tasks.

The problem of recognizing what has value for people and what it is and means for them is not only a matter of business practice. Questions about how people define value, prioritize its individual components and how they make decisions on the basis of valuation, have been the subject of scientific research for thousands of years and the search for answers to these questions has been dealt with by philosophers, sociologists, anthropologists, psychologists and economists.

B. Stępień, *The Value of Luxury*, Palgrave Advances in Luxury,
https://doi.org/10.1007/978-3-030-51218-7_1

This book assumes that people, when shopping, do so for a variety of reasons and that these actions always reflect their needs, although they may not always be realized. The rich and varying hierarchy of needs is derived from the individual's value system. This evolves and changes under the influence of the environment, although it always reflects the individual's worldview of what is good/bad, true/false, beautiful/ugly, wise/stupid etc. However economic sciences do not provide us with an answer to the question of what this value system, reflected later in economic choices, consists and how it works, because they do not explore it.[1] However since the economic foundations of the models are based on foundations whose nature is recognized by other sciences it is the task of economists to constantly observe and take into account the achievements of the sciences which are concerned with mechanisms of individual and collective behaviour.

The following are the fragments of the scientific output of philosophy, sociology, psychology and economic sciences which contain the most important findings on how expected and experienced value can be perceived, what influences it and what relationships can take place between an individual and his or her environment, that then make them recognize something as valuable and influence their respective market choices.

1.1 Value as Philosophical Category

Philosophy is the science that has researched value and what it is for the longest time, in the most in-depth and consistent but mostly ethical and then aesthetic ways. In philosophy value is identified with *virtue* and goodness. Value is the main moral or transcendent category guiding the behaviour of individuals (Tatarkiewicz and Krajewski 1990, volume 1,

[1] I intend to examine what value is, how it is formed in an individual set in a particular social context and how the mechanism of valuation is carried out. Today, however, there is a shift in the economic sciences towards drawing on other social sciences and integrating their achievements into economic analysis, especially in the field of research on consumer behaviour. An expression of such an interspecialist approach to research includes the analysis of luxury in its various versions, which is reflected in this book showing how many theoretical threads in the field of social sciences are drawn from by researchers.

p. 8). The theory of values is identified with an axiology within which it is examined/analyzed (see also Rogoziński 2011; Tischner 1993; Ingarden 1966; Znaniecki 1910):

- the nature of values: what is valuable and good and what is its nature: subjective and therefore relative, or absolute and objective;
- the sources, bases of value and the mechanisms of its creation, e.g. through valuation;
- classification and prioritization of values; distinguishing between immanent and instrumental values, which serve to achieve the former;
- shaping values in societies over a certain period of time and their impact on the lives of individuals and groups.

The above mentioned scope of axiology is a common subject of the research of philosophers, anthropologists, sociologists, cultural scientists, psychologists, or representatives of economic sciences (mainly those dealing with welfare economics or consumer behaviour), but the contribution of philosophers to the clarification and ordering of the first three aspects (apart from the analysis of valuation mechanisms) is the greatest.

This contribution of philosophy to knowing the nature of values is a consequence of the time and attention that has been devoted to it since the creation of the mother of all sciences. Questions about the nature of values have already been asked by classical philosophers and their views have become the nucleus of contemporary considerations evolving from monistic absolutism to pluralistic, epistemological, or finally post-modern value analysis.

1.1.1 The Essence and Foundation of Values in Philosophy—Immanent and Instrumental Values

The fundamental philosophical question (to which there is still no clear answer) is whether value (as a goodness, truth or beauty) exists in an objectified way or whether it is attributed to states (including things) by individuals. Philosophers have also been looking for what is the ultimate, most important value and try to determine what leads to it.

Many classical philosophical texts have attempted to prove that universal value as the supreme Goodness exists and is objective, independent of the judgement of individuals. Goodness has an immanent value, although various activities can lead to it, which by contributing to the achievement of goodness, have an instrumental value. This approach is evident in the Platonic recognition of value as a universal and transcendental category. Platonic absolutism is expressed in the claim that value exists independently of mankind and individual views and is expressed in moral standards superior even to God (Popkin and Stroll 1993, pp. 7–11). The continuators of such an approach can be found not only in classical, but also in contemporary philosophical texts. Almost all medieval philosophy was subordinated to this way of understanding reality, but it is also present in the form of categorical moral imperatives in Kant, in Rickert's neocantism, Sheler's phenomenology, or Hartmann's texts (Hartmann 1987; Scheler 1973; Rickert 1986). In these perspectives values are ideal self-contained entities, existing independently of the perception of individuals and although contemporary philosophy has not abandoned the search for a universal, objectified value, it has to a large extent abandoned the perception of it as a monistic ideal.

In opposition to the trend of objectivity of values many, including classical philosophers, saw values as being dependent on the individual and differed in what they could constitute. Aristotle, a disciple of Plato, already questioned that Goodness was universal and claimed that people, in various ways of life, could consider it good because it was happy. Aristotle was therefore one of the first subjectivists and relativists of the value theory and for its quintessence (i.e. immanent value) he considered happiness—"the action of the soul in accordance with perfect virtue" (after Popkin and Stroll 1993, p. 7 et seq., Russell, p. 205). Happiness is not a goal but is created by human actions, engaging in various activities (which have instrumental value), and performing them gives a sense of happiness. People can achieve this by trial and error. According to Aristotle they will experience it to the fullest extent by acting in moderation and avoiding drifting towards extremes in which the virtues are to help them: courage as a means between cowardice and bravado; pride as a means between vanity and humility; and finally generosity as a means between profligacy and stinginess.

In philosophy the sources of values and ways of creating them were also sought. Epicur, the creator of hedonism, considered pleasure while avoiding suffering to be the overriding value, which today is mistakenly associated with the postulate of succumbing to temptations or making up for the senses as the overriding goal of human action (see e.g. Krokiewicz 1961; Popkin and Stroll 1993, pp. 19–26). According to Epicur only "net" pleasures have value, i.e. those that bring more pleasure than suffering not only to the individual but also to the environment. Epicur's work has led to a distinction between the value of the means (an instrumental value) of achieving a goal and the value of the goal and effect itself. Thus the use of valuable, pleasant things can have a devastating effect (e.g. overeating sweets leads to obesity) and vice versa; fundamentally unpleasant activities can lead to net pleasure (e.g. tedious and painful exercises leading to improved health).

1.1.2 Value or Values, Coexistence or Hierarchy?

In almost the entire medieval philosophy the personification of the highest value; its objectified absolute becomes God. Only the revival leads to the extinction of the role of religion in human life and the considerations of values in philosophy move from teleological and moral monism to pluralism, relational theories, epistemological considerations of values, or finally the postmodern approach to this. The industrial revolution and the development of capitalism which led to the beginning of the age of consumerism, also contributed significantly to such a relativization of views on value. As Russell writes the entire history of Western philosophy can be summarized as the struggle of divine forces and the influence of reason and science on human thoughts and actions (Russell 2012). The scientific approach to value analysis dominates in contemporary value approaches and moral issues gradually cease to dominate. The debate about values is clearly moving in the direction of recognizing that many values coexist, although there is still disagreement as to whether they exist independently of individuals, are superior to them (neo-Kant, neo-idealists, representatives of pragmatism), or are only properties of the individual (e.g. Nietzsche or evolutionists). The issue of the relationship between pluralism of values and their incommensurability also remains a problem. However the assumption that the coexistence of many values is independent, lateral and non-hierarchical seems too simplistic. Such interdependence but also hierarchy is suggested, for example, by Scheler's or Hartman's classifications but it is also proven by the research of sociologists and psychologists on the composition of an individual's values. So if there is a hierarchy of values and one of them is rated higher than the other, then the former has more value, whatever it may be. In accepting this argument the debate is once again drifting towards the search for the Neo-Platonic Absolute promoted by American neo-idealists headed by Emerson.

The complexity, co-existence and interpenetration of different values manifests itself in the "heterogeneity of mental sources of satisfaction" (Wiggins 1998, p. 266) and explains the balanced evaluation of the desire for two objects, which differ in terms of their dimensions within the value itself, e.g. less intense, through longer pleasure and intense, short-term pleasure (Stocker 1990, p. 230).

Another important change concerning the analysis of values in philosophy concerns the departure from axiology towards epistemology: extinguishing the debate on what value is and what constitutes it to the search for mechanisms of valuation. Such a turn expresses a growing conviction about the pragmatic role of philosophy and the need for it to draw on other sciences. On the other hand the multiplicity of paths that analyze value enriches its understanding. However according to Dewey (1949) this ambivalence of stances leads in practice to an inability to conduct a theoretical discussion and despite the fact that more than half a century has passed since the concerns expressed by this author not much has changed in this area. Such a situation gives room in turn for development and total deconstruction in the spirit of the Nietzschean revaluation of values present in postmodern axiology (see e.g. Inglehart 1997, 2015). While deconstruction can be theoretically neutral and creative its social consequences are already a cause for historically substantiated fear.

1.1.3 Consequences of a Philosophical Debate of Value for the Understanding of Luxury

The analysis of the philosophical positions presented may lead to the frustrating conclusion that the multiplicity, mutual incomparability and interdependence of the proposed sources of values results in the impossibility of following a single course of thought without being accused of making a wrong choice.

However in this jungle of positions a wealth of findings can be identified which are difficult to find e.g. in economic sciences. Axiology shows how different understanding of values with which we deal and in which states and activities this can be found and experienced.

Philosophy's contribution to understanding the essence and sources of values is fundamental to studying luxury for luxury is not only conducive to pleasure, it is even created to that end. It therefore has instrumental value and contributes to the creation of Goodness as long as it does not cause suffering to others. Beauty, on the other hand, is considered an immanent value which justifies the creation of luxury goods with an element of artistry. Artistry—experienced aesthetically—also brings pleasure.

On the other hand some philosophical approaches to values, due to a saturation with normative components (what is goodness and what is evil), place luxury goods and services in an unfavourable light. Apart from artistic and aesthetic value the acquisition and consumption of luxury does not bring the individual closer to the ultimate Goodness in an ethical sense. It is not surprising that for centuries luxury has been, and still is, subject to negative moral judgments. However if we assume that one of the essential immanent values is the very search for a compromise between the pleasure and happiness of the individual and the non-antagonistic persistence of societies, the odium of moral condemnation becomes smaller. One of the most important distinguishing features of the luxury sector is the pursuit of beauty and artistic excellence (or at least uniqueness) while providing above-average functionality of the goods and positive consumer experience. Their utility value (treated as instrumental in leading to satisfaction) is therefore indisputable. It is the social desire for luxury and its uneven distribution and accumulation in the hands of just a few social groups that makes luxury an area prone to negative judgments of its value, just as it is not the hammer's fault that someone made it the instrument of crime, so luxury services and goods are not the carrier of immorality or negative social value. It is their use for the purpose of demonstrating wealth or emphasizing superiority over others that can cause moral controversy.

The works of philosophers in the field of axiology (although they indicate the difficulty of determining what is an immanent and objective value) clearly show that people in considering various states to be valuable, are able to hierarchize them and thus make choices. People develop (though not always consciously) valuation mechanisms in which not only co-existing and interdependent values and preferences (which depend on these values) but also current and future expectations and perceptions of the individual, influenced by the social context, play a role. The development of philosophy in the last century also clearly shows that an interdisciplinary approach is needed to explain certain phenomena. It is impossible to analyze the value of any good within one science today because it will inevitably create a narrow picture of reality. To analyze the value of luxury it is necessary at the same time to use the achievements of:

- philosophy, showing the whole ethical, aesthetic and cognitive range of value categories and their mutual coexistence, both in society and in the individual,
- sociology, illustrating the influence of the environment and historical-cultural context on the formation of certain values as superior to others and the social impact on value systems, norms and behaviours of individuals and communities,
- psychology, explaining the mechanisms of value systems, valuing and decision making, as well as the role played by personality, temperament, moods and emotions in these processes,
- economic sciences that explain (but also aspire to forecast) certain economic activities of individuals that are the consequence of a (discipline-diversified) perception of the usable value of goods or services as compared with their exchangeable value.

1.2 Sociological Value Recognitions

In philosophy the debate on values has been going on for many centuries and has evolved from one marked by normative judgments based on religion and morality, gradually moving on to a scientific debate on the coexistence and relational nature of values resulting from the combination of the biological, individual and social needs of the individual. Sociology, as a much younger science and derived (as is the case with most modern sciences) from philosophy, immediately adopted a relational and pluralistic approach to the emergence of values and their impact on the functioning of individuals. Sociologists have recognized that values are a social product although this does not mean that they are completely socially diverse. The subject of the research was the mechanisms of value creation in given communities, the processes of their rooting and the influence of values on the life of individuals in groups.

1.2.1 Social Functions of Values

Émile Durkheim and Max Weber (considered the creators of sociology as science) have already studied:

- what is the extent to which certain values influence the behaviour of people in a given society;
- what are the differences in values in individual communities and what are the consequences for their development;
- What are the relationships between values, social norms and human behaviour?

As can be expected there is no consensus in both sociology and psychology on the very definition of values (see e.g. Misztal 1980; Kloska 1982). Moreover as Hitlin and Piliavin (2004) point out sociological works focusing on values (collective or individual) have been rare since the mid-1960s. Due to the auxiliary function of the findings of sociology in defining values the detailed evolution of the varied approaches has been omitted, limiting itself to providing only the best-known and mainly contemporary definitions of the term. The values in sociological terms are:

- assumptions, largely unaware of what is right and important (Young and Mack 1959),
- generalised objectives which provide a framework for targeted human action; they define in general terms those desirable end states which serve as a guideline for human efforts (Smelser 1962),
- group concepts of relative desire for things (Leslie et al. 1976),
- the belief that something is good and worthwhile; they determine what is worth having and for what to strive (Haralambos et al. 1980),
- general concepts of good, ideas about the kinds of goals and activities that people should follow in their lives (Worsley 1984),
- situation-dependent motivators and guiding principles guiding the behaviour of a person or group which are formed from the first moments of life in a given culture and guide the individual in life (Schwartz 2007),
- general standards, higher standards (Johnson 2013).

Values in sociology are understood as the partial (apart from the individual characteristics that shape the value system) production of societies and their culture, giving direction to individuals, organizations and societies. Values are culturally accepted, internalized criteria (most often rooted in morality or religion) that guide people in their daily lives. They are a set of priorities that allow human behaviour to be categorized as proper or socially inappropriate. They are responsible for the stability of the social order, underlying social norms. The values reflect human needs and preferences in three different spheres: biological; social—concerning human interaction; social, but related to the institutional requirements needed to survive and create group welfare (Schwartz 1992). All three types of values are dealt with by both sociology and psychology. Values typically analyzed in sociology include patriotism, freedom, respect for human dignity, rationality, sacrifice, social equality, or democracy, while the very functioning of the individual in a group and the whole basis of these behaviours is much more subject to an analysis of psychology, especially social aspects.

Values as indigenous, basic components of culture, are more general and superior to the standards constituting their material. Values are often unconscious beliefs, a moral skeleton, talking about what is good and what is bad, logical—paradoxical, ugly—nice, durable—fleeting, important—irrelevant. Standards in the form of rules and orders for specific behaviour can be built from different values. The same value can also be a building block of many standards. This is the case, for example, with the sense of justice, honesty, scope of individual freedom, etc. Standards, in turn, are the building blocks of social attitudes and roles, the so-called second order components, i.e. sets of norms and values assigned to some social function (see also Sztompka 1983, pp. 128–129). Standards and values are also created by institutions: specific behaviours with a system of rewards and sanctions for compliance and violation (see North 1991). The institutions reflect in their construction the cultural elements of a given society; they are a kind of manifestation of the values and norms that society professes and through their functioning they contribute to the strengthening of the cultural elements concerned.

The culture of a given community (including the nation) is an element constituting the system of values of the society and the individuals functioning in it. Adjoining this the character and shape of the value system is influenced by the history of a given region (becoming an element of a given culture), the state and development of economy, politics or even geographical location. The social complexity of the "background" of the value system (also called ideological systems and half-baked theories about reality, see Denzau and North 1994) has contributed to a number of studies both in sociology itself and in psychology. It has explored how far the valuation and perception patterns used to interpret reality depend on environmental influences and to what extent they are common to people, regardless of where they live.

Values play an important but not always conscious and clearly visible role in action. As the foundation of the goals they stimulate individuals to act, but this stimulation occurs automatically and without the need for high energy. The system of values is a hidden, non-reflective guide to assessing and interpreting the world (see Feather 1995). It is used to formulate assessments of reality, it is a basis for setting goals, it motivates and facilitates choices in situations of internal conflicts related to equivalence of certain values or contradiction of internal values with the pressure of the environment for example.

With regard to the latter the concept of a pluralist value model, according to which, in a situation of competing values, the final choice is made not only by accounting for the benefits and losses of alternative attitudes but also by harnessing a sense of responsibility, courage and readiness to accept the consequences of a particular assessment, attitude or action.

1.2.2 Universal and Socially Diverse Values

An important research thread, both in sociology and in social psychology, is the search for areas of diversity and above and beyond the social similarity of people in the adherence to certain values. In addition to the search for these coincidences and differences there is an attempt to find an answer to the question—what criteria differentiate people with regard to their value systems?

The most important achievements in terms of arrangements for the universal values of an entity are:

- Kluckhorn and Strodtbeck's work (1961): suggesting that (1) values are beliefs about preferences (*what is desired*) and (2) internal criteria for evaluating what happens to us and *what is desirable*. The first thread examines sociology (especially when that which is socially preferred does not coincide with the preferences of the individual) and the second thread examines psychology (see also Oleś 2002).
- The work of Rokeach, the creator of groundbreaking sociological approaches to values that have inspired numerous researchers; differentiated between ultimate/important values (personal and social) and instrumental values (moral, competence) that reflect respectively the final states or goals and the means and mechanisms of reaching the former. He believed that needs under the influence of the social environment are transformed into values and he proposed a scale for measuring values (Rokeach Value Scale, RVS, Rokeach 1973, 2008).

- The work of Schwartz who developed the RVS questionnaire and used it to search for values independent of social influences, as they are shared by people regardless of their nationality or place of residence. He created a circular picture of values from which the adjacent ones, influencing each other, strengthen each other, while those lying on the opposite side contradict each other. His model has been tested and modified many times and is now the most recognized way of presenting the universal values of an individual (Schwartz 1992, 2012; Schwartz et al. 2012).

As Schwartz's work builds on and develops on the achievements of Klukhorn and Rokeach, the latest version of the circular Schwartz value model (2012) is discussed below.

Schwartz takes the view that values are relational, interdependent, but also mutually exclusive: e.g. the emphasis on values focused on each other weakens the focus on others, or the pursuit of growth is at the same time an abandonment of security and an abandonment of the status quo (self-protection). According to Schwartz all people have the full set of values described, although their composition and weight is already individual and depends on their personality and social influence and is a consequence of the external impulses and moods reaching the individual on an ongoing basis, juxtaposed with their needs. In the presented model the focus on oneself was made up of such elements as: openness to change and self-confidence. Personal safety is also a part of this area. Openness to change includes values such as self-management (associated with an inner sense of control), stimulation, identified with an inner disposition to risk and adventure and partly hedonism: egocentric sensual satisfaction. Hedonism aimed at strengthening one's wellbeing is combined with another element of self-concentration: strengthening through power and achievements and prestige. The prestige is also partly attributed to conservatism and is associated with a sense of security. Focusing on others related to the search for values within the environment includes the search for social security by referring to and respecting tradition, adaptation to the rules of the environment and submission to those rules. But humility is also part of self-improvement in the sense that the needs of the individual can be subjugated to those of the environment. The sphere of self-crossing includes so-called universalism, understood as tolerance and concern for the good of others, kindness: preserving and improving the well-being of loved ones and the general public.

According to Epstein (1989), there are two different value systems: one conscious (reflective and reporting) and the other unconscious. Such an internal dichotomy of an individual's value system explains well the internal incompatibility of choices with conscious beliefs but it is precisely because of the unconscious nature of the latter system that this ambivalence cannot be consciously and causally eliminated.

Among the studies that seek answers to the question of why and how we differ works on the search for the influence of various socio demographic characteristics on the formation of diverse value systems, and studies oscillating around intercultural ones, related to the analysis of so-called national value systems should be mentioned.

Sociological, anthropological, as well as psychological empirical research focused on the study of individual value systems in different configurations or social constellations points to areas and causes of discrepancies. According to the cited researchers the diversity of value systems is influenced by personality and biological conditions, as confirmed by psychological personality studies and animal behaviour studies (e.g. Michod 1993; Mandler 1993);

- race, ethnicity and gender:
  - Research on differences in perception of the importance of conformism and regularity, the concept of equality between white and black Americans (less important for whites, for example see Rokeach 1973),
  - Research on differences in perceptions of their own and foreign ethnic groups and family values (Waters 1990; Stewart et al. 1999; Ohbuchi et al. 1999),
  - The relationship between gender, values and social structure is inconsistent and researchers consistently report contradictory results (see e.g. Rokeach 1973; Prince-Gibson and Schwartz 1998; Struch et al. 2002 not finding gender differences vs. e.g. Beutel and Marini 1995; Xiao 2000). Although Hofstede has identified a category

that differentiates societies in terms of masculinity/femininity—goal orientation versus process orientation, the tendency to adopt certain attitudes is supposed to apply to entire societies,

- social class, occupation, level of education; there are differences in the approach to upbringing between social classes, occupation and level of education and the shaping of the children's value system (e.g. Kohn et al. 1990; Pearlin and Kohn 1966; Slomczynski et al. 1981),
- The family as a strong reference group (mainly parents, grandparents) shaping the children's value system (e.g. Gecas and Seff 1990; Simons et al. 1990), these differences also exist between countries (Silver 2002),
- Age group: there are many confirmed studies that values change with age (e.g. Hoge et al. 1981; Thompson 1981),
- Religion: despite the intuitive relationship between the system of beliefs and the system of values (as shown by the whole philosophical debate, centred for centuries around moral, ethical, religion-based guidelines on what is good/bad, etc.), research directly investigating the influence of religion on values is limited, or at least rarely published; the main reason for the unclear relationship between a particular religion and the system of values of individuals is a general, vague set of religious precepts and prohibitions, partly duplicated by many religions. According to Alwin (1986) it is better to study so-called religiousness, measured by the intensity of religious practices and identification with a given church/community than just belonging to a church or religious formation,
- Nationality: there are two approaches in the study of a country's impact on the value system of its citizens. The first stream of research concerns the identification of values at a given time within a given country. The second, much more developed, focuses on comparing countries: how certain political, social and cultural elements influence the value systems that later differentiate countries.

Researchers agree that so-called intra-national value systems are stable over time. This is due to the fact that values are fixed in the culture, norms, attitudes and informal institutions and the process of their creation and rooting often takes generations (see e.g. Berger and Luckmann 1967; Zucker 1977; Stępień 2009). Just as in the USA dating from the beginning of the country's establishment, high values of independence, equal opportunities and economic liberalism have been maintained (see e.g. Feldman and Lynch 1988), In Poland, 30 years after the fall of socialism, high values of collectivism or the status quo are still visible.

In the framework of so-called horizontal research comparing country value systems one should mention the works of Hall (1959, 1989), Head (1961), Gesteland (2002), Schwartz (2012), Hofstede (1991, 2001), or Trompeenars and Hampden-Turner (2004, 2011). For the purposes of comparative research there are also classifications of value dimensions which, being a cultural creation, differentiate the countries in which the Hofstede study is most popular, although the study itself and its analytical usefulness are often questioned.

The most empirical confirmation is found in the division into collectivist and individualist countries. Studies by e.g. Smith et al. (1996), Triandis (1995) Markus and Kitayama (1991), confirm the diversity between countries precisely on the scale of individualism/collectivism according to Hofstede. But even this dimension has been criticized. Oyserman et al. (2002), for example, raised the issue of small and undifferentiated empirical samples in the Hofstede study, based initially on employees of one concern (IBM) and later on students. Takano and Osaka (1999) or Matsumoto (1999), not only did they not find evidence that the Japanese were more collective than the Americans, but they also showed that the conclusions so far regarding differences in national value systems contain serious methodological errors. Moreover in a kind of contradiction to the focus on demonstrating cultural diversity, Schwartz and Bardi's (2001) studies show that there is a supra-continental consensus on the hierarchy of certain values. In 56 countries (over 40% of the sample) this hierarchy is as follows. The priority in 56 nations is benevolence/goodness,[2] followed by self-improvement, universalism, safety, conformity, achievement, hedonism, stimulation, tradition and finally power.

Another much more interesting direction of research (compared to research of countries according to several cultural dimensions) concerns not so much the search for differentiation as to explain the dynamics of changes in value systems in some countries. In Inglehart's research the contemporary, exacerbating social conflict between materialistic (modernist) and postmodern (postmodern) values is shown.[3] Developed Western societies are now entering a phase in which political conflicts arise as a result of tensions between materialists who prefer order, stability of the economy (with its active control) and post-materialists who, taking economic security for granted, focus on the issues of quality of life, sense of community and care for the environment (see Inglehart 1995, 2006).

In conclusion research on the influence of national culture on the individual value system still has to be treated with caution, especially if the base of comparisons is a culture categorization with methodological errors (as is the case with the Hofstede study). The influence of national culture on the system of values and later on the behaviour of individuals should not be rejected, but demonstrating it is a methodical challenge. There are at least a few reasons for this. The first is the ambiguity of the concept of value as such, which is expressed, in this book. The second problem is the measurement of the value itself (see below). The third and most important obstacle concerns the unclear relationship between the value system and the behaviour of individuals.

---

[2]The Schwartz Circle has been changing over the years, as have some of the names of individual values.

[3]The sign of equality between modernism and materialism is only justified with reference to the research of our western and contemporary civilization. Indeed the present is characterized by the dominant materialism, and the future is drawn as postmaterialism.

1.2.3 Importance of Sociological Research on Values in the Analysis of Luxury

Research in sociology and social psychology shows that the social environment has a multi-directional impact on the formation of an individual's value system. Although the research carried out by Schwartz and his colleagues shows that as people, quite unanimously, whoever they are and wherever they live consider kindness and goodness to be their core values and they value personal development and security highly, they will differ in their assessments of more specific issues. This differentiation is influenced not only by the genetically and biologically assigned personality, but also by ethnic and social origin, which later influences the level of education.

Sociologists' findings on the social impact on the individual value system are relevant to the study of luxury as those categories of goods or services whose purchase and use is motivated not by their functional usefulness but by social symbolism.

In the case of luxury it is the dimension of social evaluation of the value of these goods that determines their popularity. In this context there is a two-way relationship between individual values and social impact. Luxury goods can be viewed as valuable not because an entity classifies them as aesthetic or functional, but they acquire such a value in the entity's judgement because others judge them to be known or desirable. In other words, as in the case of goods from the area of fashion, the willingness to buy increases because a given good is considered to be fashionable, aesthetic and socially desirable at a given time. This social impact therefore shapes the value of a particular good or service, and also influences the growth of other value categories (e.g. aesthetic).

The research on the perception of the value of luxury presented in the second part of the book, also draws on studies looking for socio-demographic and cultural reasons for its diversity. The influence of e.g. age, gender, income, level of education or country of residence on the perception of the value of luxury is analysed. In addition to socio-demographic traits the influence of personality traits on the perception of luxury is also studied where the studies of psychologists provide a much richer medium for consideration, as follows.

1.3 Psychological Value and Value Judgements

Values determine the quality and meaning of human life (Oleś 2002, pp. 53–54). Psychological research on values analyses the process of their formation and the role in building life goals and needs, the choice of ways of satisfying them, as well as the influence of the system and hierarchy of values on the realization of life plans, or self-assessment (Mądrzycki 2002, p. 119 and further). As in sociology psychology assumes that both social groups themselves and certain institutional constellations can shape the values that individuals later internalize in the socialization process.

The study of values in sociology is largely consistent with the area of interest of psychology, especially in the search for the values of individuals. In contemporary texts on values both psychologists and sociologists quote authors from both sciences, treating their findings as a common basis for further analysis (Hitlin and Piliavin 2004; Oleś 2002). Although both sciences have a long tradition in value research it has not yet been established to what extent individual internal factors and elements of the environment shape the value system, how a value hierarchy is created, what causes individual value differentiation and how the value system influences the decisions of individuals. According to Hechter (1993) the difficulties in the general acceptance of individual findings both between and within sciences lie mainly on the methodological side resulting from (a) the "unobservability" of values, (b) a small number of theoretical indications of how values shape behaviour, (c) ignorance of the mechanism of value creation which makes behavioural explanations unconvincing, and (d) the resulting measurement difficulties. Hitlin and Piliavin (2004) are joined by two other factors: the inseparability of values with other elements of social systems and the still unrecognized relationship between the affective and cognitive decision-making system.

Values in psychology are defined as:

- elements of attitudes (e.g. in election and action models, as discussed in Chapter 5),
- characteristics of human potential (Maslow 1959),

- objective categories, related to morality (Kohlberg 1981),
- elements of the human system of beliefs that guide his actions (Rokeach 1973),
- the process of transforming information, energy and matter into motivation and action (Adamiec 1983).

To simplify; understanding values in psychology is reduced to what is important to a person because of what they think and feel (Rohan 2000). Modern value research focuses on exploring valuation processes. Cognitive mechanisms of evaluation are analysed, as well as those related to emotions and affective ones.

Further considerations related to the psychological treatment of values and valuation are focused on the recognition of two issues: the nature and significance of the so-called affective component in the value shaping and valuation process and an attempt to explain how individual data in the valuation process are processed by the individual.

1.3.1 The Importance of Affect in the Process of Value Creation and Valuation

On the basis of psychology values are treated as evaluation beliefs that synthesize affective and cognitive elements that direct people to the world in which they live (Oleś 2002).

Values are created in the process of socialization and are created through personal experience. This second source has a stronger impact on the way an individual behaves than socialisation (Brzozowski 2007; Cieciuch 2013). Both their own experiences and external influences are subject to "biological mediation"; the value system is in part the result of biological and genetic conditions that are reflected in the human personality.

The building blocks of values are information and emotions. Values are created through a combination of information that has been and continues to reach us throughout our lives and the emotions that accompany it. Emotions still have a scientifically underestimated influence not only on the very formation of values, but also on the process of valuation, so knowing what they are and how they influence us helps to understand how people think and function under the influence of what they feel. However the discussion on this topic should begin by presenting the main affective factors that govern our lives to a much greater extent than even the most progressive representatives of mainstream economics assume. The affective area consists of:

- emotions as primary elements, although they are gradual, merge with each other and give different variations of feeling (primary emotions have a different intensity, e.g. fear, fear, panic, pleasure, joy, euphoria; excitement as a mixture of fear and expectation of joy etc.).
- mood—a relatively long-lasting state with a certain emotional colour,
- affective style—an element of personality and identity, responsible for a certain permanent scheme of action which is the result of repeated admission/blocking of certain emotions and giving them meaning in the process of valuation and subsequent behaviour.

According to R. Shweder, "emotion is the whole story, a unity containing both somatic and affective events, experienced as a kind of insight associated with some kind of action plan" (in: *Nature of Emotions* 1994, p. 42). The basic function of emotions is modulation and selection of actions (Frijda et al. 1989). According to Zajonc (1980), affective influences can be non-cognitive; the effect is then "spilled" globally, unanalyzed, suggesting that both values and the resulting preferences do not necessarily have a cognitive component.

The determinant of most emotions are not the actual properties, the characteristics of the events, but their importance for the individual. This significance is attributed to specific events in the context of how much the condition will affect an individual's wellbeing, how much it is consistent with the individual's value system and whether it is capable of bringing the individual closer to his or her goal. For example the same music can evoke positive emotions and put us in a good mood but it can also cause irritation if, for example, we have to do some work and the melody distracts us. If we are vegetarians then an advertising billboard of a restaurant with a large shank of mutton will not have the desired effect.

Atmosphere is a long-term feeling of a certain kind of emotion but it is not accompanied by a decisional component, directing action. The function of mood is to modulate and select cognitive activities: mood changes both the way it is processed and the content itself which is the subject of the cognitive process. Under the influence of our mood we are more inclined to recall memories according to the given mood (see e.g. Mineka and Sutton 1992).

The affective style (in simple terms, temperament) is an element of identity which is partly genetically conditioned and inherited; it means a certain permanent tendency to a certain emotional response. Do not confuse mood with affective style. The mood of nostalgia, sadness and guilt can be felt by both born optimists and pessimists.

Processing information related to stimuli that cause certain emotions may be conscious or unconscious, but already experiencing emotions is a conscious experience (LeDoux 1995). People who experience certain emotions, or who are in a certain mood, feel more strongly about their condition. Moreover they better remember events that arouse strong emotions regardless of their direction. Emotions "drain" the resources of attention and information processing; a reaction to an emotional stimulus causes other emotionally neutral neural stimuli to go unnoticed.

Emotions serve as "commentators" of a given situation; thanks to them we react to a given situation, evaluate it against plans and effects. Emotions are used to signal whether a given situation coincides or diverges with expectations. Emotions are about some kind of harm or benefit resulting from the relationship between an individual and his environment (Lazarus 1991a, b); they are about scenarios of certain meanings, threads and they are embedded in the mind of the individual in a particular context.

According to Lazarus (1982) people constantly assess their relationship with their environment in terms of its importance to their overall well-being and, on the basis of this assessment, take specific actions. If these assessments are positive for the individual the level of safety is increased and the actions taken are a kind of challenge, not a threat. A positive perception of oneself in relation to one's environment evokes positive emotions which in turn intensify kindness towards the world and lead to altruistic actions (for an overview of research in this area see. Glanzmann 1985; research by Ashby and Isen 1999).

An important issue examined by psychologists is the attempt to determine how particular emotions and moods influence human behaviour. For a long time it has been claimed that a "emotionally entangled" man is no longer rational. It was assumed that emotions—especially strong ones—block the access of other, neutral stimuli to the brain and this hinders rational decision making in the face of not only a small amount of information but also its selective analysis. The last thirty years of research in this area have undermined this view.

Empirical research shows that people in a good mood:

- better recall information in line with previously developed affective and cognitive patterns (Forgas and Moylan 1991; Bodenhausen 1993);
- combine similar information more effectively, make faster and more accurate decisions (Isen and Means 1983; Isen and Daubman 1984);
- are more creative and original than when being in a neutral mood (Isen 1984).

People in a sad mood are more critical; they better differentiate the logical basis of argumentation from non-logical persuasion (Bless et al. 1990); they more accurately assess the probability and interrelationships between events/states (Sinclair and Mark 1992; Bodenhausen et al. 1994).

In other words positive emotions and moods increase the likelihood of actions that do not conform to the stereotype and negative emotions encourage refraining from actions. The special feature of sadness is the preservation of resources. The research on sad moods has indirectly led to the belief that people in a happy mood are simply less critical of the world and thus will find it more difficult to reach logical conclusions than if they were not positively stimulated. For a long time it has been assumed that perpetual sadness and prolonged joy "produce" mirror effects in the form of judgments and the resultant behaviour. This conviction which has lasted for years can be illustrated by the stereotypes of a cheerful fool and a gloomy intellectual.

Many years of research by Isen and her colleagues (Isen 1984; Ashby and Isen 1999; Isen 2001, 2003) prove that a positive affect stimulates creative and flexible behaviour[4] and that a good mood makes it possible to take into account and consider different, not only schematic, information. Positive emotions increase the integration of concepts and the ability to see the links between ideas. People in a happy mood work harder and try harder if they see that their work makes sense. They are also more motivated because they see more clearly the benefits of completing the job. According to the theory of evoking events in harmony with the mood, when we are cheerfully disposed we do see the world through slightly rosier glasses but it does imply that we cease to be rational and base our conclusions solely on cognitive heuristics.

Even ardent supporters of linking joy to a lack of rationality are already inclined to admit that there is not enough evidence that people with a positive attitude ignore or omit details that are important for the situation under assessment (Bless et al. 1996). Although people in a positive mood show a greater tendency to use heuristics in organizing data it cannot be proven that a good mood reduces cognitive ability, motivation and information processing to an extent that would indicate less rationality/logic (Bless et al. 1996, p. 665).

The argument that a cheerful mood which increases the tendency to use simple cognitive heuristics makes choices less rational therefore seems to be misguided. First, less frequent use of cognitive heuristics in a sad mood does not exclude their use at all. Moreover cognitive heuristics also means sticking to established valuation patterns, proven successful and efficient in the past. Being sad we are more critical and less inclined to act inconsistently with our pattern which may mean a total lack of rationality in the face of a non-standard situation.

Secondly, it has been proven so far that a man in a neutral mood aims at a designated, rather than optimal, level of satisfaction in his choices (Simon 1956). The moods may modify this level of satisfaction (to lower,

[4]Compared to control groups not in a positive mood. In this study moderate joy, not its extreme state of euphoria, is dealt with. Extreme emotions block, for example, long-term conceptual considerations and focus on preserving basic functions. What is more, if you feel strong emotions, your body blocks the functioning of the organs and vital functions that are not necessary for survival at that moment.

increase, redirect, etc.) but further evaluation may aim at satisfaction to meet temporary needs and in this sense be rational. The question of whether decisions made at time t will be satisfactory at time $t + n$ is a debate on a completely different topic as it concerns the effects and not the process of rational or heuristic evaluation. Another final argument is rather a question of whether, with the current state of knowledge, we are able to find in practice such a valuation scheme that would be free of heuristics?

1.3.2 Information Processing in the Evaluation and Decision Making Process

According to Domurat (2009):

- individual values are part of the individual's cognitive system,
- value systems motivate and control human behaviour,
- each individual is characterised by a subjective system and the way values are linked to objectives that are compatible with them and the behaviour that results from these links,
- the relationship between value and motivation and the value of objects and subsequent behaviour is influenced by the situational context.

Epstein (1989) drew attention to a possible duality of evaluation: cognitively conscious and unconscious. The first consists generally of a free choice from a variety of options after consideration of their consequences, subject to individual assessment as to whether they are consistent with its beliefs, accepted by others and lead to the desired goal. In the case of the operation of the pre-conscious system we are still not able to give the exact mechanism of its operation.

What is more, even in the case of the conscious valuation, there are various tactics, mechanisms of valuation, exploited by an individual depending on whether it involves a situation that is known to him/her or a new one, important/significant or a routine and whether the set of information needed for his/her analysis is possible to solve mentally. However regardless of how the process of valuation takes place and whether it is conscious or in a way detached from the individual's consciousness, it includes the processes of cognition, interpretation and evaluation—giving meaning and motivation to act (or refrain from acting). The conscious system of valuation leading to consumer choices is focused on in Chapter 4 (as it is also a matter subject to analysis by economic researchers). Here more space has been devoted to issues that are primarily dealt with by psychologists working with medical diagnostic researchers and trying to find an answer to the question:

Why do people remember and feel differently about the same event?

This question refers directly to the process of unconscious valuation and frustration of opinion polling researchers. The explanation why people when answering questions do not tell the truth for various reasons can be found in the discrepancy between the conscious and unconscious value system and analogous valuation processes.

Decision making is a process that involves many areas of the brain, mainly the prefrontal cortex (Lee et al. 2007; Krawczyk 2002). In the periorbital cortex emotional and motivational relationships with decisions are created. That is where preferences are born. The perioriorbital cortex also tells us what is socially compatible or incompatible with the expected social mores, allowing us to adapt to the environment. The dorsal-lateral prefrontal cortex is responsible for the operating memory and execution functions. It gives a cognitive sense to the situation and surroundings. The front bark of the rim bend is harnessed to work in a situation of cognitive conflict when there are different, equivalent choices and the possibility of making mistakes with consequences. In this area an analysis is made of the "cost-effectiveness of decisions" in the face of their potential effects (Jaracz and Borkowska 2010).

Therefore we are dealing with the processing of information by different parts of the brain and the way it is processed depends on where it occurs. There are at least two ways of remembering.

Memory (either explicit or declarative) is the ability to consciously reflect on past experiences. The hippocampus is responsible for this kind of memory. The almond body is responsible for emotional memory (strength and direction of meaning given to a given past event, often unconscious). Recording and then playing back the events takes place simultaneously in both centres; it is independent and past records can be cognitively and emotionally divergent. Emotional memory does not have to be consistent with emotional memories because the latter are written down (recorded) by the hippocampus (LeDoux 1995).

1.3.3 The Importance of Psychological Achievements in the Analysis of Luxury

The findings of psychology on value and valuation show how complicated and still unrecognized the matter remains. From the point of view of research on valuing luxury two issues in particular are relevant. The first is the area of emotions shaping the evaluation of these goods in the context of their demand, purchase and use. There are questions:

- to what extent value, manifested by the desire to purchase luxury goods and services, is a consequence of joy, self-fulfilment and well-being resulting from their possession and use?
- to what extent does the potential joy and satisfaction of purchasing and using a luxury item affect the subjective well-being?

One of the significant concepts in humanistic psychology is the organismic valuing process (OVP, Rogers 1964). OVP refers to the innate ability to know what is important, relevant and will bring a more satisfying life for the individual. This process occurs automatically: we constantly evaluate our experiences and actions in the context of what we would like to see and the result of this evaluation is a motivating factor to change (in case of discrepancies) or to continue and strengthen the belief in the relevance of our own views and actions (Carver and Scheier 2000). Importantly OVP is not only the ability to recognize an individual's personal interests but also the ability to know and choose what is important to others. "*It is an individual's characteristic to prefer up-to-date and socialised targets*" (Rogers 1964, p. 166).

In other words the creator of OVP suggests that OVP encourages individuals to pursue their development with social interests in mind. The concept of the so-called *subjective well—being* (SBS) has been the subject of many studies from which it generally results that people experiencing happiness take into account in their systems of values and actions the interests of others and the general—social interests. What is unproven and thus not permissible is to combine a high level of SBS with only the selfish motives and interests of the individual. Hedonistic and social reasons for the sense of individual wellbeing caused by contact with luxury will be analysed in the empirical part of the book.

The second important issue is a short review of the research on the very recognition of the valuation mechanism, especially the unconscious one. The following conclusions are drawn:

- Surveys on opinions about the components of values and perceptions of luxury should be treated with a certain amount of caution because people may be inclined to express their opinions in the context of what they remember and of which they are cognitively aware rather than reflect on the actual emotions they have felt and are feeling by evoking situations in which they have experienced luxury as well as goods and services they consider to be luxurious,
- The mood, emotions and temperament of individuals will influence the perception of the value of luxury and the assessment of how much such shopping and use brings long-term satisfaction and builds a sense of well-being.

Both threads are addressed in the empirical part of the book in the study of the influence of psychographic features on the perception of luxury.

1.4 Recognition and Study of Value in Economic Sciences

The views on value before economics was established as a science considered an analysis of its roots: work, land, or capital and what role money (not creating, but determining the exchange value) plays in the exchange process. The review of economic value views started again with Aristotle who differentiated between the usable and exchange value of goods. Aristotle analysed how the characteristics of objects and states and their attributes contribute to an individual's feeling of happiness. He considered the utility value to be a complex substance of things or activities and its magnitude was determined by the individual. The utility value gave meaning to the certain state or good and contributed to a certain level of (un)happiness.

However while Aristotle skillfully described utility value he was unable to specify the source of exchange value (Fleetwood 1997). This value was measured by both needs and money which made it possible to compare the value of different goods or services. Ultimately however, he rejected the needs as not quantifiable because they are individually determined and thus difficult to objectify. For Aristotle the inability to quantify needs made it impossible to express them with money. Although economic sciences have tried to solve this problem by formulating a theory of utility and marginal utility only technical success has been achieved, even though it is a crucial prerequisite for economic diagnosis and forecasting. However the classical philosophical dilemmas about values were not resolved, not least because it was conventionally accepted that it is possible and feasible to identify and then quantify human needs.

In the early Middle Ages scholars proclaimed that it is God who is the absolute value and emanation of Goodness and that private property, money and work are the necessities and activities needed to obey the commands of God and the rulers. People are to live in virtue, to work, though not to desire the wealth that is given to the chosen, anointed divine majesty. Private property and the primacy of the state and the ruler to give value to money were sanctioned. The value of money reflected not only the content of bullion but also the power of the ruler.

In subsequent eras in history mercantilists, due to analyzing the function of money, spoke about its value, identified with the amount of ore, while physiocrats, in turn, saw it in the ground, as the only capable of creating value with the participation of human labour. Later on work became the main source of value creation which is reflected in the definition of such views by the Labor Theory of Value (Lipiński 1981; Godłów-Legiędź 2010). The goods produced by work reflected its value. They also performed a variety of functions to meet needs and were therefore useful. However both the appearance and the satisfaction of needs were treated (until the time of the marginalists) as a kind of monolith, a black hole, not subject to analysis in which the matter of needs, satisfied by exchange, arises and it is on the analysis of the instrumental exchange value that the considerations were focused while developing Smith's works or disputing them.

1.4.1 Value in the Work of Early Economists

Before going into the analysis of this period in the history of economics it is worth noting the views of Smith himself, who, in addition to writing about economics, was also a philosopher involved in developing the moral theory of values. However the non-economic part of his work was marginalized by economists. Smith believed that the individual was rational but succumbed to a variety of passions and needs that could not be explained by rationality. Smith therefore assumed that people strive for rationality if they succeed in winning the battle against the passions that lead them astray and just as Smith's philosophical approach to values was ignored, reducing them to usable and interchangeable, so too much importance was given to the concept of market self-regulation which Smith did not analyse, to just once mention the enigmatic hand that seems to invisibly guide the market.

Ricardo has developed an analysis of the exchange value of goods based on direct costs; the amount of work involved over time. This narrow approach, based only on the quantitative approach to work, culminating in the creation of the comparative cost theory was later extensively complemented and developed by including further value-creating factors (e.g. Hekscher's, Ohlin's and Samuelson's [H-O-S] theory of relative abundance of resources, neo-factoral theories with human capital). However it was not only Ricard's work that led to the creation of H-O-S or neo-reactive theories, but also the findings of Nassau Sr. and the Mill family—father and son.

During many years of economic development it was not the land or capital but the work was the subject of an analytical concentration of researchers. Marx even made the manual labour of the workers the only force that multiplied value. As he argued it is not the workers but the capitalists who profit from the work of the worker and the profit is nothing more than a surplus between the useful value of the good (measured by the amount of work needed to produce it) and labour costs. The usable value is understood by Marx in many ways and yet inconsistently. On the one hand it is measured by the degree of satisfaction of specific needs while on the other the value of the product is determined by the amount of abstract work (physical and mental) and furthermore the value of the product is measured by the time needed for specific work: a set of activities necessary to produce a given object (Stankiewicz 2000).

The subjective-marginalist direction has grown out of the polemics with Marx, Engels and other representatives of the socialist economy, which drew on the achievements of the Epicurean philosophy. In defining values marginalists focused on usability as a function of satisfying the individual, subjective needs of the individual, who determines what he or she needs and what importance he or she attaches to those needs. Value in use is subjective for marginals and it is the market (not the way or time needed to produce it) that allows the exchange value of goods to be determined. By analysing goods as carriers, instruments for satisfying needs, a term and a theory of declining end-use were created. At the same time it was assumed that individuals knew their preferences and needs and were able to measure and compare them with alternatives. This simplification (which later turned out to be too far-reaching) has allowed the creation of aggregated forecasting models with respect to, consumer preferences and the development of demand and supply in different types of markets. Economics has become more and more mathematically sophisticated reducing its scope to finance while ignoring deviations of model arrangements from reality (see e.g. Ratajczak 2014a, b; Wojtyna 2008; Krugman 2009).

It was Marshall who initiated the direction of economic development which buried the analysis of values for centuries. This is because it brought the exchange value down to a category that is determined by the game of supply and demand. According to Giza, Marshall's position on the understanding of values is a manifestation of its relational treatment in axiology (see Giza 2016). Value is treated in two ways; it is objectified in goods and manifested in the act of exchange. Thanks to this approach the value has been quantified although the question of what it is has been abandoned.

1.4.2 Towards a Revolution in Economic Values? From J. R. Hicks to This Day

With the emergence of neoclassical economics and the theory of decreasing marginal utility it was considered that there was no further need to address the issues already established concerning the "origin" of utility value. The mainstream economists persistently ignored the arguments of heterodox economists concerning excessive abstractionism and the unrealism of value-oriented approaches. Certain assumptions were made[5] that allowed for the development of forecasting models which also made it possible to maintain that any deviation of model solutions from reality is a consequence of the simplifying assumptions made necessary for such modelling. The decreasing predictive force of the models was minimized by switching on additional factors (e.g. measurement error). Fortunately for the development of economics as a science the strong opposition of institutional, neo-institutional or welfare economics and behavioural economics to the neoclassical approach has resulted in an enriching of the economic understanding of the value, usefulness and rationality of management of entities. Table 1.1 presents the most important findings of the researchers related to the understanding of values from the moment the neoclassical economy was established to modern times.

The criticism of past and contemporary analyses within the framework of neoclassical economics concerns mainly:

- the abstract nature of economic models based on the axiom of rationality of all the entities involved in economic exchange,
- considerations of the behaviours of communities composed of rationally-managed individuals, while rejecting social or environmental influences on these behaviours,

[5]This refers to the assumptions of neoclassical models such as: rationality of individuals; acting on the basis of accurate and complete information and unlimited possibilities of its processing; comparability, transience and measurability of needs and preferences; the objectives are to maximize the profit of companies and maximize the expected usefulness of consumers; the environment has no impact on the activities of the market and the objectives of entities; making decisions using Bayes's conclusions of the total interchangeability of assets for money.

Table 1.1 Views on the value from the moment of the neoclassical economy

First name, last name	Position on values
John Richard Hicks (1904–1989)	The theory of extreme utility analyzed through the prism of praxeology; departure from subjectivity and psychological sources of evaluation. Introduction of the marginal substitution rate and the marginal transformation rate
Arthur Cecil Pigou (1887–1959)	The concept of optimum economic welfare; equating marginal social effects in all uses of capital based on the assumption that consumer preferences can be measured and compared
Thorstein Veblen (1857–1929)	Values created by communities within institutions. It is the social rules that give value to certain entities and things; they determine the hierarchy of social importance, status by giving value to wealth. Individuals want goods as instruments, tools to achieve socially produced value to achieve social status. The theory of conspicuous consumption
John Maynard Keynes (1883–1946)	In his essay "Economic Possibilities for our Grandchildren", he draws attention to the relativism of the value of money: money as an instrumental value, a means to satisfy other needs. In "Essays in Persuasion": people's needs seem to be insatiable and are divided into two types: absolute needs and relative needs, and the satisfaction of their consumption brings a sense of uniqueness. The latter satisfy the need for vanity, exaltation and are insatiable and infinite, as opposed to absolute needs
Clarence E. Ayers (1891–1972)	Two concepts of value: monetary (price) and real (technological) The price is not a monetary expression of total value as it does not reflect objective technological utility criteria. Prices are affected by institutional pseudo-effects, and these do not contribute to the increase in social and desirable utility
Kenneth Arrow (1921–2017)	Creator of social choice theory. Collective welfare as a value different from the sum of individual satisfaction. It is the preferences of the central authority that determine collective welfare and may not take into account the preferences of individuals, nor do they have to shape social welfare at an optimal level
Maurice Allais (1911–2010)	An experiment proposed in 1953, undermining the predictions of the theory of expected utility. People are not consistent in their view of usability: with a high probability of an event, people avoid loss, prefer certain solutions, with lower probability of an event they are more likely to take risks

(continued)

Table 1.1 (continued)

First name, last name	Position on values
Herbert Simon (1916–2001)	The concept of limited rationality and value-adjustment, not seeking to maximize usefulness due to the informational, computational limitations of individuals combined with the wealth of their sphere of values and preferences, beyond economic exchange
Daniel Ellsberg (1931–...)	The Ellsberg paradox; related to decision theory and experimental economics, It illustrates that most people do not act according to the theory of expected utility. Evidence that people try to avoid making judgments about the value of probabilities. He undermined the assumption that people are guided by the principle of maximizing the value of expected utility. In order to make usability theories realistic, there is a need for psychology of risk, not just economics linked to mathematics
Daniel Kahneman (1934–...) Amos Tversky (1937–1996)	The ultimate challenge to the theory of utility; the proposal to replace it with the prospect theory, originally called by the authors the theory of values. People are guided by two types of thinking: fast, based on cognitive heuristics (rule of thumb) and slow, rationalized. The most important findings of the prospect theory: • certainty effect: preference is given to those forecasts that give a certain profit, even if the alternative forecast gives a higher than expected (but uncertain) profit • reflection effect: the loss forecast is treated differently than the profit forecast. Where only loss-making forecasts are available, the participants in the study looked for risks and showed the inverse effect of certainty • isolation effect: people simplify complicated problems by focusing on what the different alternatives have in common The way the problem is formulated influences the chosen ways of solving it. This may result in an inconsistency of preferences
Gary Becker (1930–2014)	One of the first economists to examine racial discrimination, crime, marriage or drug addiction through the prism of economics. Many different types of human behaviour can be seen as rational and maximising usability if it is defined accordingly. According to Becker, people are guided by the principle of rationality because they consider certain aspects of a given behaviour to be valuable, even if it is fundamentally destructive (e.g. supporting a regime that destroys a nation, committing crimes, getting drugged, or being in an unhappy marriage); it brings more benefits than costs at a given time. He considered education to be the main value shaping human capital. The concept of good and bad social inequalities: the former lead to increased prosperity, the latter to decreased prosperity

(continued)

Table 1.1 (continued)

First name, last name	Position on values
Amatrya Sen (1933–...)	Criticism of welfare economics based on narrowly understood utility. Value is a social category; it is subjective; in economics, one cannot ignore the cultural and social conditions of a community's existence and functioning to assess how people value certain goods or certain states. "*Value judgement must lead us far beyond the functional utility category... we should focus on the violation and fulfilment of people's rights to freedom and development*" (Sen and Hahn 1996, p. 26)
Robert Aumann (1930–...)	He was the first to introduce the notion of so-called common sense and so-called general knowledge into the theory of games within the framework of so-called repetitive games. Like Becker he claims that people are fundamentally rational, even though their choices are burdened by a lack of knowledge and ability to process information. People rationalize their choices (not only economic) by adding values to various issues that are important to them at a given time or in the long term, and this rationalization is carried out with the best (although limited and even leading to catastrophic choices) intentions of rational behaviour. The utility value is not transferable; see also Thaler
Richard Thaler (1945–...)	It has proven the existence of mental accounting, which proves that utility functions are not continuous and fully interchangeable. The metal accounting system works before and after consumer choice: it provides input for cost–benefit analysis and influences the evaluation of the choice made. Mental accounting also involves assigning activities to a specific mental budget/account (money for food, entertainment, etc.) Accounts are created and evaluated individually and in different time perspectives. The value function is defined on the basis of profits and losses relative to a specific, but time-moving, individually determined reference point. The focus on change rather than wealth levels, as in the theory of expected utility, reflects the fragmented nature of mental accounting. Transactions are often evaluated individually, not holistically. Mental accounting also concerns sunk costs and has an impact on the way and length of use of a given good. Thaler also proved that consumers are guided in their choices by their sense of morality. Thaler's works, which use and develop the work of Kahneman and Tversky, show that the palette and the way of human valuation of goods goes beyond the concept of neoclassical utility

Source Own study using Godłów-Legiędź (2010), Sen (1999), Becker (1976, 1993), Aumann (1985), Aumann and Shapley (2015, Chapter 1), Thaler (1985, 1999, 2018), Tversky and Kahneman (1981), Kahneman et al. (1990), Orléan (2014), Bochańczyk-Kupka (2014)

- a focus on looking for general economic regularities so that they can forecast phenomena rather than explain them.

Using increasing references and drawing on sociology and philosophy in the research of contemporary economists show how far the neoclassical perception of values in economics has been simplified and, in fact, did not allow a solution to social problems or even understand economic cooperation (Rand and Nowak 2013).

As Sen writes, "*a man with a purely economic approach is in fact a social idiot. Economic theory was largely concerned with such a rational fool*" (Sen 1977, p. 336). According to this Nobel Prize winner the main values for people, which in turn promote the development of societies and their prosperity, are freedom, democracy or equal rights. They are the ones that foster the operation of markets in such a way that they multiply not only wealth but also social welfare. In Sen's works there is a clear reference to values understood philosophically, socially shaped and internalized by the individual. Economists should take greater account in their analyses of human attachment to freedom as a fundamental value that guarantees its social and economic development Orléan (2014) also points to the social and culturally conditioned shape of the market mechanism. In their work on economic models and laws of demand and supply and the hypothesis of efficient markets, Orléan refers, to the achievements of institutional economics. The works of the institutionalists show that it is the societies that shape certain values, contained in social norms and institutions (understood here as rules of play in a given environment with their apparatus of rewards and sanctions) which regulate social behaviour. Both usable and interchangeable values, as well as the market itself, are socially determined institutions; they have a social context and not a universal dimension. This approach calls into question the assumption of mainstream economics that markets are not affected by the environment. Orléan also uses mimetism in Girard's philosophical approach to its analyses (Orléan 2014, p. 51 et seq., but also Palaver 2013), which allows an understanding as to why entities (individuals and organisations) reproduce behaviours similar to them and those which they consider as a model and point of reference. Despite the unquestionable beauty of its argumentation contained not only in its factual elegance but also in its support by empirical analyses, such an approach does not explain why there are such entities that act against the accepted behaviour. Admittedly Orléan attempts to prove that the mimetic hypothesis allows an analysis of both stability and instability, as well as transitions from one state to another. According to him, in the face of a breakdown of the system or loss of social legitimacy for a given mode of action, a strong tendency to imitate triggers a set of corrective actions thanks to the "*creation of an infectious* imitative *dynamic*" (see Orléan 2014, pp. 60ff.). This, however, does not show where the non-conformist disembowelment, which acts against the wave and leads to the annihilation of the model, comes from. While the argument of mimetism explaining the behaviour of the community in the market (including the acceptance of prices or the regulation of the exchange itself) can therefore be accepted it should be treated with caution in relation to luxury, let alone art.

The view about the social origin of market mechanisms; consumption, demand and, as a result, supply,[6] is shared by many contemporary researchers who come from philosophy, sociology and political science, but and who analyze economic issues. At this point I will quote only a few researchers who clearly demonstrate that it is the social evolution of tastes and socially shaped individual value systems that guides the market by giving it a specific social meaning.

Appadurai defines demand as a function emerging from various social practices and social classification (Appadurai 1986, p. 29). A necessary consequence of demand is consumption, driven by "*eminently social, relational and active, not private, atomic, passive*" demand (Appadurai 1986, p. 31). According to this author demand must be seen as embedded in the political and social logic of consumption.

There is a circular relationship between demand, consumption and the social environment in which they are formulated. On the one hand demand and consumption are social products that go beyond the equation of price and utility, regardless of whether we refer to functional or symbolic value. On the other hand, demand and consumption themselves change social relations because of the role that goods play in

[6]Although it is supply that can shape demand, which is also identified and discussed.

creating and maintaining social relations and shaping supply through the emergence of social taste creators and ambassadors of new trends.

In classic economic terms of consumption and demand, a good—as a good offered to the consumer—leaves the market after production and purchase and its importance for the economy ends; at this point it becomes a private sphere, irrelevant to social life. In addition to their basic utility value, however, goods, consumed and used in public, have a social significance and communicate many socially relevant contents (Douglas and Isherwood 1979). In such an approach goods become not only a tool of exchange but an active participant in shaping culture and social relations.

Similarly Bourdieu (1984) writes about the social symbolism of goods, going even further in his considerations of the mutual relationship between consumption and demand and supply. According to Bourdieu the logic of production and consumption is independent and is organised on the basis of a homogeneous competitive struggle between producers and a similar, albeit separate, struggle between the social classes, which shapes consumer demand.

The tendency to consume selected types of products and services is a basic indicator of a certain social class. The universe of goods offered for consumption allows the social classes to distinguish themselves from others by defining and socially manifesting their taste. However these tastes are highly dependent on the goods currently offered by the producers. The expansion of production makes it easier to satisfy different tastes, but at the same time creates changes in tastes, as a result of constant competition between classes and drives competition between producers (Bourdieu 1984, p. 232).

The consumption of certain types of goods and services as a marker of social class does not only concern what is acquired and publicly displayed but also how it is used. Decoding to which particular social class the user belongs therefore requires knowledge of what and how to consume properly (Bourdieu 1984, pp. 320–323). This is particularly important for the consumption and use of goods with a high social symbolic potential, such as luxury goods. It is not enough to be an owner of luxury goods, you still need to know how to display them in order to be identified with a certain social class.

While the adoption of a broader sociological and philosophical perspective on value has led to a broadening of the scope of analyses, mainly on the subject of social welfare (see G. Becker or A. Sen), the basis for a new understanding of usable and interchangeable value in the context of consumer behaviour was provided primarily by psychology. As early as the 1950s Simon proved (1957) that people have limited rationality and are guided in their choices not by the search for the optimum but for what is good enough for them. In other words an entity does not seek to optimise the value in use of the goods it purchases in the marketplace because:

- there is no complete information on their value,
- does not have the appropriate apparatus and analytical mechanisms to assess the value of the goods in each case,
- does not have sufficient time to consider the costs and benefits of the transactions concerned, because
- in addition to economic exchange it has a number of other social roles and activities that are important and valuable to it.

The assessment of the rationality of consumer actions should therefore take place in the context and within the limits set by the possibilities of cognition and the environment (see also Kieżel 2003; Mazurek-Łopacińska 2003). Rationality can also be seen as an attempt to satisfy a wide range of needs, satisfaction and pleasure.

As Thaler (2018) wittily and convincingly writes the world is filled with people, not *Econs* and it is the former who show a number of "defects" and deviations from model, rational behaviour. Many of the findings of economists to date, especially those concerning consumer behaviour, are based on idealised assumptions. It can be assumed, however, that consumers, guided by their daily shopping habits do not prove their lack of rationality due to, for example, the small importance and consequences of such small value choices. Even if we find this argument convincing, it is to be expected that individuals, motivated by their propensity for rationality, will start a prefrontal cortex thought process and come close to the homo oeconomicus model in their choices. As behavioural economics show, this is not the case.

Thanks to the joint findings of psychologists and economists it was possible:

- to challenge the theory of maximizing marginal utility (Aisley and Ellsberg paradoxes, prospect theory of Kahneman and Tversky),
- to prove that in economic elections people are guided not only by profit maximisation but also by morals; for example, they are willing to lose out in the face of unfair practices in order to punish opportunists (see e.g. Etzioni 2010; Kahneman 2003; Camerer 1999),
- people make mental accounting (acts of mental accounting), as opposed to the assumption of fungibility of assets and money and are guided by the effect of possession, showing an "irrational" attachment to so-called sunk costs (see e.g. Thaler 1985, 1999; Henderson and Peterson 1992),
- people are susceptible to influences and suggestions (nudges) that change their choices (and thus the estimation of the usefulness of goods), as opposed to the assumption of money and property interchangeability (Sunstein and Thaler 2008; Leonard 2008).

As Thaler (1999) writes the value function, described by Kahneman and Tversky, can claim that it is built on the basis of hedonic framing. The assessment of the situation, in order to maximise the utility of the unit, shall be based on the following principles:

1. segregation, disconnection of profits (the gain function is concave),
2. the combination, the accumulation of losses (the loss function is convex),
3. combining smaller losses with larger profits (to offset the aversion to losses),

4. separating small gains from large losses (the gain function is the steepest at the beginning: the utility of a small gain can be rated higher than the utility of a small reduction of a large loss).

Based on the findings described here, Thaler (1999, pp. 188–189) proposes a clarification of the term of utility by introducing definitions of acquisition utility and transaction utility. Purchasing utility is a measure of the value of a good and represents a so-called consumer surplus: it is the gift left to the consumer after he deducts from the benefits the cost namely the price of the good. The transaction value is measured by the perceived "transaction" value. It is defined as the difference between the amount paid and the 'reference price' of the good; the normal price the consumer intends to pay for that product. Thaler illustrates this with an example of buying beer which we want to drink on the beach. If you buy it in a nearby restaurant you will find that a higher price is justified (e.g. the cost of operating the facility), as opposed to buying the same beer in a nearby shop (also Thaler 1985).

The assessment of transaction value is an example of mental accounting as is the approach to the use of goods in the context of sunk costs assessment. The more we spend on a given good, the more we will feel pressure to use it more often and longer (which is rational if the alternative is to buy another, equally expensive good)—but—even if we do not use this good according to our original ideas (because we do not like it anymore), we still feel a reluctance before getting rid of it, as if this were the case with cheap substitutes (Thaler 1999; Arkes and Blumer 2000). Further examples of mental accounting related to the perception of sunk costs include the decoupling of payment from consumption (see e.g. Gourville and Soman 1998; Soman and Gourville 2001), or the perception of price as appropriate, reasonable (Bolton et al. 2003).

Summarising the contribution of economics to what value is and how it is established a great deal has been done to try to establish and forecast how the actors will operate under certain market conditions, at the cost of abandoning the analysis of the mechanisms and causes of value creation (whatever it is). Perhaps the focus on finding trends in the actions of entities rather than what lies behind them, stems from economists' desire to consider economics as a pure science, free from normative value judgments. On the other hand, this approach is restrictive. One may fully agree with the Godłów-Legiędź, who writes: "*Economists, wanting to create pure science, deny themselves value, even though they call the science they practice the theory of choice. Given that the choice is based on valuation, it is logically impossible to consistently produce economic theories without value*" (Godłów-Legiędź 2010, p. 41).

An interesting justification for such a praxeological, pragmatic approach to values is given by von Mises, according to whom, in order to understand the economy properly one has to relate it to the motivation and actions of people who choose, sell and buy. Economics according to this author is the science of human action, changeable in time. However it is not a matter of economics to study the causes, motives and objectives of human action, but of exploring the methods and means to achieve them.

1.4.3 Consequences of the Understanding of Value in Economics for the Analysis of the Value of Luxury

As presented above the attempt to determine what is value to an individual has been almost excluded from economic debate for many years but the question of how the notions of value translate into economic decisions has been addressed. Apart from what constitutes consumer value, economists have been exploring how it is valued and exchanged. Fortunately researchers developing consumer theories have long since revealed that in order to measure consumer willingness to buy, their satisfaction or loyalty, it is necessary to first deconstruct the concept of value and then try to measure it. Today even mainstream economists are aware that consumer behaviour deviates from the rational behaviour model. The economists' understanding of values is too hermetic (limited) for the considerations in this book, although it is not without merit.

This relative utility stems from the dual nature of the concept of luxury: luxury is not only an individual concept, defined by the individual, but also business. In the latter sense it is a specific model that creates, communicates and spreads the value proposition of goods and services to monetize them. The final value of the company is built by the proposal of the utility value but also its consequence in the number of customers who have so far considered these products to be valuable enough to purchase them. The scale of monetization depends directly on the attractiveness of the offer and (let us consider Girard et al. 2003) the mimetic wave of demand. This broadly understood offer, including a set of circulating pulses, starts and accelerates this wave. The value in use is therefore instrumental to the exchangeable value for businesses and it is thanks to the latter that businesses determine their value over time measured by various indicators always reduced to money.

The term value as used is treated in this book as a result of an individual's beliefs and calculations about the ability of a given good/service to satisfy his or her conscious needs and not always conscious desires. The value in use is therefore:

- subjectively defined by the individual; reflects ideas about past, present and future desires and needs (*I always wanted to have it; I need it now; I don't need it now, but in the future it will be useful to have it*[7]);
- is subject to the influences of the environment; both past and present; it is also an idea of how the future influences of the environment will affect the individual (*others I have admired, have it; it is not appropriate not to have it; if I show it in public they will admire me*);
- is changeable over time; under the influence of the environment, experience, it leads to a change in the system of value and valuation (*I used to wear Louboutin shoes, now I still like them, but I don't buy them because it's hard to run after a small child and I don't work now…; I haven't heard about this brand but my friend convinced me that it's very popular, a sort of must have…; after the accident I stopped appreciating all these gadgets and focused on family and travelling*);

[7]The texts marked in italics are fragments of interviews conducted with consumers of luxury and their methodology, scope, content and conclusions are presented in Chapter 4. Quoting here the statements of the respondents is intended to illustrate the understanding of the utility value of luxury.

- value in use is the sum of: the value given by the entity to both the item/service it purchases; an assessment of the circumstances surrounding the expectation of purchase; an assessment of the purchase act and its consequences;
- The value is created by the characteristics of the good/service and the experiences, experiences and emotions associated with this good before, during and after its purchase (*I couldn't wait for this bag to reach me, the purchase itself was a pleasure—I felt appreciated; when I was strolling with a Hermés' shopping bag, everyone was paying attention to this characteristic packaging*, etc.).

It is also assumed that the relationship between the value in use and interchangeability is as follows:

- The willingness to purchase is a combined effect of: the current perceived value in use and interchangeability, the result of valuing a given good/service in the past and the expected value (in use and interchangeable) in the future;
- The act of purchase itself, as well as the circumstances accompanying it, create (increase/decrease) the usable value of the good;
- The value in use is compared with its exchangeable value: the price and costs of purchase and use and the price for which the goods can be sold in the future;
- The result of the comparison between the exchangeable value and the value in use is analysed by the consumer with regard to the purpose for which he or she purchases the good (privately used luxury vs. acquired for investment purposes).[8]

This book is written from an economic perspective. The perception of values through the prism of business pragmatism is characteristic for economists. The study of what it is like is intended to draw conclusions on how it should work in order to optimise the benefits for the company measured by money. However the main research perspective in this book

[8]The book does not analyse directly the declared purposes for which consumers purchase luxury goods. All categories of empirically analysed luxury goods belong to the so-called core of private luxury (cars, jewellery, fashion).

is consumers—the other side of the coin; a source of money for business. It is on understanding their behaviour and perception of value that the volume of this money and the economic success of companies depends.

1.5 The Inclusion of Values in Research in the Areas of Management and Consumer Behaviour[9]

The conceptualisation of customer value perception (CVP) is a challenge for both academia and practice (Woodall 2003; Zubac et al. 2009; Leroi-Werelds et al. 2014). The reasons for these difficulties are already set out in detail above and come down to five main ones:

- Value is an individually, subjectively and socially constructed phenomenon (e.g. Holbrook 2006; Sánchez-Fernández and Iniesta-Bonillo 2006),
- The components of values overlap and influence each other (in addition to the philosophical relational value approaches the Schwartz circular model, see also Woodall 2003; Tynan et al. 2010),
- Consumers may have mixed or even conflicting perceptions of certain goods or services at the same time, may not realise the reasons for these different opinions or may hide their preferences for different reasons (see also Dubois et al. 2001),
- The perception of values is evolving; people change their views, preferences and behaviours over time (see also Woodall 2003; Holbrook 2006; Tynan et al. 2010; Leroi-Werelds et al. 2014),
- We do not know exactly the mechanism linking value to purchasing decisions; the actions of the buyer may be partially inconsistent with the opinions expressed about the attributes of the value of a good or service.

A detailed description of the construction and value of components is a prelude to further measurement procedure. The right tools and

[9]The content of this subsection was partially published in the article Stępień (2017).

measures must be selected, validated and then tested. Another already practical challenge is to translate the obtained results into operational and strategic activities of companies. Finally, all these detailed and time-consuming procedures may prove inadequate in the face of rapidly competing markets. Companies don not need information on what and how customers value today. It is definitely more important what these customers will value in the future (see also Narver et al. 2004). Drawing lessons from the past and extrapolating results to future trend developments is logically questionable in a turbulent environment.

Despite the obstacles both business scientists and managers are looking for precise constructions and measures of the value perceived by the consumer which will not only allow them to precisely diagnose but also to accurately predict its nature in order to be able to monetize it effectively (Slater and Narver 2000; Woodruff 1997).

1.5.1 Defining Customer Perceived Value (CVP) in the Area of Management and Consumer Behaviour Theory

Exploring the value perceived by the client in business has led to an impressive number of publications describing the term as:

- customer value (Woodruff 1997), consumer value (Holbrook 2006; Sánchez-Fernández et al. 2009),
- value for customer (Woodall 2003),
- perceived value (e.g. Chang and Wildt 1994; Patterson and Spreng 1997; Agarwal and Teas 2001; Sanchez-Fernandez and Iniesta-Bonillo 2007),
- consumer perceived value (Grönroos 1997; Eggert and Ulaga 2002; Yang and Peterson 2004; Sinha and DeSarbo 1998; Chen and Dubinsky 2003).

The most misleading term is "customer/consumer value". It may refer either to the individual assessment of goods by customers (e.g. Woodruff 1997; Holbrook 2006) or to the company's profits from the value offered on the market as measured by the number of customers (e.g. Berger and Nasr 1998; Venkatesan and Kumar 2004). In the latter sense the customer base serves as a basis for calculating goodwill based on customer loyalty. The customer is a resource, a component of the measure and it does not matter how he perceived the value of the offer. It is enough for him to purchase the products in question to show that he values their value in use at least as much as their exchangeable value. The customer's life value (CLV, CLTV), the customer's lifetime value (LCV) or the life time value (LTV) serve as the basis for assessing the company's profit and financial value (see e.g. Venkatesan and Kumar 2004; Dobiegała-Korona and Doligalski 2011). Current and future revenues and the expected length of customer relationships and retention rates are used here as variables to calculate the ratios. This approach assumes, however, that the customer does not change his preferences over time and assumes that companies know and monitor customer satisfaction. In this sense the perception of value by the customer/consumer (CVP) is a prerequisite and necessary condition for an accurate assessment of the "customer value" for the company.

In the case of customer/consumer perceived value (CVP) the subjective perception of goods or services is measured. This book is dedicated to this perspective. In business literature on consumer behaviour, customer/consumer value (CVP) is defined from different perspectives (Ng and Smith 2012; Moliner et al. 2007; Mazur and Zaborek 2014):

- companies:
  - value as a consequence of utility of goods: utility value created by companies for customers/consumers, valued by companies (exchangeable value) and converted into income;
  - economic value for goodwill: the customer is a component of goodwill through loyal acquisition of its products;
  - value as the sum of perceived satisfaction: providing the customer/consumer with an above-average offer compared to the competition (which results in the above-average satisfaction of the offer recipient) creates a competitive advantage for the company;
- of the consumer:

- value as a net benefit: the compromise between the benefits and costs associated with the acquisition, use and disposition (post-consumer condition) of a product or service;
- value as a measure of achieving a goal, meeting customer/consumer needs through tangible and intangible attributes of the goods;
- Phenomenological value: existing not so much in the product as in the images, feelings, experiences of individuals; in this sense value is co-created by the customer/consumer in the process of experience; companies offer value proposals.

Table 1.2 shows the most popularly cited definitions of CVP showing different research perspectives, sources of values and its components. The table omits the value perspective as a consequence of usability and economic value in which the customer/consumer is a component of goodwill, as such accounting is not and will not be developed in the book.

The variety of definitions of CVPs presented in Table 1.2 is due to the different perspectives of looking at this construct. This book adopts a phenomenological approach in which the value is placed on the consumer's perceptions, both unconscious and cognitively aware, of his impressions, feelings, emotions, symbols related to the commodity and its current or future use, including the benefits and costs it will/have brought about by expectation and consumption. Value can be created at different levels of awareness (see Block 1977):

- pre-conscious, phenomenological, when an individual senses stimuli, absorbs symbols, experiences impressions, creates images of what jointly shapes the value of a given good/state, etc. but this value is not yet categorized and hierarchically hierarchized by it;
- cognitively aware: perception, introspection, reflection on meaning, benefits, costs, possibilities of meeting expectations, achievement of goals through possession/consumption of a given good or service.

Ng and Smith (2012) describe the four components, the conditions for this first, pre-conscious phase of value creation. The first is the offer itself, its existence. The second is the ability of this offer to do something,

Table 1.2 Definitions of the value perceived by the customer/consumer from different research perspectives: value attributes

Research perspective/approach	A value definition typical of a given perspective	Components of values
The perspective of the company: Value as a measure of customer satisfaction **Selected representatives**: Gale et al. (1994), Ravald and Grönroos (1996), Narver and Slater (1990), Ballantyne et al. (1995), Porter (1985), Vandermerwe (1993)	Gale et al. (1994): value is perceived quality versus price A measure of customer satisfaction with the company's offer compared to that of other companies in the industry. The level of satisfaction affects the competitive advantage. Companies create an offer of value, consumers/customers evaluate it in comparison with other available offers on the market	Value for the customer = relative overall quality score of the offer *x* quality weight (in a given industry and in case of a company) + relative price compared to the competition; competitive score *x* price weight (in a given industry and in case of a company)
The consumer perspective: Value as net benefit **Selected representatives**: Anderson and Narus (1998), Butz and Goodstein (1996), Chen and Dubinsky (2003), Dodds et al. (1991), Grönroos (1997), Woodall (2003), Zeithaml (1988)	Zeithaml (1988) General assessment of the utility of a product based on the perception of what is offered and what is given in return	Value as a game effect, trade off between costs and benefits; individual, subjective, empirical; is the consumer's assessment. It takes into account both internal and external CVP sources. Perceived, generally understood quality affects the perceived value and determines the intention to purchase
	Butz and Goodstein (1996). The emotional bond established between the customer and the manufacturer after the consumer bought the product	Value as a hedonic, emotional construction that is influenced by attributes of a higher level and not just material benefits and costs
	Chen and Dubinsky (2003) Consumers' perception of net benefits obtained in exchange for costs incurred to obtain the desired benefits	A conceptual model of perceived customer value in business-to-consumer e-commerce, where the key value components are: experience in online shopping, perceived product quality, perceived risk and product price

(continued)

Table 1.2 (continued)

Research perspective/approach	A value definition typical of a given perspective	Components of values
	Woodall (2003): A personal perception of the benefit of a customer's relationship with an organization's offering: may occur as a reduction in sacrifice, an increase in benefit (defined and expressed rationally or intuitively); or the aggregation of any of these components over time	Five notions of value: net worth, marketing value, delivered value, sales value and reasonable value. The value can also be categorised temporarily: ex-ante, ex-post, transaction value, sales value
	Smith and Colgate (2007): For consumers, value is what they receive in relation to what they have to give up	Dimensions of the value: functional/instrumental, empirical/hedonic, symbolic/expressive and cost/size of sacrifice. Value is created by the activities of the value chain; Value sources are: information, products, interactions, environment, chain participants
Customer/consumer perspective: Value as a measure of achievement **Selected representatives**: Beverland and Lockshin (2003), Woodruff (1997)	Woodruff (1997) Customer preferences for assessing product attributes and consequences; the extent to which products/services facilitate (or block) the achievement of customer objectives	Value is reflected not only in the attributes of the product and its use, but also in the process of distribution, purchase or general communication (or cooperation) between the company and the customer
The consumer perspective: Value as a phenomenological construction: felt, experienced and co-created by the consumer **Selected representatives**: Holbrook (1996, 2006), Pine et al. (1999), Mazur and Zaborek (2014), Prahalad and Ramaswamy (2004), Schmitt (2010) Szymura-Tyc (2006) Vargo and Lusch (2004, 2008)	Holbrook (1996, 2006) Interactive, relativistic experience of preferences	Three dichotomies shape consumer value: (1) external and internal signals, (2) self-centered perception and perception by others and (3) active and reactive behaviour. These dichotomies form a unique constellation of attributes (joy, aesthetic, social, functional, etc. see also below)

(continued)

Table 1.2 (continued)

Research perspective/approach	A value definition typical of a given perspective	Components of values
	Vargo and Lusch (2004, 2008): The value is idiosyncratic, empirical, contextual and meaningful; always unambiguously and phenomenologically determined by the beneficiary	Vargo and Lusch (2008): Companies do NOT provide value, they offer a value proposition. Customers co-create value, value creation is a relationship, an interactive process between the perception and experience of a good during consumption in a given context, occurring on many levels
	Szymura-Tyc (2006) Value is a subjective category, situational, perceived by the consumer, dynamic (pp. 75–76). It is co-created by the consumer. The value obtained may be different from the expected value (where it is created, among others, by marketing communication of the company)	Customer/consumer value is also a marketing category (p. 64), as it is shaped, among other things, in the process of communicating and offering goods on the market, but it is the consumer who creates it thanks to his or her ideas about the characteristics of the goods and the benefits they can obtain

Source Own study

the ability to meet expectations, both functional ones and everything else (affordance, see also Gibson 2002). In this sense the LV bag is not only supposed to be comfortable (practical) and enjoyable, but also to be recognizable and raise social status. The latter expectation is closely linked to the third value-building condition—context. For example, in the early 1990s colourful plastic advertising bags or carbonated beverage cans were not so much bought for their packaging in Poland as they were synonymous with luxury for average citizen (Boćkowska 2017). Value is created by context; role, applicable standards, or structure or social relationship with other market participants and is related to the use of the commodity in the given circumstances (Archpru Akaka and Chandler 2011). The use of a Bentley by the Queen of England adds prestige to this brand while the possession of such a car by a rapper who is famous for his scandals, generally weakens this prestige.

The last element that creates value at the pre-conscious level is the ability of the consumer to interact with a given commodity (agency, see also Arnould and Thompson 2005; McCracken 1986; Bourdieu 1977). In relation to luxury it is not enough to be surrounded by luxury in order to be automatically recognised as a member of an elite society. It is still necessary to have certain social competences, a sense of taste and taste, etc., in order for luxury goods to properly fulfil their role by emphasizing the qualities and status of their owner (see Bourdieu 1977).

Value at the conscious level is an individual assessment of value formed at the pre-conscious level (both at the waiting and consumption stage). This is where the cognitive calculation of the benefits and costs associated with the purchase and consumption of a given good comes into play in the context of the objectives and expectations set for it. For a long time the development of literature on customer and consumer value has focused on the cognitive, evaluative level. It was only Holbrook, Vargo and Lusch and researchers of the so-called culture of consumption that drew attention to the earlier stage of shaping values, which is a dynamic category shaped by the consumer's perceptions and experiences in a given context.

The understanding of values presented here is in line with the S-D, service—dominant logic, (Vargo and Lusch 2004, 2008; Lusch and Nambisan 2015; Brodie et al. 2019), where it is the consumer who co-creates the value of a given good on the basis of a value proposition provided by the company. Such an understanding means at the same time a process-oriented and interactive approach to value creation which assumes that we may have a different perception and assessment of the value of a good or service by the consumer:

1. before consumption—*expected value*;
2. during consumption—the value consumed in a specific context (*value in use and value in context*).

Both the expected and consumed value is shaped at the pre-conscious level and cognitively assessed at the cognitive, conscious level. It is also worth noting that only when the consumer is waiting to buy a given good or service, which he has not experienced before, can we speak of the lack of influence of the consumed value on the one expected. But even when the consumer shapes the value of a given good before its consumption he or she refers not only to the ideas about the future benefits (and costs) associated with it, but also recalls the experience and context associated with the purchase and consumption of similar or completely different goods (as a kind of counterpoint to future purchase and consumption). In other words, the expected value is, inter alia, the product of the consumer's past experience of consuming similar or the same goods or services.

Through the use of goods consumers create value in a given social and relational context (*co-create value*) but do not necessarily *co-produce the* good. They give it social significance, e.g., they show new applications of a given good in a specific context, they spread information about goods or services but do not have to participate in the process of creating an offer by the company.

1.5.2 Components of Value Perceived by the Consumer

The definitions and characteristics of the CVP listed in Table 1.2 also indicate the value components. Benefits and sacrifices/costs related to the purchase, use and disposal of a given good can be both tangible and intangible. Regardless of the location of a particular value element (internal, personalized in the product/service or autonomously created by the entity or external; provided by vendors, other consumers, etc.), the value element is not necessarily the same as the value element itself.), the range of benefits can be divided into functional, emotional or social. However these three basic value components are further delimited. Table 1.3 shows the different CVP components/components identified by the authors who developed these categorisations for the purpose of creating measurement tools.

The most elaborate typology of value components was proposed by Holbrook (1999, 2006) basing it on extensive studies and achievements in psychology, anthropology and sociology. He proposed three dimensions: external values in relation to internal values; self-centred and oriented to others and: created by an individual (so called active) vs.

Table 1.3 Customer/consumer value components (CVP)

Value components	Meaning	Authors, creators and propagators
Price as a value indicator	Viewing price as an indicator of the value in use of a good	Zeithaml (1988), part of the utility value at Sweeney and Soutar (2001)
Cost/sacrifice	Tangible and intangible costs associated with the purchase and use of goods	Zeithaml (1988), Smith and Colgate (2007)
Usable/economic	Received benefits at a price	Sweeney and Soutar (2001)
Functional	Expected performance, technical parameters, durability, efficiency, etc.: degree of satisfaction of the needs for the performance of specific, defined activities	Sheth et al. (1991), Sweeney and Soutar (2001), Smith and Colgate (2007), Sanchez-Fernandez and Iniesta-Bonnilo (2006), Wiedmann et al. (2009); part of Brand Luxury Index (Vigneron and Johnson, 2004)
Epistemic	innovation, novelty, element of novelty, new technical knowledge	Sheth et al. (1991), Pura (2005)
Contextual	Generated by the situational context	Sheth et al. (1991), Pura (2005), Vargo and Lusch (2004, 2008)
Social	Ability to build a specific social image of the owner of a given good	Sheth et al. (1991), Sweeney and Soutar (2001), Pura (2005), Sanchez-Fernandez and Iniesta-Bonnilo (2006), Sanchez-Fernandez et al. (2009), Wiedmann et al. (2009); part of Brand Luxury Index (Vigneron and Johnson 2004)
Emotional/hedonic	Effectively created by referring to feelings of comfort, safety, intensity and consequences of use; excitement, joy, satisfaction, fear, guilt caused by purchase, possession, use, public exposure	Sheth et al. (1991), Sweeney and Soutar (2001), Pura (2005); Sanchez-Fernandez and Iniesta-Bonnilo (2006), Holbrook (1999, 2006); part of Brand Luxury Index (Vigneron and Johnson 2004)

(continued)

Table 1.3 (continued)

Value components	Meaning	Authors, creators and propagators
Experience	Hedonic, social, conditional and epistemic: built through the assessment of pleasure and cost to the individual in a social context	Holbrook (1999—as a joy); Smith and Colgate (2007); part of Brand Luxury Index (Vigneron and Johnson 2004)
Altruistic/ethical	evaluation of benefits and costs through the prism of individual morality and moral social principles	Holbrook (1999), Sanchez-Fernandez et al. (2009)
aesthetic	Beauty, artistry, aesthetic experience	Holbrook (1999), Sanchez-Fernandez et al. (2009), Gallarza et al. (2015), Mathwick et al. (2001), part of Brand Luxury Index (Vigneron and Johnson 2004)
Symbolic/expression	Closer to society; benefits to the individual from owning, using, displaying the good in public	Kapferer (1997), Smith and Colgate (2007)

Source Own study

		Extrinsic	*Intrinsic*
Self – oriented	Active	**Utilitarian** Efficiency (eg. Convenience)	**Emotional** Play (eg. Fun)
	Reactive	**Excellence** (eg. Quality)	**Aesthetic** (eg Beauty)
Other- oriented	Active	**Social** Status (eg. Impression Management)	**Altruistic** Ethics (eg. Justice)
	Reactive	**Esteem** (eg. Posession)	**Spirituality** (eg. Sacredness)

Fig. 1.1 Typology of values according to M. Holbrook (*Source* Holbrook [1999, p. 12])

reactive, resultant types of values, created by external stimuli. The dimensions thus presented allowed to create a matrix with eight categories of customer values: effectiveness (functionality), excellence, status, respect, play, aesthetics, ethics and spirituality (see Fig. 1.1).

Holbrook's typology includes all types of value components, modified and subsequently operationalised by other authors. But this multidimensional structure, deeply rooted in psychological and behavioural axiology, was difficult to operate because of overlapping categories. As the author himself points out all types of values can coexist within a single consumption experience and are related to each other. Waiting for a Birkin bag (one of Hermés' most iconic products) may cause frustration and excitement but these emotions will probably increase the level of joy caused by possession and public exposure. Joy reinforces the feeling that the Hermés bag has the ability to signal social status and gives the owner esteem. In 2017 the Holbrook typology, although it has repeatedly served as a starting point for others to create their own measuring scales, has finally been fully operationalised and described in an article by Gallarza et al. (2017).

The diversity of the components of the value, shown in Table 1.3, reflects the multidimensional and subjective nature of the CVP. Created by an individual the CVP is the result of the individual's ideas, needs, preferences, subject to environmental influences.

There are several types of external influences that shape CVP. The first are the entities participating in the value system: co-creating, communicating and delivering a value proposition to the customer.[10] They emit different types of information, which are partly embodied in products/services. Another important centre of influence is other consumers; having their own ideas about the value of the goods in question, they issue information about the level of expectations and satisfaction with the use of the goods (e.g. by displaying the goods publicly in a specific context), or they express their support for the various activities of the companies creating the value proposition. The social perception of a company's value proposition is also shaped by the cultural, institutional, political and economic influences of the place (e.g. country, region, specific special location) and the group within which consumers function and will function (Overby et al. 2005). CVP can also change dynamically depending on the specific situational context (Holbrook 1996;

[10] Participants in the supply system (linked by supply chain relationships) create a value proposition for the customer/consumer, hence the term value system is used.

Ravald and Grönroos 1996; Flint and Woodruff 2001) or the given availability of options (Anderson and Narus 1998; Eggert and Ulaga 2002). Research on these externalities can therefore be carried out through the prism of cultural, institutional, chain or value system input, industry business models or the strategic perspective of a particular company. Figure 1.2 shows a simplified evaluation process and the influence of internal (individual) and external (context) factors on the final character of the CVP.

However the separation of internal and external signals does not reveal the nature of their interaction and does not fully reflect the causal logic of shaping the value perceived by the consumer. Both the evaluation of a proposal for the value of a given good and its subsequent consumption takes place in a specific situational and social context. Both expected and experienced value is influenced by an individual's perceptions of the characteristics of the good itself linked to the purposes to be achieved through them. This assessment is also influenced by the public perception of the good itself, as well as its owner who consumes/exposes the product in a particular social space and time.

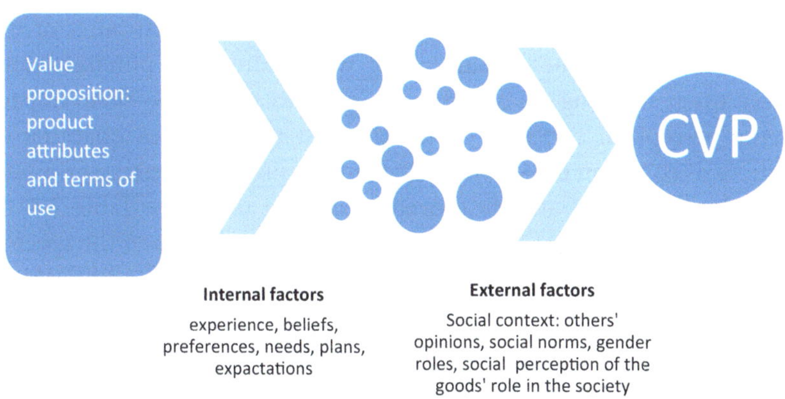

Fig. 1.2 Influence of internal (individual) and external (context) factors on CVP (*Source* Own study)

1.6 Measuring Tools for Consumer Value Perception—Why Do Quantitative Methods Prevail in Research?

The type, methods and tools of empirical research on CVP should be determined by research needs. For example, qualitative research, in the form of participatory observation or hidden purchases, will make it possible to track, for example, the purchasing process of the consumer and identify the empirical, hedonic value created by this particular process. However they will not answer the question of what components of the value of a good is valued by the consumer and how he or she prioritises them, as the act of purchase and the emotions accompanying it can influence this assessment. Quantitative studies on the assessment of benefits/costs related to the purchase and consumption of goods are, in turn, the resultant of the expected and experienced value: past consumption experiences, perceptions of these goods in relation to expectations of possible future purchase plans (Churchill and Surprenant 1982; Spreng et al. 1996).

Different sets of methods should be used when examining the perceived value of an object/service (as the sum of the attributes of the good itself and all the circumstances surrounding the purchase) and others when focusing on specific processes to determine their impact on the perception of value. While the first type justifies quantitative methods as common the second type requires qualitative testing or mixed methods. The use of already proven measuring tools (see Table 1.4) is justifiable, provided that they allow the value components of the specific goods to be measured in full. The use of PERVAL or SERV—PERVAL is justified if the individual scales actually reflect the specific characteristics of industry/sector/segment goods and are tailored to the context of the country in which the measurement is made. For example, the use of validated scales in the tourism sector to measure health care satisfaction in Germany and Saudi Arabia requires far-reaching modifications, as both the content of the statements do not fully correspond to the sector under consideration and the importance of the components varies greatly due to the culture and institutional differences in these countries.

Table 1.4 Most common CVP measurement tools for science and business practice

Authors	Approach, characteristics	Scales, measurement components/comment
Zeithaml (1988)	One-way model (quality/cost—value—willingness to buy)	Value as a derivative of quality; distinction between perceived and objective price, quality and cost. Distinction between external/internal signals, hierarchy of influencing factors, but not their interaction
Dodds et al. (1991)	Five questions about the overall value of a product or service	The simplicity of this method is its main advantage and main disadvantage at the same time. It focuses on the quality and cost of a given good
Gale et al. (1994)	Multidimensional; CV seen as a relative value for money. Value = perceived market quality (MQ)/perceived price (MPP). One of the measures used to assess a company's position in a competitive market	The tools and indicators are given and recommended by the author as relevant, comprehensive and effective for the company's strategy and management development. The main challenge is to correctly use the analysis to develop/redefine the business model of a particular company
Sweeney and Soutar (2001)	Multidimensional PERVAL model Four dimensions, linked: emotional value; social value (social concept); economic value (price/value for money); functional value (performance/quality)	The scales have developed partly on Holbrook's typology; multi-stage validated, universal, cover a wide range of PWK components, consumer approach

(continued)

Table 1.4 (continued)

Authors	Approach, characteristics	Scales, measurement components/comment
Richins and Dawson (1992), Richins (2013)	MVS scales; materialism as the main element influencing consumers' purchasing decisions	Dimensions: success, centricity and happiness15 recommended scales (5 scales for each dimension) Simple, validated, useful, omits the intangible side of CVP
Petrick (2002)	SERV—PERVAL; Development of a measurement tool to study value perception in the service sector	5 categories in SERV—PERVAL; quality of service, emotional response, reputation, money price, price. Quality of service perceived as a direct and best predictor of perceived value
Baker et al. (2002)	Comprehensive model of the effects of perceived value of goods and cost of purchases from a service perspective (retail)	quality of interpersonal service, quality of merchandising services, money price, cost/time expenditure, psychological cost
Gallarza and Gil-Saura (2008)	A combination of internal and external variables (using the Holbrook model); the SEM model for: generally perceived value, satisfaction and loyalty	Efficiency, service quality, social value, hedonic value
Martín-Ruiz et al. (2008)	Dimensions of the value of the service, a list of benefits and costs tested for many services (medical, chemical cleaning, auto repair, health club, fast food)	Quality of service, perceived costs (monetary and non-monetary), equity (image, reputation), trust (as a relationship value)
Yi and Gong (2013)	Development and validation of a first set of scales of customer behaviour leading to co-creation of value; a multidimensional hierarchical dependency model with two higher levels of factors), tested in several service industries	Behaviour related to consumer participation and value creation: seeking information, sharing information, responsible behaviour, interaction, opinions, assistance
Gallarza et al. (2016)	A structural model combining the PERVAL scale dimensions of values (functional, emotional, social dimensions of values) with satisfaction and loyalty of the cognitive and affective type	Value: emotional, social, quality of workmanship, price/performance ratio

Source Own study

The complex and dynamic nature of the value concept suggests the use of various complementary qualitative (e.g. observations, narrative-style open-ended interviews, FGI) and quantitative studies to measure this construct, which would allow a better recognition of the causes and mechanisms of CVP formation, together with the discovery of the interdependencies between the different components of this construct.

Table 1.4 presents several commonly used CVP measurement methods with some management implications resulting from their use, while Table 1.5 presents the most frequently cited research papers on the measurement of customer perception in recent years (1996–2020). Both tables clearly reflect the prevalence of quantitative, questionnaire-based CVP measurement methods.

The last twenty-five years still mainly focusing on quantitative research on CVP has brought one significant change. The focus on the attributes of goods was shifted away from the focus on the customer's experience of value. This is due to the groundbreaking work of Pine and Gilmore (1999) and Vargo and Lusch (2004, 2008) who stress that the company only provides a value proposition and that it is the customer himself who creates it in the consumption process: he experiences it. Companies, by offering different product and product-related solutions, accompany and support the consumer in experiencing value and achieving satisfaction with consumption.

This little survey, the results of which are shown in Table 1.5, covered the last 25 years. The key words of the study are "customer/consumer value measurement", "customer/consumer perception of value and measurement" and "empirical". The table shows only the most frequently cited articles containing original empirical research. It clearly shows that the results of quantitative research have a greater impact on subsequent researchers analyzing CVP. However to question the potential argument that perhaps the popularity of quantitative research (measured by the number of citations) is due to its greater scientific quality of conclusions, I will refer to Flint and Woodruff's (2001) article in a special edition of the Industrial Marketing Management Journal on the measurement of CVP in a business context. The authors present very interesting results of qualitative research carried out in the spirit of the grounded theory and applied in the American automotive

Table 1.5 Most frequently cited empirical studies, focused on CVP measurement in the last 25 years

Authors	Number of quotations[a]	Scope, test method	Main results, conclusions
Kim et al. (2007)	1664	A value-based Adaptation Model (VAM) that explains how mobile customers perceive the value of online tools Survey; the initial tests with the questionnaire consisted of groups of statements already developed, followed by an e-questionnaire; 167 responses analysed	Value as a ratio of benefits (usefulness, pleasure) and sacrifices (technical difficulties and perception of the fee) The greater the value, the greater the tendency to use the tool
Yang and Peterson (2004)	2446	Online survey of users of online services, content analysis of 848 consumer opinions on their online banking experience through Etnograph 5.0 software package	Companies seeking customer loyalty should focus primarily on satisfaction and perceived value. Switching costs reduce customer satisfaction and perceived value

Authors	Number of quotations[a]	Scope, test method	Main results, conclusions
Eggert and Ulaga (2002)	1784	Relationship between the perception of value and satisfaction; Cross-cutting survey (questionnaire) with purchasing managers in Germany	Two models have been developed and tested; value and satisfaction are separate but complementary constructions
Baker et al. (2002)	2903	Influence of the shop environment on the perception of the value of goods; proposal and empirical testing of a comprehensive model of shop selection; two independent groups watched the video and completed the survey. The scales were subject to validation	Tested model to study the distribution, exposure of goods, as a result of perception of the value of the environment/atmosphere of the store
Mathwick et a. (2001)	2645	EVS (scale of values for experience, element of fun, aesthetics, "return on investment" and service excellence) developed and tested in an online questionnaire and a shopping/email survey; scales developed using qualitative research	EVS—a scale useful for testing the value of experiments as significant components of the overall utility value
Walter et al. (2001)	1289	The supplier/customer relationship perspective on value creation within the value chain. Empirical survey of more than 200 companies; mixed methodology; first 30 partially structured interviews, followed by telephone interviews using a questionnaire	Creating value as the core of customer-supplier cooperation. Both direct (volume, profit, transaction security) and indirect (innovation, market size, access to products and information) measures of customer relations contribute to the value offered by suppliers

(continued)

Table 1.5 (continued)

Authors	Number of quotations[a]	Scope, test method	Main results, conclusions
Cronin et al. (2000)	8461	Interdependence between dedication (SAQ), service quality (SQ), service value (SV), satisfaction (SAT) and purchase intentions (BI) in the service sector; 2 large surveys in 6 sectors	Indirect relationships between constructions SQ -> SV/SAT -> BI SV-> SAT -> BI
McDougall and Levesque (2000)	2661	The relationship between the quality of basic services, the quality of the relationship services and the perceived value and their impact on customer satisfaction and future intentions. Empirical research in four service industries	The declared quality of basic services and perceived value are the most important factors influencing customer satisfaction. Indeed the quality of the relationship services provided is a significant but less important factor of satisfaction
Oh (1999)	1572	Integrated service quality model, customer value and customer satisfaction Research sample: luxury hotel services sector; modified SERVQUAL	Customer perception of value is an important construct for service quality creation and consumer satisfaction research; service quality and customer value mediate customer satisfaction; price perception has a negative impact on value
Patterson and Spreng (1997)	1672	Relationship between satisfaction, perception of value and intention to buy back; mixed methodology: expert interviews as a basis for designing questionnaires	Value is a function of satisfaction; both factors influence the repeatability of purchases; Six dimensions of value used by customers to evaluate business services

[a]Quotes in Google Scholar, access 10.06.2020
Source Own study

industry. They also propose a clearly defined instrumental framework for conducting CVP analysis; a diagnostic tool to analyse the perception of value by business customers. The method allows for "*capturing the changes desired by customers in the current value proposition, which would help sellers to anticipate more accurately what customers may value in the future*" (Flint and Woodruff 2001, p. 315). While the entire issue of the magazine is quoted more than 2500 times in Google Scholar, the quote from this article is 249 (as of 10.06.2020).

The simplicity of quantitative measurement of CVP while undoubtedly appealing, does not offer a deeper understanding of the causes of the interrelated relationships between the different CVP components. We are left with precise statistical evidence of the advantage of one attribute over another but we still observe only the surface of this phenomenon. We can probably answer the questions as to what attributes of the offer consumers value or how this assessment varies from country to country, region to region, demographic or cultural context, but can we fully understand why they are composed the way we capture them, let alone how they were created?

However if we look at CVP as a result of a dynamic process of continuous, subjective reinterpretation under the influence of the environment a set of qualitative methods will be a natural way to observe and understand them. One of the approaches to an in-depth CVP analysis is VALCONEX (value-in-context, see Helkkula et al. 2009; Helkkula and Kelleher 2010). Inductive, phenomenological and intra-subjective methods make it possible to measure how value is experienced and continuously transformed by consumers in the context of networks and the environment as postulated by Vargo and Lusch (2004) as the appropriate research method. A phenomenological approach using the method of narrative or evocation of so-called critical events in open, partially structured interviews can lead to a better understanding of value creation mechanisms.

Understanding how value is co-created and transformed by specific situations and environmental contexts also has a practical dimension. The presentation of the nature of these hermeneutic, curvilinear relationships between past experiences and expectations of value propositions can serve as a signpost for its skillful monetization. In order to better capture the complex and dynamic nature of CVP, the use of a mixed methodology seems not only cognitively more promising but simply more cost-effective. For better understanding the quantitative analysis of the CVP should be preceded and then deepened by qualitative research.

1.7 Value as Research Category—Summary

Value is a category constructed by an individual, functioning in a specific moral, ethical and social, including economic, context. Value is a measure of significance: it determines what is important or insignificant. In the philosophical context value can be reduced to perceiving in phenomena, objects, situations or people the elements of individually defined goodness, beauty and truth. We can consider values in terms of their stability and variability. An individual's system of values: what is important to him/her in life takes precedence over a set of temporal values which depend on the context and are not always identical with it. The value of a given good may be the result of a given situational context and the importance and intensity of a perceived, unmet need; it may change radically as soon as it is satisfied.

The system of superior values, although evolving with age and the social role played by the individual, is a relatively permanent phenomenon that does not change radically over time.

What has a specific value for an individual and what are the mutual relationships between values (of the nature of lateral, hierarchical and causal relationships, i.e. the relationship between immanent and instrumental values) decide the following:

- the characteristics of the individual:
  - personality, shaped as a result of genetic and social conditions; among others, the tendency to be guided in elections by intuition, emotions and logical rationalization; level of optimism/pessimism, tendency to egoism/altruism, development of individualism/social fit, etc.
  - age, linked to gender (and social expectations of gender) and the social role played at a given moment of life,

- intellect and knowledge, such things as catalysts of personality tendencies and social roles shaping the value system,

- a given system of moral codes generally considered appropriate and binding, historically shaped, rooted in culture, legitimized and promoted by e.g. religion, which is part of the collective system of worldview of a given country or region,
- a set of historically and culturally shaped aesthetic codes,
- social environment:
  - A socially legitimized hierarchy of values related e.g. to the functioning of the state, approach to the rights of individuals, specific social groups, environment,
  - a system of values, norms and codes of behaviour for the social groups within which the individual operates: family, ethnic group, professional, hobby, residency, etc.,
- own and social assessment of an individual's position in society in the context of his or her suitability for social and moral values and his or her importance/status/evaluation in the community.

Figure 1.3 shows the mutual relations and influences of the areas shaping the unit's value set.

The personal and social set of values is an overarching and often subconsciously used reference system. The assessment of a given phenomenon, object, good or service shall be made by reference to the characteristics, functions of the object to a separate value system. However the effect of this assessment is not a simple reflection of the value system and especially the superior one. For example, a momentarily intense feeling of lack, dissatisfaction affects the system of assessing the value of an object that we do not have (but want to) and contributes to a rapid increase in its significance.

The process of evaluation therefore takes place in a specific situational context and emotional state and constitutes a complex system,[11] which results in an impulse to act. The relationship between the system of

[11]This is a complex, but not as many models of consumer behavioural choice as proposed, based, for example, on unrealistic rationalizing comparison of all available options. It is a

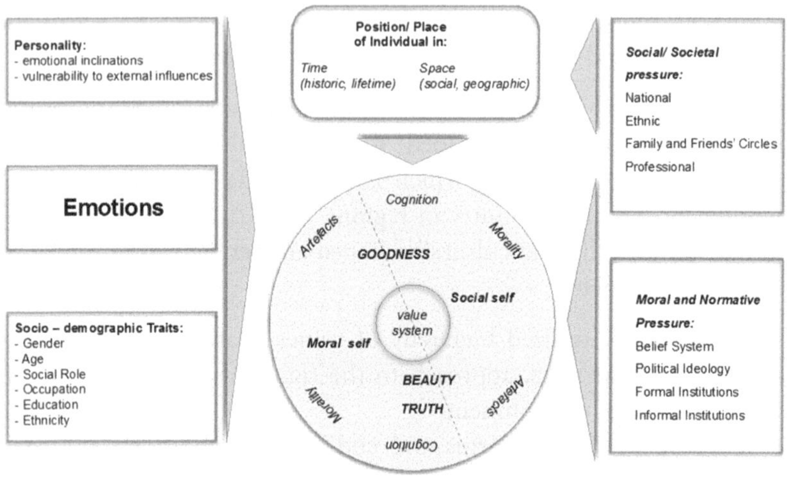

Fig. 1.3 Value as a relational social category (*Source* Own study)

values, motivations, needs, etc. and consumer choices and behaviour is described in more detail in Chapter 4. It is worth noting here that within the process of valuation an idea of the set of benefits and costs that a given good brings: its broad and contemporary, though not neoclassical, utility value. We are informed of the acquisition costs by the exchange value which consists of the price and the costs of: obtaining information on where and how to acquire the goods; the acquisition, use and post-consumer disposal or disposal itself.

complex and still undiscovered mutual relationship of emotions felt and remembered nowadays, coded experiences and collision of the situational context with the system of values developed in the process of socialization. These collisions and—still undiagnosed psychologically, compounds—produce information of the type—do yes, refrain from action, etc.

References

Adamiec, M. (1983). Działanie, wartość, sens-zarys systemu pojęć. *Przegląd Psychologiczny, 26*(1), 3–23.

Agarwal, S., & Teas, R. K. (2001). Perceived value: Mediating role of perceived risk. *Journal of Marketing Theory and Practice, 9*(4), 1–14.

Alwin, D. F. (1986). Religion and parental childrearing orientations: Evidence of a Catholic-Protestant convergence. *American Journal of Sociology, 92*, 412–440.

Anderson, J. C., & Narus, J. A. (1998). Business marketing: Understand what customers value. *Harvard Business Review, 76*, 53–65.

Appadurai, A. (1986). Commodities and the politics of value. In A. Appaduarai (Ed.), *The social life of things: Commodities in cultural perspective*. Cambridge: Cambridge University Press.

Archpru Akaka, M., & Chandler, J. D. (2011). Roles as resources: A social roles perspective of change in value networks. *Marketing Theory, 11*(3), 243–260.

Arkes, H. R., & Blumer, C. (2000). The psychology of sunk cost. *Judgment and decision making: An interdisciplinary reader* (pp. 97ff). Cambridge: Cambridge University Press.

Arnould, E. J., & Thompson, C. J. (2005). Consumer culture theory (CCT): Twenty years of research. *Journal of Consumer Research, 31*(4), 868–882.

Ashby, F. G., & Isen, A. M. (1999). A neuropsychological theory of positive affect and its influence on cognition. *Psychological Review, 106*(3), 529.

Aumann, R. J. (1985). An axiomatization of the non-transferable utility value. *Econometrica: Journal of the Econometric Society, 53*(3), 599–612.

Aumann, R. J., & Shapley, L. S. (2015). *Values of non-atomic games*. Princeton, NJ: Princeton University Press.

Baker, J., Parasuraman, A., Grewal, D., & Voss, G. B. (2002). The influence of multiple store environment cues on perceived merchandise value and patronage intentions. *The Journal of Marketing, 66*(2), 20–141.

Ballantyne, D., Christopher, M., & Payne, A. (1995). Improving the quality of services marketing: Service (re) design is the critical link. *Journal of Marketing Management, 11*(1–3), 7–24.

Becker, G. S. (1976). Pride and prejudice. In G. S. Becker (Ed.), *The economic approach to human behavior*. Chicago: University of Chicago Press.

Becker, G. S. (1993). *Human capital: A theoretical and empirical analysis, with special reference to education* (3rd ed.). Chicago: The University of Chicago Press.

Berger, P., & Luckmann, T. (1967). *The social construction of reality: A treatise in the sociology of knowledge* (pp. 52–54). Garden City, NY: Doubleday.

Berger, P. D., & Nasr, N. I. (1998). Customer lifetime value: Marketing models and applications. *Journal of Interactive Marketing, 12*(1), 17–30.

Beutel, A. M., & Marini, M. M. (1995). Gender and values. *American Sociological Review, 60,* 436–448.

Beverland, M., & Lockshin, L. (2003). A longitudinal study of customers' desired value change in business-to-business markets. *Industrial Marketing Management, 32*(8), 653–666.

Bless, H., Bohner, G., Schwarz, N., & Strack, F. (1990). Mood and persuasion: A cognitive response analysis. *Personality and Social Psychology Bulletin, 16*(2), 331–345.

Bless, H., Clore, G. L., Schwarz, N., Golisano, V., Rabe, C., & Wölk, M. (1996). Mood and the use of scripts: Does a happy mood really lead to mindlessness? *Journal of Personality and Social Psychology, 71*(4), 665–679.

Block, J. (1977). Advancing the psychology of personality: Paradigmatic shift or improving the quality of research. *Personality at the crossroads: Current issues in interactional psychology*, 2.

Bochańczyk-Kupka, D. (2014). Luksus i dobra luksusowe. *Studia Ekonomiczne, 176,* 97–108.

Boćkowska, A. (2017). *Księżyc z Pewexu.* Wydawnictwo Czarne: O luksusie w PRL-u.

Bodenhausen, G. V. (1993). Emotions, arousal, and stereotypic judgments: A heuristic model of affect and stereotyping. In D. M. Mackie & D. L. Hamilton (Eds.), *Affect, cognition and stereotyping* (s. 13–37). San Diego, CA: Academic Press.

Bodenhausen, G. V., Sheppard, L. A., & Kramer, G. P. (1994). Negative affect and social judgment: The differential impact of anger and sadness. *European Journal of Social Psychology, 24*(1), 45–62.

Bolton, L. E., Warlop, L., & Alba, J. W. (2003). Consumer perceptions of price (un) fairness. *Journal of Consumer Research, 29*(4), 474–491.

Bourdieu, P. (1977). *Outline of a theory of practice* (Vol. 16). Cambridge University Press.

Bourdieu, P. (1984). *Distinction: A social critique of the judgement of taste.* Cambridge, MA: Harvard University.

Brodie, R. J., Löbler, H., & Fehrer, J. A. (2019). Evolution of service-dominant logic: Towards a paradigm and metatheory of the market and value cocreation? *Industrial Marketing Management, 79,* 3–12.

Brzozowski, P. (2007). *Wzorcowa hierarchia wartości: polska, europejska czy uniwersalna? psychologiczne badania empiryczne*. Wydawnictwo Uniwersytetu Marii Curie-Skłodowskiej.

Butz, H. E., & Goodstein, L. D. (1996). Measuring customer value: Gaining the strategic advantage. *Organizational Dynamics, 24,* 63–77. https://doi.org/10.1016/S0090-2616(96)90006-6.

Camerer, C. (1999). Behavioral economics: Reunifying psychology and economics. *Proceedings of the National Academy of Sciences, 96*(19), 10575–10577.

Carver, C. S., & Scheier, M. F. (2000). On the structure of behavioral self-regulation. In M. Boekaerts, P. R. Pintrich, & M. Zeidner (Eds.), *Handbook of self-regulation* (s. 41–84). New York: Cambridge University Press.

Chang, T. Z., & Wildt, A. R. (1994). Price, product information, and purchase intention: An empirical study. *Journal of the Academy of Marketing Science, 22*(1), 16–27.

Chen, Z., & Dubinsky, A. J. (2003). A conceptual model of perceived customer value in e-commerce: A preliminary investigation. *Psychology & Marketing, 20,* 323–347.

Churchill, G. A., Jr., & Surprenant, C. (1982). An investigation into the determinants of customer satisfaction. *Journal of Marketing Research, 19,* 491–504.

Cieciuch, J. (2013). *Kształtowanie się systemu wartości od dzieciństwa do wczesnej dorosłości*. Warszawa: Wydawnictwo Liberi Libri.

Cronin, J. J., Brady, M. K., & Hult, G. T. M. (2000). Assessing the effects of quality, value, and customer satisfaction on consumer behavioral intentions in service environments. *Journal of Retailing, 76*(2), 193–218.

Denzau, A. T., & North, D. C. (1994). Shared mental models: Ideologies and institutions. *Kyklos, 47*(1), 3–31.

Dewey, J. (1949). Theory of valuation, and Urban's beyond realism and idealism.

Dobiegała-Korona, B., & Doligalski, T. (red.). (2011). *Zarządzanie wartością klienta w przedsiębiorstwach w Polsce*. Warszawa: Oficyna Wydawnicza Szkoła Główna Handlowa w Warszawie.

Dodds, W. B., Monroe, K. B., & Grewal, D. (1991). The effects of price, brand and store information on buyers' product evaluations. *Journal of Marketing Research, 28*(3), 307–319.

Domurat, A. (2009). *Identyfikacja wartości osobistych w badaniach psychologicznych Wartości jako cele działań i wyborów*. Warszawa: Wydawnictwo Uniwersytetu Warszawskiego.
Douglas, M., & Isherwood, B. C. (1979). *The world of goods: Towards an anthropology of consumption*. New York: Basic Books.
Dubois, B., Laurent, G., & Czellar, S. (2001). Consumer rapport to luxury: Analyzing complex and ambivalent attitudes (Consumer Research Working Paper, 736). Jouy-en-Josas, France: HEC.
Eggert, A., & Ulaga, W. (2002). Customer perceived value: A substitute for satisfaction in business markets? *Journal of Business & Industrial Marketing, 17*(2/3), 107–118.
Ekman, P., & Davidson, R. J. (Eds.). (1994). *Series in affective science. The nature of emotion: Fundamental questions*. Oxford University Press.
Epstein, S. (1989). Values from the perspective of cognitive-experiential self-theory. In N. Eisenberg, J. Reykowski, & E. Staub (Eds.), *Social and moral values: Individual and societal perspectives* (s. 3–22). London: Routledge.
Etzioni, A. (2010). *Moral dimension: Toward a new economics*. New York: The Free Press.
Feather, N. T. (1995). Values, valences, and choice: The influence of values on the perceived attractiveness and choice of alternatives. *Journal of Personality and Social Psychology, 68*(6), 1135–1151.
Feldman, J. M., & Lynch, J. G. (1988). Self-generated validity and other effects of measurement on belief, attitude, intention, and behavior. *Journal of Applied Psychology, 73*(3), 421–435.
Fleetwood, S. (1997). Aristotle in the 21st century. *Cambridge Journal of Economics, 21*(6), 729–744.
Flint, D. J., & Woodruff, R. B. (2001). The initiators of changes in customers' desired value: Results from a theory building study. *Industrial Marketing Management, 30*(4), 321–337.
Forgas, J. P., & Moylan, S. J. (1991). Affective influences on stereotype judgements. *Cognition and Emotion, 5*(5–6), 379–395.
Frijda, N. H., Kuipers, P., & Ter Schure, E. (1989). Relations among emotion, appraisal, and emotional action readiness. *Journal of Personality and Social Psychology, 57*(2), 212.
Gale, B., Gale, B. T., & Wood, R. C. (1994). *Managing customer value: Creating quality and service that customers can see*. Simon and Schuster.
Gallarza, M. G., & Gil-Saura, I. (2008). The concept of value and its dimensions: A tool for analyzing tourism experiences. *Tourism Review, 63*(3), 4–20.

Gallarza, M. G., Ruiz, M. E., & Gil, I. (2016). Stretching the value-satisfaction-loyalty chain by adding value dimensions and cognitive and affective satisfactions: A causal model for retailing. *Management Decisions, 54*(4), 981–1003.

Gallarza, M. G., Arteaga, F., Del Chiappa, G., & Gil-Saura, I. (2015). Value dimensions in consumers' experience: Combining the intra-and inter-variable approaches in the hospitality sector. *International Journal of Hospitality Management, 47*, 140–150.

Gallarza, M. G., Arteaga, F., Del Chiappa, G., Gil-Saura, I., & Holbrook, M. B. (2017). A multidimensional service-value scale based on Holbrook's typology of customer value. *Journal of Service Management*.

Gecas, V., & Seff, M. A. (1990). Families and adolescents: A review of the 1980s. *Journal of Marriage and the Family, 52,* 941–958.

Gesteland, R. R. (2002). *Cross-cultural business behavior: Marketing, negotiating, sourcing and managing across cultures*. Copenhagen: Copenhagen Business School Press.

Gibson, J. J. (2002). A theory of direct visual perception. *Vision and mind: Selected readings in the philosophy of perception,* 77–90.

Girard, R., Oughourlian, J. M., & Lefort, G. (2003). *Things hidden since the foundation of the world*. Stanford, CA: A&C Black.

Giza, W. (2016). O ewolucji ekonomicznej teorii wartości. *Studia Ekonomiczne, 259,* 49–59.

Glanzmann, P. (1985). Anxiety, stress and performance. In B. D. Kirkcaldy (Ed.), *Individual preferences in movement*. Lancaster, England: MTP Press.

Godłów-Legiędź, J. (2010). *Współczesna ekonomia: ku nowemu paradygmatowi*. Warszawa: Wydawnictwo C.H. Beck.

Gourville, J. T., & Soman, D. (1998). Payment depreciation: The behavioral effects of temporally separating payments from consumption. *Journal of Consumer Research, 25*(2), 160–174.

Grönroos, C. (1997). Value-driven relational marketing: From products to resources and competencies. *Journal of Marketing Management, 13*(5), 407–419.

Hall, E. T. (1959). *The silent language*. New York: Doubleday.

Hall, E. T. (1989). *Beyond culture*. New York: Doubleday.

Haralambos, M., Holborn, M., & Heald, R. (1980). *Sociology: Themes and perspectives*. Slough: University Tutorial Press.

Hartmann, N. (1987). *Systematyczna autoprezentacja*. przeł. J. Garewicz, „Literatura na świecie" 1987, nr 4, s. 330.

Head, W. (1961, March). Adaptive sociology. *The British Journal of Sociology, 12*(1), 23–40.
Hechter, M. (1993). Values research in the social and behavioral sciences. In R. Michod, L. Nadel, & M. Hechter (Eds.), *The origin of values* (s. 1–28). New York: Aldine de Gruyer.
Helkkula, A., & Kelleher, C. (2010). Circularity of customer service experience and customer perceived value. *Journal of Customer Behaviour, 9*(1), 37–53.
Helkkula, A., Pihlström, M., & Kelleher, M. (2009). From customer perceived value (PERVAL) to value-in-context experience (VALCONEX). In *The 2009 Naples forum on service. Service-Dominant logic, service science and network theory, Napoli*. Napels, Italy: Giannini Editore.
Henderson, P. W., & Peterson, R. A. (1992). Mental accounting and categorization. *Organizational Behavior and Human Decision Processes, 51*(1), 92–117.
Hitlin, S., & Piliavin, J. A. (2004). Values: Reviving a dormant concept. *Annual Review of Sociology, 30,* 359–393. https://doi.org/10.1146/annurev.soc.30.012703.110640.
Hofstede, G. (1991). *Organizations and cultures: Software of the mind*. New York: McGrawHill.
Hofstede, G. (2001). *Culture's consequences: Comparing values, behaviors, institutions, and organizations across nations* (2nd ed.). Thousand Oaks, CA: Sage.
Hoge, D. R., Luna, C. L., & Miller, D. K. (1981). Trends in college students' values between 1952 and 1979: A return of the fifties? *Sociology of Education, 54,* 263–274.
Holbrook, M. B. (1996). Special session summary customer value C a framework for analysis and research. In K. P. Corfman & Jr. G. L. John (Eds.), *NA—Advances in consumer research volume 23* (s. 138–142). Provo, UT: Association for Consumer Research.
Holbrook, M. B. (1999). *Consumer value: A framework for analysis and research.* London: Routledge.
Holbrook, M. B. (2006). Consumption experience, customer value, and subjective personal introspection: An illustrative photographic essay. *Journal of Business Research, 59*(6), 714–725. https://doi.org/10.1016/j.jbusres.2006.01.008.
Ingarden, R. (1966). *Przeżycie, dzieło, wartość*. Kraków: Wydawnictwo Literackie.
Inglehart, R. (1995). Changing values, economic development and political change. *International Social Science Journal, 145,* 379–404.

Inglehart, R. (1997). *Modernization and postmodernization: Cultural, economic, and political change in 43 societies*. Princeton: Princeton University Press.
Inglehart, R. (2006). Pojawienie się wartości postmaterialistycznych. In P. Sztompka & M. Kucia (red.), *Socjologia: Lektury*. Kraków: Znak.
Inglehart, R. (2015). *The silent revolution: Changing values and political styles among Western publics*. Pronceton: Princeton University Press.
Isen, A. M. (1984). Toward understanding the role of affect in cognition. In Jr. R. S. Wyer & T. K. Srull (Eds.), *Handbook of social cognition* (Vol. 3, s. 179–236). Mahwah, NJ: Lawrence Erlbaum Associates Publishers.
Isen, A. M. (2001). An influence of positive affect on decision making in complex situations: Theoretical issues with practical implications. *Journal of Consumer Psychology, 11*(2), 75–85.
Isen, A. M. (2003). Positive affect, systematic cognitive processing, and behavior: Toward integration of affect, cognition, and motivation. In F. Dansereau & F. J. Yammarino (Eds.), *Research in multi-level issues, vol. 2: Multi-level issues in organizational behavior and strategy* (s. 55–62). Oxford: Elsevier Science.
Isen, A. M., & Daubman, K. A. (1984). The influence of affect on categorization. *Journal of Personality and Social Psychology, 47*(6), 1206–1217.
Isen, A. M., & Means, B. (1983). The influence of positive affect on decision-making strategy. *Social Cognition, 2*(1), 18–31.
Jaracz, M., & Borkowska, A. (2010). Podejmowanie decyzji w świetle badań neurobiologicznych i teorii psychologicznych. *Psychiatria, 7*(2), 68–74.
Johnson, H. M. (2013). *Sociology: A systematic introduction*. London: Routledge.
Kahneman, D. (2003). Maps of bounded rationality: Psychology for behavioral economics. *American Economic Review, 93*(5), 1449–1475.
Kahneman, D., Knetch, J., & Thaler, R. (1990). Experimental tests of the endowment effect and coase theorem. *Journal of Political Economy, 98*(6), 1325–1348.
Kapferer, J.-N. (1997). Managing luxury brands. *Journal of Brand Management, 4*(4), 251–260.
Kieżel, E. (red.). (2003). Zachowania konsumpcyjne a racjonalność – ujęcie teoretyczne. In E. Kieżel (red.), *Zachowania konsumentów – determinanty, racjonalność*. Katowice: Wydawnictwo Akademii Ekonomicznej w Katowicach.
Kim, H. W., Chan, H. C., & Gupta, S. (2007). Value-based adoption of mobile internet: An empirical investigation. *Decision Support Systems, 43*(1), 111–126.

Kluckhorn, F. R., & Strodtbeck, F. L. (1961). *Values in values orientations*. Evanston, IL: Row Paterson.

Kloska, G. (1982). *Pojęcia, teorie i badania wartości w naukach społecznych*. Warszawa: Państwowe Wydawnictwo Naukowe.

Kohlberg, L. (1981). *Moral stages and the idea of justice: Essays on moral development*. New York: Academic Press.

Kohn, M. L., Naoi, A., Schoenbach, C., Schooler, C., & Slomczynski, K. M. (1990). Position in the class structure and psychological functioning in the United States, Japan, and Poland. *American Journal of Sociology, 95*, 964–1008.

Krawczyk, D. (2002). Contributions of the prefrontal cortex to the neural basis of human decision making. *Neuroscience and Biobehavioral Reviews, 26*, 631–664.

Krokiewicz, A. (1961). *Hedonizm Epikura*. Warszawa: Instytut Wydawniczy „Pax".

Krugman, P. (2009). *How did economists get it so wrong?* From z. https://www.nytimes.com/2009/09/06/magazine/06Economic-t.html.

Lazarus, R. S. (1982). Thoughts on the relations between emotion and cognition. *American Psychologist, 37*(9), 1019–1024.

Lazarus, R. S. (1991a). *Emotion and adaptation*. New York: Oxford University Press.

Lazarus, R. S. (1991b). Progress on a cognitive-motivational-relational theory of emotion. *American Psychologist, 46*(8), 819–834.

LeDoux, J. E. (1995). Emotion: Clues from the brain. *Annual Review of Psychology, 46*(1), 209–235.

Lee, D., Rushworth, M. F., Walton, M. E., Watanabe, M., & Sakagami, M. (2007). Functional specialization of the primate frontal cortex during decision making. *The Journal of Neuroscience, 27*, 8170–8173.

Leonard, T. C. (2008). Richard H. Thaler, Cass R. Sunstein, Nudge: Improving decisions about health, wealth, and happiness. *Constitutional Political Economy, 19*(4), 356–360.

Leroi-Werelds, S., Streukens, S., Brady, M. K., & Swinnen, G. (2014). Assessing the value of commonly used methods for measuring customer value: A multi-setting empirical study. *Journal of the Academy of Marketing Science, 42*(4), 430–451. https://doi.org/10.1007/s11747-013-0363-4.

Leslie, G. R., Larson, R. F., & Gorman, B. L. (1976). *Introductory sociology: Order and change in society*. New York: Oxford University Press.

Lipiński, E. (1981). *Problemy, pytania, wątpliwości: z warsztatu ekonomisty*. Warszawa: Państwowe Wydawnictwo Ekonomiczne.

Lusch, R. F., & Nambisan, S. (2015). Service innovation: A service-dominant logic perspective. *MIS Quarterly, 39*(1), 155–176.
Mądrzycki, T. (2002). *Osobowość jako system tworzący i realizujący plany*. Gdańsk: Wydawnictwo Uniwersytetu Gdańskiego.
Mandler, G. (1993). Approaches to a psychology of value. In R. E. Michod, L. Nadel, & M. Hechter (Eds.), *The origin of values* (s. 228–258). New York: de Gruyter.
Markus, H., & Kitayama, S. (1991). Culture and the self: Implications for cognition, emotion, and motivation. *Psychological Review, 98*, 224–253.
Martín-Ruiz, D., Gremler, D. D., Washburn, J. H., & Cepeda-Carrión, G. (2008). Service value revisited: Specifying a higher-order, formative measure. *Journal of Business Research, 61*(12), 1278–1291.
Maslow, A. H. (Ed.). (1959). *New knowledge in human values*. Oxford, England: Harper.
Mathwick, C., Malhotra, N., & Rigdon, E. (2001). Experiential value: Conceptualization, measurement and application in the catalog and Internet shopping environment. *Journal of Retailing, 77*, 39–56. https://doi.org/10.1016/S0022-4359(00)00045-2.
Matsumoto, D. (1999). Culture and self: An empirical assessment of Markus and Kitayama's theory of independent and interdependent self-construals. *Asian Journal of Social Psychology, 2*, 289–310.
Mazur, J., & Zaborek, P. (2014). Validating DART model. *International Journal of Management and Economics, 44*(1), 106–125.
Mazurek-Łopacińska, K. (2003). *Zachowania nabywców i ich konsekwencje marketingowe*. Warszawa: PWE.
McCracken, G. (1986). Culture and consumption: A theoretical account of the structure and movement of the cultural meaning of consumer goods. *Journal of Consumer Research, 13*(1), 71–84.
McDougall, G. H. G., & Levesque, T. (2000). Customer satisfaction with services: Putting perceived value into the equation. *Journal of Services Marketing, 14*(5), 392–410.
Michod, R. E. (1993). Biology and the origin of values. In M. Hechter, L. Nadel, & R. E. Michod (Eds.), *The origin of values* (s. 261–271). New York: de Gruyter.
Mineka, S., & Sutton, S. K. (1992). Cognitive biases and the emotional disorders. *Psychological Science, 3*, 65–69. https://doi.org/10.1111/j.1467-9280.1992.tb00260.x.
Misztal, M. (1980). *Problematyka wartości w socjologii*. Nauk: Państwowe Wydawn.

Moliner, M. A., Sánchez, J., Rodríguez, R. M., & Callarisa, L. (2007). Perceived relationship quality and post-purchase perceived value: An integrative framework. *European Journal of Marketing, 41*(11/12), 1392–1422.
Narver, J. C., & Slater, S. F. (1990). The effect of a market orientation on business profitability. *Journal of Marketing, 54*(4), 20–35.
Narver, J. C., Slater, S. F., & MacLachlan, D. L. (2004). Responsive and proactive market orientation and new-product success. *Journal of Product Innovation Management, 21*(5), 334–347.
Ng, I. C., & Smith, L. A. (2012). An integrative framework of value [Special issue]. In *Toward a better understanding of the role of value in markets and marketing* (pp. 207–243). Bingley: Emerald Group.
North, D. C. (1991). Institutions. *Journal of Economic Perspectives, 5*(1), 97–112.
Oh, H. (1999). Service quality, customer satisfaction, and customer value: A holistic perspective. *International Journal of Hospitality Management, 18*(1), 67–82.
Ohbuchi, K.-I., Fukushima, O., & Tedeschi, J. T. (1999). Cultural values in conflict management: Goal orientation, goal attainment, and tactical decision. *Journal of Cross-Cultural Psychology, 30,* 51–71.
Oleś, P. (2002). Z badań nad wartościami i wartościowaniem: niektóre kwestie metodologiczne. *Roczniki Psychologiczne, 5,* 53–75.
Orléan, A. (2014). *The empire of value: A new foundation for economics.* Cambridge, MA: MIT Press.
Overby, J. W., Woodruff, R. B., & Gardial, S. F. (2005). The influence of culture upon consumers' desired value perceptions: A research agenda. *Marketing Theory, 5*(2), 139–163.
Oyserman, D., Coon, H. M., & Kemmelmeier, M. (2002). Rethinking individualism and collectivism: Evaluation of theoretical assumptions and meta-analyses. *Psychological Bulletin, 128,* 3–72.
Palaver, W. (2013). *René Girard's mimetic theory.* East Lansing: MSU Press.
Patterson, P. G., & Spreng, R. A. (1997). Modelling the relationship between perceived value, satisfaction and repurchase intentions in a business-to-business, services context: An empirical examination. *International Journal of Service Industry Management, 8*(5), 414–434.
Payne, A., & Holt, S. (2001). Diagnosing customer value: Integrating the value process and relationship marketing. *British Journal of Management, 12,* 159–182.
Pearlin, L. I., & Kohn, M. L. (1966). Social class, occupation, and parental values: A cross-national study. *American Sociological Review, 31,* 466–479.

Petrick, J. F. (2002). Development of a multi-dimensional scale for measuring the perceived value of a service. *Journal of Leisure Research, 34*(2), 119–134.

Pine, J., & Gilmore, J. (1999). *The experience economy.* Boston: Harvard Business School Press.

Pine, B. J., Pine, J., & Gilmore, J. H. (1999). *The experience economy: Work is theatre & every business a stage.* Harvard Business Press.

Popkin, R. H., & Stroll, A. (1993). *Philosophy made simple.* New York: Three Rivers Press.

Porter, M. E. (1985). Value chain. *The value chain and competitive advantage: Creating and sustaining superior performance.*

Prahalad, C. K., & Ramaswamy, V. (2004). Co-creation experiences: The next practice in value creation. *Journal of Interactive Marketing, 18*(3), 5–14.

Prince-Gibson, E., & Schwartz, S. H. (1998). Value priorities and gender. *Social Psychology Quarterly, 61,* 49–67.

Pura, M. (2005). Linking perceived value and loyalty in location-based mobile services. *Managing Service Quality, 15,* 509–538.

Rand, D. G., & Nowak, M. A. (2013). Human cooperation. *Trends in Cognitive Sciences, 17*(8), 413–425.

Ratajczak, M. (2014a). Ekonomia i edukacja ekonomiczna w dobie finansyzacji gospodarki. *Ekonomista, 2,* 207–219.

Ratajczak, M. (red.). (2014b). *Współczesne teorie ekonomiczne.* Poznań: Wydawnictwo Uniwersytetu Ekonomicznego w Poznaniu.

Ravald, A., & Grönroos, C. (1996). The value concept and relationship marketing. *European Journal of Marketing, 30*(2), 19–30.

Richins, M. L. (2013). The material values scale: Measurement properties and development of a short form. *Journal of Consumer Research, 31,* 209–219.

Richins, M. L., & Dawson, S. (1992). A consumer values orientation for materialism and its measurement: Scale development and validation. *Journal of Consumer Research, 19*(3), 303–316.

Rickert, H. (1986). *The limits of concept formation in natural science: A logical introduction to the historical sciences (abridged edition).* Cambridge: Cambridge University Press.

Rogers, C. R. (1964). Toward a modern approach to values: The valuing process in the mature person. *The Journal of Abnormal and Social Psychology, 68*(2), 160–167.

Rogoziński, K. (2011). *Zarządzanie wartością z klientem.* Warszawa: Wolters Kluwer.

Rohan, M. J. (2000). A rose by any name? The values construct. *Personality and Social Psychology Review, 4*(3), 255–277.

Rokeach, M. (1973). *The nature of human values*. New York: Free Press.
Rokeach, M. (2008). *Understanding human values*. New York: Simon and Schuster.
Russell, B. (2012). *Dzieje zachodniej filozofii*. Warszawa: Wydawnictwo Aletheia.
Sánchez-Fernández, R., & Iniesta-Bonillo, M. Á. (2006). Consumer perception of value: Literature review and a new conceptual framework. *Journal of Consumer Satisfaction, Dissatisfaction and Complaining Behavior, 19,* 40–58.
Sánchez-Fernández, R., & Iniesta-Bonillo, M. Á. (2007). The concept of perceived value: A systematic review of the research. *Marketing Theory, 7*(4), 427–451.
Sánchez-Fernández, R., Iniesta-Bonillo, M. Ã., & Holbrook, M. B. (2009). The conceptualization and measurement of consumer value in services. *International Journal of Market Research, 51,* 93–113.
Scheler, M. (1973). *Formalism in ethics and non-formal ethics of values: A new attempt toward the foundation of an ethical personalism*. Evanston, IL: Northwestern University Press.
Schmitt, B. H. (2010). *Customer experience management: A revolutionary approach to connecting with your customers*. John Wiley & Sons.
Schwartz, S. H. (1992). Universals in the content and structure of values: Theoretical advances and empirical tests in 20 countries. In M. P. Zanna (Ed.), *Advances in experimental social psychology* (Vol. 25, s. 1–65). New York: Academic Press.
Schwartz, S. H. (2007). Universalism values and the inclusiveness of our moral universe. *Journal of Cross-Cultural Psychology, 38*(6), 711–728.
Schwartz, S. H. (2012). An overview of the Schwartz theory of basic values. *Online Readings in Psychology and Culture, 2*(1). https://doi.org/10.9707/2307-0919.1116.
Schwartz, S. H., & Bardi, A. (2001). Value hierarchies across cultures: Taking a similarities perspective. *Journal of Cross-Cultural Psychology, 32,* 268–290.
Schwartz, S. H., Cieciuch, J., Vecchione, M., Davidov, E., Fischer, R., Beierlein, C., et al. (2012). Refining the theory of basic individual values. *Journal of Personality and Social Psychology, 103*(4), 663.
Sen, A. K. (1977). Rational fools: A critique of the behavioral foundations of economic theory. *Philosophy & Public Affairs*, 317–344.
Sen, A. K. (1999). Human rights and economic achievements. In J. R. Bauer & D. A. Bell (Eds.), *Bell the East Asian challenge for human rights*. Cambridge: CUP.

Sen, A., & Hahn, F. H. (1996). On the foundations of welfare economics: Utility, capability and practical reason. *Ethics, Rationality and Economic Behavior*.

Sheth, J., Newman, B. I., & Gross, B. L. (1991). *Consumption values and market choices: Theory and application*. Cincinnati, OH, USA: South-Western Publishing Co.

Silver, C. B. (2002). Japanese and American identities: Values and their transmission in the family. *Sociological Inquiry, 72*, 195–219.

Simon, H. A. (1956). Rational choice and the structure of the environment. *Psychological Review, 63*(2), 129.

Simon, H. A. (1957). *Models of man: Social and rational*.

Simons, R. L., Whitbeck, L. B., Conger, R. D., & Melby, J. N. (1990). Husband and wife differences in determinants of parenting: A social learning and exchange model of parental behavior. *Journal of Marriage and Family, 52*, 375–392.

Sinclair, R. C., & Mark, M. M. (1992). The influence of mood state on judgment and action: Effects on persuasion, categorization, social justice, person perception, and judgmental accuracy. In L. L. Martin & A. Tesser (Eds.), *The construction of social judgments*. Hillsdale, NY: Lawrence Erlbaum.

Sinha, I., & DeSarbo, W. S. (1998). An integrated approach toward the spatial modeling of perceived customer value. *Journal of Marketing Research, 35*, 236–249.

Slater, S. F., & Narver, J. C. (2000). Intelligence generation and superior customer value. *Journal of the Academy of Marketing Science, 28*(1), 120.

Slomczynski, K. M., Miller, J., & Kohn, M. L. (1981). Stratification, work and values: A Polish-United States comparison. *American Sociological Review, 46*, 720–744.

Smelser, N. J. (1962). *Theory of collective behavior*. New York: Putnam Publishers.

Smith, J. B., & Colgate, M. (2007). Customer value creation: A practical framework. *The Journal of Marketing Theory and Practice, 15*, 7–23.

Smith, P. B., Dugan, S., & Trompenaars, F. (1996). National culture and the values of organizational employees: A dimensional analysis across 43 nations. *Journal of Cross-Cultural Psychology, 27*(2), 231–264.

Soman, D., & Gourville, J. T. (2001). Transaction decoupling: How price bundling affects the decision to consume. *Journal of Marketing Research, 38*(1), 30–44.

Spreng, R. A., MacKenzie, S. B., & Olshavsky, R. W. (1996). A reexamination of the determinants of consumer satisfaction. *The Journal of Marketing, 60,* 15–32.

Stankiewicz, W. (2000). *Historia myśli ekonomicznej.* Warszawa: Polskie Wydawnictwo Ekonomiczne.

Stępień, B. (2009). *Instytucjonalne uwarunkowania działalności przedsiębiorstw międzynarodowych.* Poznań: Wydawnictwo Uniwersytetu Ekonomicznego w Poznaniu.

Stępień, B. (2017). In search of apprehending customers' value perception. *International Journal of Management and Economics, 53*(1), 99–117.

Stewart, M. S., Bond, M., & Chung, S. F. (1999). Intergenerational patterns of values and autonomy expectations in cultures of relatedness and separateness. *Journal of Cross-Cultural Psychology, 30,* 575–593.

Stocker, M. (1990). *Plural and conflicting values.* Oxford: Clarendon Press.

Struch, N., Schwartz, S. H., & van der Kloot, W. A. (2002). Meanings of basic values for women and men: A cross-cutural analysis. *Personality and Social Psychology Bulletin, 28,* 16–28.

Sunstein, C., & Thaler, R. (2008). *Nudge: The politics of libertarian paternalism.* New Haven: Yale University Press.

Sweeney, J. C., & Soutar, G. N. (2001). Consumer perceived value: The development of a multiple item scale. *Journal of Retailing, 77,* 203–220.

Sztompka, P. (1983). Zmiana strukturalna społeczeństwa: szkic teorii. *Studia Socjologiczne, 2*(39), 128–129.

Szymura-Tyc, M. (2006). Marketing we współczesnych procesach tworzenia wartości dla klienta i przedsiębiorstwa. *Prace Naukowe/Akademia Ekonomiczna w Katowicach.* Katowice: Wydawnictwo Akademii Ekonomicznej w Katowicach.

Takano, Y., & Osaka, E. (1999). An unsupported common view: Comparing Japan and the U.S. on individualism/collectivism. *Asian Journal of Social Psychology, 2*(3), 311–341.

Tatarkiewicz, W., & Krajewski, J. (1990). *Historia filozofii* (Vol. 1). Warszawa: PWN.

Thaler, R. (1985). Mental accounting and consumer choice. *Marketing Science, 4*(3), 199–214.

Thaler, R. H. (1999). Mental accounting matters. *Journal of Behavioral Decision Making, 12*(3), 183–206.

Thaler, R. (2018). *Zachowania niepoprawne: Tworzenie ekonomii behawioralnej.* Poznań: Wydawnictwo Media Rodzina.

Thompson, K. S. (1981). Changes in the values and life-style preferences of university students. *The Journal of Higher Education, 52,* 506–518.

Tischner, J. (1993). *Myślenie według wartości*. Kraków: Znak.

Triandis, H. C. (1995). *Individualism and collectivism*. Boulder: Westview.

Trompenaars, F., & Hampden-Turner, C. (2004). *Managing people across cultures*. Chichester: Capstone.

Trompenaars, F., & Hampden-Turner, C. (2011). *Riding the waves of culture: Understanding diversity in global business*. New York: Nicholas Brealey International.

Tversky, A., & Kahneman, D. (1981). The framing of decisions and the psychology of choice. *Science, New Series, 211*(4481), 453–458.

Tynan, C., McKechnie, S., & Chhuon, C. (2010). Co-creating value for luxury brands. *Journal of Business Research, 63*(11), 1156–1163.

Vandermerwe, S. (1993). Jumping into the customer's activity cycle: A new role for customer services in the 1990s. *Columbia Journal of World Business, 28*(2), 46–66.

Vargo, S. L., & Lusch, R. F. (2004). Evolving to a new dominant logic for marketing. *The Journal of Marketing, 68,* 1–17.

Vargo, S. L., & Lusch, R. F. (2008). Service-dominant logic: Continuing the evolution. *Journal of the Academy of Marketing Science, 36*(1), 1–10.

Venkatesan, R., & Kumar, V. (2004). A customer lifetime value framework for customer selection and resource allocation strategy. *Journal of Marketing, 68*(4), 106–125.

Vigneron, F., & Johnson, L. W. (2004). Measuring perceptions of brand luxury. *Journal of Brand Management, 11*(6), 484–506.

Walter, A., Ritter, T., & Gemünden, H. G. (2001). Value creation in buyer—Seller relationships: Theoretical considerations and empirical results from a supplier's perspective. *Industrial Marketing Management, 30*(4), 365–377.

Waters, M. C. (1990). *Ethnic options choosing identities in America*. Berkeley: University of California Press.

Wiedmann, K. P., Hennigs, N., & Siebels, A. (2009). Value-based segmentation of luxury consumption behavior. *Psychology & Marketing, 26*(7), 625–651.

Wiggins, D. (1998). Weakness of will, commensurability, and the objects of deliberation and desire. In *Needs, values, truth: Essays in the philosophy of value* (3rd ed.). Oxford: Oxford University Press.

Wojtyna, A. (2008). Współczesna ekonomia-kontynuacja czy poszukiwanie paradygmatu? *Ekonomista, 1,* 9–32.

Woodall, T. (2003). Conceptualising "value for the customer": An attributional, structural and dispositional analysis. *Academy of Marketing Science Review, 12,* 1–42.
Woodruff, R. B. (1997). Customer value: The next source for competitive advantage. *Journal of the Academy of Marketing Science, 25,* 139–153.
Woodruff, R. B., & Gardial, F. S. (1996). *Know your customer: New approaches to understanding customer value and satisfaction.* Cambridge, MA: Blackwell.
Worsley, P. (1984). *The three worlds: Culture and world development*. Chicago: University of Chicago Press.
Xiao, H. (2000). Class, gender, and parental values in the 1990s. *Gender & Society, 14,* 785–803.
Yang, Z., & Peterson, R. T. (2004). Customer perceived value, satisfaction, and loyalty: The role of switching costs. *Psychology & Marketing, 21*(10), 799–822.
Yi, Y., & Gong, T. (2013). Customer value co-creation behavior: Scale development and validation. *Journal of Business Research, 66*(9), 1279–1284.
Young, K., & Mack, R. W. (1959). *Sociology and social life.* New York: American Book Company.
Zajonc, R. B. (1980). Feeling and thinking: Preferences need no inferences. *American Psychologist, 35*(2), 151.
Zeithaml, V. A. (1988). Consumer perceptions of price, quality, and value: A means-end model and synthesis of evidence. *The Journal of Marketing, 52,* 2–22.
Znaniecki, F. (1910). *Zagadnienie wartości w filozofii.* Wydawnictwo Przeglądu Filozoficznego.
Zubac, A., Hubbard, G., & Johnson, L. W. (2009). The RBV and value creation: A managerial perspective. *European Business Review, 22*(5), 515–538.
Zucker, L. G. (1977). The role of institutionalization in cultural persistence. *American Sociological Review, 42,* 726–743.

2

From Traditional to Post-modern Value of Luxury

2.1 Definition of Luxury—What Is It and What Is It not?

Luxury comes from Latin *luxuria*, which means luxury and splendour. Dictionary entries of luxury emphasize its following features:

- abundance, excess, superfluity for pleasure and comfort (Merriam Webster 2018),
- a state of rare, though great, comfort or elegance; hardly accessible pleasure; an object that is not necessary, though desirable, expensive and difficult to obtain (Oxford Dictionary 2018);
- conditions or goods for comfortable living and pleasure; accessible for few (PWN Dictionary 2018).

In many studies which try to define the features of luxury goods their rarity, artistry, polysensuality, excellent quality, uniqueness and high price are emphasized (Cristini et al. 2017; Kapferer and Bastien 2009; O'Cass and Frost 2002; Dubois et al. 2001; Vigneron and Johnson 1999). Luxury is unnecessary but desirable and its purchase, usage

B. Stępień, *The Value of Luxury*, Palgrave Advances in Luxury,
https://doi.org/10.1007/978-3-030-51218-7_2

and experiencing it brings pleasure, self-confidence and highlights high social status (Chevalier and Mazzalovo 2008; Tsai 2005; Wong and Zaichkowsky 1999; Dubois and Paternault 1997; Berry 1994).

Although there are some common features of luxury the blurred categorization criteria fail to build clear demarcation lines between what is luxury and what is not. The most important features of luxury are described below showing at the same time that the separate use of certain features to describe goods, services or even experiences may lead to an erroneous classification.

When referring to the term objectivity it is worth emphasizing the fundamental difficulty in proving that objective luxury does actually exist. The first difficulty has already been outlined in the analysis of value and valuation itself. Like value luxury is primarily a relative, individual category, depending on the situational and social context (see e.g. Holbrook 1996, 2006; Dubois and Paternault 1997; Dubois et al. 2001; Chevalier and Mazzalovo 2008). The coincidence is due to the fact that the term luxury itself contains a valuation component. When we say "*wheelbarrow*," we are able to imagine the object, to list its functions while refraining from automatically assessing whether we generally like wheelbarrows, whether we want it or whether we condemn those who have wheelbarrows or even display them publicly. Moreover by "*wheelbarrow*" we can mean our own *wheelbarrow* without thinking about how privileged we are because of its possession or socially considered worse because we bought ours at a Tesco sale. If we use the word luxury instead of a wheelbarrow the whole emotional and social context of the statement changes.

An example of a wheelbarrow as a reversal of a luxury good probably is going to be considered scientifically unconvincing thus I am going to use the work of Popper (1979) and his three layers of entities, the dichotomy and simultaneous coexistence of which was already raised earlier by philosophers (see Chapter 1). According to Popper the world is made up of (1) a material layer (objects, people, or generally materialized entities), (2) a domain of subjective experience of individuals, including thoughts, emotions, perceptions, preferences (3) a sphere of very broadly understood culture resulting from (scientific) cognition, production of material and spiritual experiences. In this context luxury is the goods and services that give rise to the possibility that individuals (by coming into contact with them, by experiencing them) create a specific image of them and that the social environment shares and legitimizes this impression.

The difficulty in objectivizing luxury results not only from the subjective feelings of individuals (the second layer of the Popper world) or the state of social knowledge about what is luxury and how to judge it (the third layer), but also from quite revolutionary transformations of this business as discussed below. Over the centuries, including the last decades, dynamic growth of different, previously considered luxury goods and services has made them democratic which should almost automatically exclude them from the luxury sphere. Following such a definition luxury is rare; not democratic. Clear distinction between luxury and its substitute or imitation is currently very difficult due to the emergence of many brands at the lowest level of the luxury ladder (so-called masstige—prestige for mass, Silverstein and Fiske 2003) and to a quite revolutionary stage of luxury business which we now observe. But let us go through these traditional and emerging categorizations of luxury, see how it evolved and what could be the consequences of this transformation.

Appadurai (1986, p. 86) lists five features of luxury:

1. restricting consumption to elites according to price or other right of access,
2. supply complexity—which may or may not reflect a real shortage of these goods/services,
3. semiotic virtuosity,
4. codes of use requiring specific expertise,
5. a high degree of linkage between consumption and the body, person and personality.

Only such goods which meet all the above conditions are transferred to the so-called "luxury register".

Consumption is not only limited by high prices but other forms of access restriction are also often used. For instance Hermés bags (Birkin and Kelly) are sold outside the stores of the brand due to the fact that demand that exceeds supply. You usually have to queue up and you cannot get on the waiting list by simply going to the shop and ordering a particular item. The same is true for niche luxury car brands—they are created and customized for consumers who, regardless of the money they are ready to spend (although there are probably exceptions) wait in line until his car leaves the factory stylized as a sanctuary of creation. Here in referring to the last comparison we are dealing with semiotic virtuosity: building an aura of uniqueness not only around the good itself but also around the whole process of its creation, sale and use. This aura is created by brand owners, other participants in the luxury value chain, as well as crowds of people who are not even potential consumers. It is those who, having heard about a product, shape its meaning as luxurious and openly or secretly desire it. The purpose of semiotic virtuosity is to create a symbolic meaning: a value expressed in social desire combined with knowledge of what a product is and how it can be used. The last feature concerns privacy: luxury is the good intended for individuals to fulfill their desires. However as Bourdieu writes the mere acquisition of a luxury good does not yet determine that its holders belong to a particular social class. This is because class diversity concerns not only material status but also a lifestyle, the use of similar practices and even the following of similar fashion trends (Bourdieu and Wacquant 2013). Although there are activities aimed at distinction from the group within the same class the search for difference takes place within an invisible, yet existing and impassable framework of what is appropriate within the group or social class.

A. Appadurai (as well as P. Bourdieu), defines this by coding: it requires knowledge to be able to decode which luxury goods are valued higher by a given social class than others and which styles of use are considered elegant and "worthy of this class". The meaning and functioning of such codes, concerning the use of luxury goods and the use of luxury services, are referred to in Chapter 6. However the most frequently cited characteristics of luxury are commented on: rarity, high price, mastery of workmanship, excellent quality, artistry, polysensuality and social desire all of which are in parallel with moral stigma.

2.2 Rarity, High Price and Master Craftsmanship—Does It Still Exist or Matter?

Luxury goods and services should be rare and therefore unavailable, which increases their value. Conversely the relative abundance of goods reduces their value and often their price. Although the price is treated as a reflection of value in use the price itself also suggests what value a good may have (see e.g. Smith and Nagle 1995; Naylor and Frank 2001). This common economic rule, called demand law (the higher the price the lower the demand) does not apply to luxury business. Instead of falling demand for luxury goods increases with their prices and results in an upward-sloping demand curve. This is because the price of a luxury is not the mere the result of supply–demand interplay but much more subtle dependencies. High price becomes an emblem of social desire and hence its social value and serves here as an indicator of wealth for those who can afford these goods, transforming luxury goods as proofs of belonging to a wealthy class.

This anomaly is called a Veblen paradox named after probably the most quoted author in studies on luxury who described the bourgeoisie's consumption practices and defined them as conspicuous consumption (Veblen 1899: 2008). However while studying this phenomenon Veblen did not shy away from moralizing remarks and was quite effective in reinforcing public condemnation of the public exposure of luxury (see also Mruk and Stępień 2018).

Rarity, analyzed as a socially constructed criterion, disqualifies the objective rarity as an absolute measure of luxury as it is also used to describe the intensity of deprivation in a certain situational and environmental context. Orléans (2014, p. 85) referring to anthropological and sociological analyses of the life of nomadic and conqueror tribes claims that in principle these people did not experience a sense of rarity. Living in a certain way they developed such a set of needs that did not make them suffer from deprivation of comfort, food and so on and allowed them to consider their modest resources to be sufficient for life.

Deprived of something, according to the prospect theory (Tversky and Kahneman 1981), we value the desired object much higher than while we possess it or already get satisfied by its usage. First however we need to know that a given set of goods or services exists and then assimilate and internalize their meaning as important to us.

Deprivation as a relative measure of rarity may also change ordinary goods into desirable (thus considered luxurious) items although only in the so-called private register of luxury. A piece of bread, a bottle of water, an old blanket or a dream becomes a luxury in a situation of hunger, thirst, hypothermia or physical exhaustion. Some people when asked what is luxury indicate free time or health as these are impossible to buy (Hoffmann and Coste-Marniere 2013; Hung and David 2020), The paradox of rarity and value in use has already been raised by A. Smith in comparison with the low price (and exchange value) of water as a highly usable good and the high price (and exchange value) of diamonds with a low value in use but understood narrowly through the prism of functionality. Although marginalists have explained this paradox by developing a marginal theory of usefulness the feelings of an individual who is deprived of, and desires, a good (despite the fact that it is universal, for example) may increase its value.

On the other hand the rare occurrence of a good does not determine that it will automatically be assessed as luxurious. One of the rarest elements in nature are lanthanides (scandium, yttrium, lanthanum, cerium, praseodymium, neodymium, promethium, samarium, europium, gadolinium, terbium, dysprosium, holmium, erbium, thulium, yttrium and lutetium). They are rare and valuable (here: expensive) and are used in the aerospace industry, in the manufacture of lasers, magnets, liquid crystal displays or ceramics. Despite this they are not called luxurious because they are not an object of social desire, like gold, platinum or recently titanium.

Luxury as a term is also not used to describe goods that are associated with superior values such as life and health. We will not call an extremely expensive life-saving operation a luxury although the conditions in which it will take place and in which the patient will convalesce can be graded from Spartan to luxurious.

Rarity is not only socially constructed but also a variable category both geographically and over time. For example crawfish, lobsters and shrimps are simply cheaper where they are abundant and can be fished at low cost.[1] In colonial times in the USA lobsters were considered to be food for the poor. Servants from Massachusetts successfully sued their masters for being served seafood too often for their daily meals resulting in agreements restricting lobster consumption to three times a week (Khan 2016). However it would be too simplistic to prove that the contemporary recognition of seafood as a delicacy and culinary luxury was influenced by the extinction of these species. The perception of this type of food as luxurious was influenced not only by its rare occurrence but also by scientific discoveries about its positive health properties combined with the fashion for taking care of the personal silhouette and although it can be considered that lobster or red royal crab is nowadays an objective luxury good (due to its rarity, high price and social desire) there are yet many people who consider it a luxury only in the face of imminent starvation.

Consumption of luxury goods has been divided at the level of the individual consumer into two distinct patterns of behaviour: the first is the pursuit of the crowd or the bandwagon effect (see e.g. Sirgy 1985; Belk 1988; Dittmar 1994; Miller et al. 1993; Brewer and Gardner 1996; Kastanakis and Balabanis 2014). The second is the snob effect (see e.g. Leibenstein 1950; Corneo and Jeanne 1997; Brewer and Gardner 1996; Kastanakis and Balabanis 2014). The snob effect is created among this group of consumers who want to stand out, but at the same time perceive themselves as exceptional and are characterized by the so-called internal locus of control (according to the principle—the most important factor is how I feel and perceive myself, see also Phares 1976; Wong and Ahuvia

[1] It is about both the abundance and the possibility of obtaining the goods in question. For example red royal crabs, the world's most expensive crab, are fished in the Bering Sea region, near Alaska, although they are an invasive species in the Barents Sea region. The price is not so much dependent on their occurrence as on extreme fishing conditions. The profession of shellfish fisherman has been hailed as one of the most dangerous in the world but since 2005 when the documentary series "Deadliest Catch" was broadcast, fishing conditions have improved. Fortunately for fishermen the price of royal crabs is still high. However the most expensive seafood are shark fins, bluefin tuna, or fugu fish. About 80% of the bluefin Atlantic and Pacific tuna caught is consumed in Japan. In 2008 a sales record was set; USD 247,000 was paid for a Bluefin tuna at the Tsukiji fish market in Tokyo.

1998; Tsai et al. 2013). The willingness to buy luxury goods from this group decreases the more popular and publicly desirable they are. Rarity is the impulse that produces both effects. While the snob inclination is driven by objective rarity, crowd chasing stems from the subjective perception of rarity, shaped by individual deprivation combined with public desire.

In the light of the above relationships the question arises whether luxury can be a good at a low price available to the public or free of charge. Considering the relativism of consumers' perception of luxury the answer to the question whether luxury can be cheap and universal should be positive. An example of such "cheap luxury" is the awarding of a Michelin star (synonymous with high quality food, culinary craftsmanship, aesthetics of serving, manner of serving) for the second consecutive year to street bars (so-called food stalls) in Singapore. The stands "The Hong Kong Soya Sauce Chicken Rice and Noodle" and "Hill Street Tai Hwa Pork Noodle" served quickly, but prepared on an ongoing basis (taking into account the wishes of customers) dishes with pasta, chicken, pork or duck at a price of about 2–8 USD per serving. The aforementioned rarity, understood as a deprivation effect, gives a luxurious character to everyday objects or activities which are not luxurious. However without falling into the postmodern tones of relativism and constructivism one can point to the emergence of such phenomena (mainly in the service sector) which can be called free of charge luxury. This is due to the growing trends of redirecting consumers' attention from the functional value of goods to ephemerality and the uniqueness of experiences, combined with strengthening the importance of transient impressions. Luxury becomes the experience and not necessarily the possession of a given good.

The studies on luxury unanimously emphasize that one of the most important characteristics of luxury goods and services is their high quality and above-average functionality. Before discussing the quality and functionality of luxury it is worthwhile to refer to the interrelation of these terms. While for the Japanese (although certainly not all) quality is an ideal entity, perfection, which should be pursued through continuous improvement of the existing condition within the kaizen philosophy in the North American perspective quality is a subjective construct formulated by an individual as a result of comparing his needs (before purchase) with experiences related to the degree of satisfaction after purchase. Apart from the subjective feelings, in the assessment of quality, objective measures are used concerning the technical characteristics of materials, components, technological excellence of the manufacturing process, or durability, effectiveness of the operation of a given good and the adequacy of action in relation to the functional assumptions of the construction of a given product. Such an objective concept of quality is characteristic to the European, especially German, understanding of this construct (for an overview of the definition of quality see Borys 1980). In the latter context the functionality of a given good becomes a component of quality but it concerns the technical functions, meeting the most important needs (from the so-called product core). Quality can therefore be seen as an attraction to the buyer, as a reflection of technical mastery, or as an unsurpassed being—the ideal type.

When it comes to assessing the quality and functionality of luxury goods these two components are not the same. High-quality luxury goods are referred to by the nobility and rarity of the materials used in their manufacture combined with the mastery of their manufacture. In the case of fashion goods, especially haute couture, clothes are hand sewn and decorated which involves making a limited number of tailor-made items for an equally small number of customers. Hermés Kelly and Birkin bags are made of the highest quality crocodile and cowhides and the whole process is done by hand which reflects the long period of waiting for these items. Rolls Royce, Aston Martin and even Audi or Mercedes cars are equipped with materials and equipment to increase the comfort of use and provide the right aesthetic or sensory experience for the future buyer.[2]

[2]For example one of the offered options in Audi is the possibility to choose the sound produced by the engine. You can choose a car of this brand, for example, get a leather styling package for 20,000 EUR or Bang and Olufsen Advanced Sound System for 10,000 EUR. Mercedes offers, for example, 17 Swarovski crystals in each headlamp for 18,000 EUR and a Rolls-Royce star headliner available from 13,000 EUR See also: https://www.auto-motor-i-sport.pl/wydarzenia/Najdrozsze-opcje-wyposazenia-w-samochodach,19946,1.

While the high quality of materials or a unique way of manufacturing increases the value (and price) of these goods the evaluation of their functionality (understood as convenience of use, comfort, safety), especially in comparison with similar goods for example premium class is debatable. Natural and rare materials generally require greater maintenance than their synthetic or less noble natural counterparts (e.g. Vicuna[3] wool, cashmere or angora compared to wool, chamois[4] or lamb nappa compared to cattle leather). The size of luxury yachts makes it impossible to moor in many marinas and their fuel consumption like that of luxury sports cars, has nothing to do with the cost efficiency of travel. In the case of luxury goods, the issue of comfort is not obvious either. Shoes from Luoboutin, Jimmy Choo or Mahnolo Blanick are rated by many fashonists as objects of exceptional beauty and workmanship but they are difficult to consider comfortable. The same is true of Lamborghini driving in the city. Just try getting into this car gracefully and then take a ride on a cobblestone road to see that using luxury can be a combination of humiliation and discomfort. Even though they can be considered as merely anecdotal examples of the discomfort associated with the use of luxury goods it does do not discredit the overall care taken to produce them. However luxury goods are not just about quality, let alone functionality, but about combining beauty with mastercraftsmanship and material care while ensuring a quality and functionality that creates the feeling of their uniqueness. Functional value is not the main reason for luxury shopping. These are social and hedonic values embodied in luxury goods that are the main causes of acquisition and public exposure (Wong and Zaichkowsky 1999; Scholz 2014; Stępień et al. 2016; Stępień and Hinner 2018; Jiang and Shan 2018, see also Chapters 5, 6, 7).

Moreover today many goods promoted as luxurious have little in common with the traditional understanding of high quality or mastery of workmanship. Mass-produced goods bearing the logo of luxury brands are nowadays offered to a wide range of less affluent, aspiring consumers living in developing regions of the world. Standards of workmanship and

---

[3]Vicuna—an animal from the alpaca family living wild in the Andes Cut every two years the wool of this alpaca is several times thinner and thus more delicate than the wool of lamas. Used in the production of clothing, by Loro Piana, and recently in Poland by Tomasz Ossoliński.

[4]Chamois—thin, very delicate goat leather.

the quality of materials have decreased and production has been relocated to off shore or near shore countries (see e.g. Robinson and Hsieh 2016; Stępień and Młody 2020). The democratization of luxury deprives the traditionally understood functional value of luxury, especially in terms of its quality and rarity.

2.3 Artistry and Polysensuality—From Possession to Reliving the Experience?

Apparently when asked what luxury is, Coco Chanel said, "*it is where necessity begins, when the necessity ends*".[5] For her (and for many other supporters and consumers of luxury goods and services) the creation, possession or mere contact with luxury is a positive aesthetic and emotional experience which, while having nothing to do with the satisfaction of basic biological or even material needs, is essential for the full enjoyment of the richness of human creativity. This value of luxury places it quite high in the hierarchy of goods/services that instrumentally provide people with so-called superior values. While it is difficult to see moral good or truth in them,[6] luxury objects embody (though not always) beauty.

Beauty includes artistic and aesthetic components. Both, although long regarded as a monolith, were from the beginning of philosophy considered a pure need of the human soul. Aristotle wrote about beauty as a superior value while Kant valued beauty at the same level as morality. Aesthetics[7] analyzes relationships between objects (the artists, their work and the recipients), the processes of artistic creation and aesthetic values;

[5]The quote is distributed mainly in online forums, fashion magazines and appears in the film about Coco Chanel. However it is difficult to consider this as a credible confirmation, hence the word—supposedly.

[6]I am omitting here a discussion about the relationship between truth, moral value and beauty. See for more details e.g. Mandler (1981), Baumgartner and Pasquerella (2004), Guyer (2005).

[7]Aesthetics, like sociology or economics, grew out of the mother of all sciences—philosophy. As a separate branch of philosophy it appeared only in the eighteenth century thanks to A.G. Baumgarten, in the work of Aesthetica (bars 1–2, 1750–1758), although the considerations about beauty, as emphasized above, were conducted already in antiquity or probably even earlier which we cannot prove. Initially the considerations about beauty were ontological in

sense of artistry filtered by the sense of individual aesthetics (Gołaszewska 1985; Chailan 2018).

Luxury goods are traditionally associated with artistry and the fact that they provide many positive experiences caused by the contact with beauty. An artistic value embodied in a product or service is the contribution of the creator and may be subject to objectivity. The experience of artistry as an attribute of a given good or service is the relationship between this object and its creator and its recipient and its effects in the form of polysensual sensations depend on the individual perception of the recipient. Works of art are an excellent example of a combination of artistic and aesthetic values whilst illustrating at the same time how their exchange value is shaped by a subjective component of aesthetic feelings (see also Białynicka-Birula 2003; Mandler 1981; Baumgartner and Pasquerella 2004; Guyer 2005). While the paintings of F. Goya, H. Bosch, Rembrandt, P. Picasso, V. van Gogh, J.C. Monet, V. Kandinski and J. Pollock are recognized (and thus objectified) works of art of exceptional artistic value their reception by individuals varies.

Luxury—like art—is supposed to evoke emotions. However the combination of artistry with the offer of aesthetic feelings in the case of luxury looks a bit different than in art (see Jelinek 2018). While for centuries human creativity was considered to be art only when it represented the beauty of nature and aroused positive emotions, since the age of Enlightenment the task of art has been to evoke various emotions, including strong, extreme and not necessarily positive ones, while gradually moving away from copying nature in favour of searching for new forms and means of expression (see e.g. Guyer 2005).

The purpose of luxury goods and services is to maximize the pleasure of their users. This is even the case with turpistic works of art which bring the collectors the pleasure of having and experiencing them, although this is in contrast to what they present.[8] In the case of luxury

nature (what it is). To the greatest extent, in the "pre-esthetic" epoch, beauty was described as part of axiological considerations concerning values (see also Table 1.2, Chapter 1).

[8]Works of art become a luxury as soon as their artistic value is widely recognized which is usually accompanied by a sharp rise in their prices. In order for an art object to become a luxury it is necessary to generate demand for it, but not demand similar to the demand for

the creators of these (mainly) goods in the personas of designers and brand owners do not stop making the suggestions that artistry lies at heart of both the effect and the process of their creation. In order to strengthen the connection between the world of luxury and art the entire system of communication and sale of luxury goods is carried out in cooperation with the world of artists. The marriage of art and luxury is well-established, strong, cultivated and seems to benefit both groups (see e.g. Lagier and Godey 2007; Kapferer 2014). Just as exports are considered to be a multiplier of economic growth so the element of artistry is a multiplier of the future margin in the luxury sector; it acts as a trigger for many positive emotions and has social consequences. The element of artistry contained in luxury goods favours aesthetic exaltations, brings joy, but also confirms the individual's conviction that besides his biological nature or egoistic material desires he also has a soul hungry for exaltation and it may be this very need to commune with art that is the main reason (or interesting excuse) for purchasing very expensive and doubtless useful things. In the case of luxury goods we deal with art only in relation to those rare and valuable goods, most often from the very top of the pyramid, which contain a large component of a unique contribution in the form of creative work combined with its unusual work or above-average quality of materials which in turn is another essential feature of traditionally understood luxury.

Luxury goods and all the aura that accompanies the process of their creation, sale and subsequent public demonstration are intended to evoke many positive emotions in the owner of these goods, some of which are aesthetic. However it is questionable whether the mere possession of luxury goods enhances the aesthetic feeling? It seems that the admiration for the beauty of a good is not directly related to its possession. Would we be more delighted with a Monet painting if it were ours? Do we like the bag more after its purchase? In order to experience positive aesthetic emotions we do not have to be owners of the goods that arouse them but their frequency can be greater the more often we deal with the object which in turn is more likely when we own it. On the other hand

ordinary goods as well as demand characterized by the symbolism of rarity and uniqueness, see more widely Dewey (2005).

the law of diminishing marginal utility may work here; we simply get used to its beauty and do not appreciate it so much as at the beginning.

Ownership therefore becomes a problem if we want to experience strong aesthetic elation again and again. New goods or services, due to their novelty component, provide a high level of such experiences to a greater extent.

Contemporary developing trends of luxury for rent or shared luxury result not only from the concern for sustainable development of the planet but also grows because it allows consumers to enjoy new (for the user) goods for a short time; when the component of delight in the beauty of a given object is still strong and cannot fade away over time; for we have it for just a short time. By sharing a given good we multiply the level of positive feelings without straining the budget and without blaming ourselves for a possible lack of use of the good for which we paid a lot (see Thaler 2005).

While the search for new strong aesthetic sensations is probably not the most important reason for the development of luxury for rent trend in the second hand luxury trade (or pre—owned, pre-loved luxury), the need to have something special and considered fairly objectively as artistic sounds clear as one of the main reasons for the desire to have something special, unique (and thus to underline our own uniqueness, see also Fox 2018). All these three ways to experience luxury are growing quickly but the artistic or aesthetic component varies in importance (Joy et al. 2012; Zhan and He 2012; Chandon et al. 2016).

Luxury for rent is mainly about fashion or cars; it meets the need for novelty and social, public exposure of what is fashionable, desirable and timely and is developing among the not richest, mainly aspiring consumers. The trend of luxury vintage is, in turn, the domain of people who appreciate the craftsmanship of the design of a given good and at the same time want it (if the good is not part of the collection, but is intended for personal use) to emphasize their individualistic style. Shared luxury is primarily based on the idea of sustainable development. However the use of luxury, whether it concerns a good purchased or consumed for a certain period of time, is a source of many positive and not only aesthetic emotions: it gives joy, satisfaction and enhances well-being (Hudders and Pandelaere 2012; Prentice and Loureiro 2018).

2.4 Luxury as a Symbol of Social Desire and Moral Stigma

Luxury symbolizes wealth, social prestige, belonging to an elite group of elected people. It is not so much a collection of goods as their socially constructed meaning. Perception, social symbolism, built thanks to the spread of information about the characteristics and significance of goods, socially recognized and legitimized defines probably the most important category of luxury value. It is thanks to a social label that certain goods or services are included in the register of goods or services considered to be luxurious. Let me once again refer to Girard and Orléans (2014) and the role of social mimicry in value creation. Desire requires the creation of a positive meaning. It is thanks to brand owners, manufacturers, designers that a set of features symbolizing luxury is proposed and embodied in the form of some kind of good, which is to be the basis of later social desire. After enterprises propose a value the process of its co-creation in the social space follows. Only a part of co-creators (apart from brand owners or salesmen) consciously participate in this process. Mimicry occurs simultaneously in two directions: as a consequence of reference, comparison of the individual to the environment and as a pressure of the environment to reformulate, adapt the individual to his requirements, trends, fashions and so on (see also Palaver 2013; Urbańska 1997).

Almost every definition of luxury indicates its social desire (see Sect. 2.1 but also Kapferer and Valette-Florence 2018; Chandon et al. 2016; Wong and Zaichkowsky 1999; Berry 1994). The reason for desire is their artistry, quality, rarity and high price but also the very fact that those considered to be "better" have them, which in turn increases the desire of the others who aspire to join the former group.

We are talking about the two effects here which have already been described when discussing the rarity of luxury: the effect of standing out from the crowd and imitation. The latter was proclaimed by Girard as the most important motive for the development of humanity and the cause of its disasters (see also Romejko 2003). According to this philosopher people want what others have, following the logic—the more people recognize that a given good/action/state is good for them (i.e. it meets their expectations, needs) the less likely they are to be wrong.

A bandwagon effect occurs when consumer demand grows with the growing popularity of a good. It is not so much expressed in the attitude "*I want what others want*" as it means "*I want it because others want it*". Scholars have explored the bandwagon behaviour in-depth in political science to explain election biases for example (see Simon 1954; Nadeau et al. 1993). Academics have furthermore analyzed the effect in economics; as one of the anomalies of consumer behavioural patterns which mainly stem from the lack of sufficient information about the product price-quality ratio. However this explanation seems highly inadequate because it abstracts from the sociological and psychological antecedents of the purchase decisions of such goods. According to Festinger's (1954) social comparison theory humans tend to evaluate their opinions, abilities, or social status and prefer to compare themselves with others similar to themselves. Especially Western societies are characterized by a "unidirectional drive upward" and therefore feel pressurized to improve continuously. The need to compare leads to affiliation, the need to conform motivates uniformity, while the unidirectional drive upward enhances competition. Even though Festinger emphasized accurate self-evaluation as the purpose of social comparison many sociological and psychological studies question this assumption (see Wood 1989 for the analysis of the amplifications and replenishments of Festinger's theory).

Firstly self-evaluation may serve different goals; people compare with others either to self-improve or self-enhance. While self-improvement inclines towards upward comparisons—with people perceived as superior (Wheeler 1966)—self-enhancement prompts downward comparisons with those who are perceived as inferior (Wills 1981). Secondly, even though humans strive for accuracy in their self-evaluation process, social comparison may occur automatically and therefore be biased because the objects of comparison may be random; namely people may as well compare themselves with a stranger passer-by (Brickman and Bulman 1977; Allen and Wilder 1977; Guiot 1978). Thirdly there may be various multiple reference groups used as the basis for self-evaluation. One may be under pressure of the implicit requirements of one's group but at the same time be attracted by the standards or way of life of another (Holt 1995).

Leibenstein (1950) defined the bandwagon effect as typical for lower-end luxury brand extensions which scholars further conceptualized as the antecedent of the snob effect (Miller et al. 1993; Berry 1994). This may suggest that bandwagoners would rather buy masstige luxuries while the snobs would rather purchase brands from a higher tier of the luxury pyramid. This may further imply that there are more bandwagon-prone consumers in the new luxury markets than in the old "luxury" homebase countries.

While bandwagoners want to conform to the public image of the upper class by virtually copying their purchase behaviour, the snobs tend to publicly manifest their individual sophistication and superior taste. The aim of the luxury purchases and their public exposure in both groups is the same: the quest for prestige and social recognition which seems to be one of the most important value categories in luxury. Both groups want to differentiate themselves from the groups that they perceive as inferior, but their methods to achieve this are different. While bandwagon behaviour is a mere copycatting strategy of the "wannabe" class, the snobbish strategy is to positively bewilder the public by non-conformist activities or appearances. The desire to differ is to express individuality which seems to be highly valued by such consumers.

Thus the reason behind snob behaviour is to gain public applause that would come from the self-evaluation of the snob's individual superiority. Social recognition seems to be a necessary, even if auxiliary condition, for the snob to enjoy their good public image of oneself.

The social desire for luxury which triggers the demand for these goods (both snobbish and imitative) is practically inseparable from its moral, generally negative evaluation. Studies on luxury date from thousands of years ago and for most of the time have been a debate on the moral meaning of consumption and the public exposure of luxury based primarily on normative religious and ideological judgments (Berry 1994; Cloutier 2015). The stigmatisation and much less numerous attempts to disenchant luxury were focused on the way in which consumption and public exposure were consumed. They are not objects but people have been stigmatized for the usage and public exposure of luxury. Traditional understanding of goods themselves was positive; for centuries they were associated with mastery of workmanship, the use of the highest quality materials, artistry and functional perfection.

The oldest views of luxury in the context of its usefulness and social symbolism are visible in the writings of classical philosophers. Socrates saw luxury as a public necessity; the final stage and effect of social development in which these goods serve the general public. He opposed the human tendency to cultivate carnal pleasures to such an extent and since these desires are stronger in the individual than the desire to serve society, luxury, as a private good, should be limited and controlled. Plato in his work Republica, recalling Socrates' conversation with Glaukon (in the treatise The City of Pigs), explains that when there are no legal restrictions on human desires cities turn into "tryphosa polis" consuming and frenetically surrounding themselves with luxury goods in a constant pursuit of new and more sophisticated desires (see Plato; 372 BC/2005; McKeen 2004). Similarly Aristotle believed that living in luxury is unworthy of the individual because it does not contribute to the prosperity of society (Berry 1994). The scale of the dichotomy between how citizens should behave and their actual behaviour was highlighted by laws prohibiting the public display of luxury costumes, jewellery or bans on the collective delight of the palate and other senses (e.g. Lex oppia, 215 BC, after: Culham 1982; Braund 1994).

Interestingly in Ancient Greece and Rome the reprehensible customs of the monarchs of the East and South of the area were considered to be the source of moral decay caused by excessive consumption. The ostentatious luxury surrounding the courts of Persia, Egypt and the Far East unprecedented in Europe aroused a mimetic desire among the rich Greek and Roman bourgeoisie. The merchants of that time conducting international trade activities not only supplied goods from distant lands but also skillfully marketed them arousing demand and social desire for these rarities (e.g. spices, porcelain, silk, exotic skins or jewellery). The explanation of demoralisation as being caused by external influences is an interesting example of the attribution error of ancient thinkers who apparently had difficulties with admitting that their fellow citizens have a fragile moral structure giving into desires of a completely non-metaphysical nature. The legislative struggle of the state against social desire and public exposition of luxury lasted in Europe until the seventeenth century.

The regulations against excesses were supposed to counteract excessive expenses that constituted a threat to souls, a reversal from God and a spoilage of public order. Luxury as a measure of size and grandeur was to remain the domain of a few privileged members of society and legitimize their greatness and power. For example a regulation of the French King Philip II in 1279 forbade townspeople to wear dormice and ermine fur, expensive stones and gold and silver diadems and an English law in 1336 provided that the wearing of clothes and fur imported from outside England, Ireland, Wales and Scotland was allowed only for members of the royal family, high-born nobility and clergy (McNeil and Riello 2017, p. 70). Italian legislation from the sixteenth century limited the consumption of superfluous fabrics, clothes, dishes, interior furnishings and means of transport. The regulations provided for a system of financial and corporal penalties (public beat ing) not only for consumers but also for craftsmen producing these goods (McNeil and Riello 2017, p. 71).

The desire for luxury goods was not only a secular domain. The position of the medieval Catholic Church was ambivalent towards luxury. On the one hand the view on the necessity of living in virtue was proclaimed (and one of its measures was supposed to be the lack of desire for temporal goods) and on the other hand monumental sacral objects were built using expensive materials, sculptures and paintings to emphasize the greatness of the divine absolute. In the thirteenth century the rule of modest clothing outside the church and decorative during liturgical ceremonies was introduced (Miller 2014, p. 41).

Early agrarian capitalism from the seventeenth and eighteenth centuries coincided with what Berry calls the "demoralisation" of luxury (1994, pp. 169–173). Intensive industrialization and the dynamic development of trade combined with the emergence of early forms of promotion, favoured the growth of consumption of luxury goods. A growing number of people had access to products that beautified their homes and the development of technologies such as printing, weaving or craftsmanship in general allowed for mass production and the lowering of prices.

Bernard Mandeville, David Hume, Adam Smith[9] and later W. Sombart (see Marshall 2000; Mandeville 1714: 2005; Franchetti 2013) saw the economically useful side of luxury. They stressed that thanks to the development of this market and business more and more people have jobs which contributes to economic development and the spread of luxury itself is an expression of the general growing social welfare and although the industrial revolution and the beginning of capitalism did not stop the debate about the moral overtones of luxury its tone has certainly diminished significantly (see also Armitage's and Roberts' interdisciplinary analysis of the "spirit of luxury" throughout history, 2016).

Despite the tendency of the privileged classes to surround themselves with luxury due to their birth or entrepreneurship (we are talking here mainly about craftsmen, merchants and bankers), in most pre-modern societies the rigid social hierarchy was not associated with a dichotomy of moral values. The accumulation of wealth allowed the privileged to surround themselves with luxury but it was not so much the common stigmatization that dominated as the lack of approval for the imposition of luxury, even among the privileged classes. In antiquity and in the Middle Ages the aristocracy's tasks were not limited to collecting tributes, inventing more and more sophisticated entertainment or searching for unusual goods. Kings, aristocrats, knights and noblemen were responsible for defending the state and winning in the armed struggles was a good opportunity for a rapid enrichment.[10]

---

[9]A. Smith was not a supporter of luxury because he saw it as a demoralising element but like Hume he saw it as an innovative and driving force for the economy.

[10]Henry VIII (1491–1547) showed a peculiar innovation in his rapidly increasing wealth by liquidating the Catholic Church in England, which allowed him not only to marry his wives, but also by taking over the church property made his capital several times greater and enabled him to enjoy himself in luxury. The ruler was famous not only for his weakness towards women, but also for his lavish life in the form of organizing tournaments, feasts, decorating his fancy clothes with hundreds of jewels and surrounding himself with luxurious furnishings in numerous residences. His daughter Elisabeth I developed this style on a grand scale by decorating her dresses with even more precious jewels (an example is her Portrait with the Armada in which the queen is dressed in a dress decorated with almost a thousand jewels). However scientific objectivity requires us to point out that the most luxurious ruler was Louis XIV. For more details about the lifestyle and clothing of English rulers see Hayward (2017).

As Stearns (2006) points out until the eighteenth century the history of mankind has shown great cohesion in the system of values of pre-modern societies determined by obligations to the state, land and ruler and the subordination of temporal life to strict religious orders. All these in turn—from Christianity, through Islam, Buddhism, Hinduism to Confucianism (rather than religion)—propagated humility, virtue and moderation in manifesting and satisfying needs other than the basic.

In the historical moral outline of the assessment of luxury two threads dominate:

- stigmatization of the ostentatious consumption of the lower classes who are not entitled to this privilege because of their place in the social hierarchy determined by birth;
- a religious imperative to live in poverty but not binding on the ruling circles for whom surrounding oneself with luxury was a legitimization of the power of the state (and the church).

Nowadays the burden of moral assessments of luxury consumption has shifted to the problem of social inequalities resulting from differences in the accumulation of capital. The point raised below is only an ambiguous link between luxury and the relatively new, though increasingly common, global trend towards sustainability.

According to a study on the relationship between luxury and sustainability these two areas seem to be mutually exclusive (Achabou and Dekhili 2013; Kapferer and Michaut-Denizeau 2013; Janssen et al. 2013; Kapferer and Valette-Florence 2018; Slater 1997; Hilton 2004). There are several reasons why luxury and sustainability can create separate worlds. In a sustainable approach the main objective is to use resources in such a way as to ensure maximum usability with minimal damage to the environment and to present and future generations (Kapferer 2010; Yang et al. 2017; Voyer and Beckham 2014). From this point of view the production and consumption of luxury goods is, in principle, unnecessary and harmful to the environment. The planet's limited resources are wasted on producing something that meets the sublime desires of an ever-growing, yet still small, global group of rich people (Willems et al. 2012; Dion and Borraz 2017; Thach and

Olsen 2006). The spread of production and the mass consumption of luxury not only democratise luxury but also increase the scale of wasting resources.

Describing luxury goods as unnecessary and their consumption as conspicuous leads to a moral condemnation of such behaviour (Achabou and Dekhili 2013; Kapferer and Michaut-Denizeau 2013; Janssen et al. 2013; Chevalier and Mazzalovo 2008; Atwal and Williams 2009; Kapferer and Bastien 2009). Looking at wealth is not compatible with an attitude that seeks to balance the conditions in which people live in the world, especially if we consider building 5-star hotels in countries with a high poverty rate or promoting luxury in these places. The very existence of luxury in places where the standard of living of the population is low exposes social contrasts and increases its negative perception among those who are deprived of decent living conditions.

This leads to another reason why luxury and sustainability are separate worlds. While luxury can cause social stigma its purchase and use generates a number of positive feelings and experiences among consumers. The desire to dazzle with riches does not necessarily lie at the heart of this pleasure. When buying luxury goods consumers want to enjoy their beauty, craftsmanship and above-average quality materials. The purchasing process itself should also be a pleasant experience. Worrying about the fate of the planet does not necessarily fit into the set of features creating this pleasant aura (Kapferer and Michaut-Denizeau 2013).

Despite these discrepancies luxury is not a complete denial of sustainable development. First of all luxury goods are still relatively rare and expensive (Kapferer and Michaut-Denizeau 2013; Tsai 2005; Brooke 2004). Their purchase, due to the price, is much smaller than daily purchases. For this reason the destructive impact of this sector on the environment is not as great as in the case of mass production. Secondly in the luxury sector the use of natural resources and the production of goods is characterised by greater attention to quality and precision in production and the way in which rare materials are obtained for the production of luxury goods seems to be better controlled than in the case of companies producing mass goods, not least because of the threat of losing the brand reputation as the most important marketing asset (Vermeir and Verbeke 2006).

If the actual production activities of all modern luxury goods were still in line with their traditional image the convergence of sustainable business models and luxury would be greater. However the control of supply chains alone does not guarantee that the resulting goods will be environmentally friendly.

2.5 Evolution of Luxury Business—From Class to Mass?

Humanity almost from the very beginning of its existence has produced things that can be described as luxurious because they were very rare, unnecessary but admired and the categories of goods that were considered luxurious changed although some clothes, jewellery, precious metals, rare textiles and works of art, including those decorative (i.e. paintings, furniture, lamps, carpets) are permanent residents in the private luxury register.

We can observe the consumption of luxury since the emergence of the agrarian economy when it was associated with the strict stratification of society into a small group of privileged and lords (rulers, mighty, clergy) and the rest living in poverty.

In Ancient Greece, Rome or the powers of the South and the East the surroundings of rare goods of newness, aesthetics or functionality was clearly present. However luxury goods were not only the result of the military annexation of some territory but also a derivative of commercial activity. Apparently the universal human tendency is the curiosity that prompts the desire for novelty. In ancient Greece, for example, exotic eastern spices, chicken legs or certain species of fish were considered luxurious. In ancient Rome the symbol of culinary luxury were poultry and birds, exotic fruit or spices and luxurious entertainment included lavish feasting, taking public baths, carrying exotic animals or having an ethnically diverse, beautiful group of slaves. An important part of the social signalling of wealth was also the organization of lavish funeral ceremonies (Johal 2012). Jewels and costumes belonged to an important group of goods symbolizing wealth and social status. The colour of purple was synonymous with luxury in ancient Rome. The dyes from a special species of sea snails (Murex brandaris, Murex trunculus) were used to produce fabrics ranging from deep orange to black violet.[11] In order to obtain 1.5 grams of pure purple dye it was necessary to collect about 12,000 pieces of these creatures. The dyeing of fabrics (mainly linen and silk used for ceremonial robes) left a weak, marine smell identified with the "fragrance of wealth".[12]

Discovering and exploring the interiors of ancient and medieval shipwrecks reveals the scale of the trade in luxury goods. On the decks marble, lead and bronze were found, which were to add splendour to Greek or Roman public buildings and private houses; fragrances, silks and other fabrics, mainly from India or Egypt; Baltic amber, dyes, metals and jewels or a living load of exotic animals from Africa. After the creation of the Roman Empire exotic goods such as silk, porcelain, tea and spices were also transported along the Silk Road. The jewellery offered by Arab merchants made of African precious metals and stones was also sold.

Thanks to the Crusaders sugar and sweets flourished in Europe and in the late Middle Ages coffee, chocolate, laka, more and more interior decorations and pets joined the group of luxury goods. Finding pleasure in "exotic" luxury concerned not only Europe but was also clearly visible in the courts of Mongolian rulers in the form of love for African animals (alive and dead in the form of skins or horns) and European works of art. However as highlighted in the discussion of social desire and moral condemn of luxury for both ancient Greeks and Romans the consumption of luxury was a social problem and subject of public debates on how to tame and manage its consumption to preserve the public order. This problem is particularly acute when the political system is called a democracy or a republic where one of the main principles is civil equality. Although the number of elected citizens was limited there were proportionately more of them than in later monarchic systems. In ancient Greece there were also extreme differences between city-states and their approach to luxury consumption. While in Athens or Macedonia in the

[11] See also https://www.ancient.eu/Tyrian_Purple/.

[12] Interesting information about the luxury lifestyle of ancient Greeks and Romans is contained in the BBC series Guilty Pleasures.

times of Alexander the Great this consumption was manifested almost ostentatiously, in ancient Sparta an expression of luxury was at most death for the homeland.

From the very beginning the consumption of luxury was developing in the cities which Plato has already hailed as the source of moral decay. In the Middle Ages luxury also did not migrate to the extremely poor countryside which was primarily concerned with keeping the lords and peasants themselves alive. During feudalism and the reign of the monarchy the percentage of the privileged population was limited to the rulers and aristocracy anointed with the sovereign privilege of owning and publicly displaying these goods and two groups who did not have formal permission for such consumption but enjoyed it anyhow; representatives of the clergy and a group of merchants, bankers and craftsmen.

In the Middle Ages the consumption of luxury became a sin due to the doctrine of the Christian Church although this did not prevent the clergy from private use of Church wealth. Officially condemned luxury did not serve the Church only to publicly legitimize the power of God, but also to make the temporal life of his servants more pleasant. The second group (merchants, craftsmen, bankers) was not privileged because of their position to exhibit wealth but thanks to their entrepreneurship they acquired it anyway The laws and regulations prohibiting the emanation of wealth affected this social group to the greatest extent.

In the late Middle Ages, mainly due to the art and architecture of this period, we can observe that the accumulation and consumption of luxury goods is increasingly the domain of entrepreneurs. As McNeil and Riello write (2017, p. 68 et seq.), the picture of *Arnolfino's engagement* (by Jan van Eyck 1434) shows how rich this Italian clothier was. Fresh oranges, Turkish carpets, silk robes decorated with fur or a small dog were symbols of rare, exotic luxury and prestige. At that time the collection of items from ancient Greece and Rome and travelling became synonymous with wealth combined with good taste. Initially the journeys concerned Europe and later the Far East and Africa. The fashion for goods from the Far East, although present throughout the history of luxury, developed especially during the industrial revolution.

The largest consumers of luxury were the monarchs and the aristocracy. Quite apart from the moral overtone of this consumption, the needs of the courts were the driving force behind the production and trade of these goods. Thanks to the patronage of the monarchs outstanding works of art in painting, sculpting, architecture and ornamentation or charming parks were created as well as the development of theatre and music. The demand for luxury on the part of the high-born led to the emergence of whole branches of industry, satisfying the desires of the wealthy. The demand and supply was also ensured by the class of entrepreneurs led by the inhabitants of medieval cosmopolitan cities of Venice, Genoa, Bruges and Antwerp. At the end of the sixteenth century big trading companies were established: English, Portuguese, Italian and Dutch and later French and German trading in luxury goods on an international scale. It is thanks to the Dutch merchants that tulips, hyacinths and imperial crowns ceased to be a symbol of luxury, since—after their initial import—their cultivation began to spread in Europe (McNeil and Riello 2017, p. 107). Near the manors, craft factories were established producing for their needs. The largest were workshops in the Louvre of the Gobelins brothers in the seventeenth century. In The Hague thanks to the discoveries of the practical clock pendulum in the years 1650–1670 watchmaking was developed. Porcelain factories in French Sevres (1768) and German Meissen (1708) as well as English fabric factories imitating Eastern design were established. The entire Grasse region began to specialize in perfume production after glovers discovered excellent conditions for growing plants in the area around the town, from the extracts of which they obtained perfume oils for their products. In the eighteenth century due to taxes, the tanning industry collapsed but the perfume machine was already so much developed that it still works today.

Relocation of the production of luxury goods to Europe made luxury consumption widespread. This was made possible by the spectacular inventions of the steam engine and electric energy which changed the face of the world.

According to Sombart (1967) luxury and the pursuit of it were of cardinal importance for the development of capitalism. Sombart even called capitalism “an illegal child of luxury” (Sombart 1967, p. 27). The author also puts forward a hypothesis that this change of social tastes to more feminized, focused on the appearance and aesthetics of homes triggered a demand for luxury goods. However while there is a strong and two-way relationship between the growth of demand for luxury and the development of capitalism, capitalism is neither a child nor even a spouse of luxury. Luxury flourished due to industrialization but it was only a sign of a general mass production and consumption being one of the complex foundations of capitalism (see Hartwell 2017).

Sombart (1967, p. 81) also claimed that the increase in the production and consumption of luxury during the industrial revolution was the result of the "emergence of homo novus"—a man of the bourgeoisie—who living in a hierarchical society must prove his value by, among other things, manifesting his wealth. In the seventeenth and eighteenth centuries the demand for luxury in Europe grew quite spectacularly. The goods that enjoyed special desire and popularity were the Far East thin fabrics, porcelain and lacquered furniture. Gerritsen and Riello (2015, pp. 111–112) report that while in 1615 the Dutch Company imported 24,000 pieces of porcelain to Europe annually, five years later this number rose to 63,000 and in the eighteenth century the annual turnover of porcelain was estimated at millions of pieces. At the end of the seventeenth century Asian manufactories were mass-producing goods especially for the European market. In Japan screens, crates and lacquer chests of drawers were produced specifically for the European market with shapes and ornamentation adapted to European tastes. Typical decorations depicted large ships and walking white invaders with umbrellas in the scenery of everyday street bustle. White masters had to be accompanied by their dark slaves or far-eastern servants. These goods were called by Japanese Nambans which meant southern barbarians (Curvelo 2012, after: McNeil and Riello 2017, p. 109).

The demand for the Orient, which lasted until the end of the nineteenth century, led to the successful European copying of craftsmanship and the style of Far East manufactories. Berg (2004) in his article on the history of luxury in eighteenth century England analyses the process of development of trade and later the European production of luxury goods. British manufacturers successfully imitated Asian luxury although they gave it their own English touch, which even allowed them to export products of a new stylistic category to continental Europe. Already a category of new luxury for the bourgeoisie was created. This mass-produced luxury included mainly fabrics used for decorating interiors and tailoring.

It was good to have a boudoir decorated with a lot of fabrics in the form of curtains, bedspreads, serviettes and to receive guests in a special, homemade loose-fitting outfit—déshabillé. Mass production of still life paintings, screens, chests of drawers and lamps was also started. Luxury ceased to be the domain of rich elites and although it did not go under thatched roofs richer layers of townsmen enjoyed its availability. By the very fact of being widespread luxury goods became semi-precious and not so expensive.

However such an arrangement resulted in a noticeable departure from the critical moralising associated with its consumption (perhaps apart from T. Veblen). New mass luxury has become a part of social life, style and fashion. It has ceased to be an overpowering object of monumental sacrum for the few and became a tool for delivering joy while still emitting social splendour. Much of the stigmatization that had previously been attached to luxury did not apply to tea sets, tableware, candlesticks or pillows. According to Berg (2004, p. 89), economic benefits resulting from the widespread consumption of luxury prevailed and suppressed the debate about the fears of moral corruption caused by the consumption of luxury.

Surrounding oneself with luxury has become a social phenomenon but it requires knowledge of whether a given good is fashionable and its use is in a good taste. Collins (1999, p. 114) quotes an anecdote about B. Franklin who in 1758 bought breakfast tablecloths in London and sent them to his wife together with a letter instructing her how to use them. He wrote that they should be laid out on the dining table because here (in England) nobody eats breakfast on a bare table.

The rushing machine of luxury consumption was stopped for some time by two world wars. In the ruins of war Europe reactivated the production and consumption of luxury from scratch, but—bearing in mind the cruelty of the fighting—no longer ostentatious. In the fashion sphere comfort, quality of cutting and restrained elegance (Chanel, YSL, Dior, Givenchy) come to the fore. Coco Chanel's philosophy about luxury essence was simplicity, elegance and comfort. She had a vision of offering luxury to everyone because she was convinced that surrounding oneself with beauty is a need of the human soul but most likely she did not think that this business would change so much. With the world recovering the luxury sector not only re-established itself but started expanding its activities. However the urge to increase sales in many cases resulted in ill-considered actions in the form of mass licensing and thus loss of control over the brand and eventually its collapse. It was thanks to Bernard Arnoult and similar businessmen that the luxury business entered a phase of consolidation; the fallen brands were taken over and incorporated into a conglomerate regime governed by the rules of the financial world rather than a small manufactory philosophy where goods are created like works of art.

The phase in which the luxury sector currently finds itself can be described as its "corporatization", but its democratization is really nothing new as suggested by Silverstein and Fiske (Silverstein and Fiske 2003). The trend of spreading luxury has continued since the beginning of the industrial revolution. Today we are only observing its succeeding stages.

Silverstein and Fiske (2003) present the so-called new luxury as an innovative, profitable business strategy based on the development and marketing of high quality products targeted at middle-income consumers. As demonstrated above there is not much innovation in such strategies except a few new traits.

First, even though not new but strong and developing trend, is maintaining marketing communication suggesting that goods belonging to the so-called mass luxury segment are still goods with all the characteristics of traditional luxury. Mass global production and sale of luxury goods offered to a wide range of consumers resulted in the loss of the value of rarity and uniqueness. The massed global production and sale of luxury goods offered to a wide range of consumers has resulted in a loss of rarity and uniqueness. The expansion of brands to new groups of less affluent customers was combined with artificial segmentation and the addition of a well-known logo for accessories. Such aggressive expansion strategies are the result of the brands consolidation of brands, not any more in the hands of designers or families of craftsmen—brand creators, but businessmen who adhere to the principles of finance and stock exchange to the luxury business. Many once elite luxury companies (e.g. LV, Dior, Gucci, Prada, Burberry) have adopted this style. The objective is a rapid increase in share prices combined with a geographical expansion of the scale of operations: both in the area of supply (offshoring, supply chain defragmentation) and sales; through the internationalisation of sales markets, brand expansion and sales in many, not any more prestigious locations (see also Liu et al. 2016).[13]

Until recently the consumption of luxury has concerned the so-called old cradle of luxury—Western Europe and many centuries later—the United States. Nowadays Chinese are the most numerous group of luxury consumers, being the leaders of a dynamically growing aspiring consumers' group from developing or catching up economies. The purchase and public use of luxury goods serves as an effective emblem of wealth and allows new social groups to demonstrate their material and higher class status. Many of these aspiring consumers belong to Millenialls and Generation Z. In 2019 Bain & Co pointed to eight new trends in the luxury sector related to changes in consumer attitudes, many of which refer explicitly to Generation Z, even more so than the Millennials, coexisting simultaneously in two spaces—real and virtual. These trends are: phygital (combination of physical and virtual channels of interactions with the brands), younger customers, openness and today—an emphasis on experiencing, positive emotions resulting from the whole process of interaction with luxury and this trend is closely connected with another which is emotionality—a category of value that is beginning to emerge (according to Bain& Co. forecasts) as the most important in shopping choices not only for luxury goods and services. Generation Z, which in 2020 accounts for about 4% of the total population of luxury consumers, generally differs in their purchasing choices from the older generations, putting more emphasis on experiencing, accumulating positive experiences and emotions, establishing and maintaining social ties than accumulating wealth and having. These

[13]The article shows how global brands spread their distribution network in China opening stores in locations defined as 2nd and 3rd tier cities. In other words we are dealing with the creation of luxury sales outlets, which in their expansionary capacity are similar to the global fast food activities.

experiences can be built in two spaces—real and virtual, but the offer addressed to this generation has to be customised.

Even at the end of 2019 the outlook for the luxury market was very good although there was already talk of a visible and necessary change—a greater focus on sustainable conduct and a possible slowdown in sales growth caused by regional economies and global political instability. According to Bain & Co (2019) the global luxury market reached 1.3 trillion euros ($1.5 trillion) this year with luxury services growing at a faster rate than sales of luxury goods for so-called private use. The new direction of change—towards experential and more sustainable luxury—is to take place mainly due to the expectations of Millenials, which currently account for about 35% of the market and by 2025 are expected to make up half of the recipients of luxury goods and services.

One of the important changes is the development of the idea of sharing. It is not just about luxury for rent or the second hand market (in 2019 it was worth 26 trillion EUR, see Bain 2019), but about cooperation between designers and popular brands with luxury ones. Examples are provided, for example, by the cooperation of H&M with well-known designers of luxury goods in limited collections for the general public, the creation of joint collections by Fendi and Fila, or Louis Vuitton and Supreme. So-called street wear, thanks to cooperation with luxury brands, gains a new dimension. This benefits both mass clothing manufacturers and luxury brands attracting crowds of future consumers. Today Generation Z does not have the means to purchase luxury goods, but this can change over time and with the growth of their income. The strategy for mass and luxury brands is similar to McDonalds' strategy for children: if we imprint positive memories of their birthdays spent with little friends with hamburgers, French fries and a defrosted sugar- and plastic-flavoured cake on this young clientele today, for example, then they will remain our customers for years to come.

Sharing and co-operation does not only concern luxury and popular brands within the same industry. It also shows the combination of the efforts of luxury goods' brands from the fashion or car industry with the hospitality industry. Hotels designed by designers from the luxury fashion industry (Versace, Dolce & Gabbana and Armani) or jewellery (for example, Bulgari) are being built. LVMH has increased its presence in this segment through the acquisition of Belmond and cruises.

The involvement of the luxury business in the development of the sustainability trend is also growing which is related to the desire to transform the perception of this sector into one that promotes ethical and, at the same time, creative production and sales solutions while promoting philanthropy and careful production using local, unique resources. According to Edelman's Earned Brand Report (2020) as many as 57% of consumers declare the impact of environmental and ethical issues on their purchasing choices. Let us remember, however, that these are still declarations, not purchase decisions.

However the most dynamic trend is the progressive digitization of communication and sales (see also Batat 2019). The virtual world provides new forms of artistic expression and building ties with the customer, allows the promulgation of the message about how a brand was created, how it is being developed nowadays and how it takes care of the individual needs of new consumers born in the era of Internet space. The Internet allows not only the selling of luxury goods in a new form of phygital or augmented retail but also provides an unlimited range and access to new impressions so desired by younger and younger recipients of luxury today. Although the so-called high luxury is still characterized by an ambivalent attitude towards the use of the Internet (see e.g. Okonkwo 2007; Andjelic 2017), communication and promotion in virtual reality is not so much a fact as a necessity. What is more today the sale of popular luxury is shifting from flagship stores in the best locations to the Internet or, for example, a fast growing outlet chain (see e.g. Stępień 2017, also Chapter 3).

Burberry is a frequently quoted example of a successful reorientation in line with the trend towards democracy. Faced with the threat of collapse mainly due to the stylistically quite caustic image of an ageing English elite Burberry has bravely transformed its image,[14] targeting most of the newly created brands and lines to the younger, more dynamic

[14]Burberry used the style of chavs (slang, also called scallie, ned). Chavs are young working class who are susceptible to hooliganism. Burberry has transformed the image of chavs into a rude but far from effeminate image of a young boy aware of his feisty, nonchalant and intriguing spell.

generation of aspiring customers (Bothwell 2005). Burberry is today an example of a benchmark in the use of online tools to strengthen the new brand image and online sales.

There is much to suggest that this is not the end of the dynamic changes in the luxury sector, which is migrating towards sensitivity and ephemerality (Lim et al. 2018; Batat 2019; von Wallpach et al. 2019; Kauppinen-Räisänen et al. 2019; Rosenbaum et al. 2019; Desmichel et al. 2020).

The latest COVID 19 Pandemic has strongly reshaped consumers' purchasing behaviour, not only in the luxury sector. Now, the whole business world, not only that of luxury, is looking closely at the pace and extent of the consumers return to shopping. Preliminary data show that consumers are very cautiously increasing their luxury purchases which seems quite natural. Luxury belongs to the category of the most discretionary purchases which are faded out most quickly in a situation of financial danger, which is the current situation. Many consumers will suffer not only from health problems but also financially, as one of the clear consequences of the temporary freeze on the economy are waves of redundancies and corporate bankruptcies. In addition to the rather slow pace and size of luxury shopping the Chinese are also showing greater interest in local brands. Research (e.g. Bain 2020) on consumer purchasing behaviour during and just after the COVID 19 pandemic also clearly shows the following trends:

- progressive (although forced by lockdown) virtualization of shopping,
- an overall reduction in expenditure on purchases beyond that which is necessary,
- greater willingness to buy brands whose communication and sales campaigns are adapted both to the pandemic situation and emphasizing the care of philanthropic, environmental and sustainable aspects in their actions.

Taking the instability and insecurity into consideration, that the last pandemic has caused and combining it with the growing need to experience luxury here and now, the prognosis of Unity Marketing (2020) seems justified. This research centre forecasts that the industry of broadly defined hospitality services will be the one to which most global luxury brands will turn and expand significantly after the end of the COVID 19 Pandemic.

References

Achabou, M. A., & Dekhili, S. (2013). Luxury and sustainable development: Is there a match? *Journal of Business Research, 66*(10), 1896–1903. https://doi.org/10.1016/j.jbusres.2013.02.011.

Allen, V. L., & Wilder, D. A. (1977). Social comparison, self-evaluation, and conformity to the group. In J. M. Suls & R. L. Miller (Eds.), *Social comparison processes: Theoretical and empirical perspectives* (s. 187–208). Washington, DC: Hemisphere.

Andjelic, A. (2017). *Blockchain and the internet of luxury.* From z. https://medium.com/@andjelicaaa/blockchain-and-the-internet-of-luxury-ee5c956b83bf.

Appadurai, A. (1986). Commodities and the politics of value. In A. Appaduarai (Ed.), *The social life of things: Commodities in cultural perspective.* Cambridge: Cambridge University Press.

Armitage, J., & Roberts, J. (2016). The spirit of luxury. *Public Culture, 12*(1), 1–22.

Atwal, G., & Williams, A. (2009). Luxury brand marketing—The experience is everything! *Journal of Brand Management, 16*(5–6), 338–346.

Bain & Co. (2019). *Eight themes that are rewriting the future of luxury goods.*

Bain & Co. (2020). *Global personal luxury goods market set to contract between 20–35 percent in 2020.* https://www.bain.com/about/media-center/press-releases/2020/spring-luxury-report/.

Batat, W. (2019). *Digital luxury: Transforming brands and consumer experiences.* Los Angeles: Sage.

Baumgartner, W., & Pasquerella, L. (2004). Brentano's value theory: Beauty, goodness, and the concept of correct emotion. In D. Jacquette (Ed.), *Cambridge companion to Brentano.* Cambridge: Cambridge University Press.

Belk, R. (1988). Possessions and the extended self. *Journal of Consumer Research, 15*(2), 139–168.

Berg, M. (2004). In pursuit of luxury: Global history and British consumer goods in the eighteenth century. *Past & Present, 182,* 85–142.

Berry, C. (1994). *The idea of luxury: A conceptual and historical investigation*. Cambridge, UK: Cambridge University Press.

Białynicka-Birula, J. (2003). Wartość dzieła sztuki w kontekście teorii estetycznych & ekonomicznych. *Zeszyty Naukowe Akademii Ekonomicznej w Krakowie, 640*, 63–75.

Borys, T. (1980). *Elementy teorii jakości*. Warszawa: PWN.

Bothwell, C. (2005). *Burberry versus the Chavs: BBC news*, 28. From z. http://news.bbc.co.uk/2/hi/business/4381140.stm.

Bourdieu, P., & Wacquant, L. (2013). Symbolic capital and social classes. *Journal of Classical Sociology, 13*(2), 292–302.

Braund, D. (1994). The luxuries of Athenian democracy. *Greece & Rome, 41*(1), 41–48.

Brewer, M. B., & Gardner, W. (1996). Who is this "we"? Levels of collective identity and self-representations. *Journal of Personality and Social Psychology, 71*(1), 83–93.

Brickman, P., & Bulman, R. J. (1977). Pleasure and pain in social comparison. *Social Comparison Processes: Theoretical and Empirical Perspectives, 149*, 186.

Brooke, S. (2004, 4 stycznia). Luxuries ain't what they used to be: Now the high street is full of designers labels and glittering prices, does anything count as exclusive. *The Daily Telegraph*, s. 4.

Chailan, C. (2018). Art as a means to recreate luxury brands' rarity and value. *Journal of Business Research, 85*, 414–423.

Chandon, J. L., Laurent, G., & Valette-Florence, P. (2016). Pursuing the concept of luxury: Introduction to the JBR special issue on "luxury marketing from tradition to innovation." *Journal of Business Research, 69*(1), 299–303. http://doi.org/10.1016/j.jbusres.2015.08.001.

Chevalier, M., & Mazzalovo, G. (2008). *Luxury brand management: A world of privilege*. Singapore: Wiley.

Cloutier, D. (2015). *The vice of luxury: Economic excess in a consumer age*. Washington, DC: Georgetown University Press.

Collins, B. (1999). Matters material and luxurious-eighteenth and early nineteenth-century Irish Linen consumption. In J. Hill & I. C. Lennon (Eds.), *Luxury and austerity* (s. 106–120). Dublin: University College Dublin Press.

Corneo, G., & Jeanne, O. (1997). Conspicuous consumption, snobbism and conformism. *Journal of Public Economics, 66*(1), 55–71.

Cristini, H., Kauppinen-Räisänen, H., Barthod-Prothade, M., & Woodside, A. (2017). Toward a general theory of luxury: Advancing from workbench

definitions and theoretical transformations. *Journal of Business Research, 70,* 101–107. https://doi.org/10.1016/j.jbusres.2016.07.001.
Culham, P. (1982). The Lex Oppia. *Latomus, 41*(4), 786–793.
Curvelo, A. (2012). The disruptive presence of the Namban-jin in early modern Japan. *Journal of the Economic and Social History of the Orient, 55*(2–3), 581–602.
Desmichel, P., Ordabayeva, N., & Kocher, B. (2020). What if diamonds did not last forever? Signaling status achievement through ephemeral versus iconic luxury goods. *Organizational Behavior and Human Decision Processes, 158,* 49–65.
Dewey, J. (2005). *Art as experience*. New York: Penguin.
Dion, D., & Borraz, S. (2017). Managing status: How luxury brands shape class subjectivities in the service encounter. *Journal of Marketing, 81*(5), 67–85.
Dittmar, H. (1994). Material possessions as stereotypes: Material images of different socio-economic groups. *Journal of Economic Psychology, 15*(4), 561–585.
Drabik, L., Kubiak-Sokół, A., Sobol, E., Wiśniakowska, L., Stankiewicz, A., & Wydawnictwo Naukowe, P. W. N. (Eds.). (2018). *Słownik języka polskiego PWN*. Wydawnictwo Naukowe PWN SA.
Dubois, B., Laurent, G., & Czellar, S. (2001). Consumer rapport to luxury: Analyzing complex and ambivalent attitudes (Consumer Research Working Paper, 736). Jouy-en-Josas, France: HEC.
Dubois, B., & Paternault, C. (1997). Does luxury have a home country? An investigation of country images in Europe. *Marketing & Research Today, 25*(2), 79–85.
Edelman's Earned Brand Report. (2020). https://www.edelman.com/research/covid-19-brand-trust-report.
Festinger, L. (1954). A theory of social comparison process. *Human Relations, 7*(2), 117–140.
Fox, C. (2018). Understanding the culture of consuming pre-owned luxury. In *Vintage luxury fashion* (pp. 45–61). Cham: Palgrave Macmillan.
Franchetti, C. (2013). A reconsideration of Werner Sombart's luxury and capitalism. *International Review of Social Sciences and Humanities, 5*(2), 135–139.
Gerritsen, A., & Riello, G. (Eds.). (2015). *Writing material culture history.* London: Bloomsbury Publishing.
Gołaszewska, M. (1985). *Zarys estetyki.* Warszawa: PWN.

Guiot, J. M. (1978). Some comments on social comparison processes. *Journal for the Theory of Social Behaviour.*

Guyer, P. (2005). *Values of beauty: Historical essays in aesthetics.* Cambridge: Cambridge University Press.

Hartwell, R. M. (2017). *The causes of the industrial revolution in England.* Abingdon, Oxon: Routledge.

Hayward, M. (2017). *Rich apparel: Clothing and the law in Henry VIII's England.* London: Routledge.

Hilton, M. (2004). The legacy of luxury: Moralities of consumption since the 18th century. *Journal of Consumer Culture, 4*(1), 101–123. https://doi.org/10.1177/14695405040409060167-4544).

Hoffmann, J., & Coste-Marniere, I. (2013). *Global luxury trends: Innovative strategies for emerging markets.* Basingstoke: Palgrave Macmillan.

Holbrook, M. B. (1996). Special session summary customer value C a framework for analysis and research. In K. P. Corfman & Jr. G. L. John (Eds.), *NA—Advances in consumer research volume 23* (s. 138–142). Provo, UT: Association for Consumer Research.

Holbrook, M. B. (2006). Consumption experience, customer value, and subjective personal introspection: An illustrative photographic essay. *Journal of Business Research, 59*(6), 714–725. https://doi.org/10.1016/j.jbusres.2006.01.008.

Holt, D. B. (1995). How consumers consume: A typology of consumption practices. *Journal of Consumer Research, 22*(1), 1–16.

Hudders, L., & Pandelaere, M. (2012). The silver lining of materialism: The impact of luxury consumption on subjective well-being. *Journal of Happiness Studies, 13*(3), 411–437.

Hung, K., & David, K. T. (2020). Luxury brand consumption in emerging economies: Review and implications. In *Research handbook on luxury branding.* Northampton: Edward Elgar Publishing.

Janssen, C., Vanhamme, J., Lindgreen, A., & Lefebvre, C. (2013). The catch-22 of responsible luxury: Effects of luxury product characteristics on consumers' perceptions of fit with corporate social responsibility. *Journal of Business Ethics, 119*(1), 45–57.

Jelinek, J. S. (2018). Art as strategic branding tool for luxury fashion brands. *Journal of Product & Brand Management, 27*(3), 294–307.

Jiang, L., & Shan, J. (2018). Heterogeneity of luxury value perception: A generational comparison in China. *International Marketing Review, 35*(3), 458–474.

Johal, M. (2012). The diffusion of luxury in ancient Rome: An analysis of funerary practices during the late republic and early empire. *Honors Thesis Collection*, 71.
Joy, A., Sherry, J. F., Jr., Venkatesh, A., Wang, J., & Chan, R. (2012). Fast fashion, sustainability, and the ethical appeal of luxury brands. *Fashion Theory, 16*(3), 273–295.
Kapferer, J.-N. (2010). All that glitters is not green: The challenge of sustainable luxury. *European Business Review, 2*, 40–45.
Kapferer, J.-N. (2014). The artification of luxury: From artisans to artists. *Business Horizons, 57*(3), 371–380.
Kapferer, J.-N., & Bastien, V. (2009). In the beginning there was luxury. *The Luxury Strategy*, 3–30.
Kapferer, J.-N., & Michaut-Denizeau, A. (2013). Is luxury compatible with sustainable development: The consumer viewpoint. *Journal of Brand Management, 21*(I), 1–22. https://doi.org/10.1057/bm.2013.19.
Kapferer, J.-N., & Valette-Florence, P. (2018). The impact of brand penetration and awareness on luxury brand desirability: A cross country analysis of the relevance of the rarity principle. *Journal of Business Research, 83*, 38–50.
Kastanakis, M. N., & Balabanis, G. (2014). Explaining variation in conspicuous luxury consumption: An individual differences' perspective. *Journal of Business Research, 67*(10), 2147–2154.
Kauppinen-Räisänen, H., Gummerus, J., von Koskull, C., & Christini, H. (2019). The new wave of luxury: The meaning and value of luxury to the contemporary consumer. *Qualitative Market Research: An International Journal*.
Khan, S. (2016). *The lure of luxury*. From z. http://bostonreview.net/forum/lure-luxury/shamus-khan-khan-response-lure-luxury.
Lagier, J., & Godey, B. (2007). A scale for measuring aesthetic style in the field of luxury and art products. *International Journal of Arts Management, 9*(2), 39–50.
Leibenstein, H. (1950). Bandwagon, snob, and Veblen effects in the theory of consumers' demand. *Quarterly Journal of Economics, 64*, 183–207.
Lim, H., Childs, M., Cuevas, L., & Lyu, J. (2018). Chanel's invitation to backstage: The effects of visual storytelling and content ephemerality on VIP emotions, International Textile and Apparel Association (ITAA) Annual Conference Proceedings.
Liu, S., et al. (2016). The standardization-localization dilemma of brand communications for luxury fashion retailers' internationalization into China.

Journal of Business Research, 69(1), 357–364. https://doi.org/10.1016/j.jbusres.2015.08.008.
Mandeville, B. (2005). From the fable of the bees. *Readings in the economics of the division of labor: The classical tradition*, 71–79.
Mandler, G. (1981). *The structure of value: Accounting for taste: Center for human information processing*. Department of Psychology. San Diego: University of California.
Marshall, M. (2000). Luxury, economic development, and work motivation: David Hume, Adam Smith, and J. R. McCulloch. *History of Political Economy, 32*(3), 631–648.
McKeen, C. (2004). Swillsburg city limits (the 'city of pigs': Republic 370C–372D). *The Journal for Ancient Greek Political Thought, 21*(1–2), 70–92.
McNeil, P., & Riello, G. (2017). *Historia luksusu*. Warsaw, Poland: Bellona.
Merriam Webster. (2018). *Luxury*. From z. https://www.merriam-webster.com/dictionary/luxury.
Miller, C., McIntyre, S., & Mantrala, M. (1993). Toward formalizing fashion theory. *Journal of Marketing Research, 30*, 142–157.
Miller, M. C. (2014). *Clothing the clergy: Virtue and power in medieval Europe, C. 800–1200*. Ithaca, NY: Cornell University Press.
Mruk, H., & Stępień, B. (2018). Wpływ rozwoju gospodarczego na konsumpcję dóbr luksusowych. *Konsumpcja i Rozwój, 1*(22), 55–65.
Nadeau, R., Cloutier, E., & Guay, J. H. (1993). New evidence about the existence of a bandwagon effect in the opinion formation process. *International Political Science Review, 14*(2), 203–213. https://doi.org/10.1177/019251219301400204.
Naylor, G., & Frank, K. E. (2001). The effect of price bundling on consumer perceptions of value. *Journal of Services Marketing, 15*(4), 270–281.
O'Cass, A., & Frost, H. (2002). Status brands: Examining the effects of non-product-related brand associations on status and conspicuous consumption. *Journal of Product & Brand Management, 11*(2), 67–88.
Okonkwo, U. (2007). *Luxury fashion branding*. Basingstoke: Palgrave Macmillan.
Orléan, A. (2014). *The empire of value: A new foundation for economics*. Cambridge, MA: MIT Press.
Oxford Dictionary. (2018). *Luxury*. From z. https://en.oxforddictionaries.com/definition/luxury.
Palaver, W. (2013). *René Girard's mimetic theory*. East Lansing: MSU Press.
Phares, E. J. (1976). *Locus of control in personality* (Vol. 174). Morristown, NJ: General Learning Press.

Plato, C. (2005). From the republic. In *Readings in the economics of the division of labor: The classical tradition* (pp. 43–49). London: World Scientific.
Popper, K. (1979). *Three worlds*. Ann Arbor: University of Michigan.
Prentice, C., & Loureiro, S. M. C. (2018). Consumer-based approach to customer engagement—The case of luxury brands. *Journal of Retailing and Consumer Services, 43*, 325–332.
Robinson, P. K., & Hsieh, L. (2016). Reshoring: A strategic renewal of luxury clothing supply chains. *Operations Management Research, 9*(3–4), 89–101.
Romejko, A. (2003). Teoria mimetyczno – ofiarniczna. Wprowadzenie do antropologii Rene Girarda. *Studia Gdańskie, XV–XVI*, 55–64.
Rosenbaum, M. S., Ramirez, G. C., Campbell, J., & Klaus, P. (2019). The product is me: Hyper-personalized consumer goods as unconventional luxury. *Journal of Business Research*. https://www.sciencedirect.com/science/article/abs/pii/S0148296319303297?via%3Dihub.
Scholz, L. (2014). *Brand management and marketing of luxury goods*. Hamburg: Anchor Academic Publishing (aap_verlag).
Silverstein, M. J., & Fiske, N. (2003). *Trading up: The new American luxury*. New York: Portfolio/Penguin Group.
Simon, H. (1954). Bandwagon and underdog effects and the possibility of election predictions. *Public Opinion Quarterly, 18*(3), 245–253. https://doi.org/10.1086/266513.
Sirgy, M. J. (1985). Using self-congruity and ideal congruity to predict purchase motivation. *Journal of Business Research, 13*(3), 195–206.
Slater, S. F. (1997). *Consumer culture and modernity*. Oxford: Polity Press.
Smith, G. E., & Nagle, T. T. (1995). Frames of reference and buyers' perception of price and value. *California Management Review, 38*(1), 98–116.
Sombart, W. (1967). *Luxury and capitalism*. Ann Arbor: University of Michigan Press.
Stearns, P. N. (2006). *Consumerism in world history: The global transformation of desire*. London: Routledge.
Stępień, B. (2017). The "Day-After" gleam: Reverse logistics in the luxury fashion sector and its impact on consumer value perception. In *Advanced fashion technology and operations management* (pp. 92–114). IGI Global.
Stępień, B., & Hinner, M. (2018). From love to rebuff: How culture shapes the perception of luxury goods among consumers. In S. Sarma (Ed.), *Global observations of the influence of culture on consumer buying behavior* (s. 24–47). Hershey: IGI Global.

Stępień, B., Lima, A. P., Sagbansua, L., & Hinner, M. B. (2016). Comparing consumers' value perception of luxury goods: Is national culture a sufficiently explanatory factor? *Economics and Business Review, 2*(16), 74–93.
Stępień, B., & Młody, M. (2020). Principles of reshoring development in luxury goods sector. *International Journal of Management and Economics, 56*(2): 1–19.
Thach, E. C., & Olsen, J. (2006). The role of service quality in influencing brand attachments at winery visitor centers. *Journal of Quality Assurance in Hospitality & Tourism, 7*(3), 59–77.
Thaler, R. H. (Ed.). (2005). *Advances in behavioral finance, Volume II* (Vol. 2). Princeton University Press.
Tsai, S. P. (2005). Impact of personal orientation on luxury-brand purchase value: An international investigation. *International Journal of Market Research, 47,* 429–454.
Tsai, W. S., Yang, Q., & Liu, Y. (2013). Young Chinese consumers' snob and bandwagon luxury consumption preferences. *Journal of International Consumer Marketing, 25*(5), 290–304.
Tversky, A., & Kahneman, D. (1981). The framing of decisions and the psychology of choice. *Science, New Series, 211*(4481), 453–458.
Unity Marketing. (2020). https://unitymarketingonline.com/prospects-for-home-brands-in-post-pandemic-world/.
Urbańska, A. (1997). Koncepcja mimesis Rene Girarda. *Etnografia Polska, 41*(1–2), 21–46.
Veblen, T. (2008). *Teoria klasy próżniaczej*. wydanie III. Warszawa: Wydawnictwo Literackie Muza.
Vermeir, I., & Verbeke, W. (2006). Sustainable food consumption: Exploring the consumer 'attitude—behavioral intention'. *Journal of Agricultural and Environmental Ethics, 19,* 169–194. https://doi.org/10.1007/s10806-005-5485-3.
Vigneron, F., & Johnson, L. W. (1999). A review and a conceptual framework of prestige-seeking consumer behavior. *Academy of Marketing Science Review, 1,* 1–15.
von Wallpach, S., Hemetsberger, A., Thomsen, T. U., & Belk, R. W. (2019). Moments of luxury—A qualitative account of the experiential essence of luxury. *Journal of Business Research, 116*, 491–502.
Voyer, B. G., & Beckham, D. (2014). Can sustainability be luxurious? A mixed-method investigation of implicit and explicit attitudes towards sustainable luxury consumption. *Advances in Consumer Research, 42,* 245–250.

Wheeler, L. (1966). Motivation as a determinant of upward comparison. *Journal of Experimental Social Psychology, 1,* 27–31.
Willems, K., Janssens, W., Swinnen, G., Brengman, M., Streukens, S., & Vancauteren, M. (2012). From Armani to Zara: Impression formation based on fashion store patronage. *Journal of Business Research, 65*(10), 1487–1494.
Wills, T. A. (1981). Downward comparison principles in social psychology. *Psychological Bulletin, 90,* 245–271.
Wong, N. Y., & Ahuvia, A. C. (1998). Personal taste and family face: Luxury consumption in Confucian and Western societies. *Psychology & Marketing, 15*(5), 423–441.
Wong, A. C. Y., & Zaichkowsky, J. L. (1999). Understanding luxury brands in Hong Kong. *ACR European Advances.*
Wood, J. V. (1989). Theory and research concerning social comparisons of personal attributes. *Psychological Bulletin, 106*(2), 231–248. https://doi.org/10.1037/0033-2909.106.2.231.
Yang, Y., Han, H., & Lee, P. (2017). An exploratory study of the mechanism of sustainable value creation in the luxury fashion industry. *Sustainability, 9*(4), 483. https://doi.org/10.3390/su9040483.
Zhan, L., & He, Y. (2012). Understanding luxury consumption in China: Consumer perceptions of best-known brands. *Journal of Business Research, 65*(10), 1452–1460.

3

Luxury Supply Side

Luxury is not only a collection of goods or services with certain characteristics. It is also an important part of the economy. It is neither an economic sector, nor a single industry, but a group of companies involved in the design, production, distribution and sale of goods and services aimed at affluent customers.[1] Due to the specific business models, including the way of competing, the importance of tradition and the control of supply chains in this area, the activities of enterprises offering luxury goods and services make this group quite homogeneous in several important features which distinguishes this business from non-luxury ones.

Luxury goods or services can be found in any industry such as "luxury" pet food, coffee served with gold flakes, or home grills with a wide range of functions and a very high price[2] but only those industries that have been producing luxury goods for centuries and are the backbone of luxury in the world economy are described here.

---

[1] Further on in the text and for the sake of stylistic simplification, the term 'luxury market' will be used interchangeably: whether it is a question of demand, supply or the business of luxury.

[2] Such coffee is served in Burj Al Dubai, grills and food are described by Silverstein and Fiske (2003b) as examples of new luxury.

B. Stępień, *The Value of Luxury*, Palgrave Advances in Luxury,
https://doi.org/10.1007/978-3-030-51218-7_3

The analysis of luxury supply presented in this chapter concerns the structure and dynamics of production and sales and includes a description of the goods and services considered to be the core of this business. Business models, their connection with the capital-ownership system and the evolution of competitive strategies were also discussed. The starting point for this analysis is a unique (as contradicting the rules of marketing) DNA of luxury business model (see Kapferer and Bastien 2009). The analysis reveals the extent to which modern business strategies adhere to these principles. Based on the analysis of the latest global consumer trends the summary attempts to determine the future directions of development of enterprises creating the supply of luxury.

3.1 Global Luxury Market—Sales Structure and Dynamics

The growth rate of the luxury market has been impressive over the last 30 years. It started in 1994 and Bain & Company calls this period "sortie du temple". At that time luxury goods sales began to increase dynamically, spreading geographically and socially, thanks to the widespread application of extension strategy into less affluent consumer segments while maintaining a luxurious brand image. However, the beginning of this vast dynamic can be traced back to the 1970s when Cartier created the "Les Must" jewellery series aimed at less wealthy audiences who could not afford to buy the then cult Panthère necklaces and watches (Economist 2014). In this phase of dynamic growth global sales of luxury products almost doubled from EUR 74 billion to EUR 133 billion in 2001 and slowed down when the World Trade Center towers were attacked (Bain & Company 2018). The next stage called the phase of democratization of luxury[3] began with a temporary stagnation caused by a drop in the exchange rate of the dollar where the U.S. at that time was the world's largest luxury buyer. The luxury market continued to develop

[3]The term democratisation seems somewhat misleading here. It was the "exit from the temple" of luxury for the few that initiated the growing wave of democratisation that continues to this day.

dynamically to reveal speculative stock exchange bubbles, to record small (lower than average in other industries) decreases in sales in 2016–2017, and then rapidly moving upwards due to the "Chinese luxury bulimia" (Bain & Company 2016, p. 6). 2018 was a return to normality understood as an average 4–5% annual growth of the sector, which, however was unattainable for many industries.

In 2019 sales of luxury goods and services reached approximately 1.3 trillion EUR in 2019 and its rate of growth compared to the previous year was estimated at 4% at constant exchange rates. The main forces that have driven this dynamic growth are the demand for luxury from Chinese citizens and the global Millennial group along with the dynamically growing importance of online sales channels. Even Pandemic Covid 19 in 2019/2020 does not seem to change this growing role of the Chinese and other fast growing luxury markets in the development of this sector and will possibly even strengthen this dependence. China was the starting point of the pandemic, but was also the first to deal with its subjugation. Unfortunately at the time of writing this book the world has been experiencing a global panic and both social and economic lockdown caused by the spread of the coronavirus. The first consequences of stopping the Chinese economy to allow drastic measures to be taken in the fight against the coronavirus have a very broad spectrum of impacts, both negative and positive, including in the luxury sector. One of the few positive consequences was a reduction in the level of air pollution in China caused by the stoppage or a drastic reduction of production due to quarantine. Another quite positive effect of coping with communication difficulties was the massive launch of e-learning at Chinese universities and schools. This has forced many universities to adapt quite rapidly to the new way of learning and the effects of such a change can be both permanent and global. However the range of positive changes is much smaller than the negative outcomes. While we can introduce e-learning during the quarantine to continue the education process this is still impossible to introduce for example e-sewing (especially when hand made work is a value creating factor) or e-welding to mitigate the effects of production stops. The slowdown in the Chinese economy will most probably translate into higher production and commodity prices worldwide. Although the effects of Coronavirus should not be equated with the ones of the global crisis one can expect a longer term stagnation in the dynamics of sales of luxury goods and services on a global scale.

Europe has been hit even stronger and longer than China by COVID 19 pandemic, is now (June, 2020) slowly waking up economically after a few months lockdown, while both Americas are still suffering not only from a rapidly spreading virus but also from social unrest.

The COVID 19 pandemic caused a drop in turnover in the luxury sector of 30–35% on average compared to the previous year. Bain & Co. (2020) predicts that it will take the industry at least two to three years to recover to the sales level before the epidemic although two scenarios of this recovery are assumed, depending on the region. As regards the Asian market a rapid rebound is forecast and the expected rate of recovery will be faster than in the rest of the world for two reasons. First, the Chinese are a major and growing group of luxury consumers on a global scale responsible for the 90% growth in luxury sales in 2019 (see e.g. Bain & Co. 2019). The second scenario refers to the so-called western world: mainly North America and Europe. These regions are experiencing a deep recession and a slower return to stability. These regions have been experiencing a stabilization of interest in luxury for years and sales growth has only been in the region of 1–3%, with more sales growth in hospitality and well-being services. However it should be stressed that these areas of luxury are growing everywhere at a higher rate than the so-called private core luxury. Moreover according to Unity Marketing (2020), these will become the industry of broadly defined hospitality services that will be the one to which most global luxury brands will turn and expand significantly after the end of the COVID 19 Pandemic.

3.1.1 Structure and Dynamics of Sales of Luxury Goods by Geographical Markets

According to Euromonitor (2019) estimates, most luxury goods are now sold in the Asia-Pacific region with Chinese consumers dominating. The share of Chinese purchases currently accounts for more than 30% of world sales of luxury goods. The second place is occupied by the USA followed by the so-called old Europe, which is also the cradle of luxury goods manufacturers. Japan is an important region for the sale and production of luxury goods; a country of wealthy people fascinated for decades by so-called "high" luxury (see Table 3.1).

However the size of the markets in terms of the value of sales of luxury goods in particular years does not fully reflect the dynamics of consumption. The Chinese are now the largest and consumer group of luxury but in terms of growth in demand they are outstripping India and Poland (see Table 3.2).

The dynamic growth of sales in China, BRIC countries and Central and Eastern Europe can be attributed to the emergence and development of the middle class for which to a large extent the measure of social success is the consumption of luxury.

In terms of per capita spending China ranks first in luxury shopping thanks to ever younger generations of consumers (KPMG 2018; Delloite 2019; Bain 2020). The Chinese are also the main buyers in Hong Kong, Macao and Singapore and represent an important consumer segment in the UK. The latter records such high sales dynamics thanks to the purchases of tourists from Asia and other European countries and the increase in sales of luxury goods from the weak pound sterling against other currencies. Compared to China, prices of luxury goods are on average 22% lower, even compared to Italy (21.6%) and France (21.4%, Delloite 2019). At the same time British purchases of luxury goods stagnated, as well as luxury goods sales in the USA.

The countries with the highest growth rates in luxury goods' sales include India and Poland (see Table 3.2). It is worth noting how the dynamics of the sales growth in a given country affects its importance for the global luxury supply market. In both cases there is less than a 1% share of global luxury sales from these countries. In Poland with a population of 38 million with a balanced but relatively low GDP growth rate even a high luxury sales growth rate will not result in a sudden increase in the importance of this market on the global arena. In the case of India, the world's second largest country in terms of population, almost every positive change in the internal economic situation can result in global changes in luxury consumption. On the other hand still retaining the caste system of Indian society and the existence of a large group of people (including the so-called untouchables) living on

Table 3.1 Size of the luxury market by country 2010–2020

Country	2010	2011	2012	2013	2014	2015	2016	2017	2018	2019	2020
China	133,653	164,171	180,992	183,386	193,897	196,808	220,133	247,560	*274,759*	*304,296*	*335,081*
USA	129,926	140,448	154,242	167,958	179,044	187,373	185,713	178,931	*177,456*	*176,142*	*175,249*
United Kingdom	36,929	38,454	41,216	44,356	47,817	52,589	57,369	61,155	*66,535*	*72,746*	*79,741*
Germans	50,518	53,673	54,617	53,466	54,630	57,576	61,348	63,025	*64,806*	*66,213*	*67,347*
Japan	31,354	32,218	33,382	37,524	40,094	42,707	43,357	43,561	*44,639*	*45,392*	*46,297*
France	31,620	32,583	33,519	33,384	34,141	36,136	36,971	38,137	*39,271*	*40,460*	*41,536*
Italy	30,218	29,967	28,101	28,009	28,458	30,732	32,630	34,090	*35,511*	*36,971*	*38,309*
Spain	17,559	16,463	15,705	15,818	17,590	19,915	22,568	24,889	*27,511*	*30,400*	*33,629*
South Korea	11,152	12,765	14,523	16,385	19,247	22,231	23,032	23,685	*24,631*	*25,521*	*26,345*
Russia	14,939	18,032	22,202	24,328	24,589	20,826	19,874	19,927	*20,554*	*21,856*	*22,956*
Canada	10,966	11,349	12,076	12,924	13,771	15,153	16,273	16,780	*17,207*	*17,538*	*17,831*
Australia	8585	8679	9179	11,154	12,205	13,619	14,828	14,962	*15,296*	*15,631*	*15,970*
Switzerland	10,092	10,831	11,847	12,143	12,510	13,699	13,491	13,339	*13,309*	*13,345*	*13,387*
Taiwan	6436	7532	8136	8951	9865	10,587	11,223	11,568	*12,072*	*12,576*	*13,087*
Hong Kong	10,337	12,656	13,341	14,141	13,456	12,979	11,861	11,678	*11,822*	*12,031*	*12,302*
United Arab Emirates	8559	9826	10,793	11,714	12,111	12,270	11,953	11,639	*11,570*	*11,724*	*12,241*
India	3382	4201	4699	4930	5430	6364	6644	7559	*8552*	*9603*	*10,760*
Turkey	7037	7767	8060	9763	11,206	13,196	13,167	10,509	*9527*	*9798*	*10,253*
Holland	7394	7738	8059	7727	7631	8621	8398	8629	*8768*	*8929*	*9060*
Mexico	3857	4303	4757	5069	5372	5937	6702	7066	*7522*	*7958*	*8395*
Singapore	6442	6760	7066	6934	6835	7513	7673	7622	*7750*	*7945*	*8150*
Poland	2456	2349	2543	2755	3218	3731	4594	5485	*6328*	*7056*	*7800*

Source Euromonitor (2019)
Note Italics are estimates, while others are factual numbers

Table 3.2 Annual growth rate of luxury sales in individual markets 2010–2020 (%)

Country	2010–2011	2011–2012	2012–2013	2013–2014	2014–2015	2015–2016	2016–2017	2017–2018	2018–2019	2019–2020
India	24	12	05	10	17	04	14	*13*	*12*	*12*
Poland	−04	08	08	17	16	23	19	*15*	*12*	*11*
Spain	−06	−05	01	11	13	13	10	*11*	*11*	*11*
China	23	10	01	06	02	12	13	*11*	*11*	*10*
United Kingdom	04	07	08	08	10	09	07	*09*	*09*	*10*
Romania	08	05	−03	06	12	17	06	*07*	*08*	*09*
Argentina	02	00	18	−26	10	00	18	*08*	*08*	*08*
Indonesia	13	07	07	03	06	04	06	*08*	*08*	*07*
Mexico	12	11	07	06	11	13	05	*07*	*06*	*06*
Russia	21	23	10	01	−15	−05	00	*03*	*06*	*05*
Ukraine	07	33	05	−26	−25	37	08	*04*	*05*	*05*
Malaysia	19	14	10	07	16	04	02	*05*	*06*	*05*
Turkey	10	04	21	15	18	00	−20	*−09*	*03*	*05*
Taiwan	17	08	10	10	07	06	03	*04*	*04*	*04*
Thailand	13	21	21	05	09	−02	05	*04*	*06*	*04*
United Arab Emirates	15	10	09	03	01	−03	−03	*−01*	*01*	*04*
Italy	−01	−06	00	02	08	06	05	*04*	*04*	*04*
Philippines	07	08	11	04	18	07	03	*04*	*04*	*03*
Singapore	05	05	−02	−01	10	02	−01	*02*	*03*	*03*
South Korea	15	14	13	18	16	04	03	*04*	*04*	*03*
France	03	03	00	02	06	02	03	*03*	*03*	*03*

(continued)

Table 3.2 (continued)

Country	2010–2011	2011–2012	2012–2013	2013–2014	2014–2015	2015–2016	2016–2017	2017–2018	2018–2019	2019–2020
Hong Kong	22	05	06	−05	−04	−09	−02	*01*	*02*	*02*
Japan	03	04	12	07	07	02	01	*03*	*02*	*02*
Australia	01	06	22	09	12	09	01	*02*	*02*	*02*
Brazil	20	−09	21	09	10	−22	−12	*03*	*05*	*02*
Canada	04	06	07	07	10	07	03	*03*	*02*	*02*
Germans	06	02	−02	02	05	07	03	*03*	*02*	*02*
Holland	05	04	−04	−01	13	−03	03	*02*	*02*	*02*
Sweden	09	−02	−01	12	13	11	01	*02*	*01*	*01*
Switzerland	07	09	03	03	10	−02	−01	*00*	*00*	*00*
USA	08	10	09	07	05	−01	−04	*−01*	*−01*	*−01*

Source Euromonitor (2019)
Note Italics are estimates, while others are factual numbers

the edge of or below the poverty line[4] should be taken into account as factors that would not boost the luxury demand to such an extent as in China. However observing the dynamic growth of this economy and the continuous decline in poverty in a few years' time Indians may replicate the trend of Chinese consumers from more than a decade ago and be the second country in the world to experience luxury.

3.1.2 Luxury Goods and Services Categories and Their Share of the Global Market

The supply of luxury goods is represented by companies manufacturing and selling:

- vehicles: yachts, cars, motorcycles and private planes,
- clothing and clothing accessories (e.g. handbags, belts, scarves, sunglasses, etc.),
- shoes,
- jewellery,
- watches,
- spirits and wines,
- perfumes and cosmetics,
- works of art.

Luxury services include primarily tourist services, including hotel, spa and wellness, restaurant and catering services. They are provided by five-star hotels, wellness centres of sufficiently high renown and restaurants (e.g. in the Michelin ranking).

The luxury industry in Bain & Company's analysis consists of nine segments the main part of which is the so-called luxury core accounting for more than 80% of world sales (Bain & Co. 2019). The core consists of luxury cars, so-called private luxury goods (clothing, footwear,

---

[4]In 2011—the latest World Bank data for India (as of 01.09.2018)—22% of the Indian population lived below the poverty line, i.e. had an amount equal to or less than $1.9 per day to cover their daily living needs. For the record it should be added that this indicator is falling year on year. By comparison in 2009 it was 30%. See https://knoema.com/atlas/India/Poverty-rate.

cosmetics, watches and jewellery) and the segment comprising tourist services together with spa and wellness (*hospitality*). The largest group within the luxury core are cars. This market segment is growing dynamically at a rate of about 6% annually and the demand for cars have increased mainly in developing countries. The highest growth were noted in India, China, and in Russia. The consequence of significant changes in the demand for cars in various regions of the world is the growing geographical expansion of automotive concerns through foreign direct investments. The biggest increases are in premium and luxury car sales: with Mercedes as number one, followed by BMW and Audi.

The luxury fashion market has for years recorded a stabilization of sale, with the most dynamic development of the accessories segment (bags, accessories, etc.), while the clothing market is relatively the slowest growing segment (Bain & Co. 2019; Delloite 2019).

The supply of luxury fashion goods is represented mainly by global conglomerates and fashion houses. Brands such as LV, Dior, Chanel, Hermés, Prada and Gucci have the biggest market shares. It is worth noting that the fashion market is not as consolidated as the car market and about 30% of sales in the luxury segment of the industry is covered by regional and local brands (Euromonitor 2019).

The luxury jewellery market is characterised by a high degree of fragmentation—the vast majority is dominated by non-branded goods. In 2009 the so-called brand jewellery constituted 19% of the total market compared to 60% for watches. The fifteen largest global brands accounted for 40% of the branded market while 60% accounted for about 1000 other companies in the industry. According to Macquarie Research (2016), Tiffany, Cartier (Richemont), Pandora Jewellery and Swarovski together have about 25–30% of the world's "branded" market. According to McKinsey forecasts by now (2020) about one third of the market is owned by branded sellers.

However last years the most dynamic growth is observed in the sale of luxury travel on large passenger ships and the sales of food, catering and hotel services recorded the biggest increase, but already purchases of luxury yachts or jets did not record the expected growth, which is explained by an increased tendency to charter them.

While sales of luxury goods have generally been growing rapidly in recent decades we have seen stagnation in luxury private goods except for luxury cars. There may be several reasons for this situation. The first is the decrease in the number of tourists in Europe due to the risk of terrorist attacks. France, Italy and Spain are countries where 70–80% of demand for luxury goods is generated by foreigners. In the case of the United Kingdom and Switzerland the average is between 50 and 55%. About 66% of Russian and more than 40% of Chinese luxury purchases are made abroad. The second reason is the aforementioned drop in oil and gas prices, and a large part of the demand for luxury goods is created by countries rich in natural resources such as Russia or the Middle East. The third reason is that the Chinese government has introduced restrictions to stimulate domestic consumption and halt purchases outside China (Solca et al. 2016). As a result China's share of the global market for private luxury goods (excluding cars) has stabilised despite increasing consumer purchasing power.

The fourth premise concerns the growing disagreement of a growing group of consumers (including Chinese) in respect of the trend of democratising luxury and their turning away from the frequent purchases of luxury brands sold almost everywhere and to everyone in[5] search of "quieter luxury". After the wave of luxury 2.0 characterized by democratization, the signals of the upcoming luxury 3.0 can be seen; not so much a return to the classic dimension of luxury for a few but an individualised, not epic, not hastily experienced, use of digital technologies (Wealth X 2015; Focus. Luxury 3.0).

[5]This is a a simplification because luxury goods are still expensive, but a growing number of opinions of analysts, scientists or publicists dealing with luxury note that this development trend constitutes a real threat to the luxury industry in the form of loss of image which is the greatest attribute in this business.

3.2 Competitors in the Luxury Goods Market

The global luxury market is dominated by globally listed corporations, conglomerates and family businesses. These companies account for about 70% of the market and the remaining 30% of sales are owned by local or regional companies offering brands in this range (Euromonitor 2019). The relatively largest percentage of the market in terms of revenues belongs to the automotive industry with the leading share of Audi, Mercedes and Volkswagen (including the owner of the Porsche brand). The luxury car market is therefore dominated by German companies which offer premium and luxury goods in virtually every segment. Italian sports cars, English or American limousines or even the Japanese Lexus have significantly lower market shares. The largest share relatively in the global luxury market is held by three German automobile companies (12% of the global luxury market), and in the segment of luxury goods for private use about ten companies account for less than 50% of revenues.

LVMH (Louis Vuitton Moet Hennesy), Estee Lauder and Richemont have been at the forefront of the latter group for years with double-digit profits for the last five years. Other giants such as Swatch, Ralph Lauren and Chow Tai Fook, are recording stagnant sales. Among the ten largest in terms of sales in this segment are also the two so-called masstige companies—PVH (owner of the Calvin Klein and Tommy Hilfiger brands) and Ralph Lauren Corp. which is experiencing considerable financial difficulties due to a drop in sales (Wahba 2018). The most dynamic of this group is Kering, a smaller conglomerate being a direct competitor of LVMH, recording rapid increase in revenues in last years.

The following types of enterprises operate in the luxury goods market:

- car manufacturers (e.g. Mercedes, BMW, Audi[6]) which supply cars to all market segments, including the luxury one,
- car companies with a specific production profile, creating cars exclusively for the luxury segment which are part of concerns such as Aston Martin,[7] Bentley,[8] Maserati, Ferrari,[9] Bugatti,[10] Rolls Royce,[11] or Lamborghini,[12]
- conglomerates associated companies representing various industries of luxury in the category of private goods (fashion, jewellery, cosmetics, watches, alcohol and others such as LVMH, Richemont, Kering),
- conglomerates operating in a single luxury industry (e.g. Swatch watches, Este Lauder, L'Oréal Luxe, Shiseido Prestige and Fragrance cosmetics, Chow Tai Fook jewellery, Luxottica glasses),
- family' companies[13] focused on the production of goods in one or more related industries (e.g. Prada, Chanel, Hermés, Versace),
- mixed capital companies active in different sectors (e.g. Armani, Ralph Lauren),
- mixed capital companies covering a single brand across a wide range of different but related industries (fashion and cosmetics—e.g. Dior, Chanel, Burberry, Salvatore Ferragamo).

---

[6]Audi is part of the Volkswagen Group.

[7]Aston Martin's owners include Ford, Daimler Benz, Kuwaiti investment companies and an Italian investment fund.

[8]Bentley belongs to VW AG.

[9]Mas erati and Ferrari belong, among others, to the Fiat Group.

[10]The owner of Bugatti is VW AG.

[11]Owned by BMW.

[12]Lamborghini is owned by Audi and both brands are owned by VW AG.

[13]Shares in these companies do not belong only to the founding families but it is still their founders or their heirs who shape the strategies of the companies.

- *Monobrand* companies with mixed capital operating in one industry, e.g. jewellery and watchmaking (Chopard, Graff, Rolex[14,15]) or yacht manufacturing,
- profiled companies, often family-owned, manufacturing luxury goods from various industries with local or regional coverage.

3.3 Luxury Brand

3.3.1 Characteristics and Varieties of Luxury Goods Brands

Despite numerous studies on luxury brands,[16] there is still no consensus on what a luxury brand actually is and how to measure its luxurious nature (Atwal and Williams 2009; Christodoulides et al. 2009; Fionda and Moore 2009; Kernstock et al. 2017; Ko et al. 2019). The reasons for the difficulty in developing a single luxury brand definition are due to the unclear concept of luxury and the different perspectives of its evaluation. For luxury can be seen as a the result of popularity, positive experiences and social perception (Atwal and Williams 2009) or the place in the

[14]Rolex is a company managed by the Hans Wilsdorf Foundation. According to the last will of the co-founder of the brand (the brand was created by Alfred Davis and his brother-in-law Hans Wilsdorf), part of the income from the activity is donated to charity. Although this was certainly not the intention of the founders the activity of the fund raises a number of questions and controversies. The fund's authorities have consistently refused to provide information on how much of the profits are spent on charity and doubts about the sound financial management of the company are exacerbated by the fact that Rolex is involved in the infamous Bernard Maddoff fund.

[15]Between 1997 and 2008 there was a huge increase in the number of private luxury yachts ranging from 24 to 70 meters (79 to 230 feet). Some of them can be chartered; the largest ones cost up to EUR 1 million per week. The largest private yachts in the world are the M/Y Eclipse 163.5 m (536 ft) built by Blohm + Voss for Russian businessman Roman Abramowicz and the 180 m (590 ft) Azzam launched in 2013. Amels, Feadship, Hessen Yachts, Oceanco from the Netherlands, Fincantieri Yachts, Perini Navi from Italy, Norbiskrug, Lursen, Blohm + Voss from Germany) and the United States (Christensen Shipyards), but they are also increasingly present in Australia, New Zealand, Asia and Central and Eastern Europe (e.g. in Poland). In 2016 there were about 10,000 luxury yachts with a length of more than 24 meters and annual production volume of about 150 boats.

[16]The book will continue to use the term luxury brands only for the sake of stylistic simplification.

continuum between the inaccessible absolute and inferior good (Tynan et al. 2010). In this book the following stand is taken: a luxury brand is a set of attributes of a given good/service which coincides with previously described attributes of luxury (see Chapter 2) in connection with its aura which reinforces these attributes.

Premium goods typically offer higher quality and functional characteristics than mass products but are priced higher, whereas luxury goods offer a surplus of value over premium products reflected in their (Mason 1993; Chevalier and Mazzalovo 2008; Kapferer and Bastien 2009; Dion and Arnould 2011):

- aura of uniqueness, reflected by its artistry, novelty etc.;
- aura of timelessness, guaranteed by the artistry of the project and the uniqueness of workmanship, combined with respect for the traditional way of production and the place from which the brand originates,
- the preservation of craftsmanship with often manual production methods;
- maintenance of traditional manufacturing sites, taking into account the history of the company's establishment in a given location,
- aura of rarity, which is a consequence of the manufacturing methods and the quality of the materials used,
- the aura of magic, built around all the above features, in combination with the charisma of the designers, the beauty and location of the places of sale and social desirability, legitimizing all these attributes,
- the promise of fulfilling dreams that go far beyond expectations concerning the use of a product (they are to bring joy, raise social status, improve well-being, etc.).

Luxury brands through a skilful combination of the above mentioned attributes become credibly auratic like pieces of art (see Arnould et al. 1999; Arvidsson and Malossi 2011; Heilbrunn 2006, p. 189; Dion and Arnould 2011; Featherstone 2016). This means that their aura created around magic, charisma and uniqueness, bears the traces of authenticity through original creative contribution, non-mechanical and non-mass human effort, meticulousness related to the selection of materials and respect for tradition. These qualities are supposed to make its value timeless.

Luxury brands while shaping the image of their products put varied emphasis on communicating the particular attributes of value proposition for the consumer. Moreover in this business success is not measured by copying and improving competitors' value propositions and even if it does it is unacceptable for such practices to be publicly communicated. In this market there is no place to make consumers aware that the company is cheaper/more efficient/offer more functional for the same price, etc. compared to other brands on the market. The aim is to create a unique, incomparable brand, which translates into unique way of competing. The rule in the luxury business (even though informal) is the coexistence of companies whose efforts are focused on proposing a unique offer with the imposition of a veil of silence on the cost-organisational layer of their activity and emphasizing the uniqueness, innovation, care, diligence, control over the entire process of production and sales.

Berthon et al. (2009) propose a typology of luxury brands based on philosophical aesthetic considerations. The axes of the model determine the ontological and aesthetic understanding of art and the process of its perception described by Martin Heidegger and Alfred North Whitehead (Heidegger 1993; Whitehead 1978, after: Berthon et al. 2009, pp. 50–51).

The vertical axis determines the metaphysical understanding of luxury as a permanent category, in contrast to the temporal feeling of luxury-ephemeral experience. The horizontal axis is the level of aesthetic education: at one pole there are individuals who have an in-depth knowledge of the aesthetics and the complex value of luxury (experts), and at the other there are novices who evaluate luxury on the surface on the basis of the most strongly exposed brands' attributes, which at the same time dominate the composition of the overall value proposition (Fig. 3.1).

The axes are defined by four groups of luxury brands:

- classical brands—they are characterized by history, tradition; the values of the products are the result of concentration on artistic and craftsmanship and the brand perception is primarily the result of

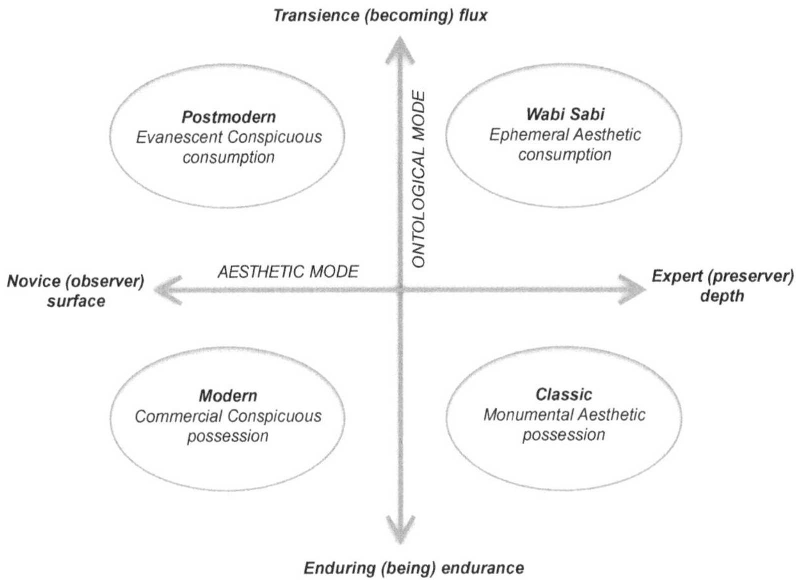

Fig. 3.1 Typology of luxury brands as a result of a differentiated understanding of their aesthetic component and the signs of timelessness (*Source* Berthon et al. 2009)

consumer education—conducted both by the brand itself and through an individual's searches. This group includes Hermés, Loro Piana, Rolls Royce, Bentley, Patek & Philippe or Schaffhausen,

- modern brands—offering prestige and status by clearly signalling through style/design, logo and communication strategy that they are expensive, unavailable to the general public but having lasting artistic values, combined with uniqueness and social desirability (intensively strengthened by marketing). The main component of their offer is, apart from the aura of uniqueness and artistry, the social value. These are examples of the so-called well-known brands, such as Gucci, Cavalli, Dolce Gabbana, Prada, Porsche, Ferrari, Lamborghini and Tag Hauer, Omega, Rolex,
- impression brands (Wabi Sabi)—their main component of value is the experiencing of contact with fleeting beauty; this is primarily the domain of services: e.g. offering culinary experiences of molecular

cuisine combining the aesthetics of the service, interior design and unusual form and flavours of the food offered (ice cream with the taste of truffle, broccoli "earth", foam from herring or caramelized larvae), a marathon at the North Pole, camping in Mount Everest, a snow safari in Antarctica, meditation classes in hammocks in an oasis and so on
- postmodernist brands—basing their value on the search for new forms of aesthetic and emotional impact. The novelty that will be accepted publicly as interesting is the main component of the value of the brands from this area. Examples of such brands include Moschino or Fog Point Vodka (advertised as made with the use of liquefied fog from San Francisco).

The typology given here does not exhaust the possible categories of brands, nor does it mean that a given area is the only place where a given brand operates. An important criterion for differentiating brand attributes which is missing here is the target segment of consumers with a given purchasing power. This is another level of luxury determined by the consumers' wallets. Brands, especially those from the classic area while striving to maintain their timeless artistic image, "migrate" to the remaining parts of the model in order to monetize their luxury potential in wider, though less affluent, segments of the market. Although Chanel and Dior with their *haute couture* collections are still undisputedly strong players in the most prestigious, traditional category of luxury brands their biggest revenues are generated by cosmetic and perfume lines sold on a massive scale under their brands. In this way they extend their brand to the remaining segments. Emphasizing the uniqueness and priceless transience of communing with luxury (in the form of using a particular lipstick or perfume) they monetize their potential while maintaining a timeless and artistic aura for the luxury fashion industry.

3.3.2 Luxury Pyramid and Brand Positioning

The model of the luxury pyramid illustrates the level of uniqueness and availability of goods. On the very top there is a "materialised perfection" (French "griffe" Kapferer 2008, p. 98). They are single, individualized objects, unique in terms of design, workmanship or materials used. These include custom-made yachts, planes, cars, jewellery and clothing for very special occasions (e.g. Oscar galas). Below that level but still at the top of the pyramid there is the so-called high, absolute luxury: a short series of expensive, masterfully made goods of exceptional aesthetic and functional qualities. In order to reach this tier of the pyramid the brands must not only have their own history, but their reputation has to stem from their tradition and manufacture in the place where the brand was established. Both "griffe" and absolute luxury, despite the evident changes in the market (resulting in pressure on global e-sale for instance), still adhere to the traditional understanding of luxury. The communication strategies are based mainly on maintaining the image with economical use of the promotional impact (Brun and Castelli 2013; Castelli and Sianesi 2015).

The lower tier is a popular/aspiring luxury available to a wider audience intensively using marketing tools aimed at creating an impression of uniqueness and exclusiveness. These are well-known brands with a long history and reputation, producing goods on a global scale. At the lowest level there is a luxury available with "masstige" brands (i.e. prestige for the masses, see e.g. Truong et al. 2009; Paul 2019). There are popular and quite widely available brands offering goods at a still high price, available for the middle classes. The lowest level of the pyramid has been undergoing the greatest changes for more than 25 years and it includes the activities of those brands which are largely responsible not so much for the redefinition as for the degradation of the concept of luxury.

The lower the tier of the pyramid, the more intense the media coverage, aimed at creating an impression of real luxury and a broader (in terms of channels and locations) mass distribution strategy. Although the lowest-level brands emphasise the uniqueness of their design and style, they are already in the category of mass products. The lower the level, the more effort it takes to convince consumers that the composition of value attributes offered is still luxurious. When rarity, the extraordinary quality of materials, or mastery of not mechanical and mass production cease to be proposed other, mainly emotional, symbolic, epistemic and social components of values must replace these deficiencies. The basis for brands at this level is technical, material innovation or the promise of positive emotions for example which will legitimize the high price and "luxury of the brand" (Hanna 2004).

3.3.3 Pyramid or Pear? The Consequences of the Democratisation of Luxury and Migration and Brand Stretching

There is no single, fully objective pyramid of luxury: there are different variations both in terms of the number of tiers[17] and the positioning of brands in each tier (Chevalier and Gutsatz 2012; Rambourg 2014). The position of brands at a certain pyramid level may also vary from market to market. In China many luxury niche brands (such as Sophie Hulme and Bottega Veneta) are becoming more and more desirable and popular. Chinese consumers increasingly want to emphasize their individuality and excellent taste. According to Rambourg (2014) Luis Vuitton is now considered a brand for well-paid Chinese secretaries. Changing Chinese tastes have forced luxury giants (such as Gucci, Chanel or LV) to introduce short-term promotions and limited collections to maintain a consumer base (China Report, Innovation in Luxury 2018).

Since the mid-1990s a steady and continuous increase in the number of luxury goods' consumers (with slight decreases in 2001–2003 and just after the outbreak of the last financial crisis) has been associated with an exponential increase in the number of new luxury brands at the bottom of the pyramid. While sales and brand sizes on the absolute luxury tier have remained fairly stable for years the revolution has taken place at the accessible luxury and masstige level. The core strategy causing dynamic changes in this tier is an artificial creation of increasingly smaller segments, such as sports and casual luxury brands, intended for various activities (leisure luxury) or for teenagers or children with the aim of creating an aura of suitability and uniqueness in this increasingly competitive part of the market (see Silverstein and Fiske 2003a, b; Paul 2019). The image of the luxury pyramid has been transformed in recent decades. The elegant form of the triangle has evolved into a thick pear, swollen from the number of brands and "about – luxury" quality products (see Fig. 3.2).

---

[17]According to the Bain & Company classification used by other researchers (e.g. Brun and Castelli 2013; Castelli and Sianesi 2015), the pyramid of luxury is divided into three levels: absolute luxury (which also includes a "griffe") aspiring and accessible.

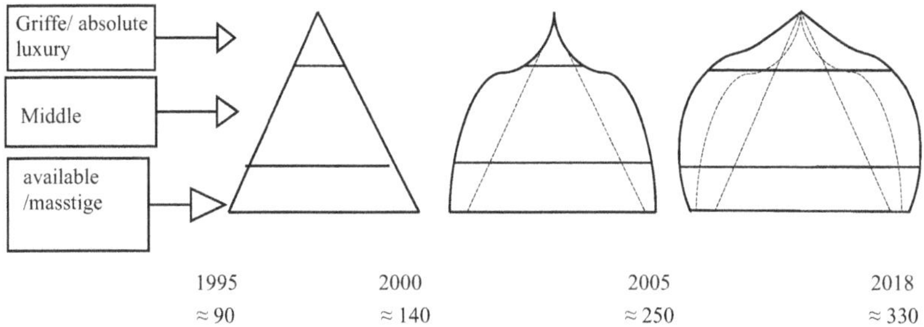

Fig. 3.2 Transformations of the luxury pyramid in the last 25 years (*Source* Own study using D'Arpizio and Levato 2014)

The pyramids of luxury deformed by the growth of the lower levels are the result of the brand owners‘ efforts to stabilize and maximize revenues while maintaining the status of a luxury brand in their so-called "core business".[18] There is therefore a general trend towards the stretching and extension of brands (Reddy et al. 2009; Ahn et al. 2018; Dall'Olmo Riley et al. 2015).

Even though stretching and extensions are often used as synonyms there are distinct types of this strategy (Bastien and Kapferer 2013). Stretching involves placing different brand variations at different levels of the luxury pyramid most often in one industry (in the fashion industry—haute couture lines, prét a porter, sports, for teenagers; in the automotive industry—Audi A 8 at the highest point of the middle level of the pyramid, Audi A2 in the lower segment). The extension of the brand is the start of activities outside the leading industry (fashion) in sectors such as lifestyle (Armani Hotels, Armani Fiori, Armani Casa), cosmetics and perfumes (Tiffany, LV perfumes), watches (Burberry or LV watches) and even outside the luxury market (the cooperation of Porsche with Acer, residences of Aston Martin' in Biscayne Boulevard Way in Miami). The probability of success in these strategies depends heavily on so called brand adjacency—the extent to which extensions are consistent with the brand value proposition (Reddy et al. 2009).

[18] LV no longer sells the number of travellers' trunks in such a quantity as to generate sufficient revenue to support itself. The bags and accessories are the main source of revenue for the company at the highest margins.

The brand is stretched mainly vertically and most often towards the bottom of the pyramid. Chanel and Dior, while still at the top, monetize their value with prét a porter lines while retaining control over distribution. As mentioned above an important source of income for Chanel and Dior is the cosmetics industry, where brand value is monetized without compromising its status as a high luxury in the fashion industry.

While downward stretching is normal there are also successful strategies for simultaneously stretching up and down the pyramid, especially in the medium tier. An example of such activities in the fashion industry is the strategy of Armani, who only after success as a designer of men suits (which placed him in the middle tier) developed his collections with women's clothing lines, including haute couture (Armani Privé). Today, the Armani brand monetizes its value in many luxury industries (hotels, sweets, home accessories etc.), significantly reducing the value of the Armani Privé. Other examples of attempts to stretch the brand upwards come from the automotive industry, although they are hardly a success. For example, VW created and promoted the Phaeton brand and after a few years gave up the production of this car because it was not able to convince consumers that VW is a brand that could offer a product similar to Bentley or Maybach.

However brand stretching is more justified (in terms of future success) if its prestige places it at the top or in the higher middle level of the pyramid. In the case of younger brands (especially when they are rapidly internationalised), they have been at the lowest level of luxury available and masstige since their inception. Then the main strategy is to extend the brand to other industries within one (middle or the lowest tier) with a narrow segmentation to selected groups of consumers (teenagers, children, seniors, etc.) with limited lines (clothing for various types of sports).

The overview in Fig. 3.3 is a compilation of the various developments in the luxury pyramids of the fashion, jewellery, watch and automotive industries, which form the backbone of the luxury supply market.

At the highest level of the pyramid in the fashion industry are clothes designed according to the individual needs of customers and those brands that create haute couture lines targeted at the wealthiest customers. In the automotive industry it is the level of cars that are the

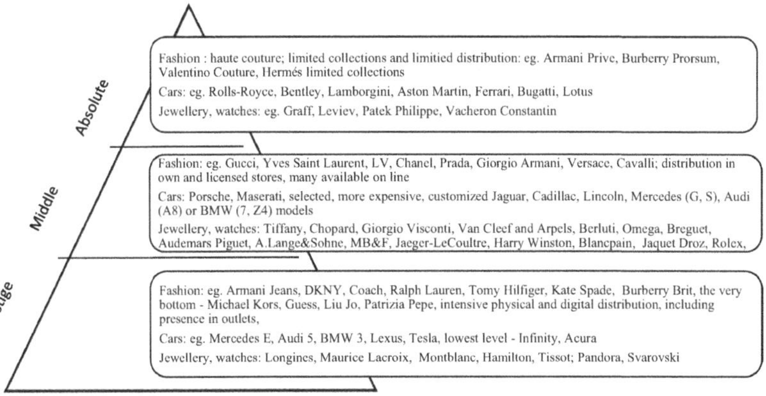

Fig. 3.3 Luxury pyramid—luxury fashion, jewellery, watches and automobiles industry (*Source* Młody and Stępień 2020)

symbol of high social status (Rolls Royce, Bentley) and unique sports cars (e.g. Aston Martin, Ferrari, Lamborghini, Bugatti). In the watchmaking and jewellery industry they are the most expensive, single exhibits or limited series of watches or jewellery. The common feature of all these brands, apart from very high prices, is their artistry, innovation (which creates uniqueness) and rarity of occurrence. This level is synonymous with traditional luxury.

The lower down the ladder the more intensive and wider the distribution and communication, the lower the price and the more it and the greater the number of potential recipients. It should be noted that while buying Michael Kors brand jeans is an expense of about 150 EUR the cars from this level of the pyramid start from 50 to 75 thousand EUR. The juxtaposition of different industries within a pyramid of luxury is therefore not so much to show what income one needs in order to acquire a given category of good as to show that the gradation of luxury takes place in different industries although a different sum of money is needed to buy a dress or a handbag at the same level as to buy a watch or a car.

3.4 Business Models in the Luxury Goods Market

The business model consists of several key elements: customers, customer value proposition, competitive strategy, position in the value network,[19] logic of revenue generation and supply chain organization with identification and development of their key competencies. Although there are many definitions of business models very often it is defined by three basic components: creation of value propositions, value architecture and revenue model, also described by means of investment processes and approaches to business development (Osterwalder and Pigneur 2010). Value creation refers to the specification of the value proposition embodied in products or services and customer segments of the company.[20] Value architecture is the activity of defining the nature (intensity, rules of cooperation, etc.) of relations with customers, within distribution channels and identifying key (for creating and monetizing value) activities, resources and partners within the company and the entire supply chain. The revenue model determines the structure of the company's costs and revenue streams.

In determining the business model it is also important to identify (see also: Fionda and Moore 2009; Teece 2010; Gutsatz and Heine 2018):

- who, what and where creates value for the customer: which department within the company and within its value chain contributes to the creation of specific components of the value proposition for the

[19]The value network is understood as that defined by Szymura-Tyc (2006, pp. 46–53). The value network, created through enterprise relationships, crosses the boundaries of the value system, i.e. the links of enterprises within one industry, creating value chains and offering products/services to a specific group of customers. The value offered to different purchasers is created through a cooperation and interaction between companies that benefit from the flow of information, technology and resources. As a supplier within one value system, for example, a company acquires competences, skills, which it then uses to function within another value system and in its own value chain.

[20]The term value creation is simplified (and therefore misleading), when used by researchers analyzing business models. As already described in the first chapter it is consumers who create value and companies only offer it. In order to clarify and justify the use of the term value creation at this point it is assumed here that it is about the creation/design of value propositions by companies.

customer; later materialized in products/services, as well as the sales process and the physical usage of the goods;

- who and how (within the company, within the value chain, on the market, etc.) should communicate the value proposition, thus co-create it, through the positive social popularization of the prestigious brand image,
- who and how should supply the products: what distribution and sales channels should be used to, on the one hand, strengthen the proposal of materialised value in the products/services and on the other—allow for the most effective management of sales;
- how to monetize value: what model of financing, investment, cost optimization to adopt in order to strengthen the company's value over time and at the same time maintain and develop the level of value offer for the client.

The market for luxury supply, regardless various ownership variants, capital structures and inter- and intra-organisational links, is based on one ideal type of a business model which is the combination of an operator and an integrator. Kapferer and Bastien (2009) named this canon the DNA of luxury business. Most of the principles of this canon are contrary to the principles that guide companies operating in the premium and mass sales' segments. The characteristics of this ideal model are described below and commented on how often they are nowadays bent or broken.

3.4.1 Strategies Related to the Supply and Production Architecture

The guiding principle in the canon of luxury business is to maintain full control of the value chain—from sourcing to retail:

- the whole process of creating value propositions, from production workshops to the use of the product by the customer, is to be closely integrated in order to ensure full cooperation between entities,

- subcontracting is to be kept to a minimum and the ultimate goal is full vertical integration so that the entire production process, from raw materials to finished goods, is controlled,
- production is to be carried out in a traditional craftsman's manner, preserving the traditional way of manufacturing from the time the brand was created. The place where the luxurious goods are manufactured is to be accompanied by the aura of a sanctuary where dreams are created,
- maintaining production in the place where the brand was established as one of the components of its value: the brand is to be an ambassador of local culture and art.

It is widely recognised that high quality throughout the supply chain from production to distribution in retail stores is one of the key requirements for the market success of these companies (Vigneron and Johnson 1999; Antoni et al. 2004; Lamming et al. 2000; Castelli and Sianesi 2015). Ensuring adequate quality control of both materials and production processes should go hand in hand with the management of close, long-term and fruitful relationships with suppliers and contractors, as well as the management of training and human resources (Christopher and Towill 2002; Caniato et al. 2009).

Ideally the whole production process, as well as the provision of materials should be carried out within a single company and at the point of origin of the brand. The origin of goods from certain countries (perceived by consumers as centres of handicraft or the gift of creating beautiful things) is a guarantee of quality, heritage, competence and high social standards for consumers (Balabanis and Diamantopoulos 2008; Money and Colton 2008; Oetzel and Doh 2009). It has been proven that with the increase in brand status (premium, luxury) the frequency and importance of the use of country of origin information in the communication strategy increases (see e.g. Chevalier and Mazzalovo 2008; Calori et al. 2000; Shukla 2011).

However the last few decades have significantly changed the configuration of corporate value chains in luxury business. The production of goods in the brand's place of origin is currently maintained in relation to the so-called strict core of business; products—icons, symbolizing grandeur, uniqueness and tradition. Hermés produces Kelly and Birkin bags in France but never in the case of accessories (belts, jewellery, blankets, toys) is this place of production disclosed.[21] The growing trend of the relocation of production is visible. It is becoming the norm, especially in the luxury fashion industry, to commission the production of collections (especially for lower segments) to countries within Europe (so-called nearshoring) or in the Far East. The principle of choosing a location for production relocation is simple: the lower the brand positioning in the luxury pyramid, the further the cost effective, but less controllable aspects in terms of the maintenance of quality of the manufacturing site.

Contact Lab together with Exane BNP Paribas (Solca 2015) analysed the "made in" labels of leading luxury brands. Brands were divided into four main groups. The first one consisted of fully transparent brands with information about production sites (information available on websites) with almost all products produced in the countries of origin of the brand (e.g. Bottega Veneta, Brunello Cucinelli, Gucci). The second group produces only product lines from the highest levels of luxury in the countries of origin of the brands (Burberry declares "Made in the UK" and "Made in Italy" for Burberry Prorsum, while Burberry Brit is "imported"; Giorgio Armani has "Made in Italy" labels and Armani Jeans has the description of "Imported"). The third group declared that they partially produce their goods in the countries of origin of the brand but this information is incomplete (Hermès, Loro Piana, Louis Vuitton, Ermenegildo Zegna). The fourth group includes companies that do not disclose the origin of the products (Chanel, Dior, Prada, Dolce & Gabbana, Hugo Boss).

Between 2017 and 2018 the author conducted her own research to examine the information about country of origin provided on luxury fashion goods' tags (see Table 3.3).

The information presented in the table above shows the departure from the traditional manufacturing site of brands located at the middle and lowest levels of the luxury pyramid. For the sake of fairness it should

[21]A few years ago Hermés officially withdrew from the project to outsource production to factories in China just after it had been announced by the media inadvertently. The company's PR department effectively cleared the Internet media of any mentions of this intention.

Table 3.3 Information on the country of manufacture of products of selected brands from the luxury fashion industry

Brand	Information about the country of manufacture on official websites	Country of origin (tag tests)[a]
Hermés	Information on the traditional place of production of "icons" goods	France: Paris
Chanel	No information available on the website	France, Italy
Bottega Veneta	No information available on the website	Italy
Dior	No information available on the website	France, Italy, men's sweaters—USA, Great Britain, some children's clothes—China, India, jeans—Japan
Luis Vuitton	No information available on the website	France, shoes—Italy
Prada	Information on the website giving the place of manufacture only for Italy, France or the United Kingdom	clothing—Italy, Japan, Peru, Scotland, India; shoes—Italy, Vietnam, purses—China, Italy
Armani Collezioni	No information available on the website	Moldova, Romania, Italy
Escada	No information available on the website	Moldova, Romania, Thailand, shoes—Italy
Just Cavalli	No information available on the website	Italy, India
Karl Lagerfeld	No information available on the website	China, Turkey
MarcCain Sports	No information available on the website	Hungary, Portugal
Armani Jeans, EA7	No information available on the website	China
Marciano Guess	No information available on the website	Italy (special logo with COO)
Versace Collection, Versace Jeans	No information available on the website	Bulgaria, India, Turkey, Italy
Hugo Boss	No information available on the website	Bulgaria, Romania, Portugal, Turkey, Turkey, China

(continued)

Table 3.3 (continued)

Brand	Information about the country of manufacture on official websites	Country of origin (tag tests)[a]
Michael Kors	No information available on the website	Vietnam, Bangladesh, China

Source Own observations
[a]Verification of tags and interviews with retailers on the country of origin were conducted in stores in Poznan, Warsaw, Krakow, Berlin, Paris, Dubai and Singapore

be noted that while in the luxury fashion industry top and middle level brands still try to maintain the image of locally produced goods, in the case of the automotive industry, or jewellery in particular, the country of manufacture loses its importance.

The jewellery industry imitates the fashion industry by reacting quickly to emerging trends and shortening the production cycle while at the same time dispersing the production sites. Outsourcing is natural especially when it comes to obtaining ores and precious stones, often extracted in poor, unstable countries, stigmatised by corruption which is a cause for concern for the more environmentally and socially engaged consumers. Most jewellery companies (including those producing and selling luxury jewellery) do not provide information about their sources of supply to the public even if they declare that they are socially responsible and controlled. The Swarovski Group (2015) says it regularly audits its factories in Thailand (The Marigot Jewellery Company and Swarovski Gemstones Thailand) and Austria (Swarovski Gemstones Business) to maintain high production standards and respect for workers' rights. Tiffany & Co. points to Russia, Thailand, Vietnam, Cambodia, Namibia, Sierra Leone and Botswana as well as Canada, the United States, Belgium and Australia as major diamond mining and supply sites. In order to increase control over its supply chain and ensure transparency for socially engaged customers, Tiffany & Co. has developed a long-term programme based on the principles developed by the Initiative for Responsible Mining Assurance (IRMA).

In 2005 the Responsible Jewellery Council (RJC) was established in order to strengthen consumer confidence in jewellery brands by offering gold and precious metals from proven, ethical suppliers. The founders were the largest miners and distributors: Tiffany & Co, BHP Billiton and Cartier, as well as trade associations (Jewellers of America). RJC's vision is "*a responsible global supply chain that promotes confidence in the world jewellery and watchmaking industry*" (RJC 2017). RJC members (14 in 2005 and 850 in 2017) are required to submit to audit procedures for corporate social responsibility of their business practices: respect for human rights, environmental responsibility, mining practices, disclosure of product information and configuration of the jewellery supply chain. However there are opinions that the organization represents low standards, certifying individual companies with its brand name and lack of control over individual firms and their practices (Hepler 2015).

On the other hand, even in the luxury segment, few consumers generally pay attention to where and to what standards jewellery has been produced (see Chapters 6 and 7). Production is widely outsourced to workshops and factories located in the Far East. Indian and Chinese companies not only produce but also often design entire collections for European, Arab and their own markets, acting as OEMs (*original equipment manufacturers*). The production is later accompanied by the logo of a large, world famous luxury brand (McKinsey 2014). Interviews conducted by the author with representatives of suppliers (mainly precious stones), jewellery manufacturers and retailers at the international fair of the jewellery and watchmaking industry in Dubai[22] in December 2016 clearly show that consumers do not ask about the place of jewellery production. According to the representatives of these links in the chain the main element that is the decisive factor in the purchase of jewellery is the style of the product, combined with skilful sales technique. The owner of the Chinese manufactory who produces jewellery for the world's most famous retailers admitted that the local, anonymous designers employed by him are responsible for the diversity of styling but they know well the preferences of Arab, American and European consumers. The Lebanese owner of a chain of jewellery stores in the Arabian Peninsula and Europe was convinced that the country of origin of stones and precious metals does not matter to the recipients. The most

[22] Dubai is a city that controls almost half of the world's trade in diamonds and gold.

important factor is the emotions that the seller will be able to evoke using the argument of exceptional product design.

As for the importance of the country of origin in the luxury segment of the car market the situation is similar to that of the fashion industry. The most prestigious cars are assembled in the place that is the cradle of the brand while maintaining strict control over the entire supply chain. As assembly in a traditional brand headquarters is the norm for the most prestigious brands this is not the case for lower-level brands. Given the complexity of a good such as a car it would be unreasonable to expect all components to be manufactured by a single manufacturer. The automotive supply chain is much more complex than in the fashion and jewellery industry. For example, the BMW Group (BMW, Mini, Rolls Royce) works with around 13,000 suppliers in 70 countries but each of them is subject to quality controls to ensure that the quality standards set by the industry and the Group are met (BMW Group 2017). On the other hand, Mercedes-Benz is trying to create a supply chain close to an assembly site. China is a good example of this strategy—the number of local suppliers has grown from five to more than 300 in the last decade in line with the slogan "Made in China for China" (Daimler 2018).

However while the cars sold on the Chinese market are essentially manufactured in China the expectations of European consumers for the car to be "manufactured" for example in Germany are already leading these companies to carry out the final stages of assembly in German factories.

3.4.2 Communication Strategies

In the DNA of business in the luxury market a lot of space is devoted to communication with current and future consumers as well as with a large number of people who will probably not be consumers for a long time to come but who form an indispensable group of luxury admirers and boost the social desire for such goods.

The most important communication rules are:

- a ban on intensive, mass advertising,

- the imperative of discreet image creation: creating an aura and a dream,
- directing the communication strategy outside the company's audience,
- establishing direct, individual customer relationships: luxury means treating all customers as VIPs, which requires personalised interaction.

The principle of abstention is now more of an indication than a practice. Although luxury brands still adhere to it within their highest placed core, they do not shy away from advertising in prestigious magazines and increasingly use Internet communication tools.

Luxury product providers recognise the importance of the Internet and its potential to create added value for customers. It is not only a valuable source of consumer information but also facilitates current communication, enables cheap and interactive image shaping, sales and development of new types of services to make the whole sales process smooth and pleasant (Vecchi et al. 2014; Soopramanien and Robertson 2007). Software packages are constantly being developed to attract consumer attention ranging from classic mobile apps designed to inform consumers about upcoming events which facilitate purchasing decisions (e.g. 3D measurement applications, style tips, interactive screening, see e.g. Okonkwo 2007; Peng et al. 2012; Vecchi et al. 2014; Samuely 2016) to co-creation and exploitation projects of virtual reality (see Wooding 2016).

Enterprises producing and offering luxury goods successfully implement the blend of the psychological of the Maletzky G communication model and a cultural mosaic model described by A. Molles[23] (Wiktor 2013, pp. 33–35). Maletzky's model is based on the assumption that only the core information is sent to the addressees of the proposal, which is usually the one highlighting the highest quality, rarity and an above-average aesthetic. The message is directed to the exceptional audience elite and aims to create an image with which a potential buyer will identify himself finding in the message her/his socially, aesthetically and emotionally desirable "me". The cultural mosaic model, on the other hand, is used in virtual space: various forms of interaction and ways

[23]A mosaic, not so much cultural as globally eclectic.

of communication with the global consumer are applied, combining elements of local cultures and artefacts in the message and creating the impression of closeness and joint experience and a co-operation in brand creation (Moore et al. 2000; Phan et al. 2011; Lee and Watkins 2016).

Social media are an important channel of communication which is now widely used by the owners of luxury brands. They help to spread the brand image desired by companies and at the same time constitute a convenient, widely available, relatively cheap (in comparison with advertising broadcast on television, for example) tool of social impact (see e.g. Godey et al. 2016).

Table 3.4 presents the results of an Internet content search on the most frequently communicated features of brands that are components of the value proposition offered by these brands for the customer. Three platforms were analysed: Instagram (I), Facebook (F), Twitter (T) and YouTube (YT) for selected luxury fashion brands and content. The results of this analysis (in the form of "tag clouds") have been simplified and only the most important components of the communicated brand value are shown in the table.

By targeting their communication strategy beyond their current audience luxury brands increase the likelihood of monetizing their value proposition by creating social desire among the multitude of people for whom this luxury is beyond their reach (see also Howarth 2018; Jain 2018; Jain and Schultz 2019). Communication strategies, especially those aimed at the mass audience, are created through the skilful use of so-called *content marketing*.[24] Walking the thin line between the need to maintain elitism and reaching a wide range of potential "followers" and admirers, luxury brands use their heritage as a focal point around which they spin stories intended to arouse emotions: to evoke aesthetic feelings, the impression of communion with something unique, unusual and noble at the same time. The Internet is an ideal place to strengthen the image although the relationship of luxury with

[24]Activities aimed at winning clients by publishing attractive and useful content (webinars, e-video, podcasts, infographics, manuals, reports), especially on the Internet which are to be of interest to a specific group. It is based on creating long-term customer relationships through interaction and commitment on both sides.

Table 3.4 Content of posts and scope of impact (measured by the number of observers) of selected luxury fashion brands in social media

Brand	Information on company websites	Communication in social media (number of followers)
Hermés	Communication puts emphasis on brand heritage, more than a century of experience/masterly workmanship, artistry and craftsmanship combined with a unique design	I—10,112,581 F—3,274,178 T—82,480 YT—117,000 There is little communication on the T-side. The main platforms are I and F. Many fancy, artistic product images and on T information about new sales outlets or sponsored events (e.g. equestrian events) Communication is focused on: elite, prestige, modernity, design
Chanel	Communication is focused on: prestige (designer and place—Paris), craftsmanship, elegance, celebrities/models	I—39,879,947 F—22,551,977 T—13,209,776 YT—1,580,000 The marketing message is consistent across all platforms. Communication is focused on: **design, elegance, celebrities, status**
Bottega Veneta	No information on the place of production Internet communication focuses on: **quality, craftsmanship, artistry**	I—2,190,242 F—795,059 YT—24,500 The marketing message is consistent across all platforms. Communication focuses on **craftsmanship, artistry, uniqueness and design**

Brand	Information on company websites	Communication in social media (number of followers)
Louis Vuitton	No information on the place of production Internet communication is focused on: **brand recognition and heritage, celebrities, emotions**	I—38,172,040 F—23,491,338 T—7,508,307 YT—425,000 The marketing message is consistent across all platforms. Communication is focused on: **celebrities, celebrities, modernity**
Burberry	On the website we can find information that the company employs 10,000 people around the world, so we can assume that production is not just in the UK Internet communication is focused on: **brand heritage, country of origin, artistry,** music	I—17,093,323 F—17,139,762 T—8,343,915 YT—341,000 The marketing communication is not as consistent as for other brands. Burberry focuses at YT on music videos with British artists and Thomas Burberry's film. On I and T they publish pictures of products and celebrities in their clothes. F combine all the approaches mentioned above. Communication is focused on: **project, artistry, celebrities, country of origin**

(continued)

Table 3.4 (continued)

Brand	Information on company websites	Communication in social media (number of followers)
Prada	Information on production sites has been found on the Prada Group's website. Internet communication only for Prada products focuses on: **design, modernity, well-known brand**	I—23,492,912 F—6,849,748 T—1,185,325 YT—160,000 The marketing message is consistent across all platforms, and YB emphasizes more fashion shows. Communication is focused on: **well-known brand, design, goals of the British**
Gucci	No information about the place of production, but there are prices in the online store Internet communication is focused on: **design, emotions, celebrities**	I—40,428,767 F—19,105,060 T—5,894,069 YT—534,000 The marketing message is consistent across all platforms. Communication is focused on: **design, modernity, exclusivity, artistry**
Karl Lagerfeld	No information on the place of production Internet communication is focused on: designer's brand, everyday emotions, exclusivity	I—6,057,380 F—1,140,070 T—1,483,517 YT—14,300 The marketing message is consistent across all platforms and YB emphasizes more daily emotions. In addition the communication focuses on: **the designer's brand, the country of origin**

Brand	Information on company websites	Communication in social media (number of followers)
Armani	Different brands can be found on the same page: Giorgio Armani, Emporio Armani, EA7, Armani Collezioni. No information on the place of production. Internet communication is focused on: **a well-known brand, accessibility, desire…**	I—16,699,232 F—8,707,787 T—3,473,531 YT—139,000 The marketing message is consistent across all platforms, and YB emphasizes more fashion shows. Communication is focused on: **well-known brand, design, everyday emotions**
Versace	No information on the place of production. On the same page you can find different collections for women, men and children Internet communication is focused on: exclusivity, but also everyday emotions, because the website is aimed at different age groups	I—21,705,922 F—5,634,237 T—4,805,305 YT—188,000 The marketing message is consistent across all platforms, and YB emphasizes more fashion shows. Communication is focused on exclusivity
Hugo Boss/Boss	No information on the place of production. Different collections can be found on the same page: Boss, Boss Orange, Boss Green, Hugo Internet communication is focused on: exclusivity, a well-known brand	I—8,047,696 F—8,305,827 The marketing message is consistent across all platforms. Communication focuses on: **celebrities, accessibility**

Source Own study, state of followers on Instagram, Facebook, Twitter and Youtube dated 14.05.2020

this powerful medium can still be described as simultaneous love and hate relationship (Okonkwo 2007; Howarth, 2018). Creating contextual online campaigns (e.g. Burberry Kisses,[25] Rolex's cooperation with National Geographic for discoveries and research on our planet[26]), aims to induce consumers to engage and independently promote the brand, bringing at the same time a blend of positive emotions and creating a sense of belonging to a community of consumers.

The image of brands is also strengthened by appropriately selected product placement as in films (e.g. Aston Martin or BMW in productions with James Bond, Chanel clothes, Manolo Blahnik shoes and other luxurious fashion goods in the series "Sex in the big city"), at big gala events (lending unique jewellery to Hollywood stars, sewing dresses for them for the annual Oscar awards ceremony or Cannes Film Festival) or other prestigious artistic or sports events.

More and more brands also turn to influencers, including Internet bloggers, to ensure greater visibility of their brands on the Internet. On the one hand luxury brands are still worried about how a given blogger or other influential person can change the brand image to an undesirable one, but on the other the temptation to use the services of these people is huge. According to the reports of Luxury Daily, about 70% of brand activity is caused by influencers and not by the brands themselves (Ramirez 2018). However according to the research conducted by L2 (Infleuncer Special Report 2018) it is not worth investing in luxury pyramid brands in people who have millions of followers on their social networks because being very popular and promoting a lot of goods, they are not perceived as being credible. While such actions may have an impact on the communication strategies of masstige products or accessories or cosmetics, the[27] higher luxury is preferred to niche, exclusive bloggers, bloggers and celebrities whose activities guarantee greater emotional attachment and loyalty of consumers.

[25] http://kisses.burberry.com.

[26] https://www.rolex.com/science-and-exploration.html.

[27] The employment of e.g. Bella Hadid by Dior to advertise Dior cosmetics on their websites was a great success and gave the brand more than 19 million page views.

3.4.3 Distribution and Sales Strategies

As regards the configuration of the distribution network the recommendations for luxury brands are identical to those for manufacturing and boil down to maintaining full control over distribution processes, including:

- concentration on sales in own networks,
- not granting licenses.

Personal contact between the seller and the buyer of a luxury product is of such great importance that it is inconceivable for products to be sold by entities that are not part of the "universe" of the brand (Kapferer and Bastien 2017; Okonkwo 2007). In practice, however, this is the case with a variety of multi-brand department stores that have obtained a licence to sell luxury brand products. The principle of direct contact with the buyer as postulated in the communication strategies has also been significantly relaxed thanks to the popularization of Internet sales' channels. Even brand-controlled online shops cannot provide the impression of traditional sales.

Physical distribution outlets for luxury products include (Moore and Doherty 2007; Moore et al. 2010):

- *bricks and mortar shops*[28] and brand retail stores,
- licensed dealers: in the case of luxury cars, offering one specific brand and in the case of watchmaking or jewellery industry also selling other competing brands,
- single-brand stores or separate stands in a multi branded space and the licence is granted to reputable chains of department stores,
- airports,
- outlet chains, usually built on the outskirts of big cities or in the so-called outlet villages several kilometres away from the metropolis,
- wholesale of surplus products by so-called jobbers.

[28]The flagship store is the largest of all types of shops, offers a full range of products, both in terms of range and depth of assortment, as well as service, or special assortment, not available in stores of lower rank (e.g. LV perfumes are sold only in selected brand's flagship stores).

In online sales we deal with:

- online shops run by brand owners,
- online sales of department stores licensed to sell,
- online sales of many luxury brands by specialised shops offering only brands from this segment and premium brands,
- Internet sales of large portals offering a very wide range of products.

The traditional and at the same time the most advantageous way of distribution in terms of maintenance of control is to sell goods in one's own shops. Architecture and the way they function are the result of well thought-out strategies and, at the same time, significant financial outlays. In the case of the most prestigious brands (including car brands), they are created in the best locations of big cities; first of all in the largest and most visited by tourists rich metropolises (*1st tier cities*). The design and furnishing of such shops is carried out by eminent architects and artists and the exhibition of goods itself—sparing in terms of the number of "exhibits", with the use of appropriate lighting, music and fragrance is to create an aura that is a combination of a visit to a church and museum. The salesmen are the ambassadors of the brand and with their combined professionalism and restrained, discreet assistance they complete the charm of the "act of purchase".

3.4.3.1 Controlled Licensed Sales

The aura of the "brand universe" can be recreated through an appropriate design and sales strategy based on individual service and direct contact with the customer in single-brand licensed stores and dealer chains but already in multi-brand department stores and jewellery stores these features are weakening. They are compensated for by the reputation of the department store itself making a visit to the esteemed buildings of Harrods, Galleries La Fayette or Bergdorf Goodman an impression of luxury. In both types of shops described above seasonal price reductions are applied, but this applies only to a small part of the less prestigious offer and the scale of these reductions is small and discreet.

3.4.3.2 Airports

Luxury is also consumed during a journey. This method of shopping, apart from the dynamically developing Internet channel, is preferred by the largest global Chinese consumers (Delloite 2018). China's preference for foreign purchases is not only due to the tariffs on luxury goods imposed in China and the yuan's exchange rates against the USD and EUR but also to the fear of fraud by Chinese consumers where the selling of counterfeit products on the pretence of selling luxury goods in prestigious city districts in their country. Delloite in its 2018 report points to the growing role of airports in the purchase of luxury goods.

The COVID 19 pandemic 2019/2020—drastically changed the direction of sales. The physical blockade of airports caused the turnover to suddenly drop almost to zero and the only source of access to luxury goods became the Internet. It is thanks to it that the luxury goods market did not collapse in the period from February to the end of May although there are many indications that, on average, more than a 30% decrease in turnover in this sector (compared to the same period of 2019) will cause the whole sector not only to return to the level of turnover before the pandemic for at least two or three years but also to undergo major strategic transformations.

3.4.3.3 Outlets[29]

The standard for the strategy of selling luxury brands is not only to refrain from price reductions but also to increase prices in subsequent seasons and years for flagship products. But not all products with brand logos are sold as a complete entity. This is especially true for the fashion, accessories, cosmetics and perfume industries. In order not to spoil the reputation of brands and at the same time to liquidate the excess of goods from previous seasons many companies decide to build their own outlets

[29]Information about these distribution channels, which are the domain of luxury, but rather spoil its image, and hence are not officially communicated by the brands, was published in Stępień (2016). This part of the subsection is a modified version of the quoted article.

or license the sale of these goods elsewhere. The principle is a geographical separation of consumers purchasing goods at full price in flagship stores from those less wealthy and at the same time not determined to own goods from the latest collections. The business model of luxury outlets, whether controlled by brand owners or licensed, has several common features;

- points of sale are located at a certain distance from the prestigious locations of flagship stores,
- the outlets sell only a fraction of the range of goods offered by the flagship shops; they offer mainly masstige products, there are relatively fewer middle-level pyramid brands and there are no top luxury pyramid brands at these locations,
- part of the collection is produced specifically for outlet stores; as a result they do not represent a reduced offer from last season and the outlet products are presented as last season's reductions to attract the attention of consumers,
- outlets serve designers and brand owners as a place to test new designs and styles before they are introduced to traditional shopping in flagship stores located in prestigious locations.

Outlets are a popular shopping destination for aspiring consumers. Since the beginning of its existence (i.e. the 1970s, when VFC, the world's largest clothing manufacturer, allowed consumers to search chests with discounted goods from previous seasons), they have been developing extremely dynamically all over the world. In the USA there are currently over 130 large stores located on 42,000 square feet, and in Europe there are about 70 centres, but they cover about one third of the area of such American outlets (Dion and Borraz 2017). The dynamic and continuous growth of such places confirms the success of this business model. Most buyers are young and retired consumers. The image of this group is complemented by crowds of enthusiastic Chinese tourists buying wholesale Ralph Lauren's T-shirts and Coach bags. Masstige brands use this business model in a wide range and with financial success but brands from higher levels seem to slowly succumb to the vision of earning money on products from previous seasons (e.g. Salvatore Ferragamo, Prada, Givenchy).

3.4.3.4 Unofficial Retail Outlets for Luxury Goods of Previous Seasons

Companies such as Marshalls, TJ Maxx (TK Maxx in Europe), DSW or Loehmann are large international discount stores. They are not interested in buying small quantities of last season's collections. Their margins are high, the contract terms are demanding enough, so it is not an option to liquidate unsold collections for smaller and new, aspiring brands. Selling 2-year-old stocks of goods with up to 80% discount often brings these companies more profit than the owner of a small luxury brand assumed when creating a collection.

Some luxury brands when selling their products off-season require the removal of labels before they are displayed in discount stores but this requirement is rather a simulation of a selective distribution policy since the reality of these discount stores shows the exact opposite. On the other hand it must be acknowledged that luxury fashion sales by discount stores (as well as online flash sales portals) are often made without the formal consent of the brand owner. This is due to the fact that surplus goods are disposed of by means of so-called jobbers who carry out mass liquidation of collections.

3.4.3.5 Jobbers' Activities and Their Impact on the Degradation of Brand Image

One of the risks associated with the sale of surplus stocks by foreign, uncontrolled entities (Internet and traditional) is the effect of cannibalism. This happens when unlicensed sellers reduce the prices of recent seasons' products more than is the case with luxury brand websites or brand-controlled physical sales sites. This is the effect of moving collections not sold in a given season abroad to the so-called emerging markets of luxury (India is a good example of such a location). Moving goods to less developed markets is done by jobbers: wholesale intermediaries.

Those trusted traders quickly and efficiently move surplus stocks to other distribution channels and entities in the country and abroad and perform this task reliably because they are interested in maintaining good relations with their principals. The goods distributed in this way are often cheaper than the discounted prices offered by brand owners but the potential damage (resulting from inconsistent pricing policies) is offset, for example, by communicating the application of a more lenient pricing policy in developing countries. However there are also some dishonest intermediaries and although a 70–80% discount is effective in helping to monetise collections it does create a sense of an inadequate basic price among consumers and encourages them to postpone purchases in anticipation of significant price reductions.

In the context of the risk posed by off-season sales many, especially those most luxurious brands, choose to destroy unsold collections. This practice is, moreover, covered by the greatest secrecy and this type of work is carried out by trusted intermediaries. Although unethical and environmentally disgraceful this practice exists and is likely to continue. According to the 2018 annual report, Burberry burned unsold products worth £28.6 million. Richemont also made the headlines in May 2018, when it turned out that it had destroyed watches worth 572 million dollars over the last two years[30] (however this is value in terms of catalogue prices, see Pinnock, 20.07.2018, Forbes). LV also admits to destroying its products, although it does not state what their value is.

3.4.3.6 Internet Sales Channels

Perhaps the most important feature of the Internet which does more harm than good to luxury brands is the lack of control over distribution channels on the Internet. To maintain this control Richemont Group purchased yoox.com and net-a-porter.com; the two largest online retailers, merged since 2015 (new name is Yoox Net-A-Porter Group S.P.A.[31]). What is even more interesting (and highlights the importance

[30]In both cases, however, it is the value at selling prices which reduces the injury picture.

[31]Yoox specializes in buying unsold items from previous seasons from reputable fashion houses (e.g. Dolce & Gabbana, Gucci, Armani, Cavalli, etc.) and selling them online at reduced prices.

of digital distribution channels) in June 2015 the CEO of Richemont invited LVMH and Kering SA to take part in an attempt to set up a luxury retail website that could compete with the global market of the largest online retailers. So far, however, nothing more has been heard about the implementation of this project.

Although the purchase of products in shops and Internet portals deprives consumers of the impressions built through the use of traditional sales methods the Internet sales of luxury goods are growing dynamically. This is primarily due to the large number of aspiring consumers for whom a visit to a traditional shop is either difficult (because it is not in the place where the consumer lives) or, despite its existence, may be a source of frustration (due to the hitherto limited experience in the consumption of luxury goods or the fear of making too many purchases beyond their means under the influence of subtle pressure from the seller). The third and perhaps the most important reason for the growing popularity of Internet sales channels is due to the possibility of buying the desired goods at significantly reduced prices, which would not be found in traditional shops. Such "opportunities" are possible on the Internet precisely because of the lack of full control over distribution channels.

Already in 2019 and even more in 2020 (due to the COVID 19 Pandemic) Internet channel developed most dynamically. It is estimated that on a global scale as much as 75% of physical and online purchases were made under the impulse provided by Internet communication. Just as in luxury shopping in general Asia has the biggest share in the development of online sales channels, with the Chinese as the most intensive users of this form of shopping.

One of the liquidation practices of unsold collections is to sell them online through flash sales and specialized, socially responsible sellers. Such sales however mainly relate to fashion and is a relatively new, innovative solution that provides brand owners with the ability to manage surpluses while maintaining the aura of uniqueness and unavailability. The French internet platform Vente Privée is considered to be the creator

---

Yoox also creates capsule collections (e.g. Hussein Chalayan, Alexandre Herchcovitch) sold as flash sales. Net - a - porter is one of the first portals selling luxury goods at slightly lower prices but not much lower than if they were sold in flagship stores.

of this business model now successfully copied by others (Gilt Group, Rue La La La, Cocosa, OutNet and over 100 other players). There are also so-called flash sales search engines (such as RetailFetish.com). The most characteristic feature of *flash* sales is that they offer luxury brands at reduced prices in a very short period of time (usually during a maximum of 2–3 days). It seems that for both websites—operators and brand owners—this is a beneficial strategy. There is still a sense of shortage, margins from the sale of off-season products are still positive and many consumers have a sense of winning the lottery. Belonging to the "lucky ones" (and even happier than buyers in traditional sales outlets due to favourable price offers) is also achieved because some sites are only available to recommended, registered members.

Another safe way for brands to reduce excess inventory is ThredUp. It was a platform originally dedicated to the sale of used goods but in the summer of 2017 ThredUp Luxe was launched, thanks to the huge demand for luxury goods among its customers. According to co-founder James Reinhart, "*demand for luxury goods at ThredUP currently exceeds supply with more than 60,000 searches for luxury brands every week*", justifying the huge social desire to own luxury goods, both new and used (see Parisi, 27.07.2017, *Luxury Daily* 2018).

3.4.4 Monetisation Strategies

The rule of luxury DNA concerning monetization of value propositions is simple—always increase the average price and this is the case with the so-called flagship, iconic brand products, especially those present at the two highest levels of the pyramid. The so-called best sellers are not subject to discounts and their price only increases with time.

Companies in the highest luxury segment apply this principle with an iron fist and the steadily increasing demand for the top luxuries (higher than the supply levels) allows them to do so. This does not mean, however, that the limited volume of production is a consequence of bottlenecks: it is a deliberate strategy to maintain the brand image of an unavailable brand. Despite Kapferer's claim that the craftsmen sewing Birkin and Kelly bags in Hermés "are not born on stone" (Doran

2015[32]), it is difficult to assume that there are no very talented purse-makers in the world including those born “in the vicinity of stones” (here: in poverty), which can be acquired from the world market and trained to work in a relatively short time. Sewing a bag, however, is a somewhat less complicated process than the analysis of atomic particles. Even in the case of car brands maintaining an annual production limit is the result of a compromise between the need to maintain the image and the desire to increase profits,[33] and expenditure on the development of so-called concept vehicles clearly shows that capacity expansion is not a problem in these companies.

The practice of liquidating unsold goods proves how important it is in this sector to maintain the image of an inaccessible, rare luxury because this image allows the generation of high margins and the ability to monetize the brand on lower tiers.

As shown in the discussion on the pyramid of luxury it is usually the products in the so-called middle price range that drive the company’s profitability. The individual and most expensive exhibits are intended only to strengthen the brand image but these individual items, combined with high production costs, are often unprofitable. On the other hand the purpose of manufacturing and selling accessories is not only to make money from their sale but also to attract future consumers who, as their income increases, will return to the company for more expensive products.

The nature, scope and intensity of brand monetization are also determined by the ownership structures and the legal status of the company. Rationalising costs and striving for profit will, as a rule, be more important for listed companies. This pressure will not be felt equally by independent fashion houses or so-called specialists. Being a unique, innovative and sustainable brand often requires a compromise in the form of

---

[32]The essence of the Kapferer’s message implies how complicated and long-lasting the process is to develop the appropriate craft skills which are one of the key resources of luxury brands.

[33]For example, despite the huge demand Lamborghini’s production capacity is officially announced as no more than 3500 cars per year. The limits apply to all brands on the top rung of the ladder but the desire for profit means that they are constantly being raised (2016.08.26), https://www.cyrkf1.pl/wyniki-finansowe-ferrari-2016/.

sales diversification, stretching and extension of the brand, although not all players are able to apply this compromise skilfully in the long term.

Ferrari has three sources of profit: the first is cars. Revenues here do not grow dynamically due to the internally maintained production limit. The second is the Formula One championship, where the brand image is created but also the rights to broadcast and use the logo during the competition are sold. A third source is the licence to place the Ferrari logo on various accessories not directly related to cars which generate considerable income allowing the company to function and grow well. Another successful way to maintain a unique brand image is through the personalization/customization of cars such as Rolls Royce which is more profitable than the production of a new standardised car.

Other ways of monetising the brand, although less successful due to its long-term development, concern its intensive extension to almost all possible industries with a luxury segment. This is the case with Armani, which, after years of utilizing this strategy successfully eventually went too far and now has been losing customers and revenues for two years. According to the head of the company, however, the reversal of this unfavourable trend was expected in 2020 due to a thorough restructuring and a change in the business model (Luxury Daily, 2018.08.03, Armani).

3.5 The Interplay Between Ownership Configurations and Business Models in the Luxury Goods Market

Below is the author's classification of the existing business models of enterprises operating in the luxury market, quite typical for certain ownership structures.[34]

[34]A protoplast typology for the one presented above (consisting of five models—consolidators, family fashion houses, 3ML sellers, specialists and multi-segment sellers) is the list created by the consulting firm Precepta on the basis of a survey conducted in 2010 (in Hoffmann and Coste-Manière 2012, p. 233). Since then, however, much has changed in the area of acquisitions and capital mergers hence the proposed business model typology and the proposed Precepta terminology was used only as a preliminary conceptual framework, complemented

3.5.1 Large Players, Consolidating and Managing Multiple Brands

1. **Luxury consolidators for private use**—international, listed conglomerates of luxury and premium brands such as LVMH, Richemont, Kering. They have large financial resources and their development is based on the constant acquisition of new or poorly operating old luxury brands and the management of their portfolio. Brands in the conglomerate retain operational and design autonomy but are subject to a common marketing strategy, guidelines for composition and control of the supply chain and adapt to an overall strategy such as sustainability.[35] Conglomerates are listed on stock exchanges which determines their strategies focused on dynamic value and revenue growth. Their portfolios include so-called milk cows—above-average revenue brands positioned as global players (LV in LVMH, Gucci in Kering, Cartier in Richemont) as well as brands that have been making losses for years but working hard to regain new lustre and become profitability stars.

   LVMH—Moët Hennessy Louis Vuitton SE is a French company founded in 1987 by the merger of Louis Vuitton's fashion house with Moët Hennessy a company created by the merger of the champagne producers Moët & Chandon and Hennessy the cognac producer. It has been managed for years by Bernard Arnoult who is considered to have contributed the most to changing the face of luxury by introducing the hard rules of world finance. LVMH controls approximately 60 subsidiaries, each of which manages a small number of prestigious brands. In 2017 Arnault also bought out Christian Dior who had been defending himself against the takeover for many years. The flagship brands in LVMH's portfolio include LV, Dior, Celine, Marc Jabobs, Fendi, Givenchy and alcoholic beverages: Hennessy, Moèt & Chandon, Vueve Clicquot t, or Belvedere; in the jewellery and watchmaking industry: Bulgari, Chaumet, Hublot;

---

with new types of models and current activities illustrating the typical way of operation of these companies.

[35]However which does not prevent destroying off-season collections and testifies to hypocrisy.

in the cosmetics industry: Guerlain, Tom Ford, Aqua di Parma, Givenchy. LVMH also has sales networks—Sephora, Le Bon Marchè in Paris, DFS in Hong Kong.

Richemont—Compagnie Financière Richemont SA is a Swiss luxury goods trading company founded in 1988 by South African businessman Johann Rupert. Through its subsidiaries Richemont designs, manufactures, distributes and sells the highest quality jewellery, watches, leather goods, writing instruments, firearms, clothing and accessories. The brands it owns are: A. Lange & Söhne, Azzedine Alaïa, Baume & Mercier, Cartier, Chloé, Dunhill, IWC Schaffhausen, Giampiero Bodino, Jaeger-LeCoultre, Lancel, Montblanc, Officine Panerai, Piaget, Peter Millar, Purdey, Roger Dubuis, Vacheron Constantin and Van Cleef & Arpels. Richemont is the owner of YOOX NET-A-PORTER GROUP S.p.A., a leading online retailer of luxury products (data from the company's official website).[36]

Kering SA—French operator of luxury and life style brands which was known as PPR until June 2013. The main brands are Bottega Veneta, Gucci, Balenciaga, Alexander McQueen, Stella McCartney, Yves Saint Laurent and Boucheron. Compared to LVMH it is a so-called late entry global player (Gucci was taken over in 1999). Like LVMH it grows through acquisitions (acquisition of Brioni in 2011; Jeanrichard and Girard Perregaux 2011; Qeelin 2012; Christopher Kane 2013; Pomellato 2013; Ulysse Nardin 2014). Half of the Group's revenues come from luxury fashion followed by the sports and life style industry with Puma as the main brand. In April 2018 however, Kering announced its intention to sell the clothing company Volcom and in May 2018 it also sold its stake in Puma, retaining only 15.7% of the package to focus on the luxury sector. An aggressive investor with a strong, globally recognizable group of brands it is dynamically developing its sales' network in Asia but the main issue of the concern is too much dependence on the one Gucci brand and a still weak development of the haute horlogerie industry.

[36] https://www.richemont.com/.

2. **Vertical integrators and consolidators of 'tech'**—this is a group of listed automotive corporations covering all consumer segments albeit in the case of BMW and Mercedes, with only premium and luxury products. Unlike consolidators gathering private luxury brands from the fashion, jewellery, cosmetics or life—style industries the main component of the value proposition is not symbolism, aura or uniqueness. In this industry technical excellence and innovation are essential, although combined with the complimentary (but crucial) attributes of luxury in areas of the emotional, social and symbolic "magic". The competition in the global automotive industry takes place through: global sales, pooling of capital of the main players in order to increase the pace and diversification of the risk of design and research activity, dispersal of the production and supply chain on a regional and global scale. The aim of such a configuration is to develop technical innovations as quickly as possible while optimising the cost and global monetisation of manufactured goods to the widest possible audience.

   The strategies of car corporations in the luxury segment are two-track: they consist in the simultaneous development of their own, traditional brands with a wide range of goods, as well as the acquisition and development of other niche brands with a clearly defined customer profile (Ferrari, Aston Martin, Bentley, Rolls Royce, etc.). The Volkswagen Group controls Lamborghini, Audi, Porsche, Bugatti and Bentley; Tata Motor owns Jaguar Land Rover; Rolls-Royce is owned by BMW; Lexus is owned by Toyota; Infinity is owned by Nissan; Lincoln is owned by the Ford Motor Company; Cadillac GM and Maserati are controlled by Fiat Chrysler Automobiles. The companies control the entire supply chain dispersed on a global scale but closely connected with intra- and interorganization and capital relationships. In the case of luxury niche brands (sport, uber-luxury), brands retain a high degree of freedom to shape their strategies, although the guiding principle is to keep the production of the number of cars in check, which helps to persuade consumers of their scarcity, unavailability and desirability.
3. **FMLG** (fast moving luxury goods) **sellers**—this group includes mainly international cosmetics' companies such as L'Oréal, Estée

Lauder or Coty, but also players from the jewellery industry with a smaller geographical reach (such as Polish Apart or Yes). Companies using this model are present in several market segments from mass market to luxury. Business differentiators include the frequent introduction of new products, intensive marketing and skilful management of the portfolio of brands (e.g. through licensing) in order to achieve economies of scale.

4. **Galaxy models for mass luxury**—this group includes e.g. Ralph Lauren, Armani, Hugo Boss, PVH (owner of Calvin Klein and Tommy Hilfiger). The strategy is based on maximising sales by creating an umbrella brand image. The galaxy is a metaphor for the coexistence of brands created under the "wings" of the founder, most often the head designer (Giorgio Armani, Tommy Hilfiger, Ralph Lauren), operating independently in different industries. The galaxy model differs from the consolidator model in the consumer segments targeted by the products. The umbrella brand while allowing it to be monetised in many industries poses a serious threat to the whole model: if one of them loses its reputation, the odium of decline extends to the others.

The good example of a galactic model is the composition of Armani umbrella brand:

- the presence of the brand at the highest level of the luxury pyramid (Armani Prive),
- extension of the original brand to groups of less affluent fashion consumers; Armani Collezioni, Emporio Armani, Armani Jeans,
- expanding the range of fashion accessories (handbags, sunglasses, wallets, scarves, etc.),
- creation of different clothing lines (e.g. sports lines) or collections for children or teenagers with different pricing strategies for smaller, profiled segments; Armani Junior, Armani Exchange, EA7,
- presence of the brand in the cosmetics and perfumery industry with the Armani logo

- extension of the scope of operations to the so-called lifestyle area (e.g. hotels, restaurants, food, interior design): Armani Casa, Armani Ristorante, Armani Hotels (e.g. in Burj al Dubai), Armani Fiori, Armani Dolci.

3.5.2 Smaller Players with Several or One Main Brand

5 **Aggressive, agile players**—The model is a combination of an independent fashion house with its own unique style and an aggressive market expansion strategy adopted from the principles of global finance. It is a hybrid of models 1 and 6 with an original addition in the form of emphasis on the fastest possible monetization of the brand while creating the aura of luxury through intensive marketing and selling goods to almost everyone (through the use of licenses and various forms of discount sales). The dynamics of action is visible not only in the pace of opening stores around the world but also in the acquisition of other brands or geographical dispersion of the value chain. The Prada Group and Michael Kors use this model.[37]

Prada was founded in 1913 in Milan and initially produced only leather products. Thanks to Miucci Prada and her dazzling husband businessman Prada became a luxury fashion company with haute couture clothing lines and then a prêt-à-porter range. Currently Prada's portfolio includes brands created or acquired and from the beginning promoted by the concern (Prada, Miu Miu, Car Shoe, Marchesi 1824) as well as other well-known brands taken over from the market (Helmut Lang, Jil Sander, Church's). Currently Prada has 250 stores in 65 countries around the world.

Michael Kors Holdings Limited is an American company from the masstige fashion industry. Founded in 1981 by Michael Kors it was initially sold by the Bergdorf Goodman department store under an exclusive licence granted by Kors. With a designer of sports and life style clothing, Kors strenuously and determinedly sought to take

[37]However they occupy other levels of the pyramid of luxury within their so-called core business.

a place in the luxury sector. As a designer Celine had the opportunity to learn how such brands work and has since then started a dynamic market expansion with his bags, accessories and fashion. It opened its first retail stores in 2006 targeting mainly young, medium affluent women seeking an aura of luxury but at the level of their financial capabilities. In 2017 the company had 827 of their own stores and 133 licensed stores (offering goods both at full price and in the outlet system). In July 2017 Michael Kors acquired Jimmy Choo Ltd.

6. **Independent fashion houses**—this group includes Chanel or Hermès, which are controlled by family capital or private individuals. They adhere to the principles of management developed by the founders of the brand and subsequent generations of successors. Heritage, tradition, uncompromising care for quality are the basic features of the model. The old-fashioned management style of Hermès (keeping the production inside the company in France, in Paris and a cautious approach to retail) proves to be extremely effective and makes the brand a symbol of "luxury inside luxury". Chanel has not only stayed in the luxury fashion segment but skilfully achieves high revenues in the cosmetics industry.

   Independence, the primacy of the artistic project in comparison with the traditional image of luxury[38] and the set of management principles developed by the founder (although not necessarily in line with global recommendations of consulting companies or popular scientific management guides) is also a typical model for small luxury brands with a localised scope of activity.

7. **Professionals**—well-known, esteemed brands operating in one industry, e.g. Rolex or Mauboussin. The model of this group is based on high margins and small volumes, developing its activities on the traditional ideal model of luxury business described above. It is worth noting that the brands comprising conglomerates (model 1), car corporations (model 2) and FMLG players placed at the top or middle of the luxury pyramid also use this model in the production, distribution and communication layers.

[38]It has nothing to do with the character of design which is supposed to be innovative although it can be avant-garde, classic and so on.

3.6 Consequences of Changes in the Structure and Dynamics of the Luxury Market Development on the Value Proposition—Summary

Luxury consumption is a reflection of wider, global changes in consumption patterns. The most important are (Global Web Index 2020; Mintel 2020; Danziger 2019),

- deconsumption trends, conscious, sustainable, ethical, ecological consumption as a reaction to consumerism surpluses,
- dematerialization of consumption for the sake of searching and experiencing,
- the abandonment of purchases for the sake of temporary use, sharing or co-creation of goods,
- glocalisation: local consumption as a reaction to global homogeneity,
- a shift away from public loud consumption, towards quiet, private, individualised consumption,
- facilitating sales and use of goods through the use of techniques from the Internet space and mobile communication: e.g. multiple channels to reach consumers to increase their satisfaction with consumption (creating an *omni-channel experience*),
- politicisation and even nationalisation of consumption (see also Halkier 2016).

The trends listed here reflect the changes that are currently taking place in many, not only mature economies, shaping postmodern consumer culture, which dimensions are: negation of universal ideologies, pluralism of views and lifestyles, changeability, hedonism, coexistence of opposing phenomena and trends, or living in hyper-reality, mainly thanks to virtual space.

The characteristics of this culture give rise to the possibility of offering new or strengthening existing types of values resulting from the possibility of the individual shaping of lifestyles. It increases the speed of response to questions and customer needs thanks to the use of space and virtual application, transformation of marketing communication into real and virtual hyper entities. Companies focus on providing ephemeral sensations and pleasure experienced by many senses, including the coexistence of real and virtual spaces.

In the luxury goods market there is a distance from traditional marketing where consumers are seen as rational decision-makers, focusing on the functional qualities and benefits of products. The present and future consumer is an emotional being focused on achieving a pleasant experience in accordance with the concept of Service Dominant Logic (Vargo and Lusch 2004, 2008). It is a postmodern homo consumericus that has grown up in the world of mass consumption, defined by this consumption and in relation to the cult of consumption, valuing not only purchases but all of itself and others (see Atwal and Williams 2008; Yeoman and McMahon-Beattie 2006; Miller 1998).

As they wrote:

- in the 50's Fromm about the marketing man (Fromm 1947, 2013),
- in the 1980s, Baudrillard (on consumer freedom as a myth within the framework of purchasing power; Baudrillard 2016),
- in the 1990s, Bourdieu (on shaping demand and production by consumption 1986, 2013) or McCracken (on consumption as a code of communication, 1986, 2005).

the world of consumption today serves the basis for determining the superior system of individual values. The body, children, spouses and even the soul become a product which, like everything else, has its price and is judged by the extent to which it pleases others.

In this context an attempt to move away from the commonness of mass consumption is an escape into an atypical, ephemeral and totally individual (and thus unique) experience. This are created by means of experience marketing or the so-called context, combining forms, channels and ways of influence (see). In the marketing of experience activities are focused on arousing and sustaining specific customer feelings related to their lifestyle. Consumers shall be provided with sensory, emotional, cognitive and relational values that are consistent with what they expect (and can expect experiences different from those of everyday life). The aim is to achieve synergy between meaning, perception, consumption and brand loyalty. The assumption of these marketing strategies is to base consumers' decisions on a combination of emotion and rationality. However experience marketing requires a wider range of research methods to understand the causes of specific consumer behaviour in order to involve them. The richness of experience and commitment depends on the interplay between the "experimental zones": entertainment, education, escape from everyday life and aesthetics (Pine and Gilmore 1999).

According to LuxeDigital (2020), Matter of Form (2020) or Bain & Co. (2020) there are at least a few interdependent trends that will change the luxury market. It is predicted that the most important force that will change the face of luxury will be the Internet and technologies based on its use. The entry of these technologies into all areas of economic and private life will also leave its mark on this market and although until recently it successfully defended itself against mass communication in the Internet media[39] it is abstracted from the level and direction of emotions, from the exploitation of this sphere depends on its existence and development.

It seems that the leading megatrend is and will be the expanding digitalization which will change the face of the luxury market even more dynamically than before. The directions of this transformation aim to intensify the use of Augmented Reality (AR) and Artificial Intelligence (AI) to integrate real and virtual realities. All this in order to facilitate the process of communication with the customer, selection and purchase and assistance during the use of the products. Using AR and AI technologies luxury brands can also provide a personalised consumer experience, reach a wider audience, deepen product consumption experiences and establish more intense customer relationships.[40] In addition to AR and AI we

[39]Okonkwo described this as a love and hate relationship, Okonkwo (2007).

[40]These expectations relate primarily to the Millennials and Generation Z group which is expected to represent 40% of the global luxury consumer group by 2025 (Delloite 2018). I am also not convinced that the intensification of virtual relationships with the customer is simply aimed at tightening ties resulting in increased shopping and loyalty, although there are studies indicating such dependencies (see e.g. Table 9, Chapter 2).

should also mention the development of virtual commerce with extensive sensory stimuli (voice, sound, image) and the Internet of Things (IoT), which makes it possible to use the services of the Internet:

- incorporation of various additional functions into the proposal for the value of luxury goods in order to increase their functionality or intensify sensations,
- use of software to create individualised products by yourself,
- participation in the process of designing and manufacturing a product (let's take a look at the Hermés workshop[41]),
- facilitate the selection process virtual fitting rooms, etc.

The marriage of virtual space and the use of modern information technologies is to support the consumer in independently creating the value of luxury goods. It is a proposal to increase the functional and emotional value of luxury goods and services and a tool for the development of the second megatrend.

The aim is to extend the range of possible experiences for the consumer before, during the purchase, use and disposal. The most important seems to be the provision of the so-called omnichannel experience: the possibility of simultaneous use of virtual and real space.[42]

Buying luxury goods online also raises the problem of checking their authenticity. Special programs and applications from the so-called blockchain category help in this. Offering such applications by the manufacturers of luxury jewellery, watches, accessories and clothing not only increases the security of purchase, but also eliminates fraudsters and increases investment in online sales channels of luxury goods.

Other trends include the shift from traditional shopping to sharing. The so-called sharing economy is also entering the luxury sector and the phenomenon of renting luxury goods is beginning to grow rapidly

[41] Patrz np. https://www.businessinsider.com/how-herms-bags-are-made-2012-7?IR=T#many-of-the-leathers-like-this-blue-crocodile-skin-are-dyed-4.

[42] In the simplest terms it is the integration of ordering in online stores combined with social media such as Instagram where photos of celebrities using the products of a given brand are placed. After "clicking" on a given product, the program is to redirect us to the online store but we can receive the goods physically in the store already.

(see e.g. Parisi 2018; Cisse 2020). Consumers and with them new, fast-responding entities operating mainly online, began to ask themselves another question—why buy luxury goods when you can enjoy using them without being their owner for the rest of your life?

Rental applies to jewellery, watches, clothes, accessories and cars. However, lending is a trend for a rather new group of consumers, other than the traditional one for whom the possession of luxury goods will remains an asset. However the traditional customer base of classic luxury lovers is not growing at the same rate as the ambitions to increase revenue for owners and managers of luxury goods businesses. The trend towards the resale of second-hand luxury goods is also developing and the spread of such an approach to luxury makes one wonder whether the existing business models should not be reformulated.

What is more, Julius Baer (2020) clearly highlights a growing trend among the richest groups in the world, being environmentally conscious are inclined to spend money on protecting environment or even for charity rather than on goods or luxury services. A good example of this is the activity of Warren Buffet who devotes over 70% of his income to charity, or the Gates couple who invest over 20% of their income in charity work.[43]

In addition to charity work the trend towards social and environmental responsibility which is increasingly present and recognised as a new kind of value for consumers should also be noted.

In the longer term it is likely that the vision of "fully automated luxury communism" will come true.[44] In a few decades' time when robots or autonomous products are widespread human working time may be limited to 10–15 hours per week it is work itself that will then become a rare commodity—a luxury, accessible to those who are most educated and who coordinate automated work. Artificially made gemstones or autonomous cars as public transport will be available to the general public as will the ability to manufacture customized clothing and accessories with 3D printers or more sophisticated technologies. Perhaps then

---

[43]See also https://www.forbes.com/pictures/59d5055e4bbe6f37dd9ff693/how-much-do-americas-rich/#46894de94a47.

[44]https://www.forbes.com/sites/bernardmarr/2016/06/30/are-we-headed-for-automated-luxury-communism/#48489fec37e3.

Socrates' vision of luxury the highest measure of which is to serve the public good will be realized. However as predicted by Harari (2018) in such a society economic stratification will be even more visible than it is today and despite the fact that goods now considered luxurious will become universally available. Luxury versions of autonomous vehicles will be produced next to them in production units or the elite access to limited virtual amusement parks will become more important. Health and beauty enhancing services will be divided into generally accessible products (although of a higher quality and scope) and also into those products and services that are the latest, most luxurious and accessible only to the few.

References

Ahn, J., Park, J. K., & Hyun, H. (2018). Luxury product to service brand extension and brand equity transfer. *Journal of Retailing and Consumer Services, 42,* 22–28.

Antoni, F., Burgelman, R. A., & Meza, P. (2004). *LVMH in 2004: The challenges of strategic integration.* Harvard: Harvard Business School Case.

Arnould, E. J., Price, L. L., & Otnes, C. (1999). Making (consumption) magic: A study of white water river rafting. *Journal of Contemporary Ethnography, 28*(1), 33–68.

Arvidsson, A., & Malossi, G. (2011). Customer co-production from social factory to brand: Learning from Italian fashion. In D. Zwick & J. Cayla (Eds.), *Inside marketing: Practices, ideologies, devices* (s. 212–233). New York: Oxford University Press.

Atwal, G., & Williams, A. (2008). Marketing in postmodern India: Bulgari meets bollywood. *Indian Journal of Marketing, 38*(1).

Atwal, G., & Williams, A. (2009). Luxury brand marketing—The experience is everything! *Journal of Brand Management, 16*(5–6), 338–346.

Bain. (2014). *Luxury goods worldwide market study fall-winter 2014: The rise of the borderless consumer.* https://www.bain.com/insights/luxury-goods-worldwide-market-study-december-2014/.

Bain. (2020). *Luxury after COVID 19, changed for (the) good?* https://www.bain.com/insights/luxury-after-coronavirus/.

Bain & Co. (2019). *Eight themes that are rewriting the future of luxury goods.*

Bain & Co. (2020). *Global personal luxury goods market set to contract between 20–35 percent in 2020*. https://www.bain.com/about/media-center/press-releases/2020/spring-luxury-report/.

Bain & Company. (2016). https://www.bain.com/insights/luxury-goods-worldwide-market-study-fall-winter-2016/.

Bain & Company. (2018). https://www.bain.com/contentassets/8df501b9f8d6442eba00040246c6b4f9/bain_digest__luxury_goods_worldwide_market_study_fall_winter_2018.pdf.

Balabanis, G., & Diamantopoulos, A. (2008). Brand origin identification by consumers: A classification perspective. *Journal of International Marketing, 16*(1), 39–71.

Bastien, V., & Kapferer, J. N. (2013). More on luxury anti-laws of marketing. In *Luxury marketing* (pp. 19–34). Wiesbaden: Gabler Verlag.

Baudrillard, J. (2016). *The consumer society: Myths and structures*. Sage.

Berthon, P., Pitt, L., Parent, M., & Berthon, J. P. (2009). Aesthetics and ephemerality: Observing and preserving the luxury brand. *California Management Review, 52*(1), 45–66.

BMW Group. (2017). *Supplier management*. Pobrane z. https://www.bmwgroup.com.

Bourdieu, P. (2013). The forms of capital by Pierre Bourdieu 1986. *Marxists Internet Archive. Np.*

Brun, A., & Castelli, C. (2013). The nature of luxury: A consumer perspective. *International Journal of Retail & Distribution Management, 41*(11/12), 823–847.

Calori, R., Melin, L., Atamer, T., & Gustavsson, P. (2000). Innovative international strategies. *Journal of World Business, 35*(4), 333–354.

Caniato, F., Caridi, M., Castelli, C., & Golini, R. (2009). A contingency approach for SC strategy in the Italian luxury industry: Do consolidated models fit? *International Journal of Production Economics, 120*(1), 176–189.

Castelli, C. M., & Sianesi, A. (2015). Supply chain strategy for companies in the luxury-fashion market: Aligning the supply chain towards the critical success factors. *International Journal of Retail & Distribution Management, 43*(10/11), 940–966.

Chevalier, M., & Gutsatz, M. (2012). *Luxury retail management: How the world's top brands provide quality product and service support*. Singapore: Wiley.

Chevalier, M., & Mazzalovo, G. (2008). *Luxury brand management: A world of privilege*. Singapore: Wiley.

Christodoulides, G., Michaelidou, N., & Li, C.-H. (2009). Measuring perceived brand luxury: An evaluation of the BLI scale. *Brand Management, 16*(5/6), 395–405.
Christopher, M., & Towill, D. R. (2002). Developing market specific SC strategies. *The International Journal of Logistics Management, 31*(1), 1–14.
Cisse, C. (2020). *In the new age of rentable luxury, consumers are less concerned with ownership than ever in.* https://www.luxurysociety.com/en/articles/2020/02/rise-sharing-economy/.
CPCStrategy. (2018). *The 2018 influencer marketing report, The rise of micro-influencers & how consumer trust drives sales.* https://learn.cpcstrategy.com/rs/006-GWW-889/images/2018%20Influencer%20Marketing%20v3.pdf.
Daimler. (2018). https://media.daimler.com/marsMediaSite/en/instance/ko/China.xhtml?oid=9265718.
Dall'Olmo Riley, F., Pina, J. M., & Bravo, R. (2015). The role of perceived value in vertical brand extensions of luxury and premium brands. *Journal of Marketing Management, 31*(7–8), 881–913.
Danziger, P. (2019). *6 global consumer trends for 2019, and the brands that are out in front of them, in Forbes.* https://www.forbes.com/sites/pamdanziger/2019/01/13/6-global-consumer-trends-and-brands-that-are-out-in-front-of-them-in-2019/#4d8d21404fe4.
Delloite. (2018). *Global powers of luxury goods 2018.* From z. https://www2.deloitte.com/content/dam/Deloitte/at/Documents/consumer-business/deloitte-global-powers-of-luxury-goods-2018.pdf.
Delloite. (2019). *Global powers of luxury goods.* https://www2.deloitte.com/global/en/pages/consumer-business/articles/gx-cb-global-powers-of-luxury-goods.html.
Dion, D., & Arnould, E. (2011). Retail luxury strategy: Assembling charisma through art and magic. *Journal of Retailing, 87*(4), 502–520.
Dion, D., & Borraz, S. (2017). Managing status: How luxury brands shape class subjectivities in the service encounter. *Journal of Marketing, 81*(5), 67–85.
Economist. (2014). *Exclusively for everybody.* From z. https://www.economist.com/special-report/2014/12/11/exclusively-for-everybody.
Featherstone, M. (2016). The object and art of luxury consumption. *Critical luxury studies: Art, design, media*, 108–127.
Fionda, A. M., & Moore, C. M. (2009). The anatomy of the luxury fashion brand. *Journal of Brand Management, 16*(5–6), 347–363.
Fromm, E. (1947). (Man for Himself, Chinese), Shanghai (Shanghai Translation Publishing House) 2013.

Global Web Index. (2020). *Consumer trends that will shape 2020*. https://www.globalwebindex.com/reports/trends-2020.
Godey, B., Manthiou, A., Pederzoli, D., Rokka, J., Aiello, G., Donvito, R., et al. (2016). Social media marketing efforts of luxury brands: Influence on brand equity and consumer behavior. *Journal of Business Research, 69*(12), 5833–5841.
Gutsatz, M., & Heine, K. (2018). *Luxury brand-building and development: New global challenges, new business models*. Springer.
Halkier, B. (2016). *Consumption challenged: Food in medialised everyday lives*. London: Routledge.
Hanna, J. (2004). *Luxury isn't what it used to be*. From z. https://hbswk.hbs.edu/item/luxury-isnt-what-it-used-to-be.
Harari, Y. N. (2018). *21 lessons for the 21st century*. Random House.
Heidegger, M. (1993). *Basic writings* (2nd ed.), D. F. Krell (Ed.). New York, NY: HarperCollins.
Heilbrunn, B. (2006). Brave new brands: Cultural branding between utopia and a-topia. In *Brand culture* (pp. 107–120). Routledge.
Hepler, L. (2015). *Tiffany & Co.'s new CSO on cleaning up the jewelry supply chain*. From z. https://www.greenbiz.com/article/tiffany-cos-new-cso-polishing-jewelry-supply-chain.
Hoffmann, J., & Coste-Manière, I. (2012). *Global luxury trends: Innovative strategies for emerging markets*. London: Springer.
Howarth, Ch. (2018). *Does luxury's response to digital create meaningful connections?* From z. https://www.luxurydaily.com/does-luxurys-response-to-digital-create-meaningful-connections/.
Jain, V. (2018). Luxury: Not for consumption but developing extended digital self. *Journal of Human Values, 24*(1), 25–38.
Jain, V., & Schultz, D. E. (2019). How digital platforms influence luxury purchase behavior in India? *Journal of Marketing Communications, 25*(1), 41–64.
Julius Baer. (2020). *Global wealth and lifestyle report 2020*. https://www.juliusbaer.com.
Kapferer, J.-N. (2008). *The new strategic brand management: Creating and sustaining brand equity long term* (4th ed.). London: Kogan Page Limited.
Kapferer, J.-N., & Bastien, V. (2009). The specificity of luxury management: Turning marketing upside down. *Journal of Brand Management, 16*(5–6), 311–322.

Kapferer, J.-N., & Bastien, V. (2017). The specificity of luxury management: Turning marketing upside down. In *Advances in luxury brand management* (pp. 65–84). Cham: Palgrave Macmillan.

Kernstock, J., Brexendorf, T. O., & Powell, S. M. (2017). Introduction: Luxury brand management insights and opportunities. In *Advances in luxury brand management* (pp. 1–24). Cham: Palgrave Macmillan.

Ko, E., Costello, J. P., & Taylor, C. R. (2019). What is a luxury brand? A new definition and review of the literature. *Journal of Business Research, 99,* 405–413.

KPMG. (2018). *China's connected consumers, the rise of the millennials.* From z. https://assets.kpmg.com/content/dam/kpmg/cn/pdf/en/2017/12/chinas-connected-consumers-the-rise-of-the-millennials.pdf.

Lamming, R. C., Johnsen, T., Zheng, J., & Harland, C. M. (2000). An initial classification of supply networks. *International Journal of Operations & Production Management, 20*(6), 675–691.

Lee, J. E., & Watkins, B. (2016). YouTube vloggers' influence on consumer luxury brand perceptions and intentions. *Journal of Business Research, 69*(12), 5753–5760. http://dx.doi.org/10.1016/j.jbusres.2016.04.171.

LuxeDigital. (2020). *The future of luxury: Trends to stay ahead in 2020.* https://luxe.digital/business/digital-luxury-trends/luxury-future-trends/.

Luxury Daily Raport. (2018). *Armani predicts 2 more years of losses before 2020 recovery.* From z. https://www.luxurydaily.com/armani-predicts-2-more-years-of-losses-before-2020-recovery/.

Macquarie Research. (2016). *Diamonds & gemstones cautious on jewellers, bullish on miners flat prices? No problem, volume takes over*. www.macquarie.com/research.

Mason, R. (1993). Cross cultural influences on the demand for status goods. In W. F. Van Raaij & G. J. Bamossy (Eds.), *European advances in consumer research, 1* (s. 46–51). Provo, UT: Association for Consumer Research.

Matter of Form. (2020). *The luxury report: The state of the industry in 2020 and beyond*. https://matterofform.com/the-luxury-report/.

McCracken, G. D. (2005). *Culture and consumption II: Markets, meaning, and brand management (Vol. 2).* Indiana University Press.

McKinsey. (2014). *A multifaceted future: The jewelry industry in 2020.* McKinsey & Company. From z. http://www.mckinsey.com/industries/retail/our-insights/a-multifaceted-future-the-jewelry-industry-in-2020.

McKinsey. (2020). *A perspective for the luxury-goods industry during—and after—coronavirus.* https://www.mckinsey.com/industries/retail/our-ins

ights/a-perspective-for-the-luxury-goods-industry-during-and-after-corona virus#.
Miller, D. (1998). *A theory of shopping*. Cornell University Press.
Mintel. (2020). *Global consumer trends, 2030*. https://www.mintel.com/global-consumer-trends.
Młody, M., & Stępień, B. (2020). Premises of reshoring development in luxury goods sector. *Journal of Management and Financial Sciences, 1*.
Money, R. B., & Colton, D. (2008). The response of the 'new consumer' to promotion in the transition economies of the former Soviet bloc. *Journal of World Business, 35*(2), 189–205.
Moore, C. M., & Doherty, A. M. (2007). The international flagship stores of luxury fashion retailers. In *Fashion marketing* (pp. 301–320). Routledge.
Moore, C. M., Doherty, A. M., & Doyle, S. A. (2010). Flagship stores as a market entry method: The perspective of luxury fashion retailing. *European Journal of Marketing*.
Moore, C. M., Fernie, J., & Burt, S. (2000). Brands without boundaries: The internationalisation of the designer retailer's brand. *European Journal of Marketing, 34*(8), 919–937.
Oetzel, J., & Doh, J. P. (2009). MNEs and development: A review and reconceptualization. *Journal of World Business, 44*(2), 108–120.
Okonkwo, U. (2007). *Luxury fashion branding*. Basingstoke: Palgrave Macmillan.
Osterwalder, A., & Pigneur, Y. (2010). *Business model generation: A handbook for visionaries, game changers, and challengers*. Wiley.
Parisi, D. (2017). *ThredUP enters luxury resale world with dedicated platform*. From z. https://www.luxurydaily.com/thredup-enters-luxury-resale-world-with-thredup-luxe/.
Parisi, D. (2018). *Donald Trump's proposed tariffs on imported cars would have major impact on luxury auto*. From z. https://www.luxurydaily.com/donald-trumps-proposed-tariffs-on-imported-cars-would-have-major-impact-on-lux ury-auto/.
Paul, J. (2019). Masstige model and measure for brand management. *European Management Journal, 37*(3), 299–312.
Peng, F., Delamore, P., & Sweeney, D. (2012). Digital innovation in fashion—How to 'capture' the user experience in 3D body scanning. *International Journal of Industrial Engineering and Management, 3*(4), 233–240.
Phan, M., Thomas, R., & Heine, K. (2011). Social media and luxury brand management: The case of Burberry. *Journal of Global Fashion Marketing, 2*(4), 213–222.

Pine, J., & Gilmore, J. (1999). *The experience economy*. Boston: Harvard Business School Press.

Rambourg, E. (2014). *The bling dynasty: Why the reign of Chinese luxury shoppers has only just begun*. Wiley.

Ramirez, S. (2018). *Influencer marketing shows no signs of slowing: Shareablee*. From z. https://www.luxurydaily.com/influencer-marketing-shows-no-signs-of-slowing-shareablee/.

Reddy, M., Terblanche, N., Pitt, L., & Parent, M. (2009). How far can luxury brands travel? Avoiding the pitfalls of luxury brand extension. *Business Horizons, 52*(2), 187–197.

RJC. (2017). *Responsible jewellery council*. From z. http://www.responsiblejewellery.com/.

Samuely, A. (2016). *Touchscreen fitting rooms revamp retail experiences*. Pobrno z. https://www.luxurydaily.com/oak-labs-exec-touchscreen-fitting-rooms-revamp-retail-experiences/.

Shukla, P. (2011). Impact of interpersonal influences, brand origin and brand image on luxury purchase intentions: Measuring interfunctional interactions and a cross-national comparison. *Journal of World Business, 46*(2), 242–252.

Silverstein, M. J., & Fiske, N. (2003a). *Trading up: The new American luxury*. New York: Portfolio/Penguin Group.

Silverstein, M. J., & Fiske, N. (2003b). Luxury for the masses. *Harvard Business Review, 81*(4), 48–57.

Solca, L. (2015). *The 'made in' dilemma: To label, or not to label*. From z. https://www.businessoffashion.com/community/voices/discussions/does-made-in-matter/the-made-in-dilemma-to-label-or-not-to-label.

Solca, L., Grippo, M., Lucarelli, G., Pozzi, M., & Borgonovo, F. (2016). *Who buys where: Decrypting cross-border luxury demand flows*. Milan: Exane BNP Paribas Research & ContactLab.

Soopramanien, D., & Robertson, A. (2007). Adoption and usage of online shopping: An empirical analysis of the characteristics of 'buyers', 'browsers', and 'non-Internet shoppers.' *Journal of Retailing and Consumer Services, 14*(1), 73–82.

Stępień, B. (2016). Oblicza pluralizmu metodologicznego w naukach o zarządzaniu–z perspektywy instytucjonalnej. *Studia Oeconomica Posnaniensia, 4*(1), 48–62.

Swarovski Sustainability Report. (2015). *Supply chain collaborating with suppliers for continuous improvement*. From z. https://www.swarovskigroup.com/S/aboutus/CSR-Responsible-Supply-Chain.pdf.

Szymura-Tyc, M. (2006). Marketing we współczesnych procesach tworzenia wartości dla klienta i przedsiębiorstwa. *Prace Naukowe/Akademia Ekonomiczna w Katowicach*. Katowice: Wydawnictwo Akademii Ekonomicznej w Katowicach.

Teece, D. J. (2010). Business models, business strategy and innovation. *Long Range Planning, 43*(2–3), 172–194.

The China Report: Innovation in Luxury. (2018). From z. https://www.luxurydaily.com/the-china-report-innovation-in-luxury-101/.

Truong, Y., McColl, R., & Kitchen, P. J. (2009). New luxury brand positioning and the emergence of masstige brands. *Journal of Brand Management, 16*(5–6), 375–382.

Tynan, C., McKechnie, S., & Chhuon, C. (2010). Co-creating value for luxury brands. *Journal of Business Research, 63*(11), 1156–1163.

Unity Marketing. (2020). *The state of luxury*. https://unitymarketingonline.com/shop/luxury/luxury-reports/state-of-luxury-2020-the-insider-view-report/.

Vargo, S. L., & Lusch, R. F. (2004). Evolving to a new dominant logic for marketing. *The Journal of Marketing, 68*, 1–17.

Vargo, S. L., & Lusch, R. F. (2008). Service-dominant logic: Continuing the evolution. *Journal of the Academy of Marketing Science, 36*(1), 1–10.

Vecchi, A., Peng, F., & Al-Sayegh, M. (2014). Assessing the applicability of a sizing framework into online fashion retail. *International Journal of Advanced Information Science and Technology, 29*(29), 102–110.

Vigneron, F., & Johnson, L. W. (1999). A review and a conceptual framework of prestige-seeking consumer behavior. *Academy of Marketing Science Review, 1*, 1–15.

Wahba, P. (2018). *Ralph Lauren is discovering how hard it is to fix a brand*. From z. http://fortune.com/2018/02/01/ralph-lauren-earnings/.

Wealth, X. (2015). State of ultra high net worth value market, luxury insight summit, prepared by L. Raynault.

Whitehead, A. N. (1978). *Process and reality* (Corrected ed.). New York, NY: The Free Press.

Wiktor, J. W. (2013). *Komunikacja marketingowa: Modele, struktury, formy przekazu*. Warszawa: PWN.

Wooding, C. (2016, June 27). *Cannes Lions: Virtual reality is the new luxury game-changer*. Retrieved from https://www.luxurydaily.com/cannes-lions-virtual-reality-is-the-new-luxury-game-changer/.

Yeoman, I., & McMahon-Beattie, U. (2006). Luxury markets and premium pricing. *Journal of Revenue and Pricing Management, 4*, 319–328.

4

Exploring Luxury—Research Scope and Methodology

The chapter consists of two parts. The first raises the issue of the relationship between values, attitudes, preferences of individuals and their consumer choices, referring these relations to luxury. On the basis of these considerations it is shown how the luxury has been analysed so far in the scientific literature and which of the threads were exploited. The research methods used by the researchers of the discussed issues are also presented.

The second part presents the methodology of the author's own empirical research presented in the remaining part of this book. A mixed research approach was used due to the analysis of both the perception of luxury value among consumers and the creation and communication of value propositions by enterprises. Quantitative method, in the form of an international survey on consumer perception of the value of luxury goods was subordinated and enhanced by qualitative interviews, focus groups and participatory observation.

The chapter is an introduction to the empirical part of the book, which presents and critically analyzes the results of others' and the author's own research on the perception of the value of luxury by consumers and the creation of value propositions.

B. Stępień, *The Value of Luxury*, Palgrave Advances in Luxury,
https://doi.org/10.1007/978-3-030-51218-7_4

4.1 Links Between Values, Norms and Preferences

Need is a conscious lack of something that would (once satisfied) increase the level of individual satisfaction (Foxal and Goldsmith 1998), but a clear distinction between need and desire should be highlighted. Need is treated as an objective lack, while desire serves a subjective feeling of lack and/or deprivation. In the author's opinion it is not possible to determine unambiguously what is an objective and what is subjective even in relation to basic goods and needs.

Need, also understood as the desire for luxury, may reflect:

- an unnecessary and unnatural need (according to Epicure's classification), on an equal footing with the pursuit of wealth or fame,
- the desire to fulfill Freud's need for pleasure,
- a need arising either from the spiritual qualities of the human being (due to the aesthetic qualities of luxury) or from the fact of being a social individual (symbolic value of luxury),
- According to Maslow—a higher need, not requiring immediate realization, being a combination of the desire to belong, respect, self-realization or aesthetic feeling,
- an envelope need (caused by a cultural, social or psychological "envelope" and not by a real lack) or an apparent need leading to the degradation of an individual (after Szczepański in: Rudnicki 2012, p. 32).

The need for luxury also refers to motifs, often classified identically as needs, divided into biological, psychological or social (see also: Rudnicki 2012, p. 63). Biological motives are of secondary importance for the consumption of luxury goods: if we want to have a meal in a restaurant with a star (or Michelin stars), we do not want to satisfy our hunger, but rather to experience many culinary, aesthetic or social experiences (to be in a place that is popular, expensive and inaccessible to many people).

The needs of luxury, more than physiological needs, are characterised by infinity, infinity, infinity and infinity and appear (at least in theoretical[1] considerations) only after basic biological and security needs have been met. In the case of purchases of luxury goods or services the combination of non-economic or functional needs and motives, such as social, symbolic, psychological, hedonic or survival motives and needs, is particularly visible (Rudnicki 2012, p. 65).

Attitudes are usually described as consisting of a cognitive and affective component. They are something more durable than needs or desires. They express both what individuals think and believe and what they feel and experience (Keller 2001; Morris et al. 2002). It is an individual's disposition to behave in a certain way and a relatively stable emotional and evaluative relationship to something (see also Zimbardo and Ruch 1988, p. 557). At the core of this is our individual evaluation system combined with motivation, but being at the same time subject to social influence (Światowy 2006, p. 73).

The term preference is also associated with attitudes. Burgiel and Sowa (2000, p. 48) define them as a manifestation of the evaluation of specific objects or states: it is a system of evaluation, which is guided by individuals when making their choices. Preferences are therefore a sign of appreciation and an immanent feature of attitudes. They are also logically linked to needs. On the one hand, they are their expression (I need it because I value it), but—in the absence of the possibility to satisfy all needs—they allow for their hierarchy (I need it more, because I value it higher).

Aspirations, in turn, are a set of needs based on values not only shaped individually, but also socially, dictated by the image of the individual of what he or she would like to achieve. They are the realisation of values

[1]In his book about urban poverty Desmond (2016) published a chapter entitled "Lobsters on food cards", in which he describes how poor people in the USA, buying seafood with food stamps, wanted to find in their lives a part of dignity, joy and uncommonness. This "luxury for the poor", although completely incomprehensible from the point of view of neoclassical rationality of choice, gave them the opportunity to feel like materially uninhibited people for a while. In a similar spirit, such a "small luxury" and the greatness of its general usefulness is illustrated by the scene from the film *Shawshank Redemption*, in which convicts drink beer on the roof of a tarred building accompanied by the guards watching them (https://www.youtube.com/watch?v=rcj2GoIbFHk).

considered relevant to the individual, the result of individual preferences and personal value hierarchies but also relate to past, present and future consumption patterns in the community. The discord between aspirations and actual possibilities of satisfying them is a motivational impulse or, in the case of too large discrepancies, a demotivating impulse to act in order to satisfy them (Światowy 2006, p. 28).

According to functional theory attitudes play an important social role in facilitating the self-expression of individuals (Grewal et al. 2004; Shavitt 1989, 1990; DeBono and Harnish 1988). The use of, or abstention from, shopping, or public stigmatisation of luxury, for example, is therefore a reflection of attitudes towards this category of goods and services. Buying certain brands due to their auratic symbolism and social perception, is a legitimacy of one's own self for the individual, because it emphasizes one's identity and socially shows one's attitude towards oneself and others. A positive or negative attitude of an individual towards a given luxury brand is related to the extent to which it symbolizes values close to the individual (allows to express oneself) and how effectively it can build the desired social image (Wilcox et al. 2009).

The cognitive attitude is based on other components of values (e.g. aesthetic, functional, ethical) than the affective attitude (mainly emotional, partly social, Zajonc and Markus 1982). It is worth noting, however, that emotions affect cognition (e.g. a good mood enhances the positive perception of particular attributes of a given good) and vice versa—cognition influences emotions (experiences, collected information create mood in relation to a given object, etc.). Attitudes towards luxury will therefore be modified depending on permanent and temporary preferences, but are also shaped by values (*I prefer this to that, because I value the first one more*).

An attitude towards luxury also depends on the extent to which the individual strives for self-expression caused by an inner desire to shape his or her social image. Purchases of luxury made mainly for psychosocial reasons are classified by Baumgartner as symbolic (Baumgartner 2010, p. 49). Motivations can be internal or external. In the first case, the motivations will reflect the values centred around the private self, oscillating around hedonism and self-fulfillment: *I want it because it expresses my personality, fits me, the aesthetics is close to me, the contact with this object gives me a sense of fulfillment, joy, and so on.* In the case of external motivation, the purchase of a given good/service is done in order to project a specific social image of oneself. Buying a something because of its name or reputation, the status granted is intended to be socially acceptable.

Valuation of luxury goods or services is carried out through the prism of at least these two views of reality. Many studies (see Chapters 5 and 6) indicate that the weight given to internal motives (identified mainly with hedonic ones) and external motives (perception of oneself through the prism of the environment, which comes to the fore in building an individual's identity) is differentiated on the basis of individual characteristics, age, place of residence or e.g. level of education.

4.2 Values and Consumer Choices

Behaviour, just like attitudes or preferences of consumers, is guided by both cognitive and affective processes. Emotional activators include instincts, emotions, motivations and attitudes—increasingly complex and interdependent constructs. One of the cognitive factors activating behaviour is the acquisition and processing of information needed to make a specific decision, supported by a set of experiences. In this context emotions are a kind of stimulus, an impulse, which is projected by its strength, duration and direction (positive, negative) on the whole process of selection and consumption. Motivations are related to needs and aspirations (imagining oneself in the context of the values one professes), they trigger action to satisfy needs and aspirations and maintain the direction of these actions, provided that the satisfaction of needs is satisfactory and is to be repeated or requires long-term action.

Consumer behaviour reflects the process of satisfying one's needs and is a sequence of responses to incentives to satisfy them. These reactions can be considered from the perspective of:

- the specificity of these needs, the order in which they emerge and consequently, the definition of objectives and aspirations,
- the volume and pattern of consumption, including the selection of appropriate goods and services to meet these needs,

- the way in which consumption is organised,
- the use of purchased goods.

In this book behaviours of consumers are considered only in relation to this first aspect, which affects the remaining ones.

Studies on the identification of the consumer choice mechanism have been carried out for at least a century. Initially they were based on the traditional distinction (drawn from philosophy and psychology) between cognition, reason, logic and affect and intuition on the other hand. An individual's choices could be guided either by reason or emotion which led to a separable, rational and emotional classification of purchase motives. When reviewing the work on consumer choice theory Holbrook and Hirschman (1982) conclude that the researchers' attention was originally focused on rational aspects of decision making except for a few exceptions to this trend in the form of analysis of motivation or product symbolism. Over time, as experimental and behavioural economists broke through the wall of neoclassical resistance, the researchers' attention has shifted towards exploring the multi-sensory and emotional aspects of the entire process of selecting and using a product. These two, quite distant research perspectives show the consumer as: (1) a decision-maker with a specific task, cognitively engaged and obtained the information needed to evaluate options available on the market or as (2) a pleasure seeker, emotionally engaged in the purchase and experience-driven, more interested in consumption than in purchase.

For example, studies by Mittal et al. (1990) and Johar and Sirgy (1991) reveal that if functional motifs prevail in choices, consumer interests focus on functional attributes and purchases are designed to meet physiological and safety needs. When the motives for expression dominate, consumers focus on what they feel and what others think about them choosing to satisfy the needs of social recognition and self-fulfilment. Moreover where the choice concerns functional characteristics, consumers will make comparisons with other products or ideal types of products with the highest value attributes. In the case of expressive motivation, self-fulfillment or social needs, the comparisons revolve around the image of oneself, one's own value or social acceptance in comparison with the images of how it will be socially perceived. The basis for comparison in the latter case is not the product but the individual. The product is to fit into this image: fill it with a value that raises the image of the present to the desired state. When non-functional needs and motivations are met the effect is more pronounced, which may explain why consumers are willing to pay a higher price for luxury brands although they can achieve equal functional benefits through cheaper brands that do not have such status (Kumar et al. 2009; Bian and Forsythe 2012).

Nowadays it is assumed that a consumer is guided by two reasons at the same time, although to a different degree, he or she engages emotions or analyses available options depending on his or her goals and preferences (Johnson and Stewart 2005). The choices resulting from these objectives and preferences are constructed in the decision-making process (Payne et al. 1992; Tversky et al. 1988) and not, as assumed in the theory of rational choice, being already shaped and in the decision-making process only referred to as a reference framework for the optimisation of usability.

Optimization in reality does not exist, it has been replaced by the pursuit of a sufficiently good, acceptable, widely defined set of benefits in exchange for the costs incurred. Consumers have limited ability to process purchasing information because of their selective memory and limited ability to do so (Simon 1955) and their choices are guided by a variety of cognitive heuristics and in the face of an abundance of information or are more inclined to act in a habitual way, referring to their previous experiences or information available to them, although not justified for use in specific calculations (Tversky and Kahneman 1991).

Over the last 50 years or so both general and specific models of consumer choice and behaviour have been developed. The former include interpretative and constructive concepts (Engel et al. 1968; Howard and Sheth 1969; Bettman 1979). Detailed elaborations or contestations of general models can be divided into: one-dimensional or multi-dimensional i.e. indicating different sets of factors influencing the choice without their hierarchy or determining forces of interconnection for example.

Madden et al. (1992) or Sagan (2011) reviewed and analysed selected models of consumer behaviour from different perspectives and note that their construction is a derivative of the theory from which they originate which has consequences for the analysis of the factors constituting these models. The earliest approaches are founded mainly on consumer theory based on neoclassical streams of rationality and usefulness, followed by models based on cognitive-psychological theories concerning information processing and the formation of consumer beliefs and attitudes (*Information Processing Theory*) and later models based on behavioural theories (*Behavioral Preference Models*) were developed. Consumer choices and behaviours are also explained using anthropological approaches and a postmodern approach combining sociological, psychological and some economic threads within the so-called *consumer culture theory*.

In this book the analysis of consumer choice and behaviour models is only relevant from the point of view of the role of value in creating needs and motivation. The review of process type behaviour models (input–output), based on the theory of information processing, shows that these models of values are not distinguished as a separate structure:

- In the Nicosia model (1966), consumer characteristics (as a set of predispositions and experiences) shape consumer attitudes, which in turn determine—in the process of evaluation—purchasing goals and means of achieving them, which in combination with motivation leads to action,
- The Howard and Sheth model (1969) assumes the rational behaviour of an individual affected by external stimuli (objective product information) that can change their symbolic meaning through the influence of social variables (family, reference groups, etc.). Values are included in independent variables, outside the model but are considered to have a material effect on entity choices,
- In the Ajzen and Fishbein model (1977), based on the so-called *theory of reasoned action (TRA)*, norms (arising as a combination of internal features and environmental pressure) are the basis of attitudes and these give an impulse to action. The Model suggests that behaviour results from the composition of attitudes and intentions of a person to act in a certain way. Attitudes reflect the individual characteristics of the individual combined with experience and the costs and benefits of

a particular decision. The moods are influenced by social attitudes and norms. What TRA assumes is independence of attitude and normative element. The latter refers to social norms and their perception; *how I feel that others want me to behave*. Both attitudes and norms shape behavioural intentions but the relative impact of these components varies according to the individual and the community in which they operate,
- In the O'Shaughnessy model (1987) depending on the type of shopping (habitual, random, or that which are preceded by a calculation), the weight of the so-called internal preferences is different. In the case of habitual or random purchases they are more important than in the case of purchases preceded by calculations of a cognitive rationalisation nature (made on the basis of an internal system of preferences, confronted with an analysis of information of an objective nature),
- In the model initiated by Kollat et al. (1970) and continued by Blackwell et al. (2001) the consumer's personality influences the selection and analysis of information, assessment criteria and attitudes but the system of external stimuli is also a moderating filter; their type, intensity and way of understanding and reception. The choices and valuation of the available options are also influenced by income, culture, family, social group, physical characteristics of the individual and everything else that is not captured *explicitly within the* model.

The structure of the described models consists of several groups of variables concerning the environment, the influence of marketing, perception, learning and the purchasing process. In these models the value system is the basis of perception and attitudes and norms.

Behavioural models do not assume the use of rational information processing. Consumer behaviour is the effect of variables (1) independent stimulating factors, e.g. the impact of information, marketing activities (2) anticipating, so called premises—feelings, feelings of lack, specific situational context (3) behavioural factors related to the individual, its social and psychological characteristics (4) consequences in the form of a specific choice (or abandonment) and the perceived level of satisfaction, loyalty.

Based on these findings, Fig. 4.1 shows the relationship between consumer preferences, attitudes and choices depending on the type of needs met and the values that shape them.

As shown in Fig. 4.1 the choices (and subsequent behaviours) of consumers depend on a range of interrelated factors. In a well-known article, which is a summary of many years of research on the subject, Bettman together with Luce and Payne (1998) identify the following areas that have an impact on the choices that determine the nature and interrelationship of a particular behaviour:

1. The choice between the options available on the market depends not only on the purpose but also on the extent to which the options are available:
   (a) minimize: our effort needed to make choices, with negative emotions while making decisions,
   (b) maximize: accuracy, accuracy of decisions taken and the possibility of justifying it.

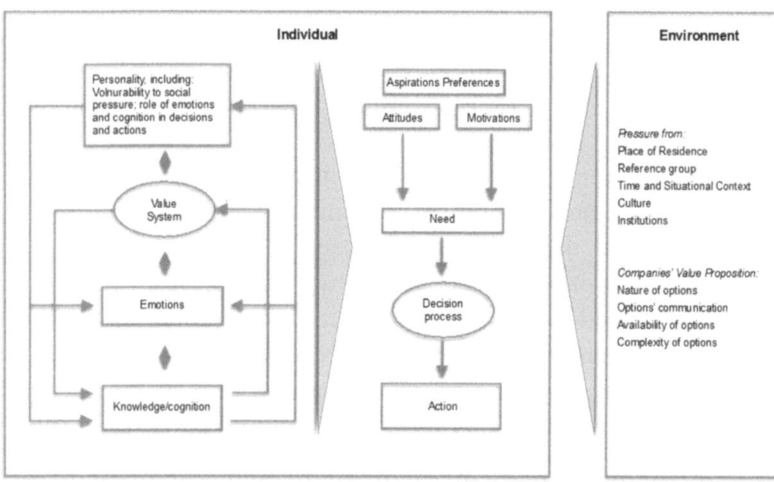

Fig. 4.1 Relations between consumer preferences, attitudes and choices (*Source* Own calculations)

2. The choice depends on the complexity of the decision-making task: the use of simple mechanisms (e.g. the most familiar, proven in the past) in the form of cognitive heuristics increases with the complexity of the task,
3. The choice depends on the relationship between the available options; the relative values of the options, not just their characteristics,
4. The choice depends on the order in which the benefits and costs of each option are presented (which has long been used in negotiation and sales techniques),
5. The choice depends on how the options are presented in terms of profit or loss over a specified period of time.

The authors of the quoted article indicate that the choice between options is made by assigning specific values to their features and that this mechanism gains in importance if a choice between two or more incomparable options is to be made (buy a watch today, or put aside money for holidays for six months).

In the decision-making process the method of valuation of the attributes: additive, comparative or eliminatory, is important for the final state of the obtained value in use. The traditional[2] model decision-making method consists in estimating the individual characteristics of the available options by assigning meaning to them. *For example, safety, aesthetics, strength, strength, colour are the most important to me* (value), *so I choose the option for which the sum of meanings, i.e. the values of attribute, is the highest.* However it is a costly process from the point of view of the need to obtain information and calculations, which additionally requires the decision-maker to unambiguously quantify the importance of particular attributes, and despite such action, the lack of a so-called superior cutting preference, concerning one attribute,[3] for

[2]Traditional—here: a derivative of the neoclassical understanding of the function of total usability as the sum of partial usabilities. The total usefulness in this case refers to the sum of the values of the attributes of the good.

[3]In the absence of a hierarchy of attributes the total value of the attributes determines the choice of a given option. Therefore it is assumed that there is no essential element which is the most important, because the highest-valued attribute can be—and often is—treated as necessarily present in the value proposition. This is the shuttering element: it eliminates options where the attribute does not or does not exist at all.

instance. Following this pattern it is possible to buy a comfortable, practical (that is possible to wear for various occasions) dress, which is solidly cut and sewn, has a dignified colour, and re resemble we our own aunt, which everyone—including family—confuses with her older brother.

If the reasons for which we buy are psycho-social motivations (based on the values of self-fulfilment and social image) or if we buy spontaneously or repetitively, it is all the more likely that the *elimination by aspects* procedure will be applied. Elimination as the overriding procedure forces the rejection of options that do not meet the minimum level for the most important attribute. This elimination process is repeated for the second most important attribute, while processing continues until one option remains (Tversky 1972). Using this way of selecting and evaluating the available purchase options a dress will probably be bought that is worn with pleasure at least once if the quality of the material and workmanship has been mentally booked by us as an important and highly ranked attribute. The sum of usability as a set of functionalities may be smaller than in the first case but the sense of satisfaction will be higher.

4.3 Scope and Methods of Luxury Research—Overview of the Existing Scientific Output

The most important, broadly described and thoroughly analyzed issue in the scientific literature on luxury are the premises, manifestations and consequences of its social desire. From the very beginning of history philosophers and later sociologists have been arguing over this trait, combined with moral stigmatization. It was mainly thanks to the pragmatic approach of economists in the seventeenth and eighteenth centuries that luxury consumption was no longer perceived as solely morally reprehensible and the industrial revolution democratized luxury, making the social desire for these goods (though not so rare, expensive or beautiful) more common and interesting in research. Due to the complexity of social desire as a cognitive construct, as well as its considerable social and economic consequences, this area is a field for analysis by scientists from many fields. Social desire is analyzed through the prism of:

- societies—what are the social and economic premises and consequences of luxury consumption?; this is the oldest and most exploited topic in terms of scientific scope. The most frequently quoted author is Veblen (2005, 2008) with his work about the leisured classes. From a sociological and cultural perspective Bourdieu's works are most frequently quoted, describing the impact of luxury consumption on the construction of social classes. From an economic perspective Leibenstein's works (1950) describing the phenomenon of bandwagon and snobbery and Bagwell's and Bernheim's (1996) discussing the premises and consequences of the influence of luxury consumption on public policy are the most frequently cited works,
- individuals—what are the individual, cultural, social, economic grounds, premises, manifestations and consequences of demonstrations, imitations, snobbish behaviours or generally luxurious purchases and uses, including
  - What is the relationship between the specific value of luxury brands and the social, psychosocial and cultural characteristics of the market?
  - What does the materialistic attitude depend on and does it bring happiness to people?

Analyses of individual attitudes and behaviour towards luxury focus primarily on the issues of perception and management of luxury brands, materialistic attitudes and cultural interpretations of individual behaviours. New, emerging themes are attitudes towards counterfeit goods or ethical and sustainable luxury. The most frequently quoted works include articles by Belk (1985, 1988) on materialistic attitudes and the power of desire, Corneo and Jeanne (1997) on conspicuous consumption, Bearden and Etzel (1982) on reference groups, Griskevicius et al. (2007) and Han et al. (2010) on the consumption of luxury as an emission of costly signals.

Scientific works by sociologists, psychologists and researchers representing economic sciences devoted to luxury are now in full swing. In recent years there have been around 150–170 publications per year in this field (see Gurzki and Woisetschläger 2017, p. 151). In their excellent article, Gurzki and Woisetschläger thoroughly reviewed the scientific literature on luxury. They identified the most important areas of scientific exploration and constructed a map of them, in which they depicted the most exploited trends in luxury research. These are: luxury foundations; luxury and public policy interconnections, areas connected with consumer culture and behaviour, such as signalling, materialism or self—concept brand relationships analysed also from the intercultural point of view and the brand and marketing management streams. Last, but not least area of investigation that develops is the counterfeiting in luxury.

As far as the methodology of luxury research is concerned the most frequently quoted works are either experimental (because they refer to social psychology) or descriptive-conceptual (because they concern sociological, anthropological, historical or cultural analyses). In the layer of research related to economic sciences, however, quantitative research dominates, based mainly on surveys using different scales of measurement and values. Due to different typologies of value components research results do not provide a basis for unambiguous comparisons.

The postmodern *consumer culture theory* (CCT) mentioned above is a relatively new approach to researching consumer attitudes and behaviour towards luxury. As Arnould and Thompson (2005) write, the methodological framework of CCT can be characterized as a heuristic mapping of common theoretical structures of interests showing a diversity of methodological approaches. Ethnography, phenomenology, different approaches to textual analysis, methods of historical analysis, drawing on sociology, anthropology, literary criticism, or even feminist studies are the theoretical foundations of this methodical post-structural epistemology in the analysis of consumer behaviour. Figure 4.2 shows a map of CCT interests that seeks to explain why people engage in a particular type and way of consumption, what this means for them and what are the links between the interpretation of their "private and social self" in the context of various historical, social and cultural influences.

Researchers, focused around the CCT current, use the analysis of the context of statements within the narrative approach and in-depth interviews as the main tool to obtain primary empirical data for their analyses.

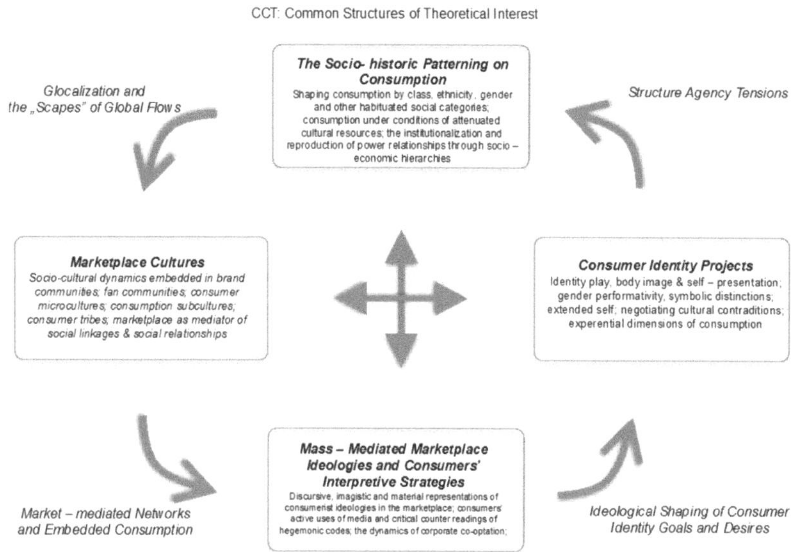

Fig. 4.2 Problems of consumer behaviour research within the framework of cultural consumer theory (*Source* Arnould and Thompson [2007])

Due to the qualitative nature of the research and the small number of examined units the findings on the basis of CCT are treated mainly as a contribution, as a prelude to further quantitative research.

4.4 Scope and Methods on Luxury Research Used in This Book

In the next part of the book the results of foreign and the author's own research will be presented in the following order:

- research on market diversity in the perception of luxury and the influence of national culture on consumers' perception of luxury (Chapter 5),

- research related to the influence of socio and psychodemographic characteristics of consumers on their perception of the value of luxury, their imitation tendencies and snobbish tendencies (Chapter 6),
- research on consumer perception of the contribution and importance of the different links in the value system to creating and communicating the value of luxury (Chapter 7).

The research presented in these chapters is international in scope and focuses on the perception of luxury value and attitudes towards luxury products. These empirical findings are mainly related to the last 20 years. Each time, while discussing the published foreign studies, the methodology used by the researchers is described.

4.4.1 Scope and Methodology of Own Research

Results the empirical research of others form the basis for the analysis of this research conducted by the author and research team within the framework of the project "Global value chains in the luxury goods sector - from the perspective of consumers and co-creators of chains".[4]

The subject of analyses in our research was:

1. perception of luxury goods as a set of different categories of values: functional, hedonic, social, aesthetic, ethical (further on the value of luxury as perceived by the consumer, CLVP), divided into:
    - the country of residence of the consumers,
    - age,
    - sex,

[4]The author was the originator of the project and acted as project manager. All research carried out as part of the project and described in the book was developed by the author in terms of concepts (goals, hypotheses, layout, course), content and tools used to obtain data. Project members—an international team of researchers from Germany, Portugal, Turkey, India, Saudi Arabia and Poland—have done invaluable work in distributing and collecting data in the quantitative research. FGI 1 and 3 studies were conducted together with Dr. Ana Pinto Lima from Porto ISCAP Polytechnic. The results of the research were published in several articles, written independently or in co-authorship. Excerpts from these publications, after being amended or supplemented by new content, are referred to in the appropriate places.

- education,
- disposable income,
- psychographic features of respondents.

2. analysis of imitative tendencies and snobbish inclinations in the approach to luxury and its consumption, taking into account the socio-demographic and psychographic features mentioned in point 1,
3. Consumers' perception of the importance of the contribution of the various components of the value system to the creation and communication of the value of luxury goods:
    - the contribution of the designers,
    - producers of goods,
    - salesmen,
    - brand owners,
    - other consumers and so-called celebrities or influential people in building the value of luxury.

In the project for a part of the results described in this book a mixed methodology was used to study the threads described above. Due to the complexity of the phenomenon studied quantitative and qualitative research was combined in order to not only diagnose the areas of convergence and diversity in CLVP but also to try to identify their possible causes.

The quantitative survey took the form of an international online survey targeted at consumers in different countries. More than 1400 responses were obtained from 20 countries, but a country analysis is done to six of them due to the biggest number of responses. Five of these countries can be classified as new, rapidly growing luxury markets (Saudi Arabia, India, Turkey, Poland, Portugal) while Germany is treated as a reference country from the old cradle luxury base. The aim of the e-mail research was to diagnose individual components of the value of luxury goods in the perception of respondents. Their opinions concerned both the evaluation of the value proposition and the experienced value.

The qualitative research consisted of:

- structured in-depth interviews: with consumers, luxury fashion and jewellery designers, representatives of suppliers and manufacturers (precious stone suppliers, owners of factories producing jewellery and clothing under foreign brands) and retailers (jewellery store owners, luxury goods sellers) of luxury goods,
- focused group interviews with consumers on the perception of luxury,
- participatory observation in the form of so-called *mystery shopping* aimed at investigating the contribution of sellers to the creation and communication of individual components of the value of luxury goods.

The research covers the years 2015–2018.

The research was international in nature. It also covered both consumers and representatives of the various links in the value system.

Table 4.1 describes which of the research methods have been used to study specific threads and where in the book the results of these studies have been analysed.

Table 4.2 shows the types of empirical research carried out, the period, place and country of origin of the respondents.

The questionnaire in electronic form (detailed structure of the sample and description of the survey below) was addressed to individual consumers using two types of reach: business and academic address databases of the project partners and placing information and a link to the survey website in English on online forums related to luxury consumption.

Interviews with representatives of value chain links and high income consumers were conducted by using a personal network to reach out to respondents and persuade them to talk to them.

Focused group interviews were conducted with the participation of students of Poznań University of Economics, University of Nottingham, Ningbo, China and Porto ISCAP Polytechnic as well as post-graduate and M.B.A. students in these units.

Due to the characteristics of the method conversations during mystery shopping were semi-structured. Each time after such an interview sellers were informed about the purpose of the research and asked for their

Table 4.1 Research threads analysed in particular types of empirical studies

Type of test	Purpose of the survey	Geographical scope of the survey	The use of results to (place in books)
International consumer survey	Investigate the importance of individual Consumer Value Assets (CLVP): embodied in luxury goods and provided by individual links in the value chain	International research, questionnaire in electronic form addressed to consumers from all over the world, including (in the case of surveys translated into local languages) Poles, Germans, Swiss, Austrian, Portuguese, Turks, Saudis, French, Indian, Chinese, etc.	(1) Survey results as a basis for determining the impact: • The place of residence (Chapter 5), • Age, gender, income, education (Chapter 6), • Psychographic features (Chapter 6): on the perception of CLVP (2) Mimicking and snobbish inclinations of respondents (Chapter 6) (3) Determining the impact of the contribution of individual links in the luxury value chains (Chapter 7)

(continued)

Table 4.1 (continued)

Type of test	Purpose of the survey	Geographical scope of the survey	The use of results to (place in books)
Structured open interviews—representatives of value systems	(1) Exploratory research (prior to the construction of the questionnaire): determining the weight of the components of the values perceived by the representatives of individual cells (2) Confirmatory research explaining the results of the survey	(1) Poland and the United Arab Emirates, including talks at jewellery and fashion fairs, (2) appointments with car dealers and luxury fashion stores agreed in advance	Fragments of interviews presented in Chapter 7 as an illustration of research results obtained with the use of other tools and methods
Structured open interviews with high income consumers	in-depth research—investigation of causes, mutual relationships between the individual composition of CLVP and social status, personality, etc.	Place of interviews—Poland: interviewees of Polish, French, Turkish and Swiss nationality	Illustrating the mutual relationships between snobbish tendencies and the tendency to imitate (Chapter 6) Extracts from the interviews illustrating the understanding of the value of luxury (Chapter 1)
Focused group interviews with consumers of generation Y (Millennials) and generation X (Millennials)	Focused group research (FGI) to explore areas of convergence/differentiation of CLVP according to age, social and family status	Polish and Portuguese consumers	Research on the impact of age, family and social status on CLVP (Chapter 6)

Type of test	Purpose of the survey	Geographical scope of the survey	The use of results to (place in books)
Mystery shopping	Luxury fashion retailers: communicating the individual components of luxury value, including sustainability value	Shops in Dubai, Berlin, Paris, Singapore. Brands: Bottega Veneta, Chanel, Dior, Gucci, Hermés, Loro Piana, LV, Prada, Stella McCartney, YSL	Value creation and communication within the supply chain (Chapter 7)

Source Own calculations

Table 4.2 Types, temporal and spatial range of empirical studies carried out

Type of test	Period of examination	Subject of the study	Language and place of testing	Country of origin of respondents[a]
International consumer survey	2015—Pretests 2016—Fundamental research 2017/2018—Indian consumer surveys 2020—Polish, Portugese, Chinese Gen Z consumer survey	Consumers of different nationalities, mainly the so-called aspiring ones: Poles, Portuguese, Saudi Arabs, Turks, Indians control group: Germans, French, Americans, Swiss, Americans	Online survey, international scale: Research language: basic questionnaire in English, translated using the back to back formula: Polish, French, Arabic, Turkish, German, Portuguese, Arabic, Polish	Results were obtained from 20 countries: Saudi Arabia Australia, Austria, Belarus, China Czech Republic, France India, Canada, Lithuania, Germany Norway, Poland Portugal, Russia, Slovakia, Switzerland Sweden, Turkey USA

Type of test	Period of examination	Subject of the study	Language and place of testing	Country of origin of respondents[a]
Structured open interviews—representatives of value systems	2015—interviews with designers and owners of fashion and luxury jewellery stores 2017—Interviews with luxury car dealers and retailers in the luxury fashion industry	Designers (fashion), Suppliers of components and materials (jewellery), owners of luxury brands (jewellery), retailers (fashion,	2015, 2017—designers and owners of luxury fashion stores—Fashion Fair, Fashion Week, Poland, 2015—Representatives of value chain links in the jewellery industry—World Diamond and Jewellery Fair Dubai 2017; Motor Showrooms: Poland, Germany	Polish women, Poles, Germans, Lebanese (fashion and jewellery designers, owners of shops, car dealerships, fashion and jewellery stores) Chinese, Pakistani, Indian, Polish (suppliers of raw materials, components, work in fashion chains and jewellry), Poles, Lebanese (owners of fashion brands and jewellery)

(continued)

Table 4.2 (continued)

Type of test	Period of examination	Subject of the study	Language and place of testing	Country of origin of respondents[a]
Structured open interviews with high-income consumers	2016, 2017—individual interviews, duration 1–3 hours	High income consumers	Polish and English	Interviewers of Polish, French, Turkish and Swiss nationalities
Focused group interviews with consumers of the Generation Z, Millennials and X Generation generations	2017/2020	Consumers with different age and income profiles	Polish, English and Portuguese	Poles, Chinese and Portuguese
Mystery shopping	2017/2018/2020	Retailers of luxury fashion stores	English	[a]Germans, French, Thais, Malaysians, Singaporeans, Chinese, English, Costa Ricans

Source Own calculations

[a]In the case of research in the form of latent purchases the vendors represented different nationalities. Especially in Singapore and Dubai salespeople were not indigenous to these places

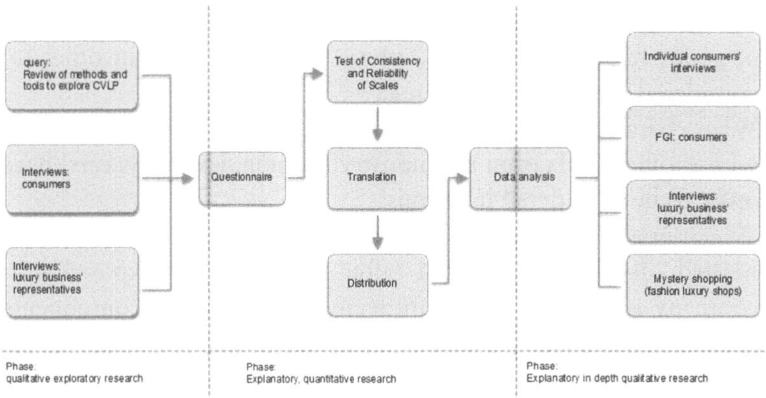

Fig. 4.3 Nature and course of own empirical research on luxury perception (*Source* Own study)

consent to include their statements in a scientific publication. All interviewees (FGI participants, individual interviewees and sellers) agreed to publish their statements. Due to the content and nature of the quoted opinions all interlocutors are anonymous.

Figure 4.3 shows the course of research over time and its logical relationships.

4.4.2 Research Protocols and Content

4.4.2.1 Interviews with Designers, Owners of Luxury Fashion and Jewellery Stores, Luxury Car Dealers and Retailers in the Luxury Fashion Industry

The interview protocol was similar in all cases and covered a wide range of issues.

Part 1 (2015) Questions concerning the perception, creation, communication and distribution of the value proposition in the company represented by the interlocutor in relation to competitors in the industry:

1. What are the characteristics of the brand you represent in terms of goods from the industry (fashion, jewellery, cars) in order to be considered luxurious? Why these?
2. What characteristics, from the point of view of the brand you represent, should goods from the industry (fashion, jewellery, cars) have in order to be considered luxurious?
3. Which qualities, features of products, how they are created, communicated, distributed, serviced (after-sales care) are exposed by the company as the most important features/components/components of luxury? Why these?
4. Is this point of view the same for the whole industry? What are the possible differences? Do these possible differences relate to product-related assets or to the features of the process of creating, communicating and selling itself? What are the reasons for such commonalities or differencies?
5. In your opinion which component of value is the most important for the recipients of goods that you co-create?
6. How do your customers differ in their perception of the value of luxury (offered by you) from that of other brands?
7. What link (e.g. designer, manufacturer, seller, celebrity, other consumers) provides the most value and what type of value (functional, social, emotional) is it (a) in your value chain (b) in your industry?

Part 2 (2017)—a request for comments on survey results concerning the contribution of individual cells to creating and communicating the value of luxury.

Table 4.3 shows the list and characteristics of interviewees with a description of their place in the value chain and the luxury industries they represented.

The most important results of the conducted talks are presented in tabular and descriptive form in Chapter 7, as part of the discussion of the contribution of particular links to the creation and communication of proposals for values.

Table 4.3 Characteristics of interviewees in direct interviews with representatives of enterprises in the luxury sector

Interviewed	Industry	Nationality/place in the value chain
A	Luxury fashion	Polish woman, owner of clothing shops—well-known Italian brand, lower level of the pyramid of luxury
B	Luxury fashion	Polish woman, fashion designer, owner of her own luxury brand, production coordinator, selling her clothes under her own brand on the Internet and in multibrand stores with Polish luxury and premium fashion
C	Luxury fashion	Pole, company director: subcontractor; cutting, sewing, picking clothes of world-famous brands from the middle and lower levels of the luxury pyramid
D	Jewels	Lebanese, owner of an international chain of jewellery stores, former jewellery designer, partial in-house production, design under the control and in the hands of the company, part of the production outsourced to workshops in China and India
E	Jewels	Indian, owner of a manufacturing plant: stone grinding and jewellery manufacturing under its own brand, mainly regional, contract manufacturing for large global retail chains
F	Jewels	Pakistani, owner of a precious stone cutting plant, wholesaler of diamonds
G	Jewels	Australian, farm owner and seller of breeding pearls
H	Jewels	Chinese, owner of a large production plant: design, stone and metal processing, production of foreign branded jewellery on behalf of European, Arab and American companies
I	Cars	German, regional sales director/representative of a premium and luxury car manufacturer (middle and lower tiers of the luxury pyramid)
J	Cars	Polish woman, salesman of premium and luxury cars (middle and lower levels of the luxury pyramid)
K	Cars	A German car dealer of the highest level of luxury pyramid

Source Own calculations

4.4.2.2 International Electronic Questionnaire on the CLVP

The most extensive in terms of thematic, temporal and geographical scope was a quantitative survey conducted by means of an electronic questionnaire. The basic language of the questionnaire was English.

The basis for creating the content of the CLVP survey questionnaire were already constructed and had validated scales of authorship:

- Holbrook's (2006)—presented in Chapter 2—components of effectiveness, play, aesthetics, ethics, perfection, esthetics, status, spirituality,
- Dubois et al. (2001); in which the quality, price, rarity, aesthetics, visibility, pleasure and value of a luxury brand were distinguished,
- Vigneron and Johnson (2004), who distinguished social value, perceived through the prism of the ability to signal status (including the Veblen effect), uniqueness (in relation to the snob effect), emotional value (hedonic) and quality,
- Wiedmann et al. (2009), who identified the following dimensions of WPK luxury: financial dimension (price, investment value), functional dimension (better usability, quality, efficiency, uniqueness), individual dimension (identity, hedonic and materialistic value), and social value (prestige and brand visibility),
- Tynan et al. (2010); distinguishing: the utilitarian, symbolic-expressive, hedonic, relational and cost-benefit component of value,
- Kim et al. (2011), who divided the value of luxury into social, aesthetic/expressive, empirical, qualitative and economic components of value.

Each of the scales considered had its own strengths and weaknesses. Although the scale of the Holbrook (2006) seemed to be the most complete categorization of values it was not yet operationalised during the construction of the questionnaire nor was it even further adapted to the study of luxury goods. Ultimately it was decided that the repeatedly tested scale of Wiedmann et al. (2009) would serve as the basis for the questionnaire, supplemented by dimensions of snobbish and

Table 4.4 Components of values measured in the international CLVP study

Categories/scale of CLVP developed by	Value component
Wiedmann et al. (2009)	Functional Hedonic Social status
Vigneron and Johnson (2004)	Snobbish inclinations Bandwagon inclinations
Holbrook (2006)	Ethics Aesthetics
Scales developed for other ingredients	Price as a result of desire/functionality

Source Own calculations

imitative inclinations exposed in the typology of Vigneron and Johnson (2004) and aesthetic and ethical components from the Holbrook scale (2006). Table 4.4 shows the components of the values to be tested in the questionnaire using scales by individual researchers.

The second part of the quantitative study concerned the perception of the contribution of individual links in chains to the preparation of value propositions for consumers. Due to the lack of previous research which comprehensively tested the role of particular types of enterprises in creating value propositions, a set of scales reflecting the composition of the luxury value chain and individual activities typical for its links was developed. Respondents were asked about the importance they attach to particular activities and cells in creating and communicating proposals for the value of luxury goods: fashion, jewellery and cars.

Preliminary tests concerning the cohesion and comprehensibility of questions in the questionnaire were conducted in Poland among 50 respondents and the results showed an acceptable level of credibility and internal cohesion (Cronbach Alfa above 0.6 for particular components).

The sample consists of 1443 responses (due to the degree of completion of the questionnaire, the variety of responses[5]) for further analysis. Table 4.5 shows the structure of the sample while showing the countries

[5]Twelve questionnaires with the same answer option (e.g. 1, 3 or 5) were rejected. 87 questionnaires were rejected and less than 50% of the questions were answered. The final questions

Table 4.5 Structure of the international sample of the CLVP international survey

		Total attempt	Saudi Arabia	Germans	Poland	Turkey	Portugal	India
Sex	Females	670	48	71	299	18	69	112
	Males	773	224	85	135	88	51	138
Generation	X (born 1966–1976)	474	30	15	233	53	54	32
	Y (born 1977–1994)	968	242	141	201	53	66	218

Source Own calculations

with the highest number of responses thus giving a reasonable possibility to analyse the results by country of residence.

The consequence of the use of the e-questionnaire is the structure of the sample due to the generational distribution. The sample consists mostly of Y generation (the so-called Millennials); consumers active in the network, considered as a globally homogeneous cohort.

Millennials represent 63% of the total sample with 76% of respondents having completed tertiary education and having an average disposable income per month ranging from around €1000 per month (mainly in Poland and Portugal), to around €1500 in Turkey and Germany and India, to over €3000 in Saudi Arabia.

The distribution of the questionnaire on the Internet and the structure and size of the sample obtained thanks to this channel do not guarantee its representativeness. The requests, which are constructed on the basis of the data obtained, therefore concern this sample. However both the sample size and the international nature of the survey (in which as many as six countries are well represented) allow for cautious generalisations. Furthermore none of the foreign studies on luxury referred to in Chapters 5–7 meets the requirements of a statistical representativeness

---

from the survey, where the drop-out rate was the highest, concerned the nature and frequency of information on luxury purchases and the frequency of purchases in various distribution channels. Results of these questions are not analysed in this book.

of the sample. Although this fact is not an excuse for the lack of representativeness of the sample described above it also illustrates how early in the exploration of the luxury area we find ourselves and how varied the conclusions (resulting from, among other things the number of respondents, the structure of respondents, or the research methods used) that can be discovered by analyzing the same or very similar threads.

4.4.2.3 Focused Group Interviews

Seven focus group studies (two in Portugal, two in China, and three in Poland) were conducted according to the same protocol (see below). The selection of respondents and the FGI scenario were the same for all groups. The motive for the FGI was to deepen the understanding of the results of the questionnaire survey. The aim of the interviews was to reveal other (than age-related) socio-demographic reasons for unanimity and possible discrepancies in the assessment of the value of luxury by the X, Y and Z generations. The structure of the FGI groups (lasting 2.5 hours each) is given in Table 4.6.

The protocol of focus-group interviews covered the following issues:

- My private definition of luxury: the characteristics of goods/services and the value categories assigned to them: the attempt at hierarchy,
- The motives for luxury shopping: my inner needs and the environment,
- An attempt to identify and assess the emergence of needs related to the purchase and use of goods and luxury services,
- Identification and assessment of the contribution of the different links in a luxury value system to the creation of consumer value: business and the environment outside the system (other consumers, media, etc.).

Table 4.6 Structure of FGI participants—study of CLVP diversity/homogeneity between generations X and Y

	FGI 1 Portugal	FGI 2 Portugal	FGI 3 Poland	FGI 4 Poland
Number of participants:	16	16	16	16
Generation Y Millennials	16	9	16	10
Generation X	0	7	0	6
Women	8	7	9	7
Men	8	9	7	9
Socio-demographic features of the participants of the generation Y	Mostly single, with no children, young, born in the 1990s, working in lower or middle positions, with an income of up to €1000	Mainly married, with children and families, older than FGI 1 and 3, born in the mid-1980s, middle or managerial positions, income higher than EUR 1300	As in the case of FGI 1, the average income is around EUR 1500	As in the case of FGI 2, mainly managerial positions, average income above EUR 1800

Source Own calculations

4.4.2.4 Interviews with Affluent Consumers

Table 4.7 presents the characteristics of the interlocutors. The interview protocol was identical to that used in focus groups with one difference: most of the interview space was devoted to exploring the motives behind luxury shopping. The aim was to identify the inclinations to imitate and snobbish inclinations in combination with the opinions expressed by the interviewees on: the hierarchy of importance of the reasons for luxury shopping and the ways of its consumption.

Table 4.7 Characteristics of interviewees—interviews on the perception of luxury among affluent consumers

Sex	Age	Occupation	(mean perhaps?) income[a]	Nationality
M	57	Businessman, owner of the company	more than EUR 20,000	Polish
M	51	Businessman, owner of the company	more than EUR 20,000	Polish
M	46	CEO, insurance sector	Approximately EUR 13,000	Polish
M	45	CEO, banking sector	Approximately EUR 11,000	Polish
M	41	Freelancer, IT, programmer	Approximately EUR 15,000	Polish
K	50	CEO, marketing	Approximately EUR 8000	Polish
K	43	CEO, Finance Sector	Approximately EUR 8000	Polish
K	47	Designer, own company	Approximately EUR 10,000	Polish
K	48	He doesn't work, family business	more than EUR 15,000	Polish
K	40	Owner, own trading company	Approximately EUR 10,000	Polish
M	42	Owner of a trading company	more than EUR 15,000	French
M	46	CEO of a multinational company	Approximately EUR 20,000	French
M	43	Director of IT, private bank	EUR 12,000	Swiss
K	34	He's not working, the wife of a restaurant chain owner	EUR 5000	Turkish
M	56	Owner of a restaurant chain	n.a. (although above EUR 5000)	Turkish
M	61	Photographer, freelancer	Approximately EUR 10,000	German

Source Own calculations
[a]Income, in order to harmonise the figures for all surveys carried out, has been converted into euros

4.4.2.5 Mystery Shopping

The research conducted in luxury fashion stores in Berlin, Paris, Dubai and Singapore was aimed at identifying the nature and manner of communication by retailers of the hierarchy (here: emphasizing the importance) of certain components of value associated with the product itself or the process of creating, communicating or using luxury goods of a specific brand. The aim of the research was to determine which components of value, according to the sellers, constitute an impulse for consumers to buy. It was assumed that sellers in luxury fashion stores who receive remuneration derived from commission on the value of purchases made by consumers would be willing to use in conversations such a set of information and incentives which, although tailored to the consumer, prove to be effective as they end with purchases. The study also aimed to examine the significance of those components of luxury values that refer to ethical and sustainable production and consumption in comparison with its other components: aesthetic, functional, social and hedonic. A detailed protocol of questions related to the components of the sustainability value component is described in Chapter 7 when the results of these studies are discussed.

4.4.3 Methods of Statistical Analysis Used

To analyze the results of the international survey on the market diversification of CLVP, descriptive statistics were used, divided into markets and individual categories/value components.

As already indicated above the scales used in the study were a deliberate modification of several CLVP typologies and their extension to include an ethical component and the perception of price as a result of social desire or a measure of functionality. Apart from the questions concerning the perception of various value components embedded in a luxury product, the questionnaire also contained consumer-oriented statements. It was expected that statements from both areas are interlinked: the assessment of luxury value reflects an individual's relationship to such purchases and consumption, and statements concerning hedonic and social components of value may be associated with snobbish or imitative inclinations. With this in mind exploratory factor analysis with Varimax rotation was used to construct segments of respondents with different psychographic features. The orthogonal factors obtained in this way, combined with the use of the Catella criterion, allowed the generation of five factors, constituting 52% of the total variance. The Kayser-Mayer-Olkin criterion is 0.89 which provides a solid basis for further interpretation (Norušis 1994). The next step in the construction of consumer segments was the k-medium analysis. The segments are described using the values of psychographic variables, demonstrating their relationship to specific demographic social characteristics: age, gender, education and nationality of respondents. These relationships were determined by using two dependency measures: Cramer V factor for nominal scales (gender, nationality) and eta (η) correlation ratio used for variables on a range or quotient scale linked by a curvilinear relationship (age, education, income).

In order to examine how each segment assesses the impact of designers, manufacturers, retailers and other market participants on the value of luxury goods, logistic regressions for each segment were carried out. Membership in a segment was a dichotomous variable (where 1 means membership in a segment) and independent variables were weights assigned to individual components of values.

The analysis of qualitative research results (interviews, FGI, hidden shopping) took the form of content and context analysis. The discussion of the results is illustrated with quotations from the statement or it takes the form of collective presentations of the main, most important slogans, keywords, repeated conversations (see: results of research on hidden purchases or interviews with representatives of enterprises, Chapter 7).

References

Ajzen, I., & Fishbein, M. (1977). Attitude-behavior relations: A theoretical analysis and review of empirical research. *Psychological Bulletin, 84*(5), 888–918.

Arnould, E. J., & Thompson, C. J. (2005). Consumer culture theory (CCT): Twenty years of research. *Journal of Consumer Research, 31*(4), 868–882.

Arnould, E. J., & Thompson, C. J. (2007). Consumer culture theory (and we really mean theoretics): Dilemmas and opportunities posed by an academic branding strategy. *Research in Consumer Behavior, 11,* 3–22.

Bagwell, L. S., & Bernheim, B. D. (1996). Veblen effects in a theory of conspicuous consumption. *The American Economic Review, 86*(3), 349–373.

Baumgartner, H. (2010). A review of prior classifications of purchase behavior and a proposal for a new typology. In N. K. Malhotra (Ed.), *Review of marketing research* (s. 3–36). Bingley: Emerald Group.

Bearden, W. O., & Etzel, M. J. (1982). Reference group influence on product and brand purchase decisions. *Journal of Consumer Research, 9*(2), 183–194.

Belk, R. (1985). Materialism: Trait aspects of living in the material world. *Journal of Consumer Research, 12*(3), 265–280.

Belk, R. (1988). Possessions and the extended self. *Journal of Consumer Research, 15*(2), 139–168.

Bettman, J. R. (1979). Memory factors in consumer choice: A review. *The Journal of Marketing, 43,* 37–53.

Bettman, J. R., Luce, M. F., & Payne, J. W. (1998). Constructive consumer choice processes. *Journal of Consumer Research, 25*(3), 187–217.

Bian, Q., & Forsythe, S. (2012). Purchase intention for luxury brands: A cross cultural comparison. *Journal of Business Research, 65*(10), 1443–1451.

Blackwell, R. D., Miniard, P. W., & Engel, J. F. (2001). *Consumer behavior 9th.* Mason, OH: South-Western Thomas Learning.

Burgiel, A., & Sowa, I. (2000). Potrzeby konsumpcyjne jako przesłanki zachowań konsumentów. In E. Kieżel (red.), *Rynkowe zachowania konsumentów.* Katowice: Wydawnictwo Akademii Ekonomicznej w Katowicach.

Corneo, G., & Jeanne, O. (1997). Conspicuous consumption, snobbism and conformism. *Journal of Public Economics, 66*(1), 55–71.

DeBono, K. G., & Harnish, R. J. (1988). Source expertise, source attractiveness, and the processing of persuasive information: A functional approach. *Journal of Personality and social Psychology, 55*(4), 541–546.

Desmond, M. (2016). *Evicted: Poverty and profit in the American city*. New York, NY: Broadway Books.

Dubois, B., Laurent, G., & Czellar, S. (2001). Consumer rapport to luxury: Analyzing complex and ambivalent attitudes (Consumer Research Working Paper, 736). Jouy-en-Josas, France: HEC.

Engel, J. F., Kollat, D. T., & Blackwell, R. D. (1968). *A model of consumer motivation and behavior*. New York, NY: Holt, Rinehart and Winston.

Foxal, G. R., & Goldsmith, E. G. (1998). *Psychologia konsumenta dla menedżera marketingu*. Warszawa: Wydawnictwo Naukowe PWN.

Grewal, R., Mehta, R., & Kardes, F. R. (2004). The timing of repeat purchases of consumer durable goods: The role of functional bases of consumer attitudes. *Journal of Marketing Research, 41*(1), 101–115.

Griskevicius, V., Tybur, J. M., Sundie, J. M., Cialdini, R. B., Miller, G. F., & Kenrick, D. T. (2007). Blatant benevolence and conspicuous consumption: When romantic motives elicit strategic costly signals. *Journal of Personality and Social Psychology, 93*(1), 85.

Gurzki, H., & Woisetschläger, D. M. (2017). Mapping the luxury research landscape: A bibliometric citation analysis. *Journal of Business Research, 77*, 147–166.

Han, Y. J., Nunes, J. C., & Drèze, X. (2010). Signaling status with luxury goods: The role of brand prominence. *Journal of Marketing, 74*(4), 15–30.

Holbrook, M. B. (2006). Consumption experience, customer value, and subjective personal introspection: An illustrative photographic essay. *Journal of Business Research, 59*(6), 714–725. https://doi.org/10.1016/j.jbusres.2006.01.008.

Holbrook, M. B., & Hirschman, E. C. (1982). The experiential aspects of consumption: Consumer fantasies, feelings, and fun. *Journal of Consumer Research, 9*(2), 132–140.

Howard, J. A., & Sheth, J. N. (1969). *The theory of buyer behavior*. New York: Wiley.

Johar, J. S., & Sirgy, M. J. (1991). Value-expressive versus utilitarian advertising appeals: When and why to use which appeal. *Journal of Advertising, 20*(3), 23–33.

Johnson, A. R., & Stewart, D. W. (2005). A reappraisal of the role of emotion in consumer behavior. In *Review of marketing research* (pp. 3–34). Bingley: Emerald Group.

Keller, K. L. (2001). *Building customer-based brand equity: A blueprint for creating strong brands* (s. 3–27). Cambridge, MA: Marketing Science Institute.

Kim, H. S., Moon, H. K., Choo, H. J., & Yoon, N. H. (2011). The effect of fashion luxury consumption values on the intention to maintain brand relationships-differences among segmented markets based on purchasing patterns. *Journal of the Korean Society of Clothing and Textiles, 35*(4), 408–420.

Kollat, D. T., Engel, J. F., & Blackwell, R. D. (1970). Current problems in consumer behavior research. *Journal of Marketing Research, 7*(3), 327–332.

Kumar, A., Lee, H. J., & Kim, Y. K. (2009). Indian consumers' purchase intention toward a United States versus local brand. *Journal of Business Research, 62*(5), 521–527.

Leibenstein, H. (1950). Bandwagon, snob, and Veblen effects in the theory of consumers' demand. *Quarterly Journal of Economics, 64,* 183–207.

Madden, T. J., Ellen, P. S., & Ajzen, I. (1992). A comparison of the theory of planned behavior and the theory of reasoned action. *Personality and Social Psychology Bulletin, 18*(1), 3–9.

Mittal, B., Ratchford, B., & Prabhakar, P. (1990). Functional and expressive attributes as determinants of brand-attitude. *Research in Marketing, 10,* 135–155.

Morris, J. D., Woo, C., Geason, J. A., & Kim, J. (2002). The power of affect: Predicting intention. *Journal of Advertising Research, 42*(3), 7–17.

Nicosia, F. M. (1966). *Consumer decision processes: Marketing and advertising implications*. Englewood Cliffs, NJ: Prentice-Hall.

Norušis, M. J. (1994). *SPSS advanced statistics 6.1*. SPSS.

O'Shaughnessy, J. (1987). *Why people buy*. New York: Oxford University Press.

Payne, J. W., Bettman, J. R., & Johnson, E. J. (1992). Behavioral decision research: A constructive processing perspective. *Annual Review of Psychology, 43*(1), 87–131.

Rudnicki, L. (2012). *Zachowania konsumentów na rynku*. Warszawa: Polskie Wydawnictwo Ekonomiczne.

Sagan, C. (2011). *The demon-haunted world: Science as a candle in the dark*. Ballantine Books.

Shavitt, S. (1989). Products, personalities and situations in attitude functions: Implications for consumer behavior. In T. K. Srull (Ed.), *NA—Advances in consumer research* (Vol. 16, s. 300–305). Provo, UT: Association for Consumer Research.

Shavitt, S. (1990). The role of attitude objects in attitude functions. *Journal of Experimental Social Psychology, 26*(2), 124–148.

Simon, H. A. (1955). A behavioral model of rational choice. *The Quarterly Journal of Economics, 69*(1), 99–118.

Światowy, G. (2006). *Zachowania konsumentów: Determinanty oraz metody poznania i kształtowania*. Warszawa: Polskie Wydawnictwo Ekonomiczne.
Tversky, A. (1972). Elimination by aspects: A theory of choice. *Psychological Review, 79*(4), 281.
Tversky, A., & Kahneman, D. (1991). Loss aversion in riskless choice: A reference-dependent model. *The Quarterly Journal of Economics, 106*(4), 1039–1061.
Tversky, A., Sattath, S., & Slovic, P. (1988). Contingent weighting in judgment and choice. *Psychological Review, 95*(3), 371–384.
Tynan, C., McKechnie, S., & Chhuon, C. (2010). Co-creating value for luxury brands. *Journal of Business Research, 63*(11), 1156–1163.
Veblen, T. (2005). *The theory of the leisure class: An economic study of institutions*. Aakar Books.
Veblen, T. (2008). *Teoria klasy próżniaczej*. wydanie III. Warszawa: Wydawnictwo Literackie Muza.
Vigneron, F., & Johnson, L. W. (2004). Measuring perceptions of brand luxury. *Journal of Brand Management, 11*(6), 484–506.
Wiedmann, K. P., Hennigs, N., & Siebels, A. (2009). Value-based segmentation of luxury consumption behavior. *Psychology & Marketing, 26*(7), 625–651.
Wilcox, K., Kim, H. M., & Sen, S. (2009). Why do consumers buy counterfeit luxury brands? *Journal of Marketing Research, 46*(2), 247–259.
Zajonc, R. B., & Markus, H. (1982). Affective and cognitive factors in preferences. *Journal of Consumer Research, 9*(2), 123–131.
Zimbardo, P. G., & Ruch, F. L. (1988). *Psychologia i ycie*. Warszawa: PWN.

5

Consumers' Perception of Luxury Goods Value: National Context

5.1 Country of Residence, National Culture and Perception of Luxury Goods

Although the image of luxury brands and their marketing strategies are highly standardised (Kapferer 1997) many empirical studies show that the behaviour of consumers of luxury goods and services varies from region to region and from country to country. As Shukla notes (2010) people buy the same luxury products all over the world but for different reasons and the value they attribute to them varies from country to country. Despite a large number of studies claiming that national culture is the most important factor in shaping consumer attitudes many contradictory results were obtained regarding the direction and strength of this impact (see Crotts and Erdmann 2000; Shukla 2012). This suggests that the study of the impact of culture on consumer behaviour is much more complex than expected. Looking at this relationship from the point of view of the so-called cultural dimensions in which culture is reduced to a few categories, it is necessary to draw attention to these special features, leaving other types of cultural influences aside. A differentiated approach to luxury shopping on a global scale is a fact although the search for the

B. Stępień, *The Value of Luxury*, Palgrave Advances in Luxury,
https://doi.org/10.1007/978-3-030-51218-7_5

causes of these differences only in a particular culture seems to be too deterministic.

Culture is defined here as a common worldview consisting of values, norms, customs and social rules shared by the group. The worldview refers to the belief system and explains how the universe functions and the role of individuals in the universe. This in turn creates a set of values: moral (what is important in life, good or bad, beautiful or ugly, valuable or worthless); social values, related to the individual's place in a given social space; and personal values.

The adherence to values established within a group (e.g. a nation) is reflected at a lower level in the form of norms, rules and customs in order to ensure the sense of community, stability and cohesion of the group. However the foundation of culture is a broader, a metaphysical ideology of moral values widespread in a given place and time in the form of religion (Cooper et al. 2007; Samovar et al. 2014). An important feature of culture is its ability to self-establish itself over time by passing on its essential components from generation to generation as guidelines for use in the process of evaluation and behavioural retention (Klopf 1998; Cooper et al. 2007; Jandt 2015).

However culture is only one (though important) of the many components of the national market. The market is also defined by its economy, political and institutional system, or a geo-political position. National culture is the foundation of political and social ideologies which in turn influence the economic system and formal institutions but which influences these other market subsystems indirectly. National culture imprints its mark on all other market subsystems but the shape and nature of these subsystems is not just its simple carbon footprint. The political, economic and formal institutional frameworks contain an afterimage of cultural influence that passes through a funnel of moderating factors:

- the historically shaped and current scope of application of the broad economic calculation of the current and future benefits and losses resulting from the adoption of specific economic, political and institutional solutions,
- the bargaining power of different interest groups in the form of opportunities to shape market subsystems,

- the educational system and the interests of those in power,
- the political and economic position of a country in global power interplay,
- the impact of the forces of nature on the life of individuals and the economic condition of the country.

The individual value system is subject to environmental influences: it is shaped by them and changes over time. It is other individuals and social groups who influence our perception of what is important, good, true or beautiful: first by telling us that it is these spheres of life that have particular virtues and over time we value the reality around us (but also the in the future and the past), but always influenced by other people and their opinions and judgments.

As A. Sen (2004) notes, people are subject to many different cultural influences (family, peer group, professional group, etc.) that shape their value system (see also De Mooij 2010). The values developed within a given cultural area do not have to (and often do not) conform to the individual value system, not least because each individual experiences the world in a different way.

In order to cope with the complexity of the world people create categories that simplify the universe. They learn how to create cognitive, evaluative and interpretative systems through interaction, socialization but also modify or strengthen them through education. Ethnicity, gender, age and their related life role, a specific social status combined with personality traits shape the value system and the way individuals are valued.

But luxury goods are the subject of social desire which is directly linked to the meaning given to the possession of goods in a given society and how people are assessed in terms of their material status.

Not only the very fact of possessing material goods, including luxury goods, is subject to evaluation but also the way in which they are socially exposed. The social perception of purchases and consumption of luxury is subject to moral evaluation and this is a result of both history and culture but also is shaped by current economic and political transformations.

5.2 Influence of the Country of Residence and National Culture on the Perception of Luxury Goods—A Review of Published Research

Much of the research has shown that customer behaviour varies from country to country and that these differences are attributed to cultural influence (De Mooij 2010; Hall and Hall 1990; Hofstede 2001; Schneider and Barsoux 2003; Schwartz 1994; Triandis 1989; Trompenaars and Hampden-Turner 2011).

Many empirical studies (Bond 2002; De Mooij 2010; Klopf 1998; Koester and Lustig 2015; Søndergaard 1994) explain these differences between countries in relation to the cultural dimensions of Hofstede (2016): individualism versus collectivism, power distance, masculinity, avoidance of uncertainty, long and short-term orientation and indulgence.

Researchers investigating CLVP in China (Iglesias et al. 2011; Zhan and He 2012), India (Shukla and Purani 2012) or Middle East countries (Hanzaee and Teimourpour 2012) indicate that local culture strongly influences customer beliefs and purchasing behaviour in a way that differentiates them from developed markets. However many of the empirical research works do not agree with those that are commonly quoted and which refer to general cultural differences found in several basic dimensions (e.g. Hofstede 2001 or Hampden and Trompenaars 2000). What is more in many studies in the part devoted to discussion (which is supposed to convince the reader that the CLVP differences between countries are of cultural grounds), the Wong and Ahuvia paper (1998) is quoted. However his paper does not contain any empirical research on this subject being only a collection of hypotheses for further testing. Referring to a number of other studies (mainly conceptual) their authors try to convince the reader that the possible differences between the countries of the West and East in the perception of luxury have the following cultural background:

- in comparison to consumers from "Western cultures" Asian consumers will value the hedonic component of luxury to a lesser extent due to a higher inclination to collectivism and to value the group's opinion more than their own needs and desires,
- in comparison with Western cultures Asian cultures will value the social component of value to a greater extent due to the relative importance of public display of status and image building thanks to how others evaluate us—(i.e. *interdependent self construal*), reinforced additionally by the concept of facial behaviour or collectivism,
- in Western cultures it will be more important to consume luxury for private purposes (because I want it), and in Eastern cultures for social reasons (because others see it),
- Asian cultures will be more likely to consume luxury as a result of a gift exchange than Western cultures where people buy luxury goods primarily for their own use,
- in western cultures there will be a more pronounced tendency to assess the product as such (due to its technical characteristics), while in Asian cultures the assessment will be made more frequently through the prism of the so-called affiliation characteristics (e.g. brand, place of production), which is conditioned by a broader context of looking at goods (e.g. through the prism of social assessment).

Some of these assumptions have been empirically tested confirming the existing differences between the eastern and western perception of luxury. For example Liang and He (2012) and Zhan and He (2012) show that in China the need for conformism, mimicking specific social trends (distinguishing, stunning with luxury as a proof of the economic and social success achieved) is greater than in Western countries where individualism is valued more highly. Preferences for very well-known global brands among Chinese consumers confirm, according to the quoted authors, conformism and dominant a intersubjective creation of one's own identity through the prism of social relationships. Global brands provide Chinese consumers with a sense of security in terms of quality and recognition thus enabling them to increase their reputation and status. Analyzing the reasons for buying luxury fashion brands among Taiwanese women Wu et al. (2015) noticed that they want to purchase clothes and accessories to emphasize their individuality to a lesser extent than their Western counterparts and that they tend to adapt to major trends rather than act against them. In the Shukla and Purani study (2012), differences between Indian and British consumers were attributed to cultural differences at the level of Hofstede's individualism/collectivism. British consumers who gained high scores for individualism in the Hofstede dimension showed a higher level of hedonic components than Indians, the inhabitants of a country with a high rate of collectivism.

Despite these results treating all Eastern countries as a monolith only because they have a few common features seems to be a far-reaching simplification of reality. Le Monk et al. in analyzing the approach of Chinese and Japanese people to luxury, noticed clear differences between these groups in their tendency to express themselves by purchasing brands of luxury goods. While the Chinese are clearly inclined to reproduce already outlined trends in their choices, for the Japanese luxury shopping is primarily meant to help them define their own self. However there are no differences in this approach in the culture, but rather in the level of economic development and the economic clamour in a state of capitalist liberalism. Successive studies by Godey et al. (2013) provide further evidence of national differences in the perception of the various components of luxury values. The authors surveyed consumers in six nations (Italians, Germans, French, Americans, Chinese and Japanese) and observed the following differences:

- Italians have the richest and most diverse view of luxury, appreciating exclusivity, exclusivity, exclusivity, prestige and social desire as components of values,
- very much like the Italians, Americans regard luxury as exclusive, prestigious, desirable but also slightly less extravagant,
- French respondents have a traditional concept of luxury based on prestige and elitism,
- The Germans emphasize l exclusivity above all, followed by social desire and then high price and prestige,

- The Chinese were the only ones to highlight the prestige and extravagance and visibility of luxury goods as being their dominant feature and value.
- For Japanese respondents luxury is above all expensive, sophisticated, exclusive, elite and prestigious.

For Germans luxury can be not only material, but also an idealistic way of life. For the Japanese and the French luxury is important for the aesthetic component resulting from its above-average characteristics and resulting in its elitism. For the Chinese luxury allows to expose oneself in public. The authors of the cited studies, having obtained such a diversified (in terms of national affiliation of respondents) approach to the perception of luxury, do not explain it by the culture of the country but by the general socio-economic impact of the country of residence.

The analysis of Chinese attitudes towards luxury is a manifestation of global social change, when luxury goods and their public consumption are a tool for the creation of new classes and an emblem of belonging to them. According to Kapferer and Bastien (2009) contemporary luxury consumption seems particularly attractive to groups of aspiring consumers living in catching up, fast-growing economies. In these countries social classes are being reformulated and the main criterion is the level of wealth rather than class membership. The process of new social stratification based on wealth is accompanied by a global degradation of the importance of traditional social classes.

5.3 Influence of the Country of Residence on CLVP—The Author's Research Results

The results of the international luxury goods value perception (CLVP) survey are presented here. The results are analysed collectively and broken down into six countries (Poland, Portugal, Turkey, Saudi Arabia, India and Germany) from which the largest number of responses were received.

In analyzing the results an attempt was made to explain the observed diversity using the cultural dimensions of Hofstede (2016).[1]

5.3.1 Short Description of the Countries Analysed in Terms of CLVP Among Consumers

Saudi Arabia, India, Turkey, Poland and Portugal can be considered as dynamically developing and promising markets for luxury. The purchasing power of consumers in these countries is growing or is already high with a rapidly growing number of young, increasingly wealthy consumers. The forecasts for continued growth in luxury goods sales on the markets in question are mainly justified by economic progress and in the case of Germany, institutional stability. The economies of all the countries analyzed here are growing or have been stable continuously over the last decade and coped with the last global economic crisis relatively well.

Germany is an example of a country that is not part of the European cradle of luxury but is the fifth largest economy in the world in terms of purchasing power parity. It is a world leader in the production of luxury cars and a significant consumer of luxury. Germany is an economically and politically stable, safe and secure country, with one of the lowest youth unemployment rates in the EU, with an average disposable net income per capita well above the OECD average.

Although India, Turkey, Poland and Portugal consume only a small part of the world's luxury, the growth rate of this consumption is impressive (see also Chapter 3). The upper middle classes in these countries are developing quite rapidly and many young, ambitious, well-educated technocrats buy luxury items as status symbols or as rewards for their hard work. In all the countries discussed here, apart from Germany, the "public exhibition" of luxury dominates as the legitimacy of the high economic and social status of the owners. The age structure in India and Saudi Arabia (about 30% of people aged 0–14),

[1]This part of the book is based on the results of research presented in Stępień et al. The article does not present the results from India which were not collected until December 2017.

combined with rapid growth of the Indian economy and apparently inexhaustible oil and gas reserves in Saudi Arabia, is particularly important for the future of luxury markets. Although Turkey has as much as 25% of the population in this age bracket its geo-political problems do not allow for such optimistic forecasts for the development of the luxury market in this country as in the case of the other two.

While Poland, Turkey and Portugal, or India can be described as new and promising markets for luxury, Saudi Arabia seems to be already a paradise for it. The Saudis are a large and young population with a very high level of disposable income. In addition rapidly changing consumption patterns throughout the Gulf region have transformed shopping into an important and popular pastime (Kassim and Zain 2016). The growing appetite for public display of status symbols only reinforces this trend. The observable boom in department stores additionally confirms optimistic luxury sales forecasts for Saudi Arabia and the Gulf region as a whole (Alserhan et al. 2014).

Germany is a mature, sustainable market responsible for 10% of world luxury consumption although annual growth in spending on these goods is minimal (Bain & Co. 2019). The majority of luxury purchases are premium and luxury German cars and luxury consumed away from public view, such as electrical and household appliances, with purchases of jewellery and watches being the smallest segment.

5.3.2 Cultural Dimensions and Religion in the Countries Analysed

The comparison of cultural dimensions (Hofstede 2020, Fig. 5.1) shows significant differences between countries. While in Saudi Arabia and India there is a strong preference for a hierarchical social order (power distance), Turkey, Portugal and Poland perform moderately in this dimension. Germans, Poles and Indians are more individualistic than the Portuguese, Turks and Saudis. The Portuguese, Poles and Turks show a strong avoidance of uncertainty and a short-term orientation that can be used to explain the dynamic growth of luxury consumption. India,

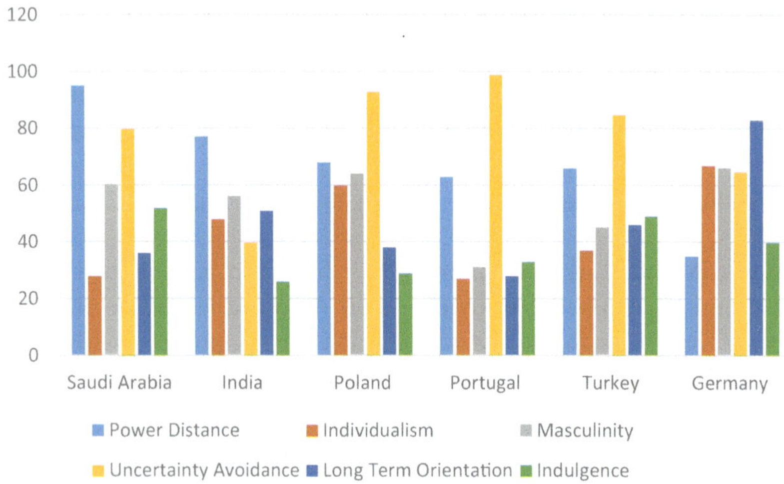

Fig. 5.1 G. Hofstede cultural dimensions for the countries analysed (*Source* Own calculations based on https://www.hofstede-insights.com/country-comparison)

Portugal and Poland are the most "reserved" cultures, characterised by a tendency to pessimism and actions controlled by social norms.

Germany has the lowest power distance of all the countries surveyed. This would mean that status symbols are not very important for the Germans. With the highest level of individualism compared to other countries (slightly higher than Poland), Germany (as interpreted by Hofstede 2016) values self-interest above group interest. The highest result of long-term orientation among the whole group of countries indicates that Germans like to save and make plans for the long term. The low level of indulgence indicates in turn that Germans try to control their desires and an open permissiveness to them is considered inappropriate.

The countries in the sample vary considerably regarding the type, significance and influence of religious beliefs on the governance of the state and daily life of its citizens.

The Kingdom of Saudi Arabia is the only country in the sample with a legal system based on religious rules derived from Koran and traditions of Prophet Muhammad. There is no legal protection of religious freedom. The strict rules of social life are based on a conservative interpretation of the rules of Koran. Turkey is a secular state guaranteeing constitutional freedom of religion and prohibiting all discrimination on religious grounds although the Islamic agenda is constantly, albeit unofficially, being introduced into the legal order. In Turkey 99% of the population are Sunni Muslims from Hanafi. Polish history and culture is strongly connected with the Roman Catholic Church. More than 85% of the 38.3 million Polish citizens are Catholics and the majority of the population are active believers. Close official and political relations with the Church confirm the importance of religion in Poland. Portugal, like Poland has a strong Christian heritage (81% of the population are Catholics), but today the Catholic Church does not play a significant role in the country.

India is an example of a multi-religious country although almost 80% of the population is Hindu. The second largest group of believers adheres to the creed of Islam (about 14%) and the third largest is Christianity (2%). Due to the historical coexistence of many religions India has a fairly high level of tolerance for different faiths, although this does not mean that there are no tensions. Interestingly the most educated and richest social class is largely made up of Jains (Jainism accounts for only 0.46% of the population).

Germany as a result of the Reformation is traditionally divided into the northern and eastern Protestant region and the western and southern Catholic regions. Protestants and Catholics make up about 34% of the total population. Around 28% of the total population has no religious affiliation and this applies to the majority of the former GDR population who declare themselves atheists. About 4% of the population is Muslim (CIA 2019).

5.3.3 Social and Ethical Components of Luxury Value Perception

The data obtained show significant differences in CLVP between the countries surveyed. Consumers in Saudi Arabia and India are the biggest admirers of luxury goods, while Germans tend not to exhibit this trait. The perception of the individual components of value by consumers in the selected countries and across the sample is presented and commented upon below.

The analysis of the social component of values, bandwagon and snobbish inclinations and the ethical dimension of luxury (see Table 5.1) shows the following differences and similarities within the analysed group:

- consumers from all the growing luxury markets in the sample consider the social component of CLVP to be important and rate it higher than the Germans,
- The Saudis and Poles demonstrate snobbish inclinations, while the Germans declare the least such inclinations in the whole sample,
- only Saudis demonstrate the positive bandwagon inclinations and Germans declare the least such inclinations in the whole sample,
- consumers in all growing luxury markets are more snobby and imitative of CLVP than Germans,
- consumers, regardless of the country, do not consider luxury shopping unethical,
- only the Portuguese believe that buying luxury goods is not a sign of snobbishness; all other respondents see such a feature in luxury purchases.

The large discrepancy in the results between Germany and the rest of the sample can be explained by the Germans' reluctance to publicly impress with luxury. Germans openly criticise the public demonstration of wealth. This probably also explains the Germans' tendency to buy luxury products mainly for domestic use. Germans who are considered distant and emotionless in public, also try to control their public image so as not to appear too ostentatious (Hall and Hall 1990).

Table 5.1 Social components of the CLVP—comparison of sample countries

	Total	Saudi Arabia	Germany	Poland	Turkey	Portugal.	India
Social component	**3.63**	**3.51**	**3.32**	**3.70**	**3.78**	**3.96**	**3.99**
Luxury products are a symbol of high social status	3.56	3.18	3.42	3.58	3.87	4.13	4.21
Luxury products make a good impression on others	3.46	3.40	2.83	3.61	3.62	3.75	3.87
Luxury products are highly desirable	3.88	3.96	3.69	3.93	3.84	4.01	3.90
Snob effect	**2.95**	**3.29**	**2.35**	**3.07**	**2.54**	**2.93**	**3.00**
I prefer to buy luxury products that are rare and not popular	3.09	3.49	2.24	3.24	2.39	3.56	3.21
I don't like it when a lot of people, even well-known people, have what I bought	2.80	3.09	2.45	2.90	2.69	2.30	2.79
Bandwagon inclinations	**2.48**	**3.19**	**1.93**	**2.45**	**2.18**	**2.62**	**2.96**
I prefer to buy luxury products that are already used by people I value and admire	2.57	3.34	1.83	2.51	2.24	2.88	3.10

(continued)

Table 5.1 (continued)

	Total	Saudi Arabia	Germany	Poland	Turkey	Portugal.	India
I love having what famous people have	2.38	3.03	2.02	2.38	2.12	2.37	2.83
Ethical components of values	**2.74**	**2.83**	**2.77**	**2.83**	**2.63**	**2.36**	**2.66**
Buying luxury products is snobby	3.19	3.00	3.04	3.53	3.15	2.62	3.22
Buying luxury products is unethical	2.30	2.65	2.49	2.13	2.12	2.10	2.10

Source Own calculations
Note The data in bold are means of the statements below for the respective components

The effect of social mirror and consumption not yet described, clearly shows that respondents from all growing markets of luxury are convinced that luxury helps to raise the social status of the owner of such goods. At the same time both Indians and Saudis are of the opinion that the purchase of these goods is essential as it determines their social status and builds public image.

Differences in the perception of social components of values in individual countries cannot be explained by the similarity or diversity of indicators in the dimension of power distance or individualism/collectivism. Poles and Germans have similar indicators when it comes to individualism but they perceive the social component of CLVP differently. Although the power distance in Germany is the lowest and in Saudi Arabia the highest, it is Indian and Portuguese who value the social component of CLVP the most which indicates that this dimension does not explain the value of luxury as a derivative of power distance.

Results on the ethical component of CLVP show that luxury consumption is perceived as more snobby than unethical by all consumers in the sample. Poles consider luxury purchases to be the most snobby amongst the entire sample of countries surveyed. However this does not prevent them from admitting to snobbish inclinations, which can be explained by a high level of individualism (according to Hofstede). Perhaps Poles do not see anything wrong in snobbism? According to Kacprzak and Dziewanowska (2015), snobbish tendencies are explained by strong individualistic features among young Poles accompanied by a relatively high level of materialism.

When analysing the ethical component percentage of respondents who expressed negative opinions about luxury was also checked. Table 5.2 shows the percentage of respondents by country who answered either 4 (I agree) or 5 (I fully agree) questions about the negative attitude/emotions towards luxury.

The analysis of the group which reveals a negative attitude/emotions with regard to luxury by country, shows significant differences. The largest group of protestors are Poles and Indians. Interestingly Polish consumers show a similar level of ethical uncertainty to the Saudis (measured by the average score).

However this does not mean that there is a more critical approach to luxury goods in countries where religion plays an important role in everyday life (e.g. Saudi Arabia, Poland, Turkey). The religious impact on consumer behaviour in this area should not be disregarded but further, in-depth qualitative research would probably serve as a better method of detecting the links between religious and moral attitudes and the perception of luxury.

5.3.4 Hedonic, Functional and Aesthetic Components of CLVP

The results of the study of the hedonic component of the luxury value initially surprise. They prove that only Saudi, Indian and Portuguese respondents admit that both shopping and luxury consumption bring them positive emotions. So what makes consumers in Poland so eager to buy luxury goods if it does not bring them joy? Do they do it only out of social coercion, regret by spending money on luxury or maybe

Table 5.2 Distribution of luxury opponents by country in the sample (%)

		Saudi Arabia %	Germans %	Poland %	Portugal %	Turkey %	India %
Buying luxury goods is snobbish	yes*	16.9	26.3	43.5	13.3	32.1	41.0
Buying luxury goods is unethical	yes*	10.7	8.3	8.3	4.2	13.2	14.1
Buying luxury goods is frustrating	yes*	14.0	6.4	13.1	10.0	15.1	13.3

Source Own calculations; * data 4 (agree) or 5 (strongly agree)

do not want to admit that such a practice "gives them wings"[2]? A closer look at the individual statements making up the hedonic component provides a possible answer: buying luxury goods brings Poles a lot of joy but they do not associate this act with taking care of oneself or feeling *"like a king/queen"*. Clearly the wording of this statement (taken from the Wiedmann et al. in 2009) seems very strong and many respondents from Poland, Turkey and Germany stated that when buying luxury goods they do not feel so exceptional or do not want to feel so.

The moderate hedonic value obtained in the study also makes one wonder whether the current direction of research so clearly focussed on not only analyzing but also emphasizing positive emotions as these (next to social) most important components of the value does not distort the perception of the value of luxury. While the sample includes responses from twenty countries (included in the data for the whole sample), the overall indicator for this component is moderate. On the other hand given the dynamically growing sales in all the growth markets for luxury covered by the study it can be assumed that it is other non-emotional components of CLVP that influence this trend.

The data presented in Table 5.3 fully confirm the dynamically growing trend of a "consumer culture" in Saudi Arabia and India. Saudis, however, more than Indians, clearly enjoy buying and owning luxury goods. Both Indians and Saudis also consider the functional elements of CLVP to be the most important of all dimensions of value. India appears to be a country where luxury consumption can flourish on an unprecedented scale if only the purchasing power of the population grows. It is noteworthy that respondents from the entire sample and all countries analysed separately positively and highly rated the quality of luxury goods as the component that contributes most to creating the value of functional luxury. Aesthetic attributes of luxury are associated by respondents (regardless the country) mainly with design and to a lesser extent with elegance.

The data also indicate that a higher level of individualism in a given country (according to the Hofstede dimension) does not correspond to

[2]This is a quotation from an interview with one of the representatives of highly paid consumers in Poland. When asked what luxury shopping gives her she expressed herself in this way.

Table 5.3 Hedonic, functional and aesthetic elements of CLVP—comparison of country averages in the sample

	Total	Saudi Arabia	Germans	Poland	Turkey	Portugal	India
Hedonic component	**2.75**	**3.32**	**2.08**	**2.68**	**2.56**	**3.09**	**3.05**
Buying luxury products brings a lot of fun	3.23	3.35	2.90	3.52	2.73	3.32	3.12
Buying luxury products is like proving that I take care of myself	2.78	3.35	2.33	2.64	2.74	3.01	2.87
Buying luxury products is very exciting; I feel like a queen /king then	2.67	3.26	2.10	2.53	2.37	3.04	3.16
Functional component	**3.21**	**3.78**	**2.66**	**3.15**	**3.33**	**3.35**	**3.96**
Luxury products provide the best value for money	3.03	3.51	2.38	2.95	3.16	3.00	3.77
Luxury products are of above-average quality	3.54	4.13	3.20	3.25	3.43	3.71	4.10
Luxurious products have above-average functionality	3.07	3.72	2.42	2.76	3.42	3.34	4.01
Aesthetics	**3.64**	**3.80**	**3.41**	**3.61**	**3.63**	**3.63**	**3.92**
Luxury products are a symbol of elegance	3.31	3.58	2.96	3.27	3.11	3.55	3.90

(continued)

Table 5.3 (continued)

	Total	Saudi Arabia	Germans	Poland	Turkey	Portugal	India
Luxury products are a symbol of the best design	3.97	4.03	3.87	3.95	4.14	3.71	3.94

Source Own calculations

the level of the hedonic component of values. The phase of public exhibition of luxury which the analysed countries, being fast emerging luxury markets, are currently passing through strongly influences the perception of CLVP and does not seem to be related to the level of individualism. The hedonic component is particularly visible in Saudi Arabia (3.32) but also in Portugal (3.09), India (3.05) and these are countries with a lower level of individualism than Poland (where the hedonic component is less important).

The Hofstede indulgence vs. restraint dimension of the analysed markets suggests (according to the author's description of this dimension) that citizens of countries where the indulgence level is high are more inclined to gratify themselves than people from countries with a low level of this dimension (e.g. Poles). The results obtained do not confirm this. Although the Saudis have a very positive attitude towards luxury the opinions of Turkish respondents (with a similar level of indulgence as in Saudi Arabia) do not confirm this tendency to reward oneself. Germany seems to deny completely in its opinions that leniency towards one's own whims (at least as regards luxury) takes place at all, which is in line with the generally low indulgence rate. In the case of Poles the hedonic dimension is quite substantial while the Hofstede indulgence level is the lowest of all the countries analysed. The explanatory power of the indulgence dimension is most strongly undermined by the results obtained from Indian consumers who positively assess almost all components of the value of luxury, including the hedonic dimension, while the Hofstede indulgence level for this country is the lowest of all the countries analysed.

Due to the importance given to the hedonic component by both luxury business practitioners and academic researchers in this area, the percentage of respondents in the analysed countries who are consumers and who derive positive emotions from luxury was checked. Table 5.4 shows the percentage of people in each country who responded in the affirmative (4—I agree or 5—I fully agree) to statements showing that the hedonic component of luxury is a significant component of their value.

The highest percentage of hedonists (consumers who value this component) is in Portugal and Saudi Arabia. However if these results are compared with the percentage of people negatively disposed towards luxury it can be seen that in fast growing luxury markets (i.e. in countries with a large group of aspiring consumers) attitudes towards luxury are polarised, which may be explained by the still evolving social stance towards consumption of these goods.

5.3.5 Price Perception of Luxury Goods in Relation to Social and Functional Components of CLVP

The survey results unequivocally indicate that for consumers price is a measure of social desire for these products while to a much lesser extent it results (or does not result at all) from the costs of their manufacture, distribution and sale (see Table 5.5). Only for Saudis and Indians is price a measure of prestige. Luxury and high price are, above all, the result of the social perception of these products and apparently stem (at least partly) from effective communication campaigns that fuel this desire. However social desire is only partly due to the prestige of the product or its brand. As the results show, apart from the prestige itself, it is aesthetic values combined with the rarity of their occurrence that allow prices to be set at levels of relative inaccessibility.

Although all consumers, regardless of country, associate luxury goods with high prices only Indians and Saudis seem to justify it with high production and distribution costs. Contrary to the rest of the sample only respondents from Saudi Arabia to the smallest extent believe that

Table 5.4 Structure (%) of hedonists by country

		Saudi Arabia %	Germans %	Poland %	Portugal %	Turkey %	India %
Buying luxury products is very exciting; I feel like a queen /king then	yes*	27.9	14.1	19.1	35.0	17.9	24.9
Buying luxury products is like proving that I take care of myself	yes*	30.5	17.9	19.4	30.0	24.5	21.2
Buying luxury products brings a lot of fun	yes*	32.0	25.0	44.0	46.7	21.7	34.6

Source Own calculations; * data 4 (agree) or 5 (strongly agree)

Table 5.5 Price perception in relation to other components of luxury value—average values

The perception of the price of luxury goods	Total	Saudi Arabia	Germans	Poland	Turkey	Portugal	India
Luxury products are very expensive	3.97	4.03	3.87	3.95	4.14	3.73	4.18
The price of a luxury product is in line with the prestige of the product	2.85	3.26	2.53	2.79	2.56	3.17	3.22
The price of a luxury product reflects the costs associated with its production, distribution and sale	2.43	3.31	2.08	2.03	2.32	2.79	3.38
The price of a luxury product reflects the consumer's desire for this good	3.70	3.39	3.85	3.74	3.59	4.03	3.82

Source Own calculations

price levels reflect the social desire for these goods. Religious influences can be found in such an approach at least in relation to Saudi Arabia. According to Islam luxury goods can be classified as Kamaliah (halal: according to the Koran, goods that increase the quality of life and improve its quality, which can be purchased and consumed) or Tarafiah (haram: goods morally reprehensible, prohibited by the Koran because they mean waste and adhering to whims). This classification is open to interpretation based on an individual assessment of what is still halal or already haram (Alserhan et al. 2014). Admitting that the price of luxury goods reflects only a social desire can be regarded as an admission that luxury goods are those of the tarafiah category.

On the subject of Indian consumer ratings the perception of luxury as a result of costs and a measure of prestige may be explained by the quite common consensus to produce and trade in low-quality goods in this country, this being one of consequences of high level of poverty. The economically enforced but also historically rooted consent to the ubiquitous presence of cheap but poor quality goods and services can serve as a counterpoint to valuing the quality of luxury goods and thus justifying their price as reasonable.

5.4 Conclusions from the Research on the Diversity of CLVP in National Markets

Consumers in the countries surveyed differ significantly in their assessment of the various components of luxury value which confirms country driven differences in value perception identified by the other researchers cited above. The assessment of all value components by consumers from fast growing luxury markets is higher than in the case of the group of German respondents. The most valued components of luxury value are social and aesthetic. The quality characteristics of luxury goods and the joy of shopping are also important at a later stage but they are not identified with the expression of self-care. The functionality of luxury goods (as a component of CLVP) is rated at an average level by Poles, Turks and Portuguese and highly valued by Saudis and Indians.

Consumers from fast growing luxury markets also show a more polarised evaluation of luxury than German consumers. This may be explained by the "delight in luxury" phase experienced by aspiring consumers for whom luxury is a category of goods with a symbolic dimension that effectively raises social status in public opinion.

Saudis and Indians are the greatest admirers of luxury and social, aesthetic, functional and hedonic elements are assessed as essential components of its value. In India, where the caste system is strongly rooted in history, public consumption of luxury can be a tool for doing something seemingly impossible until now; moving to a higher social class through material status.

The high level of these components in the Saudis' assessment of CLVP may be explained by treating consumption as one of the key elements to form identity among contemporary Muslims (Alserhan 2010). Buying luxury goods builds a positive social image by showing high material status (Tjahjono 2011; Hanzaee and Teimourpour 2012). Although luxury goods increase social status and prestige luxury consumption may be treated as religiously reprehensible, which to some extent resonates with the opinions of respondents from this country when examining the ethical component of luxury values.

However the results of the presented studies are different from those of Shukla and Purani (2012), which demonstrated the convergence of individualism with high levels of hedonism and collectivism with low levels of hedonism in a study of British and Indian consumers. The reason for the difference may be either the different scales used in both studies; (this study combines scales of different researchers, but not Tynan et al. 2010, which Shukla and Purani used) or the small Indian samples which in both studies are not statistically relevant for the country with a population of over one billion.

The Hofstede dimensions analysed for each country in the sample do not explain the nature of the differences between these markets and are often contradictory. However this does not mean that the national culture has no influence on the perception of luxury value. Culture does influences the behaviour of individuals as the data clearly show, but:

1. culture is one of many factors shaping our image of the world, besides education, age, personality, or belonging to different groups (e.g. professional, religious, social),

2. the influence of culture on an individual's behaviour, attitudes and perception of values cannot be reduced to a convergence with several dimensions that describe culture in a piecemeal way.

Although national culture may well serve as a factor explaining different perceptions of the value of luxury by consumers causes of this diversity should also be sought in the phase of economic and social development of the countries studied or in the psychographic factors of the respondents. Moreover the economic changes in developing countries which are now in a phase of "delight in luxury" as a tool to increase social prestige, make us reflect on the validity of research with the usage of cultural dimensions established and surveyed decades ago. It may turn out that with large groups becoming rapidly richer, their approach to the distance of power, individualism, or indulgence in materializing individual desires significantly changes. It can also be assumed that changes in living conditions affect the transformations of individual value systems.

Although it would seem that religion, as the foundation of the value system of many individuals, will influence the perception of such morally controversial goods as luxury, data obtained in Saudi Arabia a country regulated by Sharia law, show that even restrictive religious orders are interpreted in such a way that they do not interfere with the consumption of luxury. Moreover the results may even suggest that the high value the Saudis attribute to luxury is rather an outlet for human weaknesses in the face of the many prohibitions to which daily life in this country is subject. Shopping, as an element of social life not subject to strict religious rules, makes it possible to fulfil desires that cannot be realized publicly in other spheres of life. Not without significance for the approach to luxury is also the purchasing power of the country's inhabitants, whose income is largely due to the exploitation of huge oil and gas deposits. However this survey was not designed to investigate the relationship between religion and CLVP, hence no general conclusions can be drawn on the relationship between religion and the perception of luxury.

References

Alserhan, B. A. (2010). On Islamic branding: Brands as good deeds. *Journal of Islamic Marketing, 1*(2), 101–106.

Alserhan, B. A., Bataineh, M. K., Halkias, D., & Komodromos, M. (2014). Measuring luxury brand consumption and female consumers' religiosity in the Uae. *Journal of Developmental Entrepreneurship, 19*(2), 1450009.

Bain & Co. (2019). *Eight themes that are rewriting the future of luxury goods*. https://www.bain.com/insights/eight-themes-that-are-rewriting-the-future-of-luxury-goods/.

Bond, M. H. (2002). Reclaiming the individual from Hofstede's ecological analysis–A 20-year odyssey. *Psychological Bulletin, 128*(1), 73–77.

CIA. (2019). *The world factbook, religions*. https://www.cia.gov/library/publications/the-world-factbook/fields/401.html.

Cooper, P. J., Calloway-Thomas, C., & Simonds, C. J. (2007). *Intercultural communication: A text with readings*. Boston, MA: Pearson Education.

Crotts, J. C., & Erdmann, R. (2000). Does national culture influence consumers' evaluation of travel services? A test of Hofstede's model of cross-cultural differences. *Managing Service Quality: An International Journal, 10*(6), 410–419.

De Mooij, M. (2010). *Global marketing and advertising: Understanding cultural paradoxes*. Thousand Oaks, CA: Sage.

Godey, B., Pederzoli, D., Aiello, G., Donvito, R., Wiedmann, K. P., & Hennigs, N. (2013). A cross-cultural exploratory content analysis of the perception of luxury from six countries. *Journal of Product & Brand Management, 22*(3), 229–237.

Hall, E. T., & Hall, M. R. (1990). *Understanding cultural differences: [Germans, French and Americans]* (Vol. 9). Yarmouth, ME: Intercultural Press.

Hampden, T., & Trompenaars, F. (2000). *Building cross-cultural competence*. London: John Willey & Sons.

Hanzaee, K. H., & Teimourpour, B. (2012). Segmenting consumers based on luxury value perceptions. *Middle-East Journal of Scientific Research, 12*(11), 1445–1453.

Hofstede, G. (2001). *Culture's consequences: Comparing values, behaviors, institutions, and organizations across nations* (2nd ed.). Thousand Oaks, CA: Sage.

Hofstede, G. (2016). Culture's consequences: Comparing values, behaviors, institutions, and organizations across nations. *Collegiate Aviation Review, 34*(2), 108.

Hofstede, G. (2020). https://www.hofstede-insights.com/product/compare-countries/.

Iglesias, O., Singh, J. J., Casabayó, M., Hung, K. P., Chen, A. H., Peng, N., ... & Chou, C. L. (2011). Antecedents of luxury brand purchase intention. *Journal of Product & Brand Management*.

Jandt, F. E. (2015). *An introduction to intercultural communication: Identities in a global community*. Thousand Oaks, CA: Sage.

Kacprzak, A., & Dziewanowska, K. (2015). Does a global young consumer exist? A comparative study of South Korea and Poland. *Journal of Marketing and Consumer Behaviour in Emerging Markets, 1*(1), 47–61.

Kapferer, J.-N. (1997). Managing luxury brands. *Journal of Brand Management, 4*(4), 251–260.

Kapferer, J. N., & Bastien, V. (2009). The specificity of luxury management: Turning marketing upside down. *Journal of Brand Management, 16*(5–6), 311–322.

Kassim, N. M., & Zain, M. M. (2016). Quality of lifestyle and luxury purchase inclinations from the perspectives of affluent Muslim consumers. *Journal of Islamic Marketing, 7*(1), 95–119.

Klopf, D. W. (1998). *Intercultural encounters: The fundamentals of intercultural communication*. Englewood, CO: Morton Publishing Company.

Koester, J., & Lustig, M. W. (2015). Intercultural communication competence: Theory, measurement, and application. *International Journal of Intercultural Relations, 48*, 20–21.

Liang, B., & He, Y. (2012). The effect of culture on consumer choice: The need for conformity vs. the need for uniqueness. *International Journal of Consumer Studies, 36*(3), 352–359.

Samovar, L. A., Porter, R. E., McDaniel, E. R., & Roy, C. S. (2014). *Intercultural communication: A reader*. Boston: Cengage Learning.

Schneider, S. C., & Barsoux, J. L. (2003). *Managing across cultures*. Pearson Education.

Schwartz, S. H. (1994). Beyond individualism/collectivism: New cultural dimensions of values. In U. Kim, H. C. Triandis, C. Kagitcibasi, S-C. Choi, & G. Yoon (Eds.), *Individualism and collectivism: Theory, method, and application*. Newbury Park, CA: Sage.

Sen, A. (2004). How does culture matter? In Rao, V. & Walton, M. (Hg.), *Culture and public action*, 37–58, Stanford.

Shukla, P. (2010). Status consumption in cross-national context. *International Marketing Review.*
Shukla, P. (2012). The influence of value perceptions on luxury purchase intentions in developed and emerging markets. *International Marketing Review, 29*(6), 574–596.
Shukla, P., & Purani, K. (2012). Comparing the importance of luxury value perceptions in cross-national contexts. *Journal of Business Research, 65*(10), 1417–1424.
Søndergaard, M. (1994). Research note: Hofstede's consequences: A study of reviews, citations and replications. *Organization Studies, 15*(3), 447–456.
Tjahjono, H. K. (2011). The configuration among social capital, distributive and procedural justice and its consequences to individual satisfaction. *International Journal of Information and Management Sciences, 22*(1), 87–103.
Triandis, H. C. (1989). The self and social behavior in differing cultural contexts. *Psychological Review, 96*(3), 506–520.
Trompenaars, F., & Hampden-Turner, C. (2011). *Riding the waves of culture: Understanding diversity in global business.* New York: Nicholas Brealey International.
Tynan, C., McKechnie, S., & Chhuon, C. (2010). Co-creating value for luxury brands. *Journal of Business Research, 63*(11), 1156–1163.
Wiedmann, K. P., Hennigs, N., & Siebels, A. (2009). Value-based segmentation of luxury consumption behavior. *Psychology & Marketing, 26*(7), 625–651.
Wong, N. Y., & Ahuvia, A. C. (1998). Personal taste and family face: Luxury consumption in Confucian and Western societies. *Psychology & Marketing, 15*(5), 423–441.
Wu, M. S. S., Chaney, I., Chen, C. H. S., Nguyen, B., & Melewar, T. C. (2015). Luxury fashion brands: Factors influencing young female consumers' luxury fashion purchasing in Taiwan. *Qualitative Market Research: An International Journal, 18*(3), 298–319.
Zhan, L., & He, Y. (2012). Understanding luxury consumption in China: Consumer perceptions of best-known brands. *Journal of Business Research, 65*(10), 1452–1460.

6

Impact of Socio-Demographic, Economic and Psychographic Consumer Traits on Luxury Value Perception: Empirical Findings

6.1 Socio-Demographic and Economic Characteristics and Perception of Luxury: Preliminary Remarks

Social and demographic criteria such as age, gender, occupation, place of residence or economic status (reflected in income level for example) are often used while searching for reasons for differences in the value perception of individual goods.

These criteria are easy to apply as they are quite clear to grasp and therefore they frequently form the basis for the segmentation of consumers, not only in the luxury business. However the research presented below exploring the relationships between social and demographic characteristics and attitudes towards luxury and its valuation shows that age, gender, income and education are not necessarily linked to the perception of the value of luxury.

B. Stępień, *The Value of Luxury*, Palgrave Advances in Luxury,
https://doi.org/10.1007/978-3-030-51218-7_6

6.1.1 Age as a Criterion for the Global Segmentation of Luxury Consumers?

The fastest growing group of luxury goods consumers is Generation X, followed by the Generation Z entering the luxury shopping arena. The interest in Brands in Generations Y and Z and their characteristic features is growing in importance, not only because of their actual and potential purchasing power, but also because of the general belief that Generations X, Y and Z differ significantly from each other, while presenting an internal global homogeneity at the same time.

Despite the fact that there are several statistically significant differences in the perception of the world and the shopping habits of these generations treating generations X, Y and Z as separate from each other but internally consistent is a misleading simplification. Not every representative of generation Z will be obsessed with web searching, as well as not every representative of generation Y will be an overworked materialist.

Generation Z are people born after 1997, and in 2020 they already account for more than 2 billion. Majority of these consumers still live with their parents, but their purchasing power is visible and will grow rapidly in a near future. Now they spend most of their disposable money on small purchases such as clothes, cosmetics, grocery products and entertainment (eating out, movies, games). They are not the most important target group for luxury business yet, but they already shape some trends in the luxury fashion business, visible in co-operation between fast fashion and luxury maisons. Focused on blending physical and internet life, they search for phygital experiences, are highly influenced by their own peers, and prefer to live here and now and this is their life approach that seems to shape many of future changes in the luxury sector (see also BusinessInsider 2019; Langer 2019).

Millennials, the generation after Generation X, are considered to be the first to be born in a world of strong international interdependence reinforced by the attributes of the digital age (Bahr and Pendergast 2007; Debevec et al. 2013). Millennials—Generation Y is the largest group of consumers in the world, three times bigger than Generation X (Palmer 2008; Meredith and Schewe 2002). Millennias have $200 billion of purchasing power in the USA; they set trends in all industries and affect other age groups. With a huge contribution to the economy, they are probably the most important and simultaneously the most consumption-oriented generation in the world (Sullivan and Heitmeyer 2008; Tapscott 2008). Generation Y is also referred to as globally homogeneous cosmopolitans (see Alden et al. 1999; Nijssen and Douglas 2011; Strizhakova et al. 2008).

According to United States Census Bureau (USCB 2015) Millennials were born between 1982 and 2000. Millennials are also considered more affluent and better educated than Generation X (born between 1965 and 1981) are more involved in teamwork, accept social diversity, are more altruistic, family-oriented and pro-environmental (Howe and Strauss 2000; Maignan et al. 2005; Elam et al. 2007; Gloeckler 2008; Pew Research Center 2010; Gerzema and D'Antonio 2011). As consumers they are "digital/net natives" (Prensky 2001, Net Generation, 6 July 2008).

The features mentioned here suggest that Millennials, when valuing luxury, appreciate its social component, provided that they or their close ones do not oppose luxury consumption and do not perceive it as harmful. According to Howe and Strauss (2000, p. 184), Millennials tend to think that everything they want in life depends on their own achievements and in this sense the consumption of luxury can be treated as a reward for productive and effective work, serving as social proof of individual success and prosperity.

Today Millennials are already the largest generational segment in the luxury market in the USA. A Cue Connect study published in Luxury Daily (2018) shows that although the budgets of Generation Y consumers are smaller than those of older generations their aspirations are high. This group does not have much money at its disposal but they buy mostly products from the lowest level of the luxury pyramid in quantity. This study shows also that the greatest opportunity for luxury brands to win and retain this group of consumers is personalisation combined with the communication of the use of luxury as an experience of exceptional moments. It was mainly the needs of Generation Y that created the phenomenon of "society's luxurification and logofixation"; characterized by mass purchases of goods due to the visibility of the logo and the aura of the brand taking place in a postmodern spirit (Twitchell 2001; Chadha and Husband 2006; Yeoman and McMahon-Beattie 2006; Husic and Cicic 2009). Post-modernism refers here to the diminution of significance and functional value of goods and services for the appreciation of ephemeral experiences created by hyper-reality and sensory experience (Atwal and Williams 2009).

In the luxury market creating a global, cosmopolitan offer is not new—one of the principles of the DNA luxury business model is to create an aura and promise to fulfil the dreams embodied in standardized goods and to offer them to all those who can afford them, regardless of which country the consumers and their money come from. However it is primarily in response to the needs of the Y and Z generations that the luxury market has changed significantly as it has expanded both the geographical and product range as well as communication and distribution strategies (Delloite, Global Powers, 2018).

Recently, however, there have been increasing voices that Generation Y presents behaviour consistent with their disposal income or place of residence rather than age and the group has been found to be not as homogeneous as assumed. The importance of the probable overestimation of this homogeneity is evidenced, among others, by the Luxury Summit 2018 in New York where one of the main points of the meeting was the discussion on the manifestations and causes of the internal diversity of the Millennial generation and its business consequences.

There seem to be several reasons for this diversity. Age can be analysed in at least in two ways—as a physical, metric criterion (the most common way of understanding in the analysis of segmentation) but also as individually perceived, reflecting the psychological state of a person, the so-called mental age. A lot of research proves that physical age is not equal to mental age, and people usually feel younger than their metrics indicate (Sherman et al. 2001; Van Auken et al. 1993). The consequence of this discrepancy is that segmentation by metric age may simply not take into account those consumers who feel younger than their metrics show. Therefore, in order to prepare more precise marketing strategies, it seems appropriate to study the perceived mental age (Gwinner and Stephens 2001; Mathur and Moschis 2005; Szmigin and Carrigan 2000). The way consumers perceive themselves is an important indicator of identity and should be taken into account in communication and brand image creation (see Bian and Forsythe 2012; Stokburger-Sauer and Teichmann 2013).

Research into the process of identity development (Diehl and Hay 2011; Robins and Morley 2002) shows that attitudes and values change throughout life, modifying needs and motivations. Age is therefore an important segmentation criterion but it is worth taking into account that the period of adolescence, adulthood and expectations related to these stages are socially shaped and specific to countries, regions or religions. In some cases within a single global Millennial cohort there can be both parents and their children; people who are just entering the adult world as well as those who are already well rooted in it and due to different social roles and life responsibilities their value systems will probably distinctively differ.

6.1.2 Gender as a Differentiating Factor in the Approach to Luxury

Gender is a popular category of marketing classifications and although it refers to biological differences it also contains a number of social expectations and norms related to its role (Deaux 1985; Brewer and Lui 1989). As West and Zimmerman (1987) write gender is not an individual attribute but socially transmitted and cultivated. Women and men pursue socially conditioned gender beliefs in order to achieve a culturally defined gender identity. Social gender theory studies (Gromkowska-Melosik 2011; Ridgeway 2011; Titkow 2007; Eagly and Wood 1999) clearly demonstrate how the process of socialisation leads to the assimilation and replication of gender-related beliefs in accordance with social norms. Such beliefs concern typical or desirable features of a given gender, roles, attitudes, or even patterns of feeling (dominant, independent men, guided mainly by logic and emotional submissive, empathic women, for example). These culturally and socially conditioned beliefs concerning genderand its physical, psychological and mental predispositions lead to globally observed asymmetries related to differences in access to education, taking up positions in the business and politics or wage inequalities as examples.

The concept of culturally conditioned gender allows the search for different perceptions of luxury goods' value through the prism of social roles and status. Culturally conditioned gender identity may influence goods and the role they serve while consumed and exhibited publicly. There is a great deal of research on the causes of the differences in the social, economic and political roles of women and men (see Eagly [1995] for an overview), but only studies in which the conclusions are relevant to the question of the value of luxury will be quoted here.

Sundie et al. (2011) provide empirical evidence of the link between men's show consumption and their sexual partner search strategies. By engaging in so-called visible consumption men want to socially legitimise their economic status in order to increase their attractiveness as partners in the eyes of women. The credibility of the material position also gives the feeling of a greater possibility to select more physically attractive partners. The mechanism of the partner selection strategy itself seems also simpler for men compared to women's assessment of a man's attractiveness. Women usually perceive men in terms of economic and social status as a guide to evaluate their partner as a potential sire and life carer (see also De Block and Dewitte 2007). Men are more inclined to judge women on the basis of their physical attractiveness and although this is not the only selection criterion Buss (1989) research shows that this is a common phenomenon, independent of culture.[1]

Workman and Lee (2011) show that the perception of different characteristics and components of the good' s value (in this case fashion) is sexually differentiated and highlights the psycho-social background of this differentiation. The results of the authors' research show that men have a stronger tendency to create their own independent self while distancing themselves from the opinions of others about themselves. Women build their identity by incorporating the opinions of other people into their own image. Such an attitude manifests itself in a relatively greater sensitivity to social perception and care for their appearance. As a consequence for women and much stronger than for men,

[1] Although the canons of beauty are culturally driven.

external appearance and social image influences their self-esteem (see also Croson and Gneezy 2009).

Despite these socially and culturally conditioned differences in perception today we are dealing with a dynamic (mainly within developed economies) trend of gender equality and the abandonment of the traditional division of social roles attributed to women and men. Women increasingly hold occupations that were the domain of men whereas men take on more responsibilities and roles historically considered to be feminine. In this sense the contemporary perception of the value of goods (including luxury goods) may not be so diverse. Both women and men, especially those holding important positions in the professional and social hierarchy, can use luxury goods as emblems of social position or equally treat luxury consumption as a form of entertainment and reward for hard work.

6.1.3 Education and Perception of Luxury

According to Samovar et al. (2014), formal education creates awareness of what is considered important in a particular cultural context: what is considered appropriate, good or bad behaviour, what norms and attitudes are accepted and what are the social expectations of individuals. Through long-term exposure to a specific educational system, people (although not fully and equally) begin to share a system of similar beliefs which resembles the process of normative institutionalization (Berger and Luckmann 1967; Scott 1995; Tolbert and Zucker 1996; Stępień 2016). At the heart of this kind of institutionalisation is the professionalisation of life; the duplication of certain routines, procedures, use of a certain common code and theoretical foundations in reasoning embedded in a given scientific or ideological paradigm. Educational systems and subsequent professions shape an individual's identity. In order to successfully finish a school and then successfully pursue our profession we not only need to obtain specific information but also to use specific communication codes and the desired types of behaviour or symbolic emblems (Samovar et al. 2014; Vågan 2011). The nature of a certain type of education or having a function in a given professional circle favours the internalisation of group-specific behaviour. With regard to luxury goods this does not necessarily imply the purchase of certain brands but constitutes a kind of normative pressure to adapt to aesthetic or even ethical requirements, to present a particular lifestyle and so on and it is also a way of ensuring that the products of a certain brand are not used in any other way.

However education is not always positively correlated with the level of knowledge (or even less with the wisdom) of the individual. Certificates or diplomas of a given school or university legitimise the fact of acquiring a certain level of knowledge consistent with the profile of a certain education. The type of education may affect the perception of luxury goods. Probably technical education will allow us more competently to assess the technical values of cars, whereas artistic education will broaden the spectrum of view on the aesthetic values of such goods, while theological or philosophical education will deepen the understanding of the axiological foundations of the phenomenon of luxury consumption or may shape the perception of luxury as morally non-neutral goods.

6.1.4 Income or Materialism as a Category Differentiating the Perception of Luxury?

The level of disposable income determines the level of consumption of luxury goods. One of the most important features of luxury is the high price of these goods, hence the necessary condition for their acquisition is to have either adequate income, savings or creditworthiness.[2]

The highest revenues are achieved by suppliers of luxury goods thanks to purchases of consumers not only from highly developed economies (USA, Japan, Germany, France, Great Britain, Italy, Canada), but also due to sales of these goods in China, India or Brazil (Euromonitor, 2018, Ranked: Top 10 Countries by Consumer Expenditure).

The level of luxury sales in China, India or Poland indicates that consumers from these countries can increasingly afford such purchases while the dynamics of growth in these purchases shows that in order

[2]However, the latter option is necessarily a short-term but quite widespread.

to “catch up” with developed economies and legitimise their social status, aspiring consumers spend a relatively larger part of their budgets on luxury purchases than consumers from the so-called developed economies (Euromonitor, World Market for Luxury Goods, 2018).

However the financial capacity (or lack thereof) to make luxury purchases does not necessarily have to be linked to the higher valuation of these goods or services due to relativism and the impact of deprivation on valuation. The valuation of goods beyond our purchasing reach can be much higher providing we wish to have them. On the other hand the lack of purchasing power of the products that we like can cause frustration and this in turn can affect their perception of them as unnecessary, morally and socially harmful and their consumption can be considered unethical and snobbish. However the motives for negative assessment should not be found only in the material status of the individual. Exactly the same, generally negative or neutral attitude towards luxury goods can be shown by a wealthy consumer whose value system is much more oriented towards the environment and helping others. Moreover wealthy people accustomed to consuming luxury goods may rate their value lower than “newcomers”. Purchases of products considered to be luxurious also cease to be an experience of luxury, if they are relatively frequent. It also concerns the perception of brands from the lowest level of the pyramid, which become ordinary goods for instance. However while we can say that wealthy people spend nominally more on luxury goods, we cannot unambiguously link these purchases to a specific perception of their value.

6.2 Consumers' Perception of the Value of Luxury Goods and Their Social, Demographic and Economic Characteristics: Foreign Research Findings

6.2.1 The Perception of Luxury and Age

Dubois and Laurent (1993) in their European survey of 12,500 consumers from Germany, France, Spain, Italy and the UK and their attitudes towards 30 international luxury brands, examined the usefulness of different geographical and socio-demographic criteria in creating segments of luxury consumers. Although there are some differences (in terms of CLVP) between European countries the results show that income, education and occupation differentiate consumers much more than the country of residence. The authors also noted the nature of the relationship between luxury consumption and the age of consumers. Medium-aged consumers (aged between 35 and 49) spend the most on luxury and from that point on the interest in luxury shopping decreases. The authors explain this dependence by the relatively high purchasing power and social status of this group which encourages the consumption of luxury.

Schade et al. (2016) conducted a survey among 297 respondents aged 16–59, divided them into three age groups and investigated the purchasing motivations of luxury consumers in these groups. Four different attitudes towards luxury were distinguished: socio-adaptive, expressive, hedonic and utilitarian. It was found that age differentiates the perception of the social component of luxury values while hedonic and utilitarian components are common to all age groups. Socio-adjustment motivations are characterised mainly by the youngest group of respondents (16–25 years old), but they do not determine the acquisition of luxury brands by middle-aged people (40–59 years old). Self-expression values are relevant only for the group of young adults (26–39 years of age).

Amatulli et al. (2015) in their study of the impact of age on the perception of luxury set themselves the goal of establishing a link between the metric and mental age to denote purchasing motivation. A distinction was made between an external focus/orientation—towards status and social perception and an internal orientation/focus—towards pleasure and private consumption, not publicly displayed. The authors made older consumers (aged 65 and over) the subject of the research, where the results show the following relationships:

- the discrepancies between the declared mental and metric ages of older consumers are higher if their motivation to buy luxury goods is external and social rather than if they are internally motivated,
- when buying luxury goods purchased due to status (external motivation) the brand has a significant impact, whereas for those who buy luxury goods due to internal motivation, particular product characteristics are important but not the brand.

All the studies presented on the relationship between age and the perception of luxury values show that although age differentiates CLVP this perception is closely related to the extent to which an individual is dependent and susceptible to social influences, both regarding the role he or she plays in this society (Dubois and Laurent 1993) and his or her individual susceptibility to shape identity through the prism of social impact (Amatulli et al. 2015; Schade et al. 2016).

6.2.2 The Perception of Luxury and Gender

The most important publications aimed at exploring areas of convergence and diversity in the perception of luxury by women and men are: Stokburger-Sauer and Teichmann (2013) and Roux et al. (2017).

The authors of the first study (Stokburger-Sauer and Teichmann 2013) point out that men have a strong commitment to task-oriented life goals and are motivated by efficiency and performance in a broad sense, while women have a stronger focus on social and emotional goals. The stronger social orientation of women and the resulting increase in purchases of clothes, handbags, shoes or cosmetics justify higher margins of luxury brands targeted at women compared to luxury brands targeted at men. While men predominantly use luxury products and brands to demonstrate their economic status, women emphasize quality, uniqueness and social impact as the main components of the value of luxury brands.

The research of Roux et al. (2017) confirms the findings of Stokburger-Sauer and Teichmann (2013) and shows additional aspects moderating the gender perception of luxury values. According to these authors gender affects three aspects of luxury: elitism, exclusivity and refinement. The research was also combined with personality tests which show that women concerned with their own appearance emphasize the refinement of goods, while men with dominant characteristics attach greater importance to elitism and exclusivity. The women surveyed were more interested (compared to men) in well-being as a target for luxury shopping and were more sensitive to the opinions of others. For the men surveyed an important motive for luxury purchases was to possess exceptional, rare and elite items, as these provided them with a sense of higher status.

6.2.3 The Perception of Luxury and Education, Income and Attitude to Materialism

Dubois and Laurent (1993) point to the strength of the criteria of income, education and occupation as explanations of the volume of luxury purchases: all these variables have a positive impact on the level of luxury brand purchases. However when analysing the impact of education and professional position on CLVP, differences between countries were observed. In Spain and Italy there is a stronger link (than in the other countries surveyed) between the occupational position and the volume of luxury purchases. The authors explain this result by differences in the level of earnings of the so-called white and blue collar groups. As far as the impact of education on luxury purchases is concerned in France, Italy and Spain it is linear and positive, then in Germany and the UK there is no such clear linear relationship. The authors explain these discrepancies in the results by cultural factors. According to the authors in the countries of Latin influence (France, Italy and Spain) there is acceptance of luxury purchases, while in the puritan countries (Germany and Great Britain) social acceptance for luxury consumption is moderate. Dubois and Laurent (1993) discussed the causes and nature of the valuation of luxury by respondents but did not study this perception directly.

Psychological research provides interesting explanations on the motives for purchasing (and consequently evaluating) goods which links such consumption to the sense of materialism. Although these are studies that clearly refer to psychographic features they are discussed here because of their close relationship to wealth. Materialism refers to putting great significance on material goods which manifests itself in behaviours and life goals by the pursuit of wealth (Belk 1985; Kasser and Kanner 2004; Williams 2005; Fitzmaurice and Comegys 2006; Bywalec 2010; Hudders and Pandelaere 2012). Many studies indicate that materialism results in less satisfaction with life and even less happiness. This dependence is explained by the so-called external character of materialistic motivations. They are dictated by the formation of one's own identity through the prism of social evaluation; people who pursue material goals experience more negative feelings and tend to be less satisfied with life than people who are less materialistic about life (e.g. Kasser 2002; Polak and McCullough 2006; Kashdan and Breen 2007; Deckop et al. 2010).

But if wealth reduces the feeling of well-being and happiness why do people strive for it and buy luxury goods? Consumption of luxury now seems to be an attractive way to improve well-being and self-esteem for a growing number of consumers. This is evidenced by the dynamic growth of luxury sales in the last 25 years. Does not shopping bring joy, satisfaction and a better mood?

More light on the links between luxury consumption, materialism and mental and subjective well-being is provided by Hudders and Pandelaere (2012). The authors show that luxury consumption strengthens the materialistic lifestyle but also has positive effects. It was found that materialistic consumers are more inclined to consume luxury goods than people less materially inclined to life. But actually the consumption of luxury leads to improved moods, reduces negative emotions and increases satisfaction with life and this positive impact of luxury consumption on life satisfaction is evidently visible in the case of materialistic consumers and less evident (or non-existent) in the case of nonmaterialists. The former, being more frequent consumers of luxury, derive more satisfaction and good emotions from these purchases than the latter group although the positive effect is not long-lasting.

However the material attitude is not linked to the level of prosperity. If the discrepancy between materialistic aspirations and the impossibility of their realization grows it may lead to a reduced mood or even a feeling of being unhappy. It seems therefore that satisfaction or even happiness does not lie in a materialistic or non-materialistic approach to life but in the convergence of the individual system of values with the level of aspirations, motivation, goals and their realization.

6.3 Differentiation of CLVP in Terms of Age, Gender, Education and Income Level: Results of Own Research

The attempt of my own research was to search for significant relationships between age (analysed as generational affiliation), gender, education and income of consumers and their perception of the value of luxury.

6.3.1 CLVP Perception by Generations Y and X

The results of the following research concern possible areas and causes of convergence or differences between the perception of luxury value by generation X and Y. Two propositions are put forward:

P1 Generations X and Y have similar CLVP.

P2 The perception of CLVP in the Millennium group is internally differentiated due to its large age range, which includes people with different social and family roles.

These propositions are justified on the basis of the following arguments:

- Despite changes in the expansion and extension of luxury brands and the use of online tools (as a response to the needs of generation Y), the image of luxury is standardised worldwide and effectively supported by communication strategies of luxury brands,
- the older group of Generation Y and younger in Generation X, are more similar in their social roles which is a premise for presenting converging views and opinions in the perception of everyday life phenomena, including consumption,
- in both X and Y Generations there may be differences between metric and individually perceived (mental) age, which may affect:
  - different perceptions of luxury consumption within a single cohort,
  - a similar perception of luxury consumption regardless of the cohort.

To test the propositions data from an international consumer e-questionnaire and focused group interviews with generation X and Y were used. The characteristics of the samples and test descriptions are given in Chapter 4.

6.3.1.1 Results of the International Survey

There are no statistically significant differences between the perception of the value of luxury goods between Generation X and Generation Y except for two aspects. The results of the individual value components in the countries surveyed (see Table 6.1) reveal that Generation X in Saudi Arabia places a higher hedonic/emotional value on the worth of the value component than Millennials in Saudi Arabia. This can be explained by the higher purchasing power of the older generation and the assessment of the "playfulness factor" based on experience rather than imagination. Reverse results were obtained in Portugal. Although Portuguese Generation Y presents a low level of purchasing power respondents in this group perceive the hedonic-emotional component of value as important and positive while Generation X considers this component to be insignificant (score below 3). This can be explained by a noticeable trend in conspicuous consumption among young Portuguese and Polish Millenials.

Table 6.1 CLVP in generation X and Y in samples from the countries surveyed

Component		Total	Saudi Arabia	Germans	Poland	Portugal	Turkey	India
Functional	Generation X	3.30	3.83	2.57	3.16	3.2	3.49	3.86
	Millennials	3.51	3.85	2.83	3.13	3.59	3.38	3.95
Hedonic/emotional	Generation X	2.70	3.62	2.14	2.66	2.80	2.48	3.14
	Millennials	2.87	3.27	2.07	2.71	3.34	2.64	3.11
Social	Generation X	3.68	3.83	3.49	3.64	3.69	3.76	4.01
	Millennials	3.70	3.46	3.3	3.78	4.19	3.80	3.99
	Millennials	2.63	3.20	1.94	2.44	2.95	2.05	2.93

Likert scale, where 1 means I completely disagree, and 5 means I completely agree
Source Own calculations

No other elements differentiate the assessment of the value of luxury goods which indicates the similarity of the Millennials to older consumers in the perception of the value of luxury. The data show that functional and hedonic components of values and mimicking and snobbish inclinations among consumers of Generation Y for instance reach a slightly higher level compared to the older generation but these differences are not statistically significant.

The results clearly show that the social component (i.e. social recognition, increase in status due to public exposure to luxury) is the most important value attribute in CLVP for both generations. The second most important is the functional factor while the hedonic factor is considered to be generally immaterial. The low scores of the hedonic component contradict the author's expectations on emotions' significance as luxury value factor. However such low results can be explained by a psychologically well-known and common propensity in measuring consumers' opinions. This inclination refers to expressing rationalised opinions while weakening other stimuli that may be considered irrational or unethical (Lichtenstein and Slovic 2006; Becher 2007; Bettman et al. 1998). This trend may also explain the discrepancies between the assessment of the social component and the negative assessment of statements that would indicate snobbishness or bandwagon inclinations. Respondents admit that purchases of luxury goods visibly improve social status, are a public proof of material success and are desirable but at the same time deny that they consume luxury for snobbish or imitative reasons.

6.3.1.2 Focused Group Interview Findings

The results of the study in the form of *focus group* interviews (FGI) show the relationship between age, family status, material status and perception of the value of luxury.

6.3.1.3 Younger, Less Affluent, Single Millennials

Groups 1 and 3, consisting of younger participants, provided many more statements pointing to a hedonic approach to luxury than in FGI 2 and 4 respectively in which older consumers of Generations X and Y were involved. When asked what luxury is the participants pointed out that it brings joy, both before (emotions connected with waiting) and during the purchase. At the same time positive experiences were inextricably linked to the public exposure of these goods (as shown by the mutual relationship between the social and hedonic component), as well as the joy caused by the very fact that it is financially possible to purchase such goods.

> ...."When I think of luxury, I imagine a Duccati motorcycle... (Diogo, 24, marketer, FGI 1)
>
> "I just love the feeling when I can afford the product I want. I work hard and treat this shopping as a kind of reward... Last month I bought myself a very nice bag of Michael Kors... my friends were a little shocked ......and I feel great when I walk down the street with her." (Mariola, 27, FGI 3)
>
> "If I were rich I would go on a long vacation, buy a lot of perfume, nice clothes and maybe a house, but later, when I have a family... I don't need it now, taking care of the house is a source of stress." (Ana, 25 years old, student, FGI 1)

Importantly the FGI challenged the functional aspect of luxury and the participants during a free exchange of arguments concluded that the most important component of the value of luxury is socially constructed. This social desire contributes to the perception of joy by the individual recipient. Price and brand create a point of reference by suggesting that luxury is associated with high quality.

> "Luxury is unique, rare and very expensive but its price is not justified by its quality, but rather by its brand, its heritage." (quoted from Rita, a designer, 24, very similar statements Antonio, 25, marketer, FGI 1, Catherine, 26, PhD student, FGI 3)

> "High price and brand tell you that it's a luxury but sometimes these things are done in China." (quoted from Antonio, 28, marketer, FGI 1, very similar approach Ewelina, 29, translator, FGI 3)
>
> "Well, sometimes I don't see this quality and beauty in luxury products but they probably have something like that when others buy them. For me in many cases they are simply not worth the money, you can have much better things for far less." (Peter, 32, finances, FGI 3)

The statements quoted here suggest that the strongest component of the value proposition is an appropriately communicated image of the brand. Emphasising a brand's heritage and evoking social desire strengthened by high prices constitutes a convincing message and makes the evaluation of functional characteristics of goods less important.

The discussion about the relationship between the hedonic and social component of luxury values was caused by the moderators' question *"Would you prefer to drive a super luxurious car every day away from the roads (no one sees you and no one will know you have one) or rather use it two days a week in your city and in the area where you live?"*. Initially participants' responses indicated (vote) that the majority (10/6 in FGI 1 and 9/7 in FGI 3) preferred to drive their cars along deserted roads but the group's opinion changed after a rather fierce exchange of arguments (especially in FGI 3), and finally FGI 1 and 3 respondents stated that their joy would be greater when they were able to show themselves in the car to their friends and the general public. The opinions were altered for the following reasons.

> How do you know this car is super luxurious? You must first know that it is considered luxurious by others... society and marketing have built this image into your head so you'll be happy to drive it." (Ludwik, 33, IT programmer, FGI 3)
>
> "Oh, come on, I saw you so proud of your Gucci shirt when I told you I envy you this... Don't tell me you're just wearing it all to yourself." (Anne, 26 to Mariola, 27, close friends, FGI 3)
>
> "Can I drive my car once a week in public places and for three days off-road? I think I'd be the most happy one then... laughter. (Eduardo, 31, marketer, FGI 1)

"Joy comes when you look at yourself through a social mirror, you just feel better because others see that you are wealthy, stylish, it makes you happy and more confident." (Magda, 28 years old, married to an older, very affluent businessman, not working)

At the same time many contributions referred to the sense of frustration associated with the low purchasing power of the participants. Despite the fact that most respondents like luxury they appreciate it for its design, social impact and the positive emotions that its consumption provides, they feel bad when they visit a shop only to see luxury items. Several respondents stressed that when they entered the shop they felt rated by the sellers as consumers outside the target group (Mafalda, 22, FGI 1, Anne, 26, FGI 3, Basia, 27, FGI 3). Even before visiting such shops they have the impression that the sellers recognize their goal is only to observe, not to shop. These beliefs make them prefer to first search for desired luxury goods in e-shops and online forums, check the opinions of other Internet users about their quality and evaluation in order to "get used to" them before going to the shop or to avoid frustration—make purchases online, which is sometimes more affordable.

6.3.1.4 Older, Richer, in Long Term Relationships: Generation X and Y

The results obtained from FGI 2 and 4 show a strong relationship between the opinion of luxury and family status and professional position. The experience of luxury brings with it a comparable level of satisfaction for both older Milleniums and younger and non-Milleniums. The way the participants expressed their attitude to luxury was much more distanced compared to the two younger groups (FGI 1 and 3). The statements indicated that joy is intertwined with discomfort and pressure to consume luxury as a necessary symbol of high social standing.

"I feel a little bored with the company's existing outfits, but I wear Hugo Boss, Armani or Deni Cler's outfits and dresses to underline my position. Besides, I am the boss of 20 women, I have to look stylish, they watch me every day. Brands I wear are designed for women in corporations, they are good quality and are recognizable. When we meet at regional CEO meetings, we have a similar style, brands, but we look for new ones and talk about "new discoveries" during breaks"…. (Mariola, 40, married, CFO, FGI 4)

I am a father of two children, I "bring bread home" so I rarely buy myself something luxurious, but when I do, I want to feel joy and look a little younger and less tired. (Mirosław, 52, entrepreneur, FGI 4)

"If I were super rich, I would buy a house for my family and secure a future for my children, I would probably put aside money to study for them at the most prestigious universities. (Claudia, 34, decorator, FGI 2)

"I used to spend a lot of money on myself before I had a baby. Now I'm on maternity leave… When I look at my "Louboutin" heels that I wore to work every day I can't believe I was intentionally hurting myself but I liked it very much… now it doesn't look normal to me… but I'll probably get over it as soon as I get back to work." (Kinga, 37, chief accountant, FGI 4)

"I have a luxury car (Audi A 8), I buy luxury suits (Salvatore Ferragamo and Tomasz Ossoliński are my favorite brands), I use a Mont Blanc pen, a Rolex watch and a belt from Hermés, but I think it's part of my job, they have to build my image as a professional … or should I come to work wearing a Tesco suit? Would I look like a succesful lawyer to you then? (Dominic, 42, lawyer, FGI 4)

All these statements indicate that luxury is still a factor bringing joy and positive emotions but also an informal social duty in some professional groups where high professional social status is strengthened by the use of the symbolism of luxury goods. The personal priorities of respondents clearly indicate that luxury plays a different role in their lives than in the past when they had no families or permanent relationships. However luxury can bring back the memories of these responsibility-free days and help you feel young, stylish or elegant.

When we asked the question "*Do you prefer to drive a super luxurious car every day on deserted roads (no one will see you and no one will know that you have such a car) or rather use it two days a week, driving around the city and neighborhood*"? we obtained a strikingly different set of answers:

"It's dangerous to drive a car like this in the wilderness, somebody could kill you for it." (Jan, 48 constructor, FGI 4)

> "I'm tired of driving a car, I'd trade it for a whole day off in a week." (Sergio, 46, manager, FG2)
>
> "Definitely off-road but I'd rather not do it at all… if my employees saw me in that car, they would immediately come to my office and demand a raise while the customers would start to suspect that I'm pulling them over to buy expensive toys." (Mirosław, 52, entrepreneur, FGI 4)

The perception of the value of luxury goods is similar in the Millennial cohort and the X generation. The reason for this convergence is the internal diversity of generation Y; within one group there are people with different family and professional roles. The group interviews provided evidence that Millennials consist of at least two groups with different perceptions of luxury value. The opinions of the older Generation Y are very similar to those of CLVP Generation X and although theses results should be treated with caution (due to the fact that only two nations were included in the study) they clearly show that the evaluation of luxury is strongly dependent on the individual's social role.

Although the results of the e-questionnaire indicate that both Millennial and Generation X do not consider the hedonic component to be important in the overall CLVP the FGI results indicate that the emotional factor still plays an important role in the evaluation of luxury products and the whole experience connected with their purchase but in the case of older interviewees it is strongly related to the social context.

Treating Generation Y as a monolithic cohort of global consumers is too deterministic. Millenials are internally diverse "glocal" consumers. The concept of glocalization (Robertson 1992) shows that global and local forces overlap and young people (Generations Y and Z) create their identities under the influence of both national and global trends (Kjeldgaard and Askegaard 2006; Strizhakova et al. 2011).

6.3.2 CLVP Perception: Is It Influenced by Education, Gender or Income?

6.3.2.1 Results of the E-Questionnaire

The distribution of results for particular components of values: social, functional, hedonic and aesthetic, divided into sex, education and income was examined. Table 6.2 shows the averages of the individual responses in CLVP.

The following conclusions emerge from the analysis of the data in Table 6.2:

- there are no statistically significant differences between women and men in the evaluation of the individual components of values: for both sexes the most important are the aesthetic and social components with women valuing aesthetics and social impact slightly higher and the functional and hedonic bases of CLVP slightly lower than men,
- The value of social and aesthetic components increases with the education of the consumer,

Table 6.2 Importance of particular components of CLVP in groups by gender, education and income

Criterion	Functional dimension	Hedonic dimension	Social/status dimension/	Aesthetic dimension
Female	3.21	2.71	3.65	3.72
Male	3.45	2.79	3.61	3.56
Professional	3.20	2.78	3.54	3.56
Below and Bachelor incl.	3.68	3.14	3.59	3.61
Msc, MA and above.	3.20	2.68	3.68	3.64
>800	3.19	2.70	3.59	3.61
801–1800	3.27	2.80	3.85	3.54
1801–5000	3.44	2.91	3.59	3.67
<5000 EUR	3.80	3.13	3.95	3.72

Source Own calculations

- The assessment of functional and hedonic components is relatively highest among people with secondary (below Bachelor) education and those who earn the most in the sample (above EUR 5000),
- there is no clear linear relationship between the income and the valuation of all components of luxury, although the following trends can be observed:
  - All ingredients are important and highly valued for the top-quality group,
  - The importance of the functional and hedonic components increases with the income.

The relations between gender, education and income and snobbish and mimicking inclinations were also analysed. Table 6.3 presents the results of analyses broken down by women and men, and Figs. 6.1 and 6.2 illustrate the development of snobbish and bandwagon inclinations broken down by groups according to education and income.

As shown in Table 6.3, women show stronger snobbish inclinations than men and prefer to purchase exceptional goods, less known and less popular. Taking into account the fact that women rate the aesthetic component of value higher than men, the results obtained are consistent with the findings of Roux et al. (2017) and Stokburger-Sauer and Teichmann (2013). These studies show that women appreciate the exclusivity, refinement and uniqueness of luxury more than men.

Table 6.3 Snobbish and mimicking inclinations of women and men

Statement	N/Y[a]	Female	Male
snob 1—I don't like how many people, even well known, have what I bought	0	63.7	71.1
	1	36.3	28.9
snob 2—I prefer to buy luxury items that are rare, not very popular	0	66.5	69.9
	1	33.5	30.1
bandwagon 3—I love, as what I have is also used by known people	0	87.5	85.7
	1	12.5	14.3
bandwagon 4—I prefer to buy luxury things that people I like, see on TV, etc. have	0	81.4	79.5
	1	18.6	20.5

[a]*N*—indication below 4/ *Y*—indication 4 and above
Source Own calculations

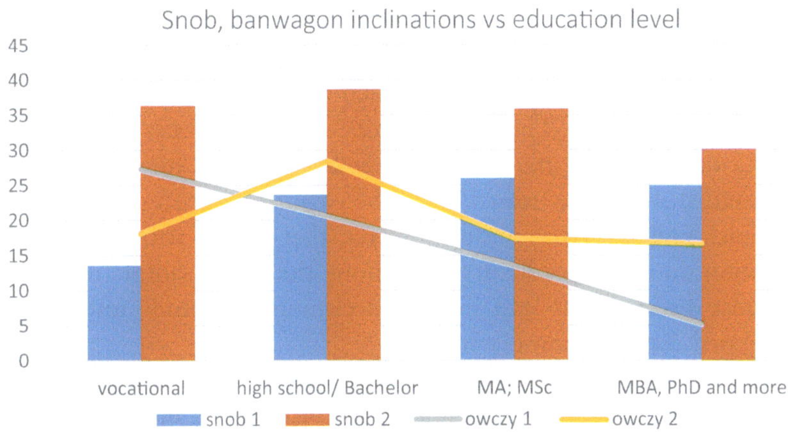

Fig. 6.1 Relationship between education and snobbish and mimicking inclinations (*Source* Own calculations)

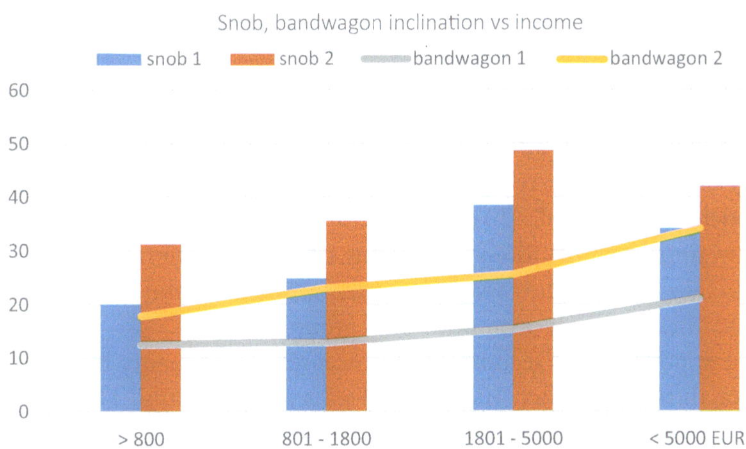

Fig. 6.2 Relationship between income and snobbish and mimicking inclinations (*Note X* axis income in EUR, *Y* axis—percentage of indications of 4 or more [statements as in Table 6.3]. *Source* Own calculations)

The Fig. 6.1. shows the relationship between the level of education and snobbish or mimicking inclinations. While snobbish inclinations do not fall drastically with the level of education the tendency to imitate is clearly diminishing. This can be explained as follows. People with higher education have tangible evidence that they represent a highly valued social characteristic, i.e. education, which is also a form of an ennobling distinguishing feature. The awareness of "*what I know and that I know*" implies that imitative trends (understood as a public manifestation of one's status) should be treated as maybe cognitively interesting, but not desirable. This does not mean, however, that people with the highest education do not enjoy luxury but among the whole sample they have the most distanced (at least in their declarations) attitude towards the accelerated consumption machine.

Figure 6.2 shows the opposite (than in the case of education) relationship between snobbish and mimicking inclinations and income. The group with the highest susceptibility to snobbish behaviour is that with incomes between 1801 and 5000 EUR, which is confirmed by global reports (Delloite 2018), indicating that it is the group of consumers aspiring and rapidly growing in wealth who purchase luxury for its status and social prestige. Apparently the stage of "hectic/ feverish consumption" is followed by calming down, not so much for the purchases themselves as for the approach to them. The information obtained from direct interviews with affluent consumers also reveals that mimicking inclinations are mainly related to one's own group of friends or peers. The article of Han et al. (2010) and Kauppinen-Räisänen et al. (2018) contains similar observations describing the consumption of so-called quiet luxury among the wealthiest accompanied by the tendency to compare oneself mainly with one's own group.

The last point in this section is the ethical reading of luxury by respondents of different gender, income and educational status. There were no differences in the ethical perception of luxury among women and men and among respondents declaring different incomes. The data show that only education is a measure of the nuance of the perceived value of luxury. Respondents with a vocational education and higher than tertiary education present the most critical attitude towards consumer goods. The lowest paid may approach the consumption of luxury as snobby and unethical because of economic deprivation. On the other hand the most highly educated respondents are able to appreciate the social values of luxury on the one hand, but also see a whole range of negative consequences related to its public exposure. It is worth recalling that the group of respondents consists mainly of the inhabitants of countries still catching up with "the old world luxury base" while Germans as a reference group from a highly developed country show the most controversial attitude towards luxury.

The influence of social and demographic features and income on the perception of individual components of luxury values is visible but ambiguous. Age is a differentiating factor in the valuation but combined with the social and occupational roles played by respondents. Similarly visible but non-linear relationships between CLVP are observed depending on gender, income or education. The diversity of CLVP of respondents due to social and demographic features is manifested by:

- a positive and the highest evaluation of the value of all luxury components among the highest-paid respondents,
- an increase in the value of the hedonic and functional components together with income,
- greater snobbish inclinations and evaluation of the aesthetic component among women compared to men,
- perceiving luxury as unethical in the lowest and highest educated groups.

The analysis of the relationship between the surveyed criteria and the CLVP of respondents did not detect statistically significant evidence that social, demographic and economic characteristics differentiate the perception of luxury. The entire theoretical analysis carried out in Chapters 1–3 shows that the evaluation of luxury is the result of many social forces and the individually shaped identity of the consumer. The next step was therefore to carry out statistical analyses which enabled the segmentation of respondents into homogeneous groups in terms of psychological similarity and only in such a way was the relationship between age, gender, education and income and the belonging to a given segment examined.

6.3.3 The Perception of the Value of Luxury and Psychographic Characteristics of Consumers

Lifestyle is a psychological term (see Wind and Green 2011; Coreil et al. 1985) and refers to everyday behavioural patterns typical of people. Lifestyle is conditioned by social background, family status for instance but it is also a resultant of personality and motivation (Horley 1992; Zalega 2013). Human identity reflected inter alia, by a specific lifestyle is created individually and socially through interactions with other people (Collier and Thomas 1988; Yep 1998). Many studies indicate how important causal and effect relationships exist between a specific, identified lifestyle and consumer purchasing behaviour (Bylok 2012; Mazur 2001; Mazurek-Łopacińska 2011).

The analysis of the lifestyle which also manifests itself in an emotional relation to specific goods and shopping behaviours reveals consumer preferences not only in relation to product attributes but also in relation to ways of communication, sales and distribution (Komor 2011; Mróz 2009). Psychographic research is a valued method in marketing as it allows the determination as to what is important for consumers and what, for example, they do not like or tolerate. Thanks to such a database of information it is known which attributes, characteristics of goods should be promoted and which products, brands are reference points for or contrasting brands.

6.3.4 International Segmentation of Consumers of Luxury Goods Based on Psychographic Characteristics: Research Review

Market segmentation can be described as the process of subdividing a large market into smaller, homogeneous markets in some way/group criteria (Weinstein 1987; Kotler and Gordon 1983; Kamakura and Wedel 1999). The similarities in each segment are intended to indicate similar purchasing behaviour. Segmental information is useful for business practitioners to effectively reach their customers with a relevant offer

(Anderson and Vincze 2000; Aaker et al. 2001). The most commonly used criteria for international consumer segmentation are education, age, income or country of residence (e.g. Helsen et al. 1993; Kale 1995). However groups identified by socio-economic factors are unlikely to be homogeneous in terms of consumer attitudes and behaviour (Sheth et al. 1991). The psychographic approach seems to be more effective for luxury goods as seen mainly through the prism of their social, aesthetic but also hedonic functions. Traditional socio-economic variables can be treated as supportive of the description of identified segments.

Despite the described growing interest of scientists in the issue of luxury consumer behaviour there is little work on the international segmentation of luxury consumers on the basis of psychographic variables.

Pioneering research on the psychographic segmentation of the international luxury market was conducted by Dubois et al. (2005). The authors analysed the consumers' responses from 20 countries and distinguished three segments: Elite, Democrats and Reserved. Respondents with Elite attitudes believe that few people own luxury goods and that knowledge is needed to fully appreciate these goods and services. According to this group luxury is very expensive, rare, selectively distributed, symbolizes "good taste" and allows users to distinguish themselves from others. Democrats show attitudes towards luxury that contrast those of the Elite group: luxury is neither rare nor reserved for the few, it does not reflect good taste nor does it require special knowledge to recognize its characteristics. For the third group—Reserved—luxury is not a subject of much interest. These consumers do not identify themselves as customers of these goods and they also perceive luxury in a somewhat negative light: these goods appear to be too expensive, useless, snobbish and flashy. A group of distanced people also feel frustrated when visiting luxury stores. In this study Polish consumers tend towards the elite, Portuguese are the most Reserved from the whole group of twenty countries (which is contrary to the research presented in the book), and German responses are fairly evenly distributed across all segments.

Another international psychographic segmentation of consumers was carried out by Hennigs et al. (2012). Analysing data from 10 countries (including Brazil, India, Hungary and Slovakia as new luxury markets), the authors identify four segments:

- Luxury lovers,
- Hedonists seeking status,
- Satisfied unpretentious,
- Rational, functionally oriented.

All segments that differ in the perception of the functional, financial, individual and social value of luxury tend to have a certain degree of national over-representation. For example luxury lovers with the highest scores of social, individual, financial and functional components of value come from the United States (25.9%), India (16.6%), Hungary (10.4) and Brazil (10.1%). Status seeking hedonists value the emotional and social categories of luxury values and come mainly from the United States (22.5%), India (16.1%), Japan (13.3) and Brazil (10.4%). The segment of the Satisfied unpretentious for whom luxury is closely related to the aspects of exclusivity and uniqueness, includes Spanish (17.9%), Hungarians (13.2%) and Slovaks (12.9%). For this group hedonic and status-related elements of consumption are not important. The smallest segment, the Rationalists, consists mainly of the USA (36.2%) and Germany (14.8%). These are consumers who value functional values most and consume these goods privately, in the privacy of their own homes.

The latest psychographic segmentation of luxury goods' customers was carried out by the Altagamma Institute (2017). Segmentation (identifying 12 groups) applies only to consumers with the highest levels of income and (apart from China) it does not include countries referred to as new luxury markets. In addition the main criteria for differentiation are age, luxury spending and the country of residence of consumers additionally described by some psychographic features. Segments are over-represented nationally and in the case of China the country's inhabitants are relatively most present in segments such as:

- Fashionists; they like to publicly demonstrate their knowledge and convergence with the latest fashion trends,
- Megacitiers: cosmopolitan hedonists, successors of the Yuppies, living in the world's largest cities) and
- Rich Upstarters: fast-growing consumers who legitimize their social status by buying luxury goods.

In each of the studies cited above a clear influence of the place of residence on belonging to segments is visible.

6.3.4.1 International Segmentation Based on Psychographic Features: Results of Own Research

This section uses the results of international e-survey to distinguish three international segments of consumers based on their perception of the value of luxury. Most of the consumers in the sample come from the so-called new, fast-growing luxury markets.

A factor analysis with Varimax rotation was used to identify the criteria (see Table 6.4). The first orthogonal factor contains statements relating to the increase in comfort, satisfaction and self-confidence associated with the consumption of luxury goods. There are mainly statements emphasizing prestige and related to social status and imitation. This factor is called a social mirror. The second factor reflects the financial and functional elements (quality, functionality, value for money). It is called functionality as in the original Wiedmann, Hennigs and Siebels scale (2009).

The third factor reflects the feeling of rarity, desire and elegance as a feature of luxury products acquired because they are popular and rare and hence make an impression on other people. This factor is called the aura of the product. The fourth category is a combination of hedonic and snobbish features: luxury goods bring a lot of joy but only if they are rare, desirable and cannot be sold in large quantities. This factor is called individualism. The fifth category reflects all the negative emotions and attitudes associated with the image, purchase and use of luxury goods:

Table 6.4 Scales forming orthogonal criteria for international psychographic segmentation

Statement	Social mirror	Functionality	Product aura	Individualism	Negation
Buying luxury products makes me feel more confident	0.666	0.164	0.136	0.356	−0.123
Buying luxury products is a must; it reflects my professional status	0.666		0.125		0.157
I prefer to buy luxury things that people I respect and admire have	0.647	0.232		0.183	
Buying luxury products is essential because people judge others on what others have	0.638		0.185		0.183
I love it when what I have is also used by famous people	0.623	0.159			0.176
Buying and owning luxury products makes me feel better in the eyes of others	0.593		0.271	0.386	
Buying luxury goods is exciting; it makes me feel like a queen/king	0.591	0.238		0.312	
Buying luxury products is proof that I take care of myself	0.542	0.331		0.118	
Luxury products of above-average quality		0.815	0.131	0.124	
Luxury products are characterized by high quality craftsmanship/workmanship		0.747	0.205	0.25	
Luxury products have above-average functionality	0.242	0.693	0.112		
Luxury products offer the best value for money	0.249	0.644	0.107		

Statement	Social mirror	Functionality	Product aura	Individualism	Negation
Luxury products are a symbol of the highest class of design	0.186	0.538	0.458	0.101	
The price of luxury goods reflects the costs and expenses associated with the production, distribution and sale of these goods	0.372	0.519			
Luxury products are a symbol of high social status			0.675	0.204	
Luxury products make a good impression on others	0.301		0.650	0.168	-0.161
Luxury products are those used by famous people.	0.22		0.639	−0.218	0.285
Luxury products are desired by people	0.227		0.579	0.19	−0.264
Luxury products are those whose brands are very well known	0.283	0.23	0.562	−0.331	0.166
Luxury products are very expensive	−0.162	0.273	0.493		0.289
Luxury products are rare; few people can have them	−0.137	0.167	0.486	0.23	0.272
Luxury products are a symbol of elegance	0.3	0.393	0.470	0.119	−0.126
I prefer to buy luxury items that are rare, not very popular…	0.355	0.148		0.654	
I don't like how many people, even well-known, have what I bought.	0.291			0.574	0.121
Buying luxury products brings a lot of fun	0.344	0.227	0.189	0.491	−0.226

(continued)

Table 6.4 (continued)

Statement	Social mirror	Functionality	Product aura	Individualism	Negation
The price of luxury goods reflects the power of desire of consumers for these goods			0.305	0.445	
Buying luxury products is unethical	0.148				0.769
Buying luxury products is frustrating; I feel intimidated by the whole process and the place of purchase	0.189				0.684
Buying luxury products is snobby		−0.164	0.253	0.201	0.622

Extraction Method: Principal Component Analysis, Rotation Method: Varimax with Kaiser Normalization, a Rotation converged in 8 iterations
Source Own calculations

Table 6.5 International luxury market segments identified on the basis of psychographic criteria by *k*-means analysis

Factors/categories	Hedonists	Reserved admirers	Status oriented
Social mirror	0.20618	−0.98982	0.66768
Financial/functional	0.05012	0.31111	−0.35351
Aura of the product	0.19769	0.12069	−0.35995
Individualism	0.91542	−0.46756	−0.70715
Negation	0.03552	−0.2473	0.18681

Source Own calculations

luxury is an unethical snobbery that causes frustration when shopping. This factor is called negation.

On the basis of such criteria, a k-mean analysis was carried out and three market segments were constructed on this basis (Table 6.5):

- Hedonists:
- Reserved Admirers;
- Status-oriented.

The first segment—Hedonists—is made up of individuals with strong internal motivations (see Schwartz, Chapter 1), for whom positive emotions and a sense of uniqueness are the main attributes of value. Luxury goods serve as a means to distinguish their owners from the crowd and highlight their individuality or good taste. Hedonists also show snobbish behaviour relatively more often than other segments. The impression that luxury products have on others (reflected in two dimensions: the aura of the product and the social mirror) is of moderate importance to this group. A slightly less important category is the functional and financial dimension of luxury. Hedonists, who treat luxury goods as a tool to increase satisfaction, do not see anything wrong with their consumption. In general they have neither negative associations with luxury nor they perceive buying or using luxury goods as snobbish.

The segment of Reserved Admirers is made up of people who see the main value of luxury products in their design and craftsmanship and because of these qualities appreciate the impression they make on others. These respondents consider luxury goods to be an object of desire, although they do not agree that possession and use of luxury goods is

Table 6.6 International luxury market segments and their structure in the analysed countries

	Total	Saudi Arabs	Germans	Poles	Portuguese	Turks	Indians	Others
Hedonists	39.2	36.3	24.6	49.8	55.4	19.1	20.6	47.6
Reserved Admirers	31.4	23.0	44.7	31.1	21.7	57.4	21.8	32.9
Status-oriented	29.4	40.7	30.7	19.1	22.9	23.5	57.6	19.5

Source Own calculations

an indicator of high social status. Moreover, they do not associate the process of buying or using luxury with a way to increase satisfaction or experience positive emotions. For this group the reason for buying luxury goods is their uniqueness but their public presentation is not associated with unethical behaviour.

The third group is strictly Status-oriented. These consumers regard luxury products as symbols of social status and prestige. Interestingly this is their main and only reason to buy luxury goods. This group of respondents emphasizes the mimic proneness most strongly and therefore perceives the uniqueness of the product as a demotivating factor. This segment associates uniqueness with low popularity and therefore insufficient social impact. As it turns out for this group buying and using luxury goods is not connected with positive emotions or taking care of oneself. Luxury goods are a tool for achieving the desired social effect: to show that their owner/user is a member of a prosperous and influential group. They justify belonging to "few", though not necessarily "happy"[3] groups.

The breakdown of the segments by country (see Table 6.6) shows the clear impact of a country on its membership of a particular group. The Portuguese and Poles are mainly Hedonists while the Turks and Germans are mostly Reserved Admirers. The most Status-oriented are Indians and Saudis. Following the crowd and trying to demonstrate one's social status by luxury purchases is of relatively minor importance in Poland, Turkey

[3]This is a reference to a frequently used statement in the analysis of luxury consumers: they belong to the group of the "happy few". See also Kapferer and Bastien (2012).

Table 6.7 Structure of psychographic segments by gender, age and education

	Sex		Generation		Education	
	F	*M*	*X*	*Y*	*Mean and below*	*Above mean*
Hedonists	46.8	36.3	40.9	41.5	44.3	40.5
Reserved Admirers	32.1	34.3	34.6	32.3	22.8	35.9
Status-oriented	21.1	29.5	24.5	26.1	32.9	23.6

Source Own calculations

and Portugal although it is strongly emphasized in Saudi Arabia and India.

There are more women than men in the Hedonist group (see Table 6.7). Reserved Admirers are more (than in other segments) people with higher education. Status-oriented, on the other hand, are more often men and respondents with primary or secondary education. There is also a difference between the average income in the Status-oriented segment (relatively highest disposable income). This is mainly due to the nationality structure of the Status-oriented segment; as much as 40% of them are Saudi Arabs and 30% are Germans, consumers from countries with much higher GDP per capita than in the other countries in the sample. At the same time, 90% of the total sample earns (or has at its disposal) less than €5000 and can be treated as aspiring consumers. There is practically no difference in segmentation between the X and Y Generations.

The scatter plots (Fig. 6.3) show how far the criteria (age, gender, education, income, country of residence) are from the identified segments. The three identified segments are characterised by a clearly differentiated approach to luxury goods due to orthogonal factors (social mirror, functional factors, product aura, individualism, negation).

Scatter plots also show that the valuation of luxury goods, although strongly dependent on the country from which the consumer comes, is not the main differentiating factor in all orthogonal factors. For example, Germans and Poles have a very similar view of luxury from an ethical point of view. However, if we take into account the aura of the product, the group that is above is Poles (usually those over 25 years of age and with higher education), while Germany does not seem to consider this criterion as important.

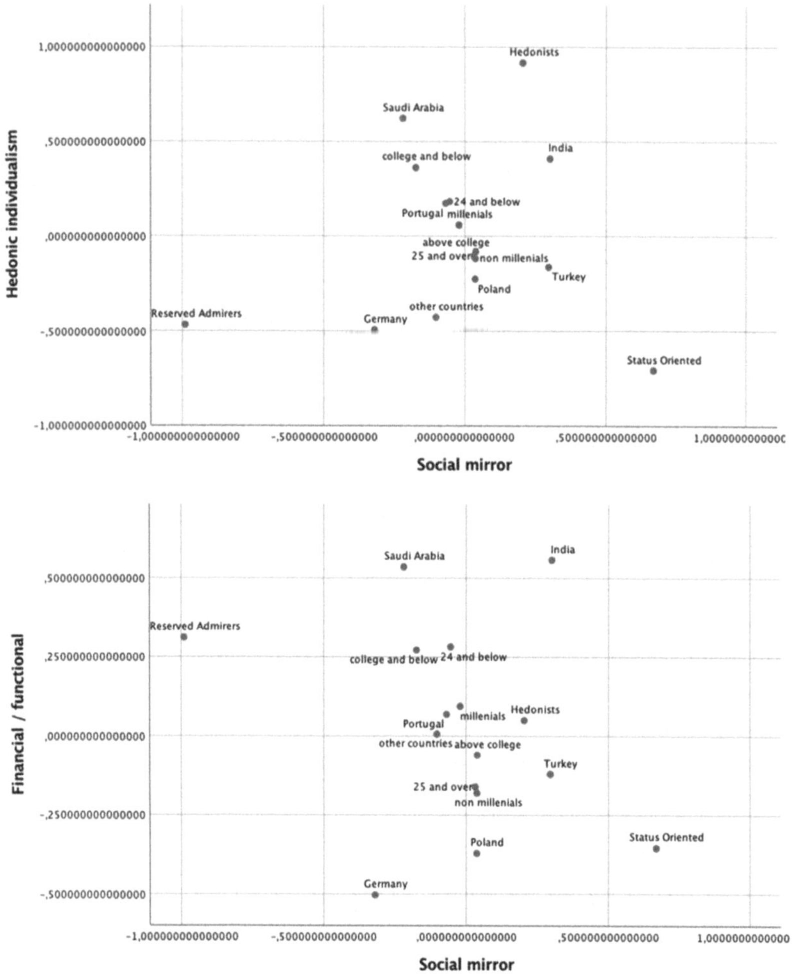

Fig. 6.3 Consumer segments—scatter plots according to orthogonal factors based on psychographic traits

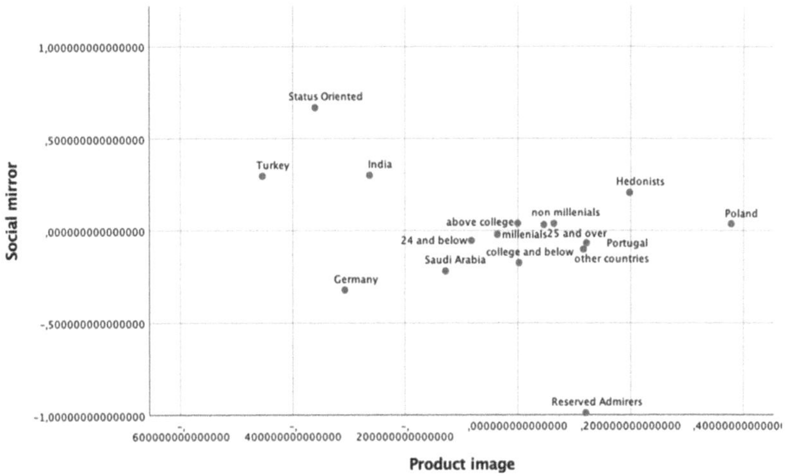

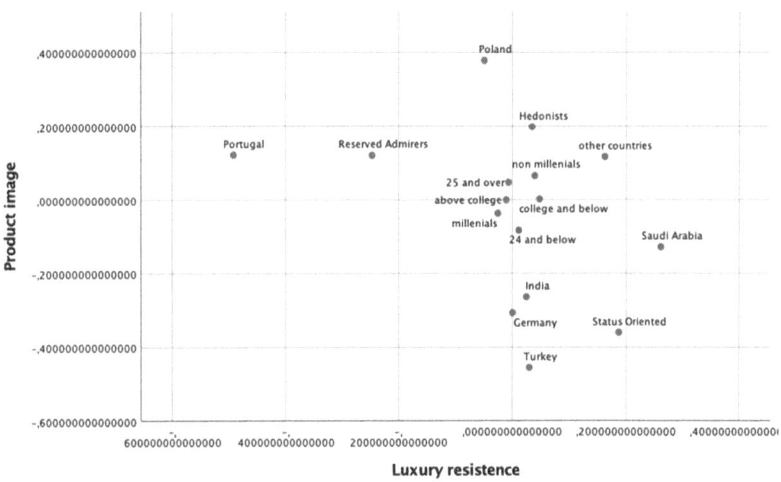

Fig. 6.3 (continued)

Chi square ($\chi 2$) with Cramer's V effect size for nominal variables (gender, nationality, generation X or Y) was used to illustrate the extent to which the country of residence, age, sex, income and education explain affiliation to a specific psychographic segment. A contingency analysis of assignment to consumer segments with nationality revealed a significant relationship between these two variables, $\chi 2$ (12, $N = 930$) $= 120.41$, $p < .001$, $V = .25$. Significant relationships were also found for age groups $\chi 2$ (2, $N = 930$) $= 12.94$, $p = .002$, $V = .12$, and for education groups $\chi 2$ (2, $N = 930$) $= 21.57$, $p < .001$, $V = .15$. A relationship with sex turned out to be not significant, $\chi 2$ (2, $N = 930$) $= 3.48$, $p = .18$, $V = .061$, same for the generation X/Y, $\chi 2$ (2, $N = 929$) $= 4{,}00$, $p = .13$, $V = .066$. The findings do not mean that age, income, gender or education does not correlate with the perception of luxury demonstrated by other studies (Schade et al. 2016; Amatulli et al. 2015; Roux et al. 2017, Stokburger-Sauer and Teichmann 2013; Dubois and Duquesne 1993). However the above analysis shows clearly that consumers share their perception of luxury on the basis of psychic similarities to a larger extent than socio-demographic characteristics.

Psychographic segmentation also reveals the role of the hedonic factor—important for one of the groups (Hedonists) and the social factor, important primarily for the Status-oriented. These two groups also present different inclinations: while Hedonists tend to be snob prone, Status-oriented demonstrate bandwagon tendencies.

6.4 Status-Oriented Consumption, Imitative Inclinations and Snobbish Tendencies in Assessing the Value of Luxury

An individual's assessment of luxury value is influenced by other people. Not only what we think and feel about a product but also how it is evaluated by other consumers—especially those with whom we like to compare ourselves becomes important (Vigneron and Johnson 2004; Kastanakis and Balabanis 2012). The importance of others' opinion depends on the individual susceptibility to the environmental social influences. In addition the reference group (with whom we compare ourselves) and the purpose of comparisons play an important role: whether they are to serve self-assessment (parallel and upward comparisons) or self-empowerment (downward comparisons).

The following are the results of research showing the extent to which externally or internally driven motivation combined with the choice of a particular reference group is combined with mimicry and snobbish tendencies to luxury consumption.

6.4.1 Conspicuous Consumption, Bandwagon and Snobbish Tendencies: A Review of Foreign Studies on Luxury Goods

Veblen (1899, 2005) was a precursor of describing the phenomenon of consumption for show, also known as *conspicuous consumption*, the purpose of which is to prove that the owners of luxury goods are affluent and socially influential. The status and wealth indication is loud or ostentatious in this case.

Status-oriented consumption, however, does not have to be loud. Luxury brands embody a specific status charge that is the result of their recognition (Vigneron and Johnson 2004, 1999; Kapferer 1997; Sikora 2012; Bombol 2012). Their purchase can only be dictated by the desire to signalize the status in society, or can result from the desire to strengthen one's own image with the use of a brand whose attributes coincide with the personal perception of oneself (Burgiel 2014). Although both show consumption aimed at emphasizing individualism they have the same effect, the rationale for these purchases is different. O'Cass and McEwen (2004) and O'Cass and Frost (2002) also perceive these different premises and propose distinguishing between show consumption (when the aim is to build an image) and status-oriented consumption (when the aim is to emphasise the status). Research by O'Cass and McEwen (2004) conducted on young consumers[4] also reveals that:

[4]Age of respondents: 18–25 years, analysis of the so-called new luxury: new brands from the lower level of the pyramid vs. old brands from higher levels and premium brands.

- there is no differentiation in status-oriented consumption between men and women,
- there are clear gender differences regarding show, image-building oriented consumption.

Women more often build their image on the basis of the opinions of others and thus are more sensitive to the attributes of goods emphasizing their uniqueness and exclusivity. Psychographic segmentation confirms these observations: women more often than men show snobbish inclinations and more often shop in order to experience positive emotions.

Kastanakis and Balabanis in two in-depth studies describe psychological premises for imitative and snobbish behaviours (Kastanakis and Balabanis 2012, 2014). Imitation (also bandwagon inclination) depends on the tendency to buy what is popular (Chaudhuri and Majumdar 2006; Vigneron and Johnson 1999) while snobbish inclinations result from the desire for rare, exceptional and unpopular things (Corneo and Jeanne 1997). Kastanakis and Balabanis demonstrate that the specified inclinations are derived from the internal or external control locus and that:

- the consumer's susceptibility to the normative influence of the environment is positively correlated with the imitation, bandwagon consumption of luxury goods,
- independence, combined with low susceptibility to external influences, is negatively correlated with a tendency to imitate,
- the internal locus of control and the independent self-concept strengthens the tendency to acquire rare and exceptional things (snobbish inclinations), and the external locus of control and the self-concept dependent on the environment weaken this tendency.

The authors also observed that the tendency to express oneself creatively is positively correlated with imitation and not snobbish inclinations. This apparent contradiction is explained by the ability of a group of imitators to combine non-luxury and luxury goods in order to create a unique image and show social status at the same time. This research result explains women's propensity to buy exceptional items while at the same time adhering to fashion which satisfies both the need for exceptionality and the need to follow popular trends (Brewer and Gardner 1996).

The relationship between snobbism and the pursuit of crowd and snobbish inclination is explained by Festinger's theory of social comparison (see also Chapter 2) and its relationship to status-oriented consumption is studied by Han et al. (2010). By segmenting luxury consumers using wealth and status criteria the authors show which consumer groups apply which reference schemes (see Fig. 6.4).

Patricians compare themselves with the members of their own group and send silent signals expressing themselves through the image. Wealthy status-oriented Parvenus use loud signals in luxury consumption. Such a strategy is supposed to clearly distinguish them from the group of the poor and not socially influential and they compare themselves with the higher (in terms of consumption sophistication and a social class) reference group of Patricians. Posers, the less wealthy of the status-oriented compare themselves primarily with richer consumers imitating their consumption patterns as much as possible (by consuming goods from the lowest level of the luxury pyramid, for example). Proletarians do not engage in luxury consumption and have neither the need to demonstrate their non-existant high status nor the means to do so. The author's own research described below analyses snobbish and imitative tendencies showing at the same time that the affluent interlocutors compare themselves within their own affluent group and accurately reflect Han et al. (2010) scheme.

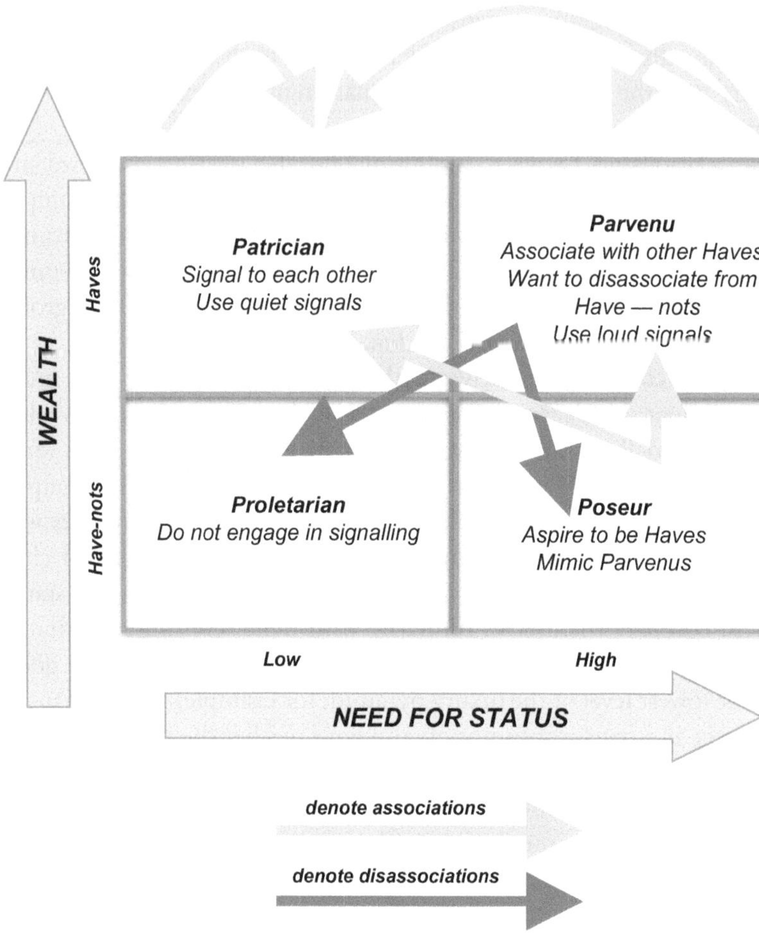

Fig. 6.4 Relationship between the level of wealth, the need to demonstrate status and the strategy for four consumer groups to signalize wealth (*Source* Han et al. [2010])

6.4.2 Between Snobbery and the Pursuit of the Crowd in the Valuation of Luxury: The Results of Our the Author's Own Research[5]

This section is devoted to exploring the grounds of snobbish and mimicking behaviour among luxury consumers and focuses on researching their possible interconnectedness. So far scholars have analysed both effects as an opposite in consumer behavioural tendencies but the findings allow a search for mutual dependencies between these trends. In order to explore and discuss these two tendencies and their possible connections two different methods were used. The first was quantitative in the form of an international e-survey among consumers (described already in previous chapters), while the second—which allowed for a more in-depth exploration of findings—a qualitative semi-structured interview with affluent consumers.

6.4.2.1 Results of the E-Survey

Table 6.8 summarises the perception of luxury by those consumers who show a clear snobbish or imitative trend (answers 4 or 5) compared to the rest of the respondents.

The respondents who show snob inclination generally value all components of luxury value higher than those who do not demonstrate such a tendency. The most valued component is of a social nature, with positive hedonic facets while these data are below average in the whole sample (less than 3). The most striking difference is reflected in the "fun factor"—a very important driver for respondents with a snobbish attitude—while less than important for the rest. Interestingly respondents with a snobbish tendency consider luxury purchases more snobbish than other respondents which may imply that they do not value it negatively.

The findings also demonstrate the interconnectedness of the snob and bandwagon tendency. The respondents who want to "stand out from the crowd" more often declare that—in their decisions on luxury purchases—they prefer luxury products that are already used by people

[5]Findings were also published in Stępień (2018).

Table 6.8 Comparison of consumer perception of luxury with snobbish and imitative inclinations with the rest of the respondents

			The bandwagon effect				Snob inclination			
			I like to have what other people have		I buy what the people I know value…		I do not like it when others have what I have		I like to buy things that are rare, not very popular…	
W	Total/responses	Total	1–3[a]	4–5	1–3	4–5	1–3	4–5	1–3	4–5
s	*Luxury products are a symbol of high social status*	3.56	3.52	3.72	3.51	3.7[illegible]	3.47	3.78	3.45	3.74
s	*They make a good impression on others*	3.46	3.38	3.88	3.33	3.88	3.41	3.59	3.28	3.76
s	*They are desirable*	3.88	3.83	4.13	3.80	4.13	3.8	4.08	3.73	4.13
h	*Buying them is a lot of fun*	3.23	3.15	3.60	3.07	3.67	3.05	3.62	2.92	3.64
h	*Buying them is proof that I am taking care of myself*	2.78	2.63	3.45	2.56	3.4	2.67	3.02	2.55	3.09
h	*Buying them makes me feel better, I feel more confident*	2.79	2.61	3.61	2.50	3.57	2.60	3.19	2.42	3.27
h	*Buying luxury is exciting: I feel like a queen*	2.67	2.47	3.56	2.40	3.43	2.5	3.04	2.33	3.13
sn	*I prefer to buy things that are rare, not very popular…*	3.09	2.97	3.64	2.90	3.63	–	–	–	–
sn	*I do not t like it when other people, even famous people, have what I have*	2.80	2.72	3.13	2.66	3.18	–	–	–	–
i	*I prefer to buy things that those I admire and value already have*	2.38	–	–	–	–	2.33	2.49	2.20	2.62

			The bandwagon effect				Snob inclination			
			I like to have what other people have		I buy what the people I know value…		I do not like it when others have what I have		I like to buy things that are rare, not very popular…	
W	Total/responses	Total	1–3[a]	4–5	1–3	4–5	1–3	4–5	1–3	4–5
i	*I like to have the same things as other famous people*	2.57	–	–	–	–	2.45	2.83	2.29	2.95

Source Own elaboration of the legend: [a]1–3—answers from completely disagree to difficult to say; 4–5—answers: agree and completely agree; s—social component of values, h—hedonic, sn—snob, i—imitation

they appreciate and admire and they “love to have the same things that well-known people have.” Even though the level of the bandwagon effect in the snob group are still below 3 the data clearly indicate that famous, well-known and socially respected members of society form the higher level reference group, whose lifestyle the snobbish respondents want to copy more frequently. This is a visible sign of the upward self-evaluation related far more to the bandwagon than the snob tendency. Similarly to snobbish respondents bandwagon- prone respondents value all components of luxury goods higher than those who do not show such an inclination. For the bandwagoners buying luxury items seems more entertaining than for the snobs. The interconnectedness between the snob and bandwagon tendency is even more visible here; the bandwagoners declare that snobbish inclinations are important in their purchase decisions of luxury goods. Buying things that are rare, not popular, seems crucial to their luxury purchases and may be explained by perception bias: even masstige goods are still labelled as luxuries and aspiring consumers do not consider them to be mass products. Self-evaluation within their own peer group probably leads the bandwagoners to the conclusion that some luxuries (irrespective of the tier) are recognized, respected and considered as desirable. These data demonstrate that bandwagoners perceive themselves distinct from their peer groups and declare that they do not like it when many, even well-known people, have what they bought.

6.4.2.2 Interviews with Affluent Consumers

This part of the empirical evidence comes from the informal semi-structured individual interviews with fourteen affluent consumers of both sexes. The author asked the individuals to comment freely on their own and their friends' attitudes towards luxury goods. A selection of excerpts regarding their bandwagon or snob inclinations is shown below. The findings generally illustrate a strong tendency to conform with their own peer group, despite individual statements. All the interviewed individuals may be categorized as snob-prone because they admit that they would rather opt for something unique, very rare, than a popular luxury label and that they do not like others—even celebrities or stars—to have the same things that they possess. At the same time they admit that they buy certain luxury brands as it is "considered improper not to have them" (female, 43, Polish). In this sense the statements about difference need to be interpreted from the point of view of the preservation of self-esteem rather than through a real search for uniqueness. Many utterances elaborated on the pressure to conform to the informal rules of their own peer group. This pressure is object-identified and either comes from externally oriented loved ones (see statement 1), the media (see statement 2), or a general, unspecified pressure to fall into line with the group (statements 1, 2, 3, 4). Such pronouncements shed new light on the bandwagon effect: for the affluent consumers, it is not anymore about following the upper-class lifestyle but conforming to their own peer group by replicating purchases, dress code, and behaviour "considered appropriate for this society" (female, 56, Polish; male, 56, and female, 34, both Turkish).

Statement 1: male (57); evidence of conformity within the peer group: *"I do not understand fashion at all but I know some luxury fashion brands because my wife makes me wear them. She thinks it's simply improper to be illiterate in this area. As far as I know from my male friends, they do the same; just dress as they are expected (of course, to certain limits; I will never wear these pastel jumpers or torn jeans). They also have quite a limited knowledge about fashion and if you asked them to recognize brands from patterns or design, most of them would simply burst out... They know only these that we all wear."*

Statement 2: female (50), pressure to conform from the peer group: *"Now I enjoy fashion much more than five years ago. My husband was sort of a VIP then and – as part of his job – we had to attend many public events. Before that I had considered myself fashion-conscious and thought that I can dress myself nicely and elegantly. But then my photo was published in some gossip magazine with the tag "how not to dress." It was a pretty devastating experience. I had to quickly learn how to conform to this "dress code" and even consulted a stylist... But I was always a bit stressed and uncomfortable before these parties... Now, I feel much more at ease but, at the same time, I must admit that these years taught me a lot. I think I know more about fashion now and can better judge upfront how to dress for certain occasions to fit in but still stay myself."*

Statement 3: female, (43), need to conform to own peer group: *"As I manage a group of mostly women now I have to pay more attention to how I dress for work than previously. This is a German MNC and we have to conform to a quite strict dress code so I wear mainly dress-suits and costumes but as I noticed that Hugo Boss [a German brand] is more respected here than Italian (which I prefer), I started to buy more of this brand."*

Statement 4: male (46), conformity within the peer group: *"To be honest when we meet we all look like clones; especially our spouses. They try so hard to find something unique for these social occasions and, eventually they all come dressed pretty much the same; either in beige suede or navy-blue wool... My wife says that it is absurd but I just see straightened blond hair and big or small bags presented as some kind of weapon or the most advanced technical novelty."*

But there are not only conformance statements. All respondents highlight their need for "unique" purchases with the fun factor being the reason for them. There is a sort of rivalry in searching for the "best items" within the membership group and the strive to stand out from their own group, yet be positively perceived and moderately followed (see statements 5 and 6).

Statement 5: male (45), evidence for upward comparison (snob effect) within the peer group: *"Well as I am not interested in fashion I find shopping for clothes either boring or frustrating. I ask either my wife or my assistant to do that for me. But as I cycle, run and ski quite actively I find it pretty relaxing and fun to search through the web for some outstanding, unique pieces. I do not always buy them for the full price, sometimes I wait till they have some sale because a new carbon bicycle can be pretty expensive... My friends do the same and, sometimes, they get pretty nice stuff. So I admit it might be a sort of competition and show-off between us. For an outsider we may look a bit like boys bragging in the sandpit but at least our devices are useful and technical... compared to these ridiculous bags."*

Statement 6: female (47), snob inclination, need to stand out from the peer group: *"I think that I have my own recognizable style although not everybody may like it. I noticed that some ladies even try to copy it which I find ... ok, as it is both flattering and a bit annoying. But I think, that as we all observe other people and look for inspiration for how to express ourselves through fashion we either set or (even subconsciously) follow the trends."*

During the interviews a differentiated approach to the assessment of their own consumer attitude by other members of society was clearly visible. The Swiss and German respondents (both male) clearly stressed that the exhibition of consumption is in their circles (and countries) considered to be a manifestation of bad taste and exaltation. One should not flaunt wealth publicly but having an expensive (preferably German brand) car or second home in the mountains is not considered as a sign of snobbish extravagance. The areas of spending for luxuries are (for both respondents) mainly travel, watches, jewellery, works of art, or technically advanced home appliances. Most of these expenditures are treated as investments; either in family and friends' relationships, comfort or as a traditional form of monetary investment monies' . For the Turkish respondents (male 56, female, 34, couple, restaurant owner and his wife), the assessment of their wealth by the community was also very important but the nature of the perception of luxury by the community seems radically different.

Statement 7: male (56), female (34), Turkish: *"Manifesting affluence by possessing luxury goods in our society is a proof of success: being resourceful, enterprising and therefore more respectable. But you must be careful with this manifestation: on the one hand, people respect you, but on the other hand, they envy you (because they probably would like the same) and probably think that you have gained this property by fraud, corruption, or other unclean methods."*

6.4.3 Individual Characteristics of Consumers and Their Perception of Luxury: Conclusions

The presented research results, both foreign and the author's own confirm the individual evaluation of luxury conditioned by age and social role, level of education, income or gender. However the most accurate evaluation of luxury is described by segmentation based on psychographic criteria. The second criterion differentiating CLVP is the country of residence. However the fact that residents of one country belong to different segments is a signal to luxury managers that (1) growing luxury markets should not be treated equally as they show clear differences in

CLVP, (2) aspiring consumers should not be treated as a homogeneous group, willing to imitate only because statistically the GDP per capita in the studied markets is lower (Poland, Portugal, Turkey, India), (3) consumers from rich economies should not be classified as snobby (Saudi Arabia, Germany).

In relation to the communication strategy of luxury brands, even in the case of the so-called *masstige* goods, it seems more effective to emphasize their uniqueness and refinement. The question is to what extent this discrepancy between communication and fact does not spoil the image of luxury. The above analysis also reveals that quantitative methods of exploring the perception of luxury values, although they provide a lot of data necessary for statistical analysis, do not show the full range of causes and the nature of their interrelationships. The interviews, although used here as a supporting method, shed more light on the subtle relationships between the individual components of CLVP.

First of all they allowed the detection of subtleties between the social role and mental age of the interviewees and their perception of luxury value. The findings indicate that treating generations X and Y as different and at the same time internally homogeneous can lead to serious cognitive and then managerial business errors. Then qualitative research also allows links between snob and imitative inclinations to be found. These two may be expressed by the same individuals in their attitude towards luxury goods and purchase preferences. There can be several reasons for this ambivalence and interconnectedness. Firstly, both snob- and bandwagon-prone consumers seek differentiation within their own peer groups and want to conform to other superior groups. The difference in snob and bandwagon behaviour lies in the different group as the basis of comparison. For bandwagoners the upper reference group is defined mainly through the prism of their affluence while for snobs the basis of comparison will be other snobs; that is loosely formed sets of individuals, who can recognize and appreciate a superior taste in other snob-prone consumers.

The next difference lies in the motivation. While bandwagoners want to be affiliated with higher social classes snobs want to be socially recognized as superior and unique, not affiliated with any specific group although still recognized as both affluent and socially influential. The reason behind snobbish behaviour can be more of a hedonic nature than for bandwagoners; so the primary motive cannot be of a social but individual hedonic nature. Thirdly, both groups value social recognition highly; although snobs may perceive it as an auxiliary condition to fulfil their hedonic needs. Even though the findings do not support the claim that snobs would value hedonic facets more than bandwagoners the reason for this can be the reverse relationship between the social and hedonic value categories for these two types of consumers. While the social recognition can give joy to bandwagoners snobs find joy in self- pampering and social recognition of what they perceive as unique taste. Moreover as Kastanakis and Balabanis (2012, 2014) report in their research the creative counter-conformity factor positively relates to the bandwagon effect. This factor refers to consumers who seek social distinction but still strive for social approval (Tian et al. 2001). In this sense snobbish behaviour can simultaneously satisfy uniqueness and social affiliation (Brewer 1991; Brewer and Gardner 1996). Festinger's social comparison theory—and its development in Brewer's optimal distinctiveness theory—explain the findings of the co-existence a tendency of both snob and peer conformity among highly affluent consumers. The next reason for the interconnectedness and ambivalence of snob and bandwagon behaviour appears in the highly subjective—and therefore hard to precisely estimate—term of "masses" in luxury goods' consumption. The popularity of any luxury brand rarely leads to its massive consumption which would lead to a lower appreciation of it among its target clients. Such brands can still maintain the image of luxurious in countries either characterized by lower economic development (such as Poland, Portugal, or Turkey) or constrained by other socio-cultural traits (such as Saudi Arabia). In the first case these goods are simply not consumed by the masses because only a small percentage of society can afford them. In the second case the consumption of popular luxury brands manifests a "Western" and (somewhat) prohibited lifestyle. This explains why newly rising luxury markets still recognize some masstige goods as upper-level brands desirable by both snobs and bandwagoners. The search for the areas of snob and bandwagon interconnectedness reveal that quantitative methods of CVPL exploration, even though informative and full with data vital to statistical analysis, do not offer much insight into the reasons for and nature of their interconnectedness. Interviews, although here only used as supportive evidence, shed much more light on the subtle relationships between snob and bandwagon inclinations.

Both e-survey findings and interviews also imply that consumers are not necessarily fully aware of the whole palette of motives that makes them purchase and use luxury goods. The discrepancy of consumer attitudes to luxury is evident but still hard for academics to explain (Otnes et al. 1997) and managers to make business sense of. The data suggest that highlighting exceptional functional features that build a unique and highly desired image of luxury products along with positive emotions forms the winning communication strategy, regardless of the market. Moreover even the bandwagoners feel distinct from the crowd.

References

Aaker, J. L., Benet-Martinez, V., & Garolera, J. (2001). Consumption symbols as carriers of culture: A study of Japanese and Spanish brand personality constucts. *Journal of Personality and Social Psychology, 81*(3), 492–508.

Alden, D. L., Jan-Benedict, E. M. Steenkamp, & Batra, R. (1999). Brand positioning through advertising in Asia, North America, and Europe: The role of global consumer culture. *Journal of Marketing, 63*, 75–87.

Amatulli, C., Guido, G., & Nataraajan, R. (2015). Luxury purchasing among older consumers: Exploring inferences about cognitive age, status, and style motivations. *Journal of Business Research, 68*(9), 1945–1952.

Anderson, C. H., & Vincze, J. W. (2000). *Cases in strategic marketing management*. Boston: Houghton Mifflin Company.

Atwal, G., & Williams, A. (2009). Luxury brand marketing—The experience is everything! *Journal of Brand Management, 16*(5–6), 338–346.

Bahr, N. & Pendergast, D. (2007). Millennial adolescent, the. *Millennial adolescent, The*, ix.

Becher, S. I. (2007). Behavioral science and consumer standard form contracts. *Louisiana Law Review, 68*(1), 117–179.

Belk, R. (1985). Materialism: Trait aspects of living in the material world. *Journal of Consumer Research, 12*(3), 265–280.

Berger, P., & Luckmann, T. (1967). *The social construction of reality: A treatise in the sociology of knowledge* (pp. 52–54). Garden City, NY: Doubleday.

Bettman, J. R., Luce, M. F., & Payne, J. W. (1998). Constructive consumer choice processes. *Journal of Consumer Research, 25*(3), 187–217.

Bian, Q., & Forsythe, S. (2012). Purchase intention for luxury brands: A cross cultural comparison. *Journal of Business Research, 65*(10), 1443–1451.

Bombol, M. (2012). *Kształtująca się polska klasa wyższa: Szkice ekonomiczno-społeczne*. Warszawa: Oficyna Wydawnicza Szkoła Główna Handlowa w Warszawie.

Brewer, M. B. (1991). The social self: On being the same and different at the same time. *Personality and Social Psychology Bulletin, 17*(5), 475–482.

Brewer, M. B., & Gardner, W. (1996). Who is this "we"? Levels of collective identity and self-representations. *Journal of Personality and Social Psychology, 71*(1), 83–93.

Brewer, M. B., & Lui, L. N. (1989). The primacy of age and sex in the structure of person categories. *Social Cognition, 7*(3), 262–274.

Burgiel, A. (2014). *Społeczne zjawiska w zachowaniach polskich konsumentów: Oddziaływania społeczne, naśladownictwo, ostentacja i snobizm*. Katowice: wydawnictwo Uniwersytetu Ekonomicznego w Katowicach.

BusinessInsider. (2019). *The state of GenZ*. https://www.businessinsider.com/gen-z-shopping-habits-kill-brands-2019-7?IR=T.

Buss, D. M. (1989). Sex differences in human mate preferences: Evolutionary hypotheses tested in 37 cultures. *Behavioral and Brain Sciences, 12*(1), 1–14.

Bylok, F. (2012). Orientacja na przyjemność w zachowaniach konsumentów. *Konsumpcja I Rozwój, 1*, 48–60.

Bywalec, C. (2010). *Konsumpcja a rozwój gospodarczy i społeczny*. Warszawa: Wydawnictwo C.H. Beck.

Chadha, R., & Husband, P. (2006). *The cult of the luxury brand: Inside Asia's love affair with luxury*. London: Nicholas Brealey.

Chaudhuri, H. R. I., & Majumdar, S. (2006). Of diamonds and desires: Understanding conspicuous consumption from a contemporary marketing perspective. *Academy of Marketing Science Review, 2006*, 1.

Collier, M. J., & Thomas, M. (1988). Cultural identity: An interpretive perspective. *Theories in Intercultural Communication, 99*, 122–147.

Coreil, J., Levin, J. S., & Jaco, E. G. (1985). Life style—An emergent concept in the sociomedical sciences. *Culture, Medicine and Psychiatry, 9*(4), 423–437.

Corneo, G., & Jeanne, O. (1997). Conspicuous consumption, snobbism and conformism. *Journal of Public Economics, 66*(1), 55–71.

Croson, R., & Gneezy, U. (2009). Gender differences in preferences. *Journal of Economic Literature, 47*(2), 448–474.
De Block, A., & Dewitte, S. (2007). Mating games: Cultural evolution and sexual selection. *Biology and Philosophy, 22*(4), 475–491.
Deaux, K. (1985). Sex and gender. *Annual Review of Psychology, 36*(1), 49–81.
Debevec, K., Schewe, C. D., Madden, T. J., & Diamond, W. D. (2013). Are today's millennials splintering into a new generational cohort? Maybe! *Journal of Consumer Behaviour, 12,* 20–31.
Deckop, J. R., Jurkiewicz, C. L., & Giacalone, R. A. (2010). Effects of materialism on work-related personal well-being. *Human Relations, 63*(7), 1007–1030.
Delloite. (2018). *Global powers of luxury goods 2018*. From z. https://www2.deloitte.com/content/dam/Deloitte/at/Documents/consumer-business/deloitte-global-powers-of-luxury-goods-2018.pdf.
Diehl, M., & Hay, E. L. (2011). Self-concept differentiation and self-concept clarity across adulthood: Associations with age and psychological well-being. *International Journal of Aging and Human Development, 73*(2), 125–152.
Dubois, B., Czellar, S., & Laurent, G. (2005). Consumer segments based on attitudes toward luxury: Empirical evidence from twenty countries. *Marketing Letters, 16*(2), 115–128.
Dubois, B., & Duquesne, P. (1993). The market for luxury goods: Income versus culture. *European Journal of Marketing*.
Dubois, B., & Laurent, G. (1993). Is there a Euro consumer for luxury goods? *ACR European Advances*.
Eagly, A. H. (1995). The science and politics of comparing women and men. *American Psychologist, 50*(3), 145.
Eagly, A. H., & Wood, W. (1999). The origins of sex differences in human behavior: Evolved dispositions versus social roles. *American Psychologist, 54*(6), 408–423.
Elam, C., Stratton, T., & Gibson, D. D. (2007). Welcoming a new generation to college: The millennial students. *Journal of College Admission, 195,* 20–25.
Euromonitor International. (2018). *World market for luxury goods*. From z. https://www.euromonitor.com/world-market-for-luxury-goods/report.
Euromonitor Research. (2018). *Ranked: Top 10 countries by consumer expenditure*. From z. https://blog.euromonitor.com/2017/10/consumer-expenditure-top-10-countries.html.
Fitzmaurice, J., & Comegys, C. (2006). Materialism and social consumption. *Journal of Marketing Theory and Practice, 14*(4), 287–299.

Gerzema, J., & D'Antonio, M. (2011). *Spend shift: How the post-crisis values revolution is changing the way we buy, sell and live*. San Francisco, CA: Jossey-Bass.

Gloeckler, G. (2008). Here come the millennials. *Business Week, 4109*, 46–50.

Gromkowska-Melosik, A. (2011). *Edukacja i (nie) równość społeczna kobiet: studium dynamiki dostępu*. Kraków: Oficyna Wydawnicza Impuls.

Gwinner, K. P., & Stephens, N. (2001). Testing the implied mediational role of cognitive age. *Psychology & Marketing, 18*, 1031–1048.

Han, Y. J., Nunes, J. C., & Drèze, X. (2010). Signaling status with luxury goods: The role of brand prominence. *Journal of Marketing, 74*(4), 15–30.

Helsen, K., Jedidi, K., & DeSarbo, W. S. (1993). A new approach to country segmentation utilizing multinational diffusion patterns. *The Journal of Marketing, 57*(4), 60–71.

Hennigs, N., Wiedmann, K. P., Klarmann, C., Strehlau, S., Godey, B., Pederzoli, D., ... & Taro, K. (2012). What is the value of luxury? A cross-cultural consumer perspective. *Psychology & Marketing, 29*(12), 1018–1034.

Horley, J. (1992). A longitudinal examination of lifestyles. *Social Indicators Research, 26*(3), 205–219.

Howe, N., & Strauss, W. (2000). *Millennials rising: The next great generation*. New York: Vintage Books.

Hudders, L., & Pandelaere, M. (2012). The silver lining of materialism: The impact of luxury consumption on subjective well-being. *Journal of Happiness Studies, 13*(3), 411–437.

Husic, M., & Cicic, M. (2009). Luxury consumption factors. *Journal of Fashion Marketing and Management: An International Journal, 13*(2), s. 231–245. https://doi.org/10.1108/13612020910957734.

Kale, S. H. (1995). Grouping euroconsumers: A culture-based clustering approach. *Journal of International Marketing, 3*(3), 35–48.

Kamakura, W. A., & Wedel, M. (1999). *Market segmentation: Conceptual and methodological foundations*. New York: Kluwer Academic Press.

Kapferer, J.-N. (1997). Managing luxury brands. *Journal of Brand Management, 4*(4), 251–260.

Kapferer, J.-N., & Bastien, V. (2012). *The luxury strategy: Break the rules of marketing to build luxury brands*. Kogan Page Publishers.

Kashdan, T. B., & Breen, W. E. (2007). Materialism and diminished well-being: Experiential avoidance as a mediating mechanism. *Journal of Social and Clinical Psychology, 26*, 521–539.

Kasser, T. (2002). *The high price of materialism*. Cambridge: MIT.

Kasser, T. E., & Kanner, A. D. (2004). *Psychology and consumer culture: The struggle for a good life in a materialistic world*. Washington, DC: American Psychological Association.

Kastanakis, M. N., & Balabanis, G. (2012). Between the mass and the class: Antecedents of the "bandwagon" luxury consumption behavior. *Journal of Business Research, 65*(10), 1399–1407.

Kastanakis, M. N., & Balabanis, G. (2014). Explaining variation in conspicuous luxury consumption: An individual differences' perspective. *Journal of Business Research, 67*(10), 2147–2154.

Kauppinen-Räisänen, H., Björk, P., Lönnström, A., & Jauffret, M. N. (2018). How consumers' need for uniqueness, self-monitoring, and social identity affect their choices when luxury brands visually shout versus whisper. *Journal of Business Research, 84,* 72–81.

Kjeldgaard, D., & Askegaard, S. (2006). The glocalization of youth culture: The global youth segment as structures of common difference. *Journal of Consumer Research, 33*(2), 231–247.

Komor, M. (2011). Segmentacja europejskich konsumentów według teorii stylu życia. *Marketing I Rynek, 7,* 14–19.

Kotler, P., & Gordon, M. (1983). *Principles of market*. Canada: Prentice Hall.

Langer, D. (2019). *Luxury 2030, part 1: Gen Z goes mainstream and disrupts luxury, in luxury daily*. https://jingdaily.com/luxury-2030-part-1-gen-z-goes-mainstream-and-disrupts-luxury/.

Lichtenstein, S., & Slovic, P. (Eds.). (2006). *The construction of preference*. Cambridge University Press.

Maignan, I., Ferrell, O. C., & Ferrell, L. (2005). A stakeholder model for implementing social responsibility in marketing. *European Journal of Marketing, 39,* 956–977.

Mathur, A., & Moschis, G. P. (2005). Antecedents of cognitive age: A replication and extension. *Psychology & Marketing, 22*(12), 969–994.

Mazur, J. (2001). *Zarządzanie marketingiem usług*. Warszawa: Difin S.A.

Mazurek-Łopacińska, K. (2011). Postmodernistyczna kultura konsumpcyjna w kształtowaniu popytu i stylów życia współczesnego. *Konsumpcja I Rozwój, 1,* 47–57.

Meredith, G. E., & Schewe, C. D. (2002). *Defining markets, defining moments: America's 7 generational cohorts, their shared experiences, and why businesses should care*. New York: Wiley.

Mróz, B. (red.). (2009). *Oblicza konsumpcjonizmu*. Warszawa: Szkoła Główna Handlowa-Oficyna Wydawnicza.

Nijssen, E. J., & Douglas, S. P. (2011). Consumer world-mindedness and attitudes toward product positioning in advertising: An examination of global versus foreign versus local positioning. *Journal of International Marketing, 19*(3), 113–133.

O'Cass, A., & Frost, H. (2002). Status brands: Examining the effects of non-product-related brand associations on status and conspicuous consumption. *Journal of Product & Brand Management, 11*(2), 67–88.

O'Cass, A., & McEwen, H. (2004). Exploring consumer status and conspicuous consumption. *Journal of Consumer Behaviour: an International Research Review, 4*(1), 25–39.

Otnes, C., Lowrey, T. M., & Shrum, L. J. (1997). Toward an understanding of consumer ambivalence. *Journal of Consumer Research, 24*(1), 80–93.

Palmer, D. (2008). *Cracking the Gen Y culinary code*. Australian Food News.

Pew Research Center. (2010). *Millennials a portrait of generation next: Confident, connected, open to change*. From z. http://assets.pewresearch.org/wp-content/uploads/sites/3/2010/10/millennials-confident-connected-open-to-change.pdf.

Polak, E. L., & McCullough, M. E. (2006). Is gratitude an alternative to materialism? *Journal of Happiness Studies, 7*(3), 343.

Prensky, M. (2001). Digital natives, digital immigrants: Part 1. *On the Horizon, 9*, 1–6.

Ridgeway, C. L. (2011). *Framed by gender: How gender inequality persists in the modern world*. New York: Oxford University Press.

Robertson, R. (1992). *Globalization: Social theory and global culture* (Vol. 16). Sage.

Robins, K., & Morley, D. (2002). *Spaces of identity: Global media, electronic landscapes and cultural boundaries*. New York: Routledge.

Roux, E., Tafani, E., & Vigneron, F. (2017). Values associated with luxury brand consumption and the role of gender. *Journal of Business Research, 71*, 102–113.

Samovar, L. A., Porter, R. E., McDaniel, E. R., & Roy, C. S. (2014). *Intercultural communication: A reader*. Boston: Cengage Learning.

Schade, M., Hegner, S., Horstmann, F., & Brinkmann, N. (2016). The impact of attitude functions on luxury brand consumption: An age-based group comparison. *Journal of Business Research, 69*(1), 314–322.

Scott, W. R. (1995). *Institutions and organizations*. Thousand Oaks, CA: Sage.

Sherman, E., Schiffman, L. G., & Mathur, A. (2001). The influence of gender on the newage elderly's consumption orientation. *Psychology & Marketing, 18*(10), 1073–1089.

Sheth, J., Newman, B. I., & Gross, B. L. (1991). *Consumption values and market choices: Theory and application*. Cincinnati, OH, USA: South-Western Publishing Co.

Sikora, T. (2012). Zachowanie nabywców produktów luksusowych. Monografie i Opracowania/Szkoła Główna Handlowa, (590).

Stępień, B. (2016). Oblicza pluralizmu metodologicznego w naukach o zarządzaniu–z perspektywy instytucjonalnej. *Studia Oeconomica Posnaniensia, 4*(1), 48–62.

Stępień, B. (2018). Pomiędzy snobizmem a pogonią za tłumem-anomalie zachowań konsumenckich w sektorze dóbr luksusowych. *Marketing I Rynek, 7*, 2–10.

Stokburger-Sauer, N., & Teichmann, K. (2013). Is luxury just a female thing? The role of gender in luxury brand consumption. *Journal of Business Research, 66*(7), 889–896.

Strizhakova, Y., Coulter, R. A., & Price, L. R. (2008). Branded products as a passport to global citizenship: Perspectives from developed and developing countries. *Journal of International Marketing, 16*(4), 57–85.

Strizhakova, Y., Coulter, R. A., & Price, L. L. (2011). Branding in a global marketplace: The mediating effects of quality and self-identity brand signals. *International Journal of Research in Marketing, 28*(4), 342–351.

Sullivan, P., & Heitmeyer, J. (2008). Looking at Gen Y shopping preferences and intentions: Exploring the role of experience and apparel involvement. *International Journal of Consumer Studies, 32*, 285–295.

Sundie, J. M., Kenrick, D. T., Griskevicius, V., Tybur, J. M., Vohs, K. D., & Beal, D. J. (2011). Peacocks, Porsches, and Thorstein Veblen: Conspicuous consumption as a sexual signaling system. *Journal of Personality and Social Psychology, 100*(4), 664–680.

Szmigin, I., & Carrigan, M. (2000). The older consumer as innovator: Does cognitive age hold the key? *Journal of Marketing Management, 16*(5), 505–527.

Tapscott, D. (2008). *Grown up digital: How the net generation is changing your world*. New York: McGraw-Hill.

Tian, K. T., Bearden, W. O., & Hunter, G. L. (2001). Consumers' need for uniqueness: Scale development and validation. *Journal of Consumer Research, 28*(1), 50–66.

Titkow, A. (2007). *Tożsamość polskich kobiet: Ciągłość, zmiana, konteksty*. Warszawa: Wydawnictwo Instytutu Filozofii i Socjologii PAN.

Tolbert, P. S., & Zucker, L. G. (1996). The institutionalization of institutional theory. In S. Clegg, C. Hardy, & W. Nord (Eds.), *Handbook of organization studies* (s. 182). London: Sage.

Twitchell, J. B. (2001). *Living it up: Our love affair with luxury*. New York: Columbia University Press.

US Census Bureau. (2015). *Millennials outnumber baby boomers and are far more diverse*. From z. https://www.census.gov/newsroom/press-releases/2015/cb15-113.html.

Vågan, A. (2011). Towards a sociocultural perspective on identity formation in education. *Mind, Culture, and Activity, 18*(1), 43–57.

Van Auken, S., Barry, T. E., & Anderson, R. L. (1993). Observations: Toward the internal validation of cognitive age measures in advertising research. *Journal of Advertising Research, 33*(3), 82–85.

Veblen, T. (2005). *The theory of the leisure class: An economic study of institutions*. Aakar Books.

Vigneron, F., & Johnson, L. W. (1999). A review and a conceptual framework of prestige-seeking consumer behavior. *Academy of Marketing Science Review, 1*, 1–15.

Vigneron, F., & Johnson, L. W. (2004). Measuring perceptions of brand luxury. *Journal of Brand Management, 11*(6), 484–506.

Weinstein, A. (1987). *Market segmentation: Using demographics, psychographics, and other segmentation techniques to uncover and exploit new markets*. Chicago: Irwin Professional Publishing.

West, C., & Zimmerman, D. H. (1987). Doing gender. *Gender and Society, 1*(2), 125–151.

Wiedmann, K. P., Hennigs, N., & Siebels, A. (2009). Value-based segmentation of luxury consumption behavior. *Psychology & Marketing, 26*(7), 625–651.

Williams, R. (2005). *Culture and materialism: Selected essays (No. 11)*. London, New York: Verso.

Wind, Y. J., & Green, P. E. (2011). In William D. Wells (Ed.), *Some conceptual, measurement, and analytical problems in life style research*. Chicago: American Marketing Association.

Workman, J. E., & Lee, S. H. (2011). Vanity and public self-consciousness: A comparison of fashion consumer groups and gender. *International Journal of Consumer Studies, 35*(3), 307–315.

Yeoman, I., & McMahon-Beattie, U. (2006). Luxury markets and premium pricing. *Journal of Revenue and Pricing Management, 4*, 319–328.

Yep, G. A. (1998). My three cultures: Navigating the multicultural identity landscape. In J. Martin, T. Nakayama, & L. Flores (Eds.), *Readings in cultural contexts* (s. 79–85). Mayfield: Mountain View.

Zalega, T. (2013). Nowe trendy i makrotrendy w zachowaniach konsumenckich gospodarstw domowych w XXI. *Konsumpcja I Rozwój, 2,* 3–21.

7

Who Creates Value of Luxury Goods Within the Value Chain? Companies vs Consumers' Perspective

7.1 The Role of the Various Components of the Value System in Creating Value Propositions for Consumers

A relatively small number of publications on luxury studies are devoted to the role played by different actors in creating value for consumers. The emphasis in these studies is placed on:

1. creating value propositions:
   - the role of designers in creating their aesthetic and emotional value (e.g. Mores 2007; Kapferer 2012);
   - the importance of the origin and quality of materials and traditional production sites in preserving the highest value in the use of luxury goods (e.g. Caniato et al. 2009; Kapferer 2012);
   - the importance of location, shop appearance and sales staff attitudes in creating emotional and social value (e.g. Moore et al. 2000, Nobbs et al. 2012);

B. Stępień, *The Value of Luxury*, Palgrave Advances in Luxury,
https://doi.org/10.1007/978-3-030-51218-7_7

- media influence on value creation and propensity to buy luxury goods (e.g. Quach and Thaichon 2017; Lee and Watkins 2016; Phan et al. 2011).

2. experiencing the value of luxury during the purchasing process itself and its subsequent public exposure (e.g. Tynan et al. 2010; Atwal and Williams 2009; Willems et al. 2012).

The first type of business entities that create the value of luxury are designers. Their contribution to the aesthetic value of the product is invaluable: it is the result of the creation of goods which shape the vision of luxury The appearance and reception not only evokes positive aesthetic impressions but also, thanks to the talent of the creator, can become a work of art. However the contribution of the designer should not be limited to the aesthetic sphere. Not only his talent creates value but also his entire charismatic personality and although it is not the case for all designers (or at least it is not exposed in the media as such), such characters such as Karl Lagerfeld, Marc Jacobs, John Galiano, Vivienne Westwood, Gianni and Donatella Versace or Alexander McQueen with their expressiveness and charisma create a symbolic and thus the aesthetic and social value of the brand. Chanel, Dior, Yves Saint Laurent, Porsche or many other brands are the names of their creators and although many of them are no longer with us their work continues in new aesthetic versions, combining the artistic heritage of the artist with his successors, based on the charismatic features of subsequent designers, dramatized by their own style and media communication (Weierter 2001; Dion and Arnould 2011).

However the strength of the designer's influence on the value of the product itself and even more so its perception by consumers, varies depending on which category of goods we deal with. While in the case of luxury fashion this contribution to the brand image is important, in the automotive, jewellery and watchmaking industries it is rather an ancillary element. While the design itself is still important in assessing the overall value of the product the designer's silhouette is not so prominent in the media as a component creating additional symbolic and social value.

An important value creating factor is the sourcing and manufacturing process and although many operations (such as the extraction of raw materials, production of components, or individual processing processes) are outsourced, the owners of brands (especially those highly positioned on the luxury pyramid) strictly control the entire manufacturing process.In analyzing supply chain configurations in international luxury companies, Caniato et al. (2015), identify three types of strategies:

- full control—production within a network of local suppliers and cells carrying out specialized operations,
- cooperation, where the design activity is still with the brand owner, but the delivery of components or workmanship takes place outside the company;
- full outsourcing, with low level of cooperation between the links and the limited level of control over the supply chain from the brand owner.

The authors state that for goods highly positioned in the luxury pyramid brand owners either carry out the production processes within their own company or subcontract the production to local networks of small suppliers with the latter not involved in the design and development of products. The priority of this integrated configuration is to ensure the highest quality and control of the entire process by the brand owner, combined with high speed and agility of response in the face of market changes in demand.

The second type of configuration is based on collaboration amongst supply chain links. It is characterized by joint product development and a regional or global scale of outsourcing where the purchase of materials is also the responsibility of subcontractors. Such a system is a compromise between the quality of manufactured goods, their control, volume and costs. Configuration based on cooperation concerns mainly mass-produced cheaper goods, mainly accessories (although identified with the logo of high-level brands).

The last so-called "virtual" configuration means full outsourcing of operations where both the geographical location of individual external links and the activities of brand owners are global. Both design and execution are outsourced. This type is characterized by low control, emphasis on the cost side of business, mass sales, relatively low prices of goods and is characteristic of the lowest level of the pyramid of luxury.

This taxonomy illustrates how the functional component of the value of luxury ceases to be a characteristic feature as the production of the product is expanded and the brand goes down the pyramid level. This is the brand that increasingly becomes a "value carrier"; built around non-functional value components, such as emotions, popularity and media-transmitted uniqueness.

The next link in the value chain are shops and retailers. These links are responsible for creating mostly an emotional value: joy from the purchase process, (the sense of uniqueness of the act itself, staying in aesthetically refined interiors, etc.) and a proper communication of functional, aesthetic or ethical value components of the goods or services offered.

Emotional value is also created through the use of artists in the design of flagship boutiques; built, equipped and exhibited as works of art (Ryan 2007). The location itself (city centres with the most expensive rents) of flagship stores also signals the social value and is a determinant of the brand's prestige (Willems et al. 2012).

An important element here is; the one who actually creates an emotional value and communicates the other value components is the seller. As Kapferer writes (1997), sellers create the universe of the brand and co-create its aura. It is sellers' skills and competences that determine the decision to purchase. The task of the seller is to make the purchasing process as pleasant as possible and an important element of this experience is to convince the consumer that all his needs and desires have been met, doubts have been dispelled and that the right choice has been made.

Taking care of the seller during the process of purchasing luxury goods is not only about providing the customer with comfort in the form of delivering further products and presenting their values but also about telling the stories that formed the basis of the product design and manufacture. During the sales process the seller becomes a brand ambassador who discreetly communicates the most important values and philosophy of the brand. However the nature of this information is highly dependent on the consumer's attitude: questions asked and willingness to learn about the history of the product or the brand itself (Tynan et al. 2010; Dion and Borraz 2017).

Further actions, which co-create the brand value concern media communication and the one done by others: actual and potential consumers. Although the principle of refraining from intense communication and promotion in the media is known in the business of luxury today it is held by just few brands. Some communication reticence only applies to the highest level of the luxury pyramid even though today all luxury brands create their social and symbolic value using various communication tools.

The in-depth literature review did not reveal publications analysing how the perception of the value of luxury products is linked to the contribution of individual actors (designers, manufacturers, retailers and other consumers) to its creation. It is only pointed out that the aura surrounding the designer or monumentality of interior design influence the perception of the brand as auric, symbolic and thus socially influential and the degree of control of the chain, place of manufacture and country of origin of the goods are the determinants of their functional value.

7.2 Which Links in the Supply Chain Contribute to Luxury Value Creation? The Results of the Author's Own Research

The aim of this part of the research was to identify the importance and hierarchy of individual operations and supply chain links in the creation of the luxury value proposition. The presentation begins with the analysis of quantitative research results in the form of an international electronic survey addressed to consumers. The next section analyses the content of interviews with representatives of particular links (designers, brand owners, suppliers of raw materials, subcontractors and shopkeepers), in the framework of which they provide answers on what is, according to the interviewees, the most important component creating value in the industry they represent.

7.2.1 Who Creates Value of Luxury Goods Within the Supply Chain? Results of an International Consumer Survey

The consumers were asked which operations and supply chain links create value for them when the purchase of luxury goods—fashion, cars and jewellery—is taken into account. Their assessment is reflected in Fig. 7.1.

According to respondents the greatest contribution to the creation of luxury value is made by the manufacturers as they ensure the quality of workmanship, manifested in the functionality of these goods. The second most important feature is design although the name of the designer is

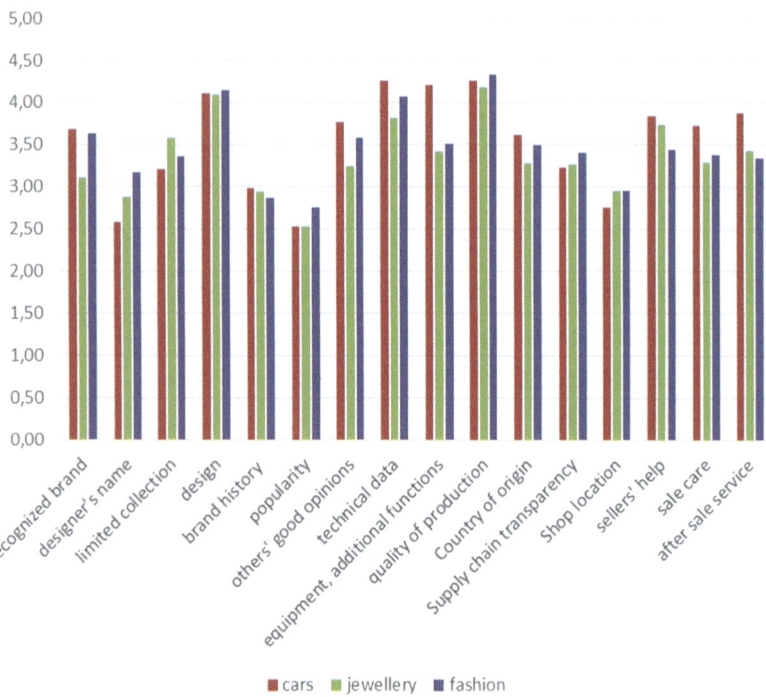

Fig. 7.1 The consumers' perception of the contribution of individual actions and links to the creation of value proposition in luxury fashion, jewellery and the car industry (*Source* Own calculations)

one of the least important factors in creating value. Designers' names are relatively most important in the fashion industry, while in the car industry the designer's persona is almost disregarded. Equally insignificant, hence not adding value for consumers, is the location of the store, the history associated with the creation of the product, or its popularity among famous people.

The results obtained show that while the evaluation of luxury as a collective category leads respondents to take a broader perspective when evaluating the value of luxury, the questions concerning the contribution of individual links to the creation of value of specific types of products (fashion, jewellery, cars) means the respondent exposing mainly functional components of value. Respondents emphasize the contribution of producers to the creation of value propositions and the aesthetic component, while reducing the influence of the creator's (designer's) person on the development of artistic values.

Moreover respondents consider that the brand owner's contribution to the creation of luxury value is important (especially in the automotive and fashion industries), depreciating the brand heritage, which seems one of the most important components of its value. The least important and thus not creating value is, according to consumers, the popularity of given goods among known people. Could it be that the owners of luxury goods brands are mistaken and wasting considerable resources on hiring actors, celebrities or recognizable bloggers to communicate the brand's value? There are at least three reasons for not so claiming. First, social opinion polls should take into account the empirically observable discrepancy between declarations and actual behaviours resulting from the (not necessarily conscious) aspiration to present oneself as a rational individual, guided by cognition rather than affect, not susceptible to external influences and thus self-determining.

Secondly, the impact of other consumers on the value of luxury is clearly indicated by the respondents that the opinions of loved ones are an important source of information about the value of these goods. While it can be cautiously assumed that popularity among many famous people does not significantly enhance social value in consumer opinions the impact is quite high for those who are liked and valued by respondents. It is therefore reasonable to assume that a popular actor whom we value, raises the value proposition of the advertised luxury good. The same may be true for a multitude of other famous people assuming that the consumer has respect or affection for them. Thirdly and finally, value and purchase are influenced by the sellers themselves which the respondents express by valuing this link quite highly, especially in the case of cars. As already agreed the more complex the selection options and the greater the number of options the more complicated the assessment of their value will be. By providing professional advice sellers can make such a choice much easier while at the same time giving the consumer the feeling that the choice was based on objective premises based on analysis of available information. However conversations with experienced luxury car dealers show that while technical information is helpful in making a choice the purchase trigger is often the evaluation of aesthetics or the mention that the queue for this model is unfortunately long…

The analysis of results by industry shows the following hierarchy of importance of individual actions and links in the creation of a luxury value proposition:

- in the automotive industry the most important is the quality of workmanship followed by technical car data, design and after-sales service/care, which indicates the dominant contribution of manufacturers to the car's value creation,
- in the jewellery industry the quality of workmanship is the most important element in creating value proposition followed by the design and technical data on the quality of raw materials,
- in the fashion industry the results are the same as in the jewellery industry: it is the quality of workmanship, design and the technical parameters of the goods that make up the most important components of the value proposition.

The analysis of results showing the impact of individual activities/links on luxury value perception in industries by country shows the following variations:

- German respondents value the technical parameters of all assessed goods the most, the quality of workmanship and design are in second and third place respectively,

- Poles have an almost identical perception of value components as the whole sample, but in fashion they value design above the quality of workmanship,
- The Portuguese are extremely different from the rest of the respondents in their perception of the contribution of the different links, especially in relation to fashion. They put the designer's name first, the brand recognition second and the opinion of other people about the brand third. They also differ in the perception of the proposed value of jewellery: design is the most important component; the second place is taken by the care of salesmen and only in third place are the technical qualities of the product,
- Turks value the technical aspects of cars the most, followed by the quality of workmanship and after-sales service; in fashion they value design the most and in jewellery the quality of workmanship,
- Saudis first of all point to the equipment in cars as the most important value creating factor and then the quality of workmanship, while in jewellery and in fashion the design is the most value creating factor,
- Indians in all analysed industries pointed to the quality of workmanship as the most important factor and immediately afterwards placed the quality of materials and design.

Overall German respondents estimates are the lowest, while Indians and Saudis give generally high scores to many value components and links.

Average scores were also analysed by income, gender and consumer education. Although there is no clear correlation between these criteria and the evaluation and impact of individual actions and links on the value of luxury women value design slightly higher than men, and more affluent consumers place quality of workmanship, country of origin, transparency of the supply chain and location of the store slightly higher than the less affluent. Brand recognition or other people's opinions are not as important to the wealthy as they are to less well-off groups. As far as education is concerned, while the functional aspects are rated slightly lower for the highest educated group than for the others brand heritage is relatively more highly valued.

In the next step the relationship between segment membership (based on psychographic criteria, explained in the previous chapter) and perception of the value created by successive links in the value chain was analysed; how the value of luxury goods relates to the design and the designer, the manufacturing phase and the technical parameters of the product, then sales, the brand's history and recognition and finally the structure of the supply chain as a whole. In order to see how these particular actions and actors (in terms of their importance in creating the value proposition) are perceived by each consumer segment logistic regression was performed in which segment membership was a dichotomous variable (meaning segment membership). The weights assigned to particular elements of the value chain were independent variables.

It has been found that only seven out of fifteen identified elements are differentiated by segment membership (absolute differences of more than 0.5 points on a five-point scale occurred for: recognizable brand, designer name, uniqueness, design, quality workmanship and aspects related to sales personnel's assistance during purchase). At the other end of the scale with differences of up to 0.3 points, were: good feedback from friends and popularity of the product with celebrities. Table 7.1 presents only the statistically significant odds ratios for each segment from the equations analyzed.

The segments identified are characterized by a diverse perception and evaluation of particular actions or characteristics specific to particular stages—links in the value chain. For Hedonists value is boosted by the product's uniqueness and design but is not created by the other actors:

Table 7.1 Segment evaluation of value created within luxury fashion value chain—odds ratios

	Hedonists	Reserved Admirerers	Status oriented
Uniqueness (e.g., limited series or one-off design)	1.466	0.794	0.768
Design	1.513		
Quality workmanship			0.629
Professional help and sales personnel's assistance		1.172	

sellers or other consumers. This has to do with the group's clear inclination to snobbery and inner self-evaluation which manifests itself through attaching higher value to personal emotions rather than to the social perception of one's own actions, behaviour or appearance. Radically different in this respect are Status-oriented consumers. The uniqueness of products may imply weak social recognition to this group so is not a desired feature for this bandwagon prone group. as it diminishes. Secondly, even though Status-oriented consumers are relatively the wealthiest their average disposable income does not put them in the group of top luxury buyers (similarly for over 90% of the sample examined). This is why quality workmanship may imply a high price of these goods and hence their relatively greater inaccessibility and lower social recognition.

In the eyes of Reserved Admirers the value of luxury goods in the luxury fashion industry is increased by professional help and sales personnel assistance whereas product uniqueness decreases it. A negative effect of product uniqueness may be explained by perceiving the display of luxury goods in public as a sort of manifestation of snobbish and unethical consumption but may be also spiritually driven. Consequently product uniqueness may be associated with making an impression of ostentation which is unacceptable to this group. Raising the value of luxury goods through professional help or sales personnel assistance may be an effect of trust in this group's professional knowledge of the value of the goods offered.

7.2.2 Interviews with Business Representatives on Their Contribution to Creating Luxury Value Propositions

In this section the conclusions of the interviews with representatives of companies involved in the design, manufacture and sale of luxury goods in the fashion, jewellery and automobile industries are presented. For the sake of clarity Table 7.2 gathers the most important information concerning the assessment of the contribution of individual links to creating value proposition in luxury business for the consumer.

Table 7.2 Hierarchy of components building luxury value in a given industry—supply chain links opinions

	Industry	Place in the value chain	The most important contribution to the luxury value is created by:	The most important component of value
A	Fashion	The store, owner	1. Brand owner, 2. Designer 3. Street—other consumers	1. Fashion—ephemeral aesthetic 2. Social component 3. Hedonic component
B	Fashion	Designer, owner of a luxury brand, own production + outsourcing, sales in foreign stores	1. Other consumers, media 2. Designer 3. Seller	1. Hedonic component 2. Aesthetics 3. Fashion—ephemeral aestehetic
C	Fashion	Subcontractor	1. Brand owner 2. Media, other consumers	1. Brand 2. Social recognition 3. Aesthetics
D	Jewellery	Owner of a chain of stores, own production and outsourcing, design sphere in the company	1. Design/nameless designer 2. Seller	1. Emotional 2. Symbolic 3. Aesthetic
E	Jewellery	Production, subcontracting to various luxury brands	1. Branded retailer 2. Designer 3. Seller	1. Emotional 2. Aesthetic 3. Capital for promoting the brand
F	Jewellery	A subcontractor, supplier of raw material	1. Quality of the raw material 2. Project 3. Quality of the workmanship	1. Aesthetic 2. Capital for promoting the brand

(continued)

Table 7.2 (continued)

	Industry	Place in the value chain	The most important contribution to the luxury value is created by:	The most important component of value
G	Jewellery	Breeder and supplier of pearls	1. Media, fashion for a specific type of jewellery 2. Design	1. Symbolic 2. Hedonic 3. Aesthetic
H	Jewellery	A subcontractor, design and production	1. Retailer's brand 2. Design 3. Quality of the workmanship	1. Social—a well-known brand 2. Aesthetic 3. Functional
I	Cars	Manufacturer's representative, premium and luxury cars	1. Brand 2. Technical excellence 3. Aesthetics	1. Social 2. Functional 3. Emotional
J	Cars	Car trader premium and luxury	1. Brand 2. Technical excellence 3. Aesthetics	1. Functional 2. Emotional 3. Aesthetic
K	Cars	Car trader of top luxury cars	1. Brand 2. Accessories 3. Approximate and after-sales care	1. Symbolic 2. Prestige 3. Hedonic

Source Own calculations

The statements refer only to the industries represented by the persons interviewed.

Several conclusions emerge from the interviews with representatives of enterprises.

Firstly, representatives of companies (involved in the design, production, communication and sale of luxury goods) see the contribution of companies in creating the value of these goods differently from consumers. Secondly, the hierarchy of importance of the individual links varies from one industry to another. Thirdly, the most important creators of value here are the brand owner, designer, seller and other consumers.

Business representatives seem to rank emotional and social components higher than consumers as motivational factors in the purchase of luxury goods. Without denying the importance of material quality, technical excellence or performance master craft business representatives appreciate the importance of the media to a much greater extent than the consumer,, brand recognition and its heritage in creating the luxury value proposition. The opinions of companies' representatives are largely consistent with the opinions of consumers on the importance of particular components (social, aesthetic, functional or hedonic) in creating the value of luxury as a collective category. According to interviewees, consumers prefer to think (and declare) that when choosing a given product they analyse the available information and are not guided by effect. The divergence in opinions and behaviours of consumers is well reflected in the statement of the interviewee D:

> *If you ask a man why he buys a necklace for his partner he will tell you that he buys it for a sort of anniversary, but it's seems a good investment, because the quality of diamonds is high (…) If you ask a woman, she will tell you more honestly that she likes it. And do you know why she likes it? Because her shopping companion together with the seller said that she looks beautiful in this necklace. She will associate this piece of metal and stone with a momentous and happy experience/moment in life. The value of the stones or even the quality of workmanship is of secondary importance here. I have been working in this business for over 20 years, I know what I'm saying, this is the way it works in every country, we only change the design and train salespeople, because sales depend on them first and foremost.*

Interviewees admit that emotions play an important role in the selection process and change the hierarchy of value components (thanks to the skills of salespeople, regardless of the industry), but they are not the sole basis for value perception in the automotive industry. This is where technical mastery combined with the brand's reputation comes to the fore. It is worth noting that interviewees from the automotive industry stressed the significant difference in the approach of consumers interested in buying premium or luxury cars from the lower level of the pyramid compared to the consumers of cars at prices higher than EUR 125,000. In the case of cheaper cars consumers devote a lot of effort to the analysis of technical data and look for the best price offers. As the price of a car increases, so does its equipment and service.

> K - *"If someone enters this show room they do it most often for two reasons. First - he wants to look at a car that he will never be able to afford for a long time or probably never. The second one - wants to order a car, the issue to determine is the date, colour, equipment, additional functions,* etc. *I don't know how to describe it to you but I am very likely to be able to determine which group the person entering the showroom belongs. The representative of the latter group knows the brand before he comes (some people send assistants first), likes it and wants it, it is only a specific model of a car, how much he will spend on it and when he can get it. And that's where we come in...".*

In the case of luxury fashion it is the popularity of style among other consumers combined with the popularity of the brand that determines the success of the collection. Although the design of luxury fashion brands is characterized by a timeless style characteristic of the brand, the success of the collection depends to the great extent on chimeric street trends.

> *I've been in the business for a long time and although I think I understand it, sometimes I can't predict what consumers will like. Although I have a group of regular and loyal clients, when the collections that were supposed to be the hit of the season do not sell, I have moments of breakdown. This industry is unpredictable and very aggressive. Styles are copied immediately and actually I'm lucky I'm not very well-known and giants don't fake my collections because I can still stand out. I don't have such a brand to have very high prices and mass sales so it happens that business brings losses...".*

7.3 (Don't) Tell Me What I (Don't) Want to Hear—Communicating Value in the Luxury Fashion Sector—Mystery Shopping Findings

This section describes the results of the research in the form of so-called mystery shopping aimed at identifying the information provided by luxury fashion sellers in communicating the proposed value of the goods offered. The type, intensity and style of the information provided were analysed. The study included luxury fashion stores and retailers from the middle and top of the luxury pyramid.

A qualitative, two stage study was conducted. The first one consisted of 46 mystery shopping visits; combining active observation and pre-structured interviews with sellers of selected brands in luxury fashion. Mystery shopping allowed the identification of the actual commitment /contribution of salespeople to customer service and examined how well they are prepared to answer questions about the value components of goods they sell, including sustainability issues.

The second part of the investigation was to:

1. reveal the scientific purpose of the interviews to sellers,
2. interview consumers about their perception of sustainable activities of the brands as an additional, important (or unimportant) value factor and purchase incentive.

All sellers and consumers were informed about the goal of the investigation at the end and were asked for permission to use the data obtained for a purely academic purpose. None of the sellers and consumers raised objections regarding the use of the information provided. Despite the fact that in all the cases the personal data of consumers (age, nationality and occupation) and the sellers were made available (in this sector the standard is the recording made of what the seller contributed to the purchase, hence the mutual presentation and an exchange of business cards or personal information is the norm), the respondents were assured of the anonymity of the study conducted.

The research was conducted in four cities: Dubai, Singapore, Paris and Berlin. The choice of places was not accidental. Singapore is one of the most developed country being both a popular destination for tourists from around the world and the base of numerous international corporations.

Dubai is a city aspiring to surprise the world with its architectural panache and the accumulation of attractions for the rich of this world thirsty for varied entertainment. The highest buildings, the most spectacular and fancy amusement parks, the largest and most modern department stores fit well into the ubiquitous and publicly demonstrated, ostentatious luxury of the inhabitants of this city, for whom shopping remains a favourite way of spending their free time.

Paris is the cradle of world luxury. Well-known and valued consumer brands as Hermés, Dior, Chanel or YSL (now Saint Laurent) are still produced there. The city is the epitome of the highest class of historic architecture, art, combining the charm of urban beauty with the accumulation of the most prestigious shops and restaurants. As in Singapore, Dubai and Berlin, Paris has inhabitants from almost all nationalities in the world. Berlin cannot be counted as one of the European capitals of luxury fashion (such as Paris, Milan or London), but it is the capital of Germany; the largest economy in the European Union. Table 7.3

Table 7.3 Mystery shopping—interviews with sellers of selected luxury fashion brands—communicated components of value propositions

Brand	The most important components of the value proposition are
Bottega Veneta	Brand for experts, quiet luxury, lack of logo, recognizable only for those who know about luxury fashion, history of the creation of the collection, care for control of the entire manufacturing process, origin of materials from the best, proven places
Chanel	Brand heritage, global brand recognition and style, distinctive design, mastery of knitwear production, innovative combinations of fabrics in bags
Dior	French, elite heritage of the brand, highest quality tailoring, artistry
Gucci	Characteristic, recognizable design, colours, combining fabrics and patterns, popularity
Hermés	Masterful workmanship, brand heritage, production site, attention to detail, timeless style, quiet luxury
Loro Piana	Exceptional material quality, style restraint, environmental care, sustainable production, brand niche
LV	Global brand recognition, acquired by well-known people
Prada	Italian bold design, global recognition
Saint Laurent	Quality of materials, French style, rarity
Stella McCartney	Original design, joy, everyday use, a close production control

Source Own calculations

presents information on the components of the proposal for the value of goods, most often communicated by sellers.

Sellers very well know what type of information consumers consider relevant and purchase persuasive. Regardless of the brand they emphasize the aesthetic values of the products in combination with the craftsmanship and excellent quality of the materials used. However sellers differ in communicating the values of the offered goods in terms of their social perception. The sellers of global brands emphasize their popularity and recognition (Dior, Chanel, LV, Gucci, Prada). In contrast retailers of Bottega Veneta, Hermés or Loro Piana consider (or at least communicate in this way) their relatively lower popularity and thus their exclusiveness as an asset. In the case of the latter group consumer service is also more attentive and reserved. It seems that the global popularity of the first group of brands results in a certain nonchalance of the sellers in customer service and devoting relatively less attention to customers than in the shops of lesser known though luxurious brands. The exception is Hermés where the service is of the highest standard despite the pressure from consumers queuing in front of the shops.

According to LV's saleswoman in Dubai the store serves about 100,000 customers a year and that the largest group of buyers are Chinese tourists who buy goods of this brand in bulk. The scale of service results in the fact that sales resemble shopping in mass fashion chains and the concern for customer service is limited to bringing a mass of clothes and shoes to the fitting room, and then efficient packaging.

7.3.1 Sustainability as the Value Factor? Official Brands' Commitment vs Shop Floor Reality

The luxury sector is associated not only with the production of expensive, rare, high quality, design and mastercrafted goods, that only a few can afford but tends to be morally condemned, as it is identified with excess and vanity. Despite such a social stigma the above average care and control of the performance and the quality and aesthetics of goods is the norm for this sector (Kapferer 2010; Achabou and Dekhili 2013; Kapferer and Michaut-Denizeau 2013; Janssen et al. 2013; Voyer and

Beckham 2014; Kapferer and Valette-Florence 2018). The sustainability concept is therefore not only coincident or complementary (at least in these aspects) with the traditional production of luxuries but also increasingly implemented in the strategies of companies that produce these goods (see also Franco et al. 2019).

The discrepancy between the social perception of luxury and its growing commitment to promoting the idea of sustainability can be offset by the effective communication of such activity to consumers (see e.g. Amatulli et al. 2018). The issue of communicating values related to sustainability by sellers in the luxury goods sector has been vaguely explored (a few examples are Risius et al. 2017), but there are several reasons why the recognition of this area is important for both academia and practice. Firstly, the sellers are considered to be a part of "brand universe" in the luxury sector. They are important promoters of the whole value that is being proposed and delivered to consumers (Willems et al. 2012; Thach and Olsen 2015; Dion and Borraz 2017), so their communication skills can help in making this value factor more visible and growing in importance. Secondly, once the sustainability becomes an important (although still complementary or emerging) part of the value proposition in luxury, it should be communicated cohesively throughout the value chain strategy in order to make this message more credible and socially recognized. Thirdly, the luxury brands perceived as marketing strategy benchmarks for other premium and mass goods can be ambassadors of sustainable practices in many industries provided that they can effectively introduce sustainability as an important value factor for consumers.

From the publicly available data it appears that the two largest conglomerates—LVMH and Kering SA undertake a number of efforts to implement the idea of sustainable development in the business model of all members within the groups. By far the most effective and comprehensive strategy in this regard is implemented by Kering SA which announced the new three pillar roadmap as part of their Strategy 2025: care (about the impact on the planet), collaboration (for long term employees) and creation (pioneering ideas to safeguard heritage and empower future generations). But Kering not only announced what it intends but has already achieved a lot in implementing the idea of sustainable development. The company was recognized as one of 100 companies in the world (Kering—47/100) most involved in the promotion and implementation of the idea of sustainable development and is the only luxury group listed in 2017 in the Dow Jones Sustainability Index (DJSI), that shows the top 10% of leading performers in this area. The holding is also a leader within the textile, apparel and luxury goods sector in the CDP Climate Performance Leadership Index and was credited by CDP Forest Ranking for its efforts against deforestation. The Kering Foundation, launched in 2009, combats violence against women, supports local international NGOs, awards local social entrepreneurs and raises sustainability awareness.

LVMH also implements the idea of sustainable, responsible development, although it began publishing information on this activity much later than its main, though smaller competitor, Kering SA. In 2012 LVMH launched its LIFE programme (LVMH Initiatives for the Environment) to increase the environmental performance of all Group members. The idea behind LIFE is that each LVMH member (maison) establishes its own sustainability action plan to ensure that the maisons will meet the following objectives by 2020: improve the environmental performance of their products; apply the highest environmental standards across 70% of their supply chains; improve the environmental performance of all sites and stores by at least 10% and reduce CO2 emissions from energy consumption by 25% compared with 2013. Regarding the last goal LVMH established the so-called 'in - house carbon fund', under which every maison was obliged to pay EUR 15 for every ton of CO2 emitted by 2017 and from 2018 this amount is increased to EUR 30. The money collected is later used to reduce the emissions of this gas.

Due to their holding structures both Kering SA and LVMH respect the artistic and strategic independence of individual fashion houses which are, to a varying degree, involved in implementing the sustainability idea within their strategies. Table 7.4 contains the most relevant information on the contribution of individual brands to sustainable development.

The information presented in Table 7.4 shows the varied involvement of brands in sustainable development. The Stella McCartney and Loro Piana brands declare the greatest commitment (both in the Kering

Table 7.4 Sustainability efforts of luxury fashion brands—information from Internet websites and officially published reports

Part of:	Brand /sustainability rank*	Sustainability features in the official mass media communication
Kering SA: Gucci Group	**Bottega Veneta** not ranked	No information on the official website, promoted as quiet luxury that shows personality, not tags. Information about the brand and its sustainability efforts reflected in Kering reports. BW sustainably active; e.g. 100% traceability of leather used, extreme care in material usage in co-operation with suppliers, elimination of chemical hazards during tanning
Wertheimer family	**Chanel** lowest score (E, 0/36)	No information on the official websites, Instagram, Facebook, etc.…
LVMH group	**Dior** ranked E (5/36)	Limited information on the official website. Dior implements some measures to reduce the environmental impact of its packaging materials, is committed to equal opportunities and the promotion of diversity and equality in the workplace

(continued)

Table 7.4 (continued)

Part of:	Brand /sustainability rank*	Sustainability features in the official mass media communication
Kering SA; Gucci Group	**Gucci** ranked D (12/36)	Information includes Gucci's commitment to: energy saving in all Gucci stores, offices, warehouses and supply chains; optimising distribution, using packaging from certified sustainably managed forests (FSC); reducing water usage throughout the whole supply chain; creating environmentally-friendly materials; sustainable sourcing and traceability of materials
Family Hermés	**Hermés** ranked (3/36)	Hermès strives to reduce greenhouse gas emissions and use renewable energy and implements measures related to its waste production. Hermès primarily uses cowhides and sheepskin exclusively sourced from European countries
LVMH group	**Loro Piana** not ranked	Sustainability as part of the brand's philosophy. On the official website there is information on the origin of raw materials and the treatment of animals, the environment and cooperation with local farmers and long term conservation programmes to safeguard the animals and their habitats. An Organization, Management and Control Model as well as a Supplier's Code of Conduct published

Part of:	Brand /sustainability rank*	Sustainability features in the official mass media communication
LVMH group	**Louis Vuitton** ranked D (6/36)	Committed to waste reduction, green gas emissions, packaging reduction and either fully certified or recycled. Sustainable efforts mostly visible in LVMH reports, not on the LV official website
Prada Group	**Prada** ranked E (3/36)	No information on the official site of Prada, On the Prada Group official website the main message concerns activities for creating beauty, supporting creativity and assuring superior quality. The actions that the Group looks at indicate that most achievements are in the use of certified or recycled packaging. The group also allocated approximately EUR 22 million to support the activities of local communities. Prada Group promotes activities connected with arts & culture, invests in a unique working environment preserving artisanal skills and supporting Prada Group brands
Kering SA; Gucci Group	**Saint Laurent**	No information on an official website but in the Kering SA website information about SL it states that it has introduced a comprehensive and exemplary programme to reduce the environmental impacts of its stores (83% by the end of 2014, excluding those in department stores). The brand has also improved its Energy impact by nearly 40% implementing LEED (Leadership in Energy and Environmental Design) requirements into its practices

(continued)

Table 7.4 (continued)

Part of:	Brand /sustainability rank*	Sustainability features in the official mass media communication
Kering SA; Gucci Group	**Stella McCartney** ranked C (16/36); the highest score of all ranked luxury fashion brands	Promoting sustainability as a very important feature of the brand image clearly visible on the official site: Stella's world of sustainability: respect for nature, animals, people: sustainable fabrics, transparency, a carefully assembled and controlled supply chain, no furs and leather etc., ranked as the most sustainable of all the luxury brands under investigation

Source Official websites of the brands under investigation, see References with websites' information about the brands
*Sustainability report on luxury brands on www.rankabrand.com, A—the highest, E—the lowest score

SA structure) to sustainability. At the other end of the spectrum are Chanel, Prada and Hermés, all being independent, mostly family—owned maisons. Despite the undeniable attention to the traditional features of luxury (artistry, mastery of craftsmanship, excellence of materials used), these fashion houses do not publicly communicate much about their sustainable efforts.

In order to check how much official information about sustainability measures is known to vendors and further communicated to customers mystery shopping was conducted. The nature and content of the questions used during these interviews was based on publicly available information about the sustainability efforts of examined fashion brands (see Table 7.4).

Table 7.5 shows the responses of brand retailers in four locations (Singapore, Dubai, Paris and Berlin). Responses from 46 mystery shopping interviews were coded, categorized and then quantified showing the level of detail, depth and nature of the sales representatives' responses about brands sustainable activities.

The results demonstrate the generally low awareness of sellers about brand activities in the area of sustainable development, although differences are visible in the following:

1. The degree of discrepancy between what brands communicate on official websites and what sellers know and say about sustainability (see also Fig. 7.2).
2. Diverse knowledge of the brands' sustainable activities: the smallest sellers' knowledge concerns reduction of an environmental footprint, while the largest portion of information regarded the country of production of the goods sold (see also Fig. 7.3).
3. Differences between the cities in terms of sellers' awareness and readiness to communicate sustainable companies' actions (see also Fig. 7.4).

Three out of ten analyzed brands conduct a coherent information policy related to sustainable development in various channels (i.e. on official websites and in stores). This is Loro Piana, LV and Saint Laurent, with only Loro Piana actually communicating its commitment to sustainable development, while LV and Saint Laurent are consistent in their

Table 7.5 Scope of information provided by luxury fashion retailers on brand engagement in sustainable development

Brand	Singapore*	Dubai	Paris	Berlin
Bottega Veneta	A—1	A—0	A—1	A—1
	B—3	B—1	B—3	B—4
	C—4	C—3	C—4	C—4
	D—5	D—4	D—5	D—5
Chanel	A—0	A—0	A—1	A—1
	B—2	B—2	B—2	B—2
	C—1	C—1	C—3	C—2
	D—4	D—3	D—4	D—4
Dior	A—1	A—0	A—1	A—1
	B—2	B—2	B—3	B—3
	C—2	C—1	C—3	C—2
	D—3	D—2	D—4	D—4
Gucci	A—1	A—0	A—1	A—1
	B—2	B—1	B—2	B—2
	C—3	C—2	C—3	C—3
	D—4	D—3	D—4	D—5
Hermés	A—0	A—0	A—0	A—0
	B—2	B—1	B—2	B—2
	C—1	C—0	C—2	C—2
	D—4	D—4	D—4	D—4
Loro Piana	A—1	–	A—1	–
	B—4		B—4	
	C—5		C—5	
	D—5		D—5	
LV	A—0	A—0	A—1	A—1
	B—2	B—1	B—3	B—3
	C—2	C—2	C—3	C—3
	D—4	D—4	D—5	D—4
Prada	A—0	A—0	A—0	A—0
	B—1	B—1	B—2	B—2
	C—1	C—1	C—2	C—2
	D—3	D—3	D—4	D—4
Saint Laurent	A—0	A—0	A—1	A—1
	B—2	B—1	B—2	B—2
	C—2	C—2	C—3	C—3
	D—4	D—4	D—5	D—4
Stella McCartney	A—1	–	A—1	–
	B—3		B—3	
	C—3		C—3	
	D—3		D—4	

A—knowledge about how shops can reduce their environmental footprint: energy savings in stores; FSC or recycled packaging
B—knowledge about the origin of the materials: fur, leather, cotton, wool and the degree of their organic character
C—knowledge of the transparency and scope of supply chain control; care for the welfare of employees and animals
D—knowledge about the place of production of clothes and clothing
0—no information; 1—very limited; very general; 2—limited, general; 3—some, specific information; 4—detailed but not exhaustive knowledge of the subject; 5—extensive knowledge of the subject
Shopping location *Orchard Road, Marina Bay; **Dubai Mall; ***Galeries Lafayette, Avenue Montaigne, Champs Elysées; ****KDW, Kurfürstendamm

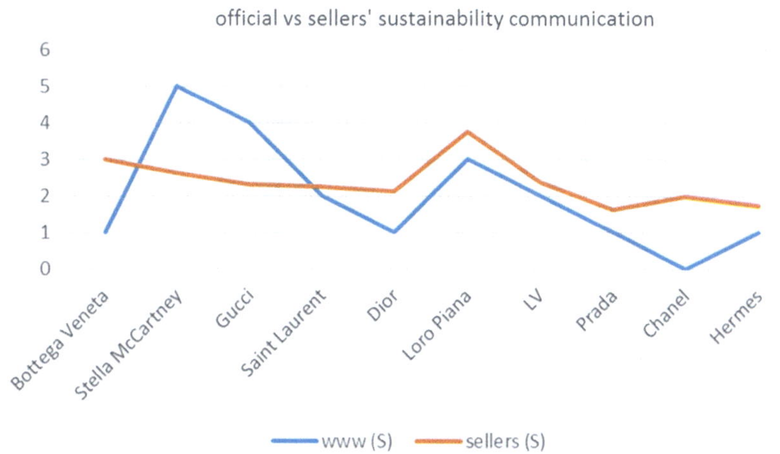

Fig. 7.2 Level of convergence between the official announcements and sellers' communication about sustainability efforts of fashion luxury brands (*Note* see Table 7.4 for official sellers' data, coded: BV (1); Stella McCartney (5); Gucci (4); Saint Laurent (2); Dior (1); Loro Piana (3); LV (2); Prada (1), Chanel (0), Hermés (1))

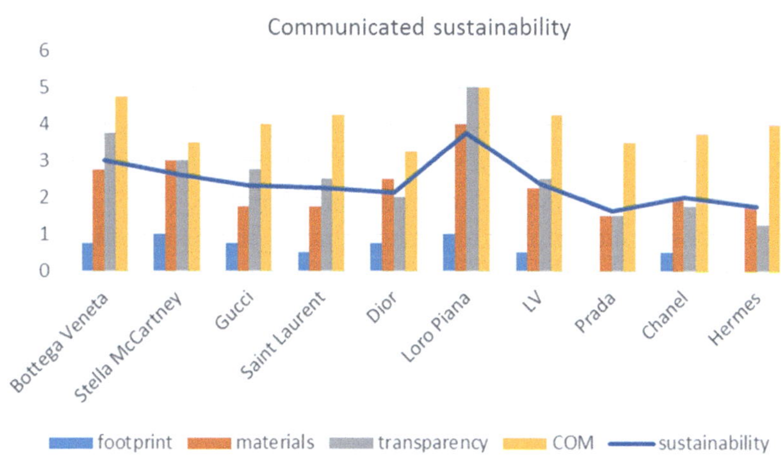

Fig. 7.3 The scope and level of information about sustainability communicated by luxury fashion retailers (*Note* see Table 7.3, sustainability (blue line)—aggregate mean of A, B, C, D results)

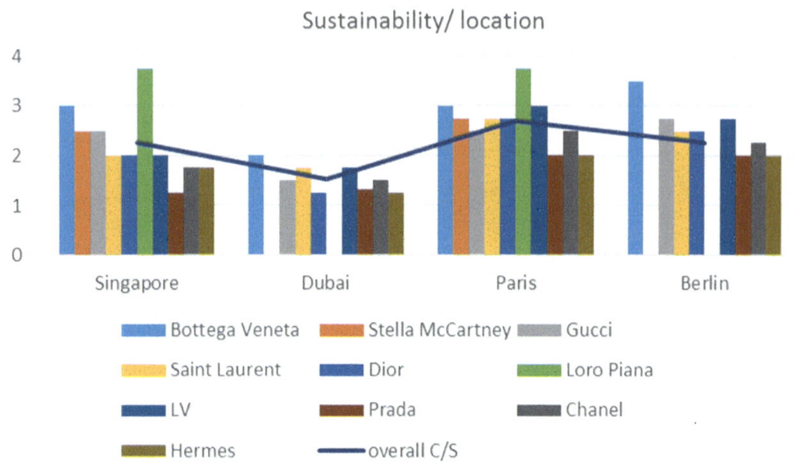

Fig. 7.4 Sustainability communication in various stores' locations

lack of commitment to this area. The biggest discrepancy between what is communicated officially and by the sellers in stores can be seen in Bottega Veneta, Chanel and Stella McCartney. While in Chanel and Bottega Veneta stores salespeople talk more about brand involvement in sustainable development than the brand itself officially communicates. In the case of Stella McCartney the opposite is true: the sellers know very little about specific brand actions in this area beyond the belief that this is an important component of value proposition.

Questions about the place of manufacture are those most often asked by consumers and therefore sellers are ready and willing to answer them. However in the sellers' opinion this interest in the country of production does not result from concern for the transparency of the supply chain but helps to gain confidence that the product is authentic. As a saleswoman in Gucci in Singapore reported Chinese consumers are justified in raising concerns about the authenticity of the goods as many counterfeit items have been sold under the Gucci logo in China (see also NYTimes 2017). LV, Dior and Prada vendors in Dubai also had similar observations.

The greatest knowledge and tendency to share information about the brand's commitment to sustainability issues with the consumer was demonstrated in Loro Piana. It is a brand whose main idea is to create clothes and accessories while respecting the environment and supporting local communities from the territory of origin of the material. The brand owns land in South America where the wild species of Vicuna live supplying the highest quality wool. The animals live wild and are shorn only once every two years. Despite providing this information the answer to the question about the origin of the chinchilla fur used to finish the clothes was: "*I do not know its origin but we do not kill them ourselves*".

Another brand whose sellers demonstrated a large amount of knowledge about sustainable activities was Bottega Veneta. Regardless of the city of research the sellers emphasized the brand's care not only for the entire process of obtaining materials, production and distribution, but also for the careful training of salespeople in this area. The seller of this brand in Singapore proudly emphasized that a part of his training was a visit to Florence where he had the possibility to learn in detail how much importance the brand pays to the selection of suppliers, quality of raw materials and control over the supply chain.

At the other end of the scale of a brand's orientation about its activities for sustainable development were Prada, Hermés, Chanel, Dior and Louis Vuitton. In none of the shops was detailed information on: the origin of materials, animal husbandry or organic sourcing provided. When asked about the scope of control of the supply chain the vendor in Hermés in Dubai responded: "*Of course we do control them … .somehow*". In the Prada shops vendors were even not able to answer the question about the sourcing of the leather used in bags, shoes or jackets.

This low level of knowledge and the sellers' inability to answer questions about sustainability may result from the popularity of these brands among buyers. The demand for these products is evidenced by queues in front of the stores, and may serve as an explanation of low quality service and sellers' ignorance on issues that are generally of little importance to their consumers.

Due to Stella McCartney's commitment to sustainability it was expected that the retailers' knowledge about the sustainable conduct of this brand would be the most extensive and the percentage of consumers asking about these issues, the highest. However it was not. To the question as to how many customers are interested in various areas of sustainability sellers replied that this is a very small group. On average one in twenty consumers asks about organic certificates or the origin of materials while I was the first customer asking about the energy footprint (which was the case in all shops in Dubai and Singapore). At the request to explain this lack of apparent interest, the saleswoman in Singapore (Stella McCartney Kids, Marina Bay) replied:

> *From what I observe consumers are mainly interested in the design, followed by the price and to a much lesser extent in all other issues. Some consumers communicate that they know the brand and its philosophy, hence they probably assume that the brand guarantees sustainable sourcing and production.*

Consumers generally rarely ask questions that indicate their commitment to sustainable development but more often these issues are raised in European stores. Sellers quite unanimously stressed that the interest in ecological, environmental and materials' issues is an emerging but growing trend and is more often expressed by the inhabitants of Europe, the United States, Canada or Australia. In Dubai the largest group of buyers are residents of the Gulf Region and the Chinese while in Singapore there are mostly Chinese buyers. Those consumers—according to shop assistants—are generally very little interested in sustainability issues. The higher level of interest of European consumers in sustainable development also results in a greater knowledge of salespeople in this field. Questions about the origin of materials, the degree of transparency of the supply chain or even the involvement of stores in the reduction of energy consumption or packaging, do not surprise them and they are able to answer them in more detail.

7.3.2 Consumers Interest in Sustainable Activities of Luxury Fashion Brands

The second part of the investigation was to inform the sellers about the goal of the investigation in the form of mystery shopping and to interview consumers about the importance of the "sustainability factor" in their luxury fashion purchases. Table 7.6 shows the characteristics of consumers and the names of brands (here shops), where the interviews took place. In order to show importance (unimportance) of sustainability

Table 7.6 The extent of consumers' interest in sustainability as a value factor and a purchase incentive—results of the interviews in the fashion luxury stores

Brand	Characteristics of consumers and their answers	Sustainability importance
Bottega Veneta	Singapore*: two consumers: • Chinese, 34 female—quality, uniqueness, quiet luxury, care about the whole production process, the brand is sustainable • Italian, 37 female, works in Singapore, knows the brand and its care about controlling the whole value chain, sustainable as an additional value factor Berlin****, two consumers: German couple, both about 50: appreciate sustainability, do not like "loud" brands, control of the value chain as the additional purchase factor	3
Chanel	Dubai**: 3 consumers: • Two Saudi Arabia females, 25 and 29—quality and French design and chic as the most important features, no awareness of sustainable activities of the brand, not interested in the activities, brand perceived as "environmentally friendly", simply because of its heritage One UAE female, about 25; interested in quality and design, the most important feature is the brand recognized style, sustainability has no importance in luxury purchases Paris***—Two Russian consumers, a couple, female around 24, male around 60, a lady not interested in sustainability, a male respondent "*Chanel maintains an extreme care for its garments, which is a sign of their sustainable production, yes, this care matters, but it was important long before the term 'sustainability' was introduced*"	2
Dior	Singapore*: 2 consumers: • One Chinese, 30, female, design, French heritage, quality of materials as important features, did not hear anything about sustainable efforts of the brand, not important to her • One American male, around 60, buying a bag for his spouse, "*I am sorry, I do not know anything about Dior being eco-friendly or sustainable, probably neither my fiance…, it's considered a social symbol of being affluent and stylish, that is why I bought it*"	0
Gucci	Singapore*—three consumers One Indian woman, 35, style and fun as important features, no interest in sustainability Two Chinese women, mother and daughter, 23 and 47: recognizable brand, no interest in sustainability, unimportant	0

(continued)

Table 7.6 (continued)

Brand	Characteristics of consumers and their answers	Sustainability importance
Hermés	Dubai**—One Saudi Arabian woman, 30, very affluent, assisted by a guard: "*I like Hermés for its quiet and very French style; they are sustainable, because they control their production and carefully select materials*" Singapore*—One German male, around 50, "*Yes, I do care about sustainability, but I have not heard much about Hermés' activities in this area, well I suppose they are more sustainable then mass brands*"	2
Loro Piana	Singapore* a couple, around 50, Italians: "*We like its style and the extreme care for quality. We also do appreciate their environmental approach. Well, it is an additional value factor, but he main reason we buy this brand is the quality of materials*"	4
LV	Dubai**—Five consumers, Two Chinese women, 25, 27—no interest in sustainability, completely unimportant Two French women, around 50—sustainability as a concept important but they think that LV does not do much about it One Canadian woman, around 40—"*I do not know anything about LV sustainable efforts, but it would be probably less painful to pay such money for the goods produced in such a way*" Singapore*—One Singaporian female, 35—sustainability is important, but not when she buys luxury clothes...	1
Prada	Singapore* Five consumers: all Chinese, two men, three female, around 30–35—no interest in sustainability, they buy Prada because of its Italian style and recognition Two local consumers, females, around 25—sustainability is important, but they did not know anything about Prada activities in this area	0
Saint Laurent	Paris*—Two female, both around 40, The brand has its heritage, style, they buy from sentiment, they have heard that SL cares about the environment, but cannot give any details, sustainability could be of an asset, but rather of a limited importance	1
Stella McCartney	Singapore*—a Russian couple around 40 with children: "*We are aware that Stella cares about environment very much, but we value this brand because of its style more than its environmental approach*"	3

Consumers knowledge and interest about sustainability
0—non-existent; 1—very limited; very general; no importance; 2—limited, general; very limited importance; 3—some detailed information about the area; limited importance; 4—a detailed, although not exhaustive knowledge and interest about the topic; 5—extensive knowledge and interest about the topic
*Orchard Road, Marina Bay; **Dubai Mall; ***Galeries Lafayette, Avenue Montaigne, Champs Elysées; ****KDW, Kurfürstendamm

as the value factor of luxury fashion goods, the similar coding as in Table 7.5 was used.

The importance of sustainability as an asset varies among consumers and the consumers' nationality seems to be the factor that differentiates its importance the most. A large part of the respondents were residents of developing economies or so called fast growing new luxury markets (Chinese, United Arab Emirates, Saudi Arabia, Singapore, Russia etc.), where the idea of a sustainable approach has just recently been promoted. For these consumers the most important traits of the luxury fashion were design and brand recognition. They reported, that they pay attention to quality of materials and the country of manufacturing but the way in which the materials are acquired and then manufactured is of minor importance to them. One Chinese consumer in LV in Dubai stated the following:

> *It's the French brand so they must take care of the manufacturing process and use sophisticated materials - they do not cheat as those in Far East.*

This statement reflects quite often expressed consumer opinions about trust in the brand they admire and purchase. Consumers believed that since the brand is known and respected it cannot afford unethical and anti-environmental actions, because it would ruin its reputation.

7.4 Impact of Enterprises on the Creation of Luxury Goods' Value Proposition—Summary

International consumer segments, constructed on the basis of common psychographic characteristics differently assess the contribution of the various links in the supply chain to building value propositions for luxury goods. The analysis of logistic regression showed not only a different scale but also a different direction of assessments. The results justify the need to create tailored marketing strategies for specific groups of customers on an international scale where the main criterion of division is lifestyle, not age or even country of residence.

The most important aspects of the value for consumers are those that appear at the design and manufacture stage. Brand recognition is considered to be much more important than its heritage.

However given that it is social value that is the most important component of the value of luxury goods for the consumers surveyed (see results presented in the previous chapters) it seems puzzling to underestimate the role of brand owners. It seems that consumers somewhat depreciate the contribution of brand owners and designers to the shaping of social prestige and a desire for luxury. Perhaps the reason for this is the recognition of these activities as not naturally belonging to brand owners and thus their underestimation. The designer's name is one of the last in terms of impact on value creation, along with shop location and shop design, which is contrary to Okonkwo (2016), Lawson (2006) and Steele (1996).

Representatives of enterprises assess the contribution of individual companies (value links) to the creation of value propositions differently than consumers themselves. Although the assessment of business representatives coincides with consumer views on the importance of individual components of the value of luxury goods it departs from consumer declarations on the contribution of particular businesses in creating this value proposition. Consumers clearly prioritize the functional qualities of luxury products as those that determine a purchase. However such consumer declarations should be treated with caution, especially as in general questions about luxury value perception they admit that social and aesthetic components are the most important components of luxury value. This discrepancy can be attributed to the tendency of us consumers to be perceived as more rational and driven solely by cognition than we actually are.

Retailers are an important link creating and communicating value of luxury to consumers. They seem to perfectly orientate to the needs of consumers by informing them during the purchase of the most important aesthetic and functional values of the goods they offer. Sellers can also contribute to raising awareness of the growing commitment of the luxury sector to sustainable development. However their role as brand ambassadors in promoting sustainability is not sufficiently exploited (see also Dekhili et al. 2019).

The presented research results show that the concept of sustainable development is still complimentary and an emerging value factor for consumers (see also Kapferer and Michaut-Denizeau 2019). Consumers' limited interest in sustainability results in a generally low level of awareness of these activities among retailers and their willingness to communicate, not to mention to promote this category of value.

While the intensive promotion of social activities by businesses may have the opposite effect and raise doubts about motives (Coombs and Holladay 2002) a distinction should be made between ostentatious and absent information. While Kotler and Lee (2008) propose to companies a minimum level of communication about activities for the public good, suggesting that others should talk about it, Van de Ven (2008) and Davies et al. (2012) prove that a lack of communication in this area exposes companies to an antisocial image.

References

Achabou, M. A., & Dekhili, S. (2013). Luxury and sustainable development: Is there a match? *Journal of Business Research, 66*(10), 1896–1903. https://doi.org/10.1016/j.jbusres.2013.02.011.

Amatulli, C., De Angelis, M., Korschun, D., & Romani, S. (2018). Consumers' perceptions of luxury brands' CSR initiatives: An investigation of the role of status and conspicuous consumption. *Journal of Cleaner Production, 194*, 277–287.

Atwal, G., & Williams, A. (2009). Luxury brand marketing—The experience is everything! *Journal of Brand Management, 16*(5–6), 338–346.

Caniato, F., Caridi, M., Castelli, C., & Golini, R. (2009). A contingency approach for SC strategy in the Italian luxury industry: Do consolidated models fit? *International Journal of Production Economics, 120*(1), 176–189.

Caniato, F., Crippa, L., Pero, M., Sianesi, A., & Spina, G. (2015). Internationalisation and outsourcing of operations and product development in the fashion industry. *Production Planning & Control, 26*(9), 706–722.

Coombs, W. T., & Holladay, S. J. (2002). Helping crisis managers protect reputational assets: Initial tests of the situational crisis communication theory. *Management Communication Quarterly, 16*(2), 165–186.

Davies, I. A., Lee, Z. I., & Ahonkhai, I. (2012). Do consumers care about ethical-luxury? *Journal of Business Ethics, 106*(1), 37–51.

Dekhili, S., Achabou, M. A., & Alharbi, F. (2019). Could sustainability improve the promotion of luxury products? *European Business Review, 31*(4), 488–511.

Dion, D., & Arnould, E. (2011). Retail luxury strategy: Assembling charisma through art and magic. *Journal of Retailing, 87*(4), 502–520.

Dion, D., & Borraz, S. (2017). Managing status: How luxury brands shape class subjectivities in the service encounter. *Journal of Marketing, 81*(5), 67–85.

Franco, J. C., Hussain, D., & McColl, R. (2019). Luxury fashion and sustainability: Looking good together. *Journal of Business Strategy*. https://doi.org/10.1108/JBS-05-2019-0089.

Janssen, C., Vanhamme, J., Lindgreen, A., & Lefebvre, C. (2013). The catch-22 of responsible luxury: Effects of luxury product characteristics on consumers' perceptions of fit with corporate social responsibility. *Journal of Business Ethics, 119*(1), 45–57.

Kapferer, J.-N. (1997). Managing luxury brands. *Journal of Brand Management, 4*(4), 251–260.

Kapferer, J.-N. (2010). All that glitters is not green: The challenge of sustainable luxury. *European Business Review, 2*, 40–45.

Kapferer, J.-N. (2012). Abundant rarity: The key to luxury growth. *Business Horizons, 55*(5), 453–462.

Kapferer, J.-N., & Michaut-Denizeau, A. (2013). Is luxury compatible with sustainable development: The consumer viewpoint. *Journal of Brand Management, 21*(I), 1–22. https://doi.org/10.1057/bm.2013.19.

Kapferer, J. N., & Michaut-Denizeau, A. (2019). Are millennials really more sensitive to sustainable luxury? A cross-generational international comparison of sustainability consciousness when buying luxury. *Journal of Brand Management, 8*(3), 1–13.

Kapferer, J.-N., & Valette-Florence, P. (2018). The impact of brand penetration and awareness on luxury brand desirability: A cross country analysis of the relevance of the rarity principle. *Journal of Business Research, 83*, 38–50.

Kotler, P., & Lee, N. (2008). *Corporate social responsibility: Doing the most good for your company and your cause*. Hoboken, NJ: Wiley.

Lawson, B. (2006). *How designers think: The design process demystified*. Routledge.

Lee, J. E., & Watkins, B. (2016). YouTube vloggers' influence on consumer luxury brand perceptions and intentions. *Journal of Business Research, 69*(12), 5753–5760. http://dx.doi.org/10.1016/j.jbusres.2016.04.171.

Moore, C. M., Fernie, J., & Burt, S. (2000). Brands without boundaries: The internationalisation of the designer retailer's brand. *European Journal of Marketing, 34*(8), 919–937.
Mores, C. M. (2007). *From Fiorucci to the guerrilla stores: Shop displays in architecture marketing and communications*. Oxford: Windsor Books.
Nobbs, K., Moore, C. M., & Sheridan, M. (2012). The flagship format within the luxury fashion market. *International Journal of Retail & Distribution Management, 40*(12), 920–934.
NYTimes. (2017). https://www.nytimes.com/2017/08/03/business/alibaba-kering-fakes-luxury.html.
Okonkwo, U. (2016). *Luxury fashion branding: Trends, tactics, techniques*. Springer.
Phan, M., Thomas, R., & Heine, K. (2011). Social media and luxury brand management: The case of Burberry. *Journal of Global Fashion Marketing, 2*(4), 213–222.
Quach, S., & Thaichon, P. (2017). From connoisseur luxury to mass luxury: Value co-creation and co-destruction in the online environment. *Journal of Business Research, 81*, 163–172.
Risius, A., Janssen, M., & Hamm, U. (2017). Consumer preferences for sustainable aquaculture products: Evidence from in-depth interviews, think aloud protocols and choice experiments. *Appetite, 113*, 246–254.
Ryan, N. (2007). Prada and the art of patronage. *Fashion Theory, 11*(1), 7–24.
Steele, V. (1996). *Fetish: Fashion, sex and power*. New York: Oxford University Press.
Thach, L., & Olsen, J. (2015). Profiling the high frequency wine consumer by price segmentation in the US market. *Wine Economics and Policy, 4*(1), 53–59.
Tynan, C., McKechnie, S., & Chhuon, C. (2010). Co-creating value for luxury brands. *Journal of Business Research, 63*(11), 1156–1163.
Van de Ven, B. (2008). An ethical framework for the marketing of corporate social responsibility. *Journal of Business Ethics, 82*(2), 339–352.
Voyer, B. G., & Beckham, D. (2014). Can sustainability be luxurious? A mixed-method investigation of implicit and explicit attitudes towards sustainable luxury consumption. *Advances in Consumer Research, 42*, 245–250.
Weierter, S. J. (2001). The organization of charisma: Promoting, creating, and idealizing self. *Organization Studies, 22*(1), 91–115.

Willems, K., Janssens, W., Swinnen, G., Brengman, M., Streukens, S., & Vancauteren, M. (2012). From Armani to Zara: Impression formation based on fashion store patronage. *Journal of Business Research, 65*(10), 1487–1494.

Summary

Value is constructed by consumers. It results from individual aspirations, expresses personal beliefs about what is good and important at a given time and in the specific social and economic environment. Value is a subjective measure depending on the environment, psychological make up, emotions felt and the possibility to obtain and process information.

An individual's choices and decisions reflect his or her value system as a set of general beliefs about what is good and important. However the relationship between the purchase of a good and an individual's overall value system is ambiguous. The evaluation of the value proposition of a particular good is influenced not only by what the consumer thinks and believes is good and important to them personally, but also by situational factors, social pressure of different reference groups or a set of affective factors (mood, momentary emotions, etc.).

It is the consumer who co-creates the value of the good, companies only offer its proposition. If the value expected by the consumer coincides with the company's offer and the financial means and circumstances allow it the purchase takes place. It is in the process of consumption that the experiential; value in use and context is shaped. However the expected value is influenced by the experience of consumption of the

B. Stępień, *The Value of Luxury*, Palgrave Advances in Luxury, https://doi.org/10.1007/978-3-030-51218-7

same or similar goods hence the assessment of the value proposition by consumers is a result of their experiences and expectations.

Luxury goods are perceived by consumers as characterized by mastery and artistry, high quality materials, are expensive, beautiful and rare. However their value is built not only on their functionality but above all on their aesthetics, social desire and the positive emotions that consumption of them brings.

From a philosophical point of view luxury has an instrumental value as it brings pleasure. The immanent value of luxury is built by the element of beauty—a combination of artistry with the intensity of aesthetic feelings. Other features of luxury products do not create value from the philosophical point of view; goodness in an ethical sense. However due to their high prices and limited availability they are the object of simultaneous social desire and moral stigma. It is therefore not surprising that luxury has been the subject of negative moral judgments for centuries.

Research in sociology and social psychology shows that it is to a big extent the environment that shapes the perception of luxury. The purchase and use of these goods, however, is not only due to their social symbolism. Luxury can be seen as aesthetic and functional but it gains additional social and symbolic value because others recognize, appreciate and desire it. As convincingly written in books such as (Bourdieu 1984; Girard et al. 2003; Orléan 2014), social impact and crowd chase over certain products or services enhances their value in the social space and in the individual's belief.

The psychological research in the field of value analysis shows that the very process of valuation—the assessment of what is important, good and rewarding for an individual—is automatic[1] and is an innate skill. Within this process the individual not only recognizes his or her individual needs and desires but also confronts them with what he or she knows and feels is socially relevant. Through the process of evaluation the individual strives for subjective well-being guided by both cognition and emotion. Emotions are not only a kind of filter in the process of evaluating goods and making purchasing choices but also an aim and value in itself. The consumption of luxury evokes positive emotions, improves

[1] Automatism does not mean irrationality.

the well-being of an individual (by dealing with goods perceived as rare, beautiful or functional) and is also a way to build social status. In the latter case we are dealing with a positive social mirror effect.

The value proposition of luxury goods is created by companies offering them on the market. They communicate this proposition exposing mainly the auric components of the products, built on artistic and aesthetic components, above-average functionality and attention to the manufacturing and San_sps@345 process. The effectiveness of spreading this aura is later reflected in the scale of monetization and depends not only on the aesthetic or functional quality of the offer but also on the mimetic wave of demand. The value proposition, created nowadays only partially in accordance with the principles of the canon of luxury business (the lower the level of the luxury pyramid, the more noticeable the deviation from these assumptions) is instrumental for companies in relation to the exchangeable value of these goods.

As presented in Chapters 5, 6 and 7 consumers when asked to assess the value components of luxury goods' value social and aesthetic components were those rated first and foremost. It is thanks to the symbolic power of social influence that consumers aspiring from new, fast-growing markets of luxury can shape their social image treating luxury goods as a public attribute of professional and life success.

However consumers from the countries surveyed (mainly from Poland, Saudi Arabia, Portugal, Turkey, India and Germany) are not homogeneous in their assessment of luxury and the components of values it embodies. One should agree with P. Shukla (2010) that when buying the same luxury goods consumers do so for different reasons and appreciate different value components in them. The assessment of all value components in countries that can be characterized as luxury fast growing markets is higher than in the case of the group of German respondents who are rather contestants than admirers of luxury.

Consumers from these growing luxury markets also present more polarized opinions on the value of luxury compared to German consumers. This may be explained by a kind of early stage of luxury consumption in these countries when the dynamic growth of consumption is associated with a certain aura of being swallowed up by the novelty and uniqueness of this hitherto unknown state—the possibility of enjoying previously inaccessible objects of dreams. Although the countries surveyed (apart from Germany, treated here as a reference group) record relatively high economic growth or an already high GDP *per capita* (the case of Saudi Arabia), it is accompanied by many social inequalities against an economic, political, religious or cultural background. In the rapidly growing markets of luxury there is a dynamic process of shaping the social assessment of luxury consumption and the co-occurrence of clearly opposing and unequivocally favourable assessments.

In the sample studied the greatest supporters of luxury are Saudis and Indians who evaluate all its components (social, aesthetic, functional, hedonic) at the highest level of the consumers from the whole sample. Such high ratings for these two countries however must be explained by different reasons. While the consumption of luxury (as a status-forming tool) in Saudi Arabia seems to be a form of balancing the strict social rules based on a dogmatic interpretation of the Koran (Alserhan 2010; Tjahjono 2011; Hanzaee and Teimourpour 2012) in India it realizes something seemingly impossible so far—to move to a higher social caste through possession and exposure of wealth.

The market-based differentiation in the perception of the value of luxury cannot be explained only by referring to the culture of the countries surveyed. National culture permanently shapes the value system of individuals but it is one of many forces, alongside individual characteristics or the institutional and economic conditions of markets.

The perception of the value of luxury, although determined by place of residence, age, level of education, income and gender, depends most heavily on the psychographic characteristics of consumers. Psychographic segmentation carried out on the basis of the results of international quantitative research concerning the consumer luxury value perception (CLVP) has identified three international homogeneous groups of consumers: Hedonists, Distant Admirers and Status-oriented. For Hedonists (individualists with an internal locus of motivation, valuing positive emotions and the sense of uniqueness) luxury is a tool to emphasize their good taste and improve their well-being. Luxury goods are supposed to be unique, have above all an aura of uniqueness and are supposed to positively enhance the Hedonist's style and personality. For this group it does not matter much how the general public evaluates luxury. The segment of Distant Admirers sees the main value of luxury products in their artistry personified in design and craftsmanship. The impression that luxury makes on others is noticed but does not create positive emotions. For a Status-oriented group luxury is a symbol of social prestige and the main reason for its purchase. In this segment a mimetic, bandwagon inclination is most evident whereas the uniqueness of the product is a demotivating factor as it suggests little recognition. Luxury does not stimulate positive emotions, it is not a sign of taking care of oneself—it is supposed to show that the owner/user of the product is a member of a thriving and influential group. Apart from psychological and lifestyle characteristics the criterion best describing the segments is the country of residence of the respondents. The group of Hedonists includes mainly Portuguese and Polish. Turks and Germans are mostly Distant Admirers and the Status-oriented group is dominated by Indians and Saudis.

The described segments also differently value the contribution of businesses in building value propositions for luxury goods. For Hedonists, value is only enhanced by the uniqueness and design of the product which is created by designers and manufacturers. The influence of other links (retailers or other consumers) is not important for this group. The opposite is true for Status-oriented consumers. The uniqueness of a product has a negative impact on its value as it means less recognition. Significantly this group seems not to notice the influence of other consumers, the name of the designer or the role of the sellers in creating the value of luxury. For Distant Admirers the luxury value is increased thanks to the professional help of salesmen, while the uniqueness of the products reduces it as it is a sign of snobbish consumption and ostentation for these consumers.

The analysis of the perception of companies' contribution to creating and communicating the value of luxury shows that the most important, most "value-creating" links are designers and manufacturers. However the representatives of enterprises have a different perspective on the contribution of individual links to the creation and communication of luxury value than consumers. More often than consumers they emphasize (although this varies from industry to industry: fashion, jewellery and cars) that the value of luxury is constructed and communicated by other consumers (fashion industry), retailers (all industries) and manufacturers (car industry).

Vendors are an important link in creating and communicating the value of luxury which can also help to promote the growing commitment of the luxury sector to sustainable development. However research shows that this element of value is still not considered important by today's consumers of luxury goods (both in their quantitative and hidden purchases).

Managerial Implications

Fast growing luxury markets should not be treated equally as they show clear differences in CLVP. Aspiring consumers do not constitute a homogeneous group, they differ significantly not only due to the country they live in, but first of all due to their individual psychological characteristics and different perceptions of luxury value.

What is more despite the great importance that companies attach to the public opinion about the differentiation of the approach to luxury by generations Y and X (it manifests itself in the differentiation of strategies), the research conducted and described in this book clearly shows that CLVP is in fact similar in the cohort of Millennials and Generation X. This is mainly due to the broad age framework and covering different family and professional roles played by consumers of these generations.

Despite the observed convergence and differences in the CLVP between consumers the dynamic growth of production volume and democratization of the luxury goods sector are still not reflected in consumers' perception of values that symbolize these goods. In spite of the increasingly clear departure of companies from the canon of luxury business which manifests itself in the spread of sales, the stretching and expansion of brands, the dispersion of supply chains and the use of multi-channel, intensive communication consumers from the growing luxury markets still perceive these goods as rare, beautiful, expensive and with above-average functionality. Although the price is for consumers more an indicator of social desire than actual cost they still have a rather traditional view of luxury. Why then does this perception persist despite the evident democratization of luxury?

The first reason may be due to effective communication campaigns emphasizing traditional features of luxury. Another reason lies in the symbolic aura of these goods. The main motive for purchase may be to build a specific public image although at the same time the functional and aesthetic values of these goods are still noticed and valued. The third reason seems to be the most important and concerns the point of reference—the basis against which consumers assess the proposal of the value of luxury goods. In the face of accelerated global consumption, which is manifested by a shortening of the life cycle of products, a continuous increase in the production volume of consumer goods and a decrease in their quality and durability, luxury goods are still perceived positively. As everything else becomes disposable luxury appears to be relatively durable and solid.

The research results presented in the book indicate that a more effective marketing strategy in the international arena is to base segmentation on psychographic criteria. In the communication strategy of luxury brands (from all levels of the pyramid) it seems justified to emphasize their uniqueness and artistic components. This is due to the interdependence of snobby and imitative inclinations shown in the research. Both groups (with snobby and mimic inclinations) highly value the uniqueness of these goods. Although the behaviour of snobs and bandwagoners are the result of comparison to different reference groups and stem from different locus of control, for both groups social recognition is important.

Limitations, Future Research Agenda

The book focuses on diagnosing and recognizing the rationale for valuing luxury by consumers and assessing the value proposition of businesses in this market. In order to achieve this goal it was necessary to deconstruct the concepts of value and luxury.

In the empirical analysis the opinions of consumers from new, fast-growing luxury markets and selected representatives of companies from the luxury supply market were the subject of research. However the sample of consumers analyzed does not include all countries that can be described as fast-growing luxury markets. Much has been written about China, although still not enough. Further research is needed for example in Russia, Brazil or other CEE countries in order to check how convergent (or diverse) the luxury perception is on these markets.

Likewise it would be useful and enriching to analyze the views of more companies operating in the luxury market with a view to gaining a more in-depth understanding of their contribution to the creation of particular value components and their importance for consumers.

An important limitation of the considerations made here is the focus on examining the perception of the value of luxury goods. It seems that the analysis of service value components would reveal more of the importance of the hedonic value component and provide more guidance for forecasting luxury brand strategies. The turbulent changes in the luxury market are caused not only by the dynamic growth in the number of aspiring consumers but also by the impact of Internet technologies and the development of sharing trends as well as the emphasis on the experience and ephemerality at the expense of ownership. The growing trend of sustainable consumption and the promotion of altruistic behaviour also points to the need to redefine existing business models and makes us reflect on the future face of luxury. If we consider that automation and robotization including the spread of autonomous products and self-production with 3D printers is a matter of the next decades the image of luxury (both of the categories of goods and the functioning of this market as a business) may undergo a significant transformation. Existing luxury products may become mass, available ones and the global luxury market will be dominated by sophisticated (and thus accessible only to the rich) ways of prolonging life and beauty, location-based enclaves for living and entertainment or the offer of sophisticated experiences in virtual reality (Harari 2018).

The book only indicates the relationship between the consumption of luxury and an individual's feeling of happiness. This area despite the already published research on the negative relationship between the propensity for materialism and the perception of one's own well-being and happiness still seems interesting and unrecognized by research, especially if the considerations are combined with the individual and social perception of well-being. We still do not know how the individual perception of well-being and the consumption of luxury are linked to the dissemination (within a country) of the idea of social equality and its individual perception in ethical terms.

The book also presents the evolution of business models in the luxury sector clearly aimed at drawing on the solutions of the world of finance and the fast moving goods sector. We are dealing with mergers, buyouts, brand expansion and progressive accession. At the time of writing this book the world has been affected by the COVID 19 pandemic which has had a significant impact on the luxury sector. Instead of the planned growth that the industry has been experiencing for many years (except during periods of mild stagnation caused by 9/11 and the last financial crisis in 2007), the luxury industry has experienced a significant fall in its sales (see Bain 2020). Purchases of luxury goods, as the most discretional ones, have been postponed by millions—both aspiring and rich consumers—for a further indefinite period. Online shopping was the industry's salvation at the pandemic time although it was only 20 to 30 percent of revenue. The world is watching closely for a return to China's new normality to estimate the pace of recovery from this. However data from China do not encourage optimism. Turnover in the luxury industry is growing at a slower-than-expected rate and Chinese interest in native luxury brands is increasing. The pandemic has also—although it is not known whether it is permanent—changed consumers' attitudes to shopping. With the real threat of income losses due to the national economies' lockdown consumers are more cautious in their purchasing choices. Awareness of life transience which has reverbed strongly during a pandemic, redirected consumers' attention to the well—being sector which is likely to develop dynamically in the near future. The COVID 19 pandemic by significantly reducing both the volume and changing the sale channel into digital one may contribute to the reshaping of business models in the sector. We will probably see a dynamic development of the virtualization of communication and sales (evident before the pandemic) and perhaps a certain return to a model of unhurried, limited production of rare, valuable but unfortunately not available for the general public.

Despite the many findings described in the book the question about the value of luxury still remains open as we live in a world where the pace of transformation surprises us and its only lasting feature is change.

References

Aaker, J. L., Benet-Martinez, V., & Garolera, J. (2001). Consumption symbols as carriers of culture: A study of Japanese and Spanish brand personality constucts. *Journal of Personality and Social Psychology, 81*(3), 492–508.

Achabou, M. A., & Dekhili, S. (2013). Luxury and sustainable development: Is there a match? *Journal of Business Research, 66*(10), 1896–1903. https://doi.org/10.1016/j.jbusres.2013.02.011.

Adamiec, M. (1983). Działanie, wartość, sens-zarys systemu pojęć. *Przegląd Psychologiczny, 26*(1), 3–23.

Agarwal, S., & Teas, R. K. (2001). Perceived value: Mediating role of perceived risk. *Journal of Marketing Theory and Practice, 9*(4), 1–14.

Ahn, J., Park, J. K., & Hyun, H. (2018). Luxury product to service brand extension and brand equity transfer. *Journal of Retailing and Consumer Services, 42*, 22–28.

Ajzen, I., & Fishbein, M. (1977). Attitude-behavior relations: A theoretical analysis and review of empirical research. *Psychological Bulletin, 84*(5), 888–918.

Alden, Dana L., Jan-Benedict, E. M. Steenkamp, & Batra, R. (1999). Brand positioning through advertising in Asia, North America, and Europe: The role of global consumer culture. *Journal of Marketing, 63*, 75–87.

B. Stępień, *The Value of Luxury*, Palgrave Advances in Luxury, https://doi.org/10.1007/978-3-030-51218-7

Allen, V. L., & Wilder, D. A. (1977). Social comparison, self-evaluation, and conformity to the group. In J. M. Suls & R. L. Miller (Eds.), *Social comparison processes: Theoretical and empirical perspectives* (s. 187–208). Washington, DC: Hemisphere.

Alserhan, B. A. (2010). On Islamic branding: Brands as good deeds. *Journal of Islamic Marketing, 1*(2), 101–106.

Alserhan, B. A., Bataineh, M. K., Halkias, D., & Komodromos, M. (2014). Measuring luxury brand consumption and female consumers' religiosity in the Uae. *Journal of Developmental Entrepreneurship, 19*(2), 1450009.

Alwin, D. F. (1986). Religion and parental childrearing orientations: Evidence of a Catholic-Protestant convergence. *American Journal of Sociology, 92,* 412–440.

Amatulli, C., De Angelis, M., Korschun, D., & Romani, S. (2018). Consumers' perceptions of luxury brands' CSR initiatives: An investigation of the role of status and conspicuous consumption. *Journal of cleaner production, 194,* 277–287.

Amatulli, C., Guido, G., & Nataraajan, R. (2015). Luxury purchasing among older consumers: Exploring inferences about cognitive age, status, and style motivations. *Journal of Business Research, 68*(9), 1945–1952.

Anderson, C. H., & Vincze, J. W. (2000). *Cases in strategic marketing management*. Boston: Houghton Mifflin Company.

Anderson, J. C., & Narus, J. A. (1998). Business marketing: Understand what customers value. *Harvard Business Review, 76,* 53–65.

Andjelic, A. (2017). *Blockchain and the internet of luxury*. From z. https://medium.com/@andjelicaaa/blockchain-and-the-internet-of-luxury-ee5c956b83bf.

Antoni, F., Burgelman, R. A., & Meza, P. (2004). *LVMH in 2004: The challenges of strategic integration.* Harvard: Harvard Business School Case.

Appadurai, A. (1986). Commodities and the politics of value. In A. Appaduarai (Ed.), *The social life of things: Commodities in cultural perspective*. Cambridge: Cambridge University Press.

Archpru Akaka, M., & Chandler, J. D. (2011). Roles as resources: A social roles perspective of change in value networks. *Marketing Theory, 11*(3), 243–260.

Arkes, H. R., & Blumer, C. (2000). The psychology of sunk cost. *Judgment and decision making: An interdisciplinary reader* (pp. 97ff). Cambridge: Cambridge University Press.

Armitage, J., & Roberts, J. (2016). The spirit of luxury. *Public Culture, 12*(1), 1–22.

Arnould, E. J., & Thompson, C. J. (2005). Consumer culture theory (CCT): Twenty years of research. *Journal of Consumer Research, 31*(4), 868–882.

Arnould, E. J., & Thompson, C. J. (2007). Consumer culture theory (and we really mean theoretics): Dilemmas and opportunities posed by an academic branding strategy. *Research in Consumer Behavior, 11,* 3–22.

Arnould, E. J., Price, L. L., & Otnes, C. (1999). Making (consumption) magic: A study of white water river rafting. *Journal of Contemporary Ethnography, 28*(1), 33–68.

Arvidsson, A., & Malossi, G. (2011). Customer co-production from social factory to brand: Learning from Italian fashion. In D. Zwick & J. Cayla (Eds.), *Inside marketing: Practices, ideologies, devices* (s. 212–233). New York: Oxford University Press.

Ashby, F. G., & Isen, A. M. (1999). A neuropsychological theory of positive affect and its influence on cognition. *Psychological Review, 106*(3), 529.

Ashby, F. G., Isen, A. M., & Turken, A. U. (1999). A neuropsychological theory of positive affect and its influence on cognition. *Psychological Review, 106*(3), 529–550.

Atwal, G., & Williams, A. (2008). Marketing in postmodern India: Bulgari meets bollywood. *Indian Journal of Marketing, 38*(1).

Atwal, G., & Williams, A. (2009). Luxury brand marketing—The experience is everything! *Journal of Brand Management, 16*(5–6), 338–346.

Aumann, R. J. (1985). An axiomatization of the non-transferable utility value. *Econometrica: Journal of the Econometric Society, 53*(3), 599–612.

Aumann, R. J. (2005). *Robert J. Aumann prize lecture*. From z. https://www.nobelprize.org/prizes/economic-sciences/2005/aumann/lecture/.

Aumann, R. J., & Shapley, L. S. (2015). *Values of non-atomic games*. Princeton, NJ: Princeton University Press.

Bagozzi, R. P. (2006). Consumer action. In N. K. Malhotra (Ed.), *Review of marketing research* (s. 3–42). Armonk, NY: Emerald Group.

Bagwell, L. S., & Bernheim, B. D. (1996). Veblen effects in a theory of conspicuous consumption. *The American Economic Review, 86*(3), 349–373.

Bahr, N. & Pendergast, D. (2007). Millennial adolescent, the. *Millennial adolescent, The*, ix.

Bain. (2014). *Luxury goods worldwide market study fall-winter 2014: The rise of the borderless consumer*. https://www.bain.com/insights/luxury-goods-worldwide-market-study-december-2014/.

Bain. (2020). *Luxury after COVID 19, changed for (the) good?* https://www.bain.com/insights/luxury-after-coronavirus/.

Bain & Co. (2019). *Eight themes that are rewriting the future of luxury goods.* https://www.bain.com/insights/eight-themes-that-are-rewriting-the-future-of-luxury-goods/.

Bain & Co. (2020a). *Global personal luxury goods market set to contract between 20–35 percent in 2020.* https://www.bain.com/about/media-center/press-releases/2020/spring-luxury-report/.

Bain & Co. (2020b). *Luxury after Covid-19: Changed for (the) good?*https://www.bain.com/insights/luxury-after-coronavirus/.

Bain & Company. (2016). https://www.bain.com/insights/luxury-goods-worldwide-market-study-fall-winter-2016/.

Baker, J., Parasuraman, A., Grewal, D., & Voss, G. B. (2002). The influence of multiple store environment cues on perceived merchandise value and patronage intentions. *The Journal of Marketing, 66*(2), 20–141.

Balabanis, G., & Diamantopoulos, A. (2008). Brand origin identification by consumers: A classification perspective. *Journal of International Marketing, 16*(1), 39–71.

Baley, S. (1959). *Wprowadzenie do psychologii społecznej.* Warszawa: Państwowe Wydawnictwo Naukowe.

Ballantyne, D., Christopher, M., & Payne, A. (1995). Improving the quality of services marketing: Service (re) design is the critical link. *Journal of Marketing Management, 11*(1–3), 7–24.

Bartkowiak, R. (2003). *Historia myśli ekonomicznej.* Warszawa: Polskie Wydaw. Ekonomiczne.

Bartosik-Purgat, M. (2011). *Kulturowe uwarunkowania zachowań konsumentów na przykładzie młodych Europejczyków.* Poznań: Wydawnictwo Uniwersytetu Ekonomicznego w Poznaniu.

Bastien, V., & Kapferer, J. N. (2013). More on luxury anti-laws of marketing. In *Luxury marketing* (pp. 19–34). Wiesbaden: Gabler Verlag.

Batat, W. (2019a). *Digital luxury: Transforming brands and consumer experiences.* Los Angeles: Sage.

Batat, W. (2019b). *The new luxury experience.* New York: Springer International Publishing.

Baudrillard, J. (2016). *The consumer society: Myths and structures.* Sage.

Baumgartner, H. (2010). A review of prior classifications of purchase behavior and a proposal for a new typology. In N. K. Malhotra (Ed.), *Review of marketing research* (s. 3–36). Bingley: Emerald Group.

Baumgartner, W., & Pasquerella, L. (2004). Brentano's value theory: Beauty, goodness, and the concept of correct emotion. In D. Jacquette (Ed.), *Cambridge companion to Brentano.* Cambridge: Cambridge University Press.

Bearden, W. O., & Etzel, M. J. (1982). Reference group influence on product and brand purchase decisions. *Journal of Consumer Research, 9*(2), 183–194.

Becher, S. I. (2007). Behavioral science and consumer standard form contracts. *Louisiana Law Review, 68*(1), 117–179.

Becker, G. S. (1976). Pride and prejudice. In G. S. Becker (Ed.), *The economic approach to human behavior*. Chicago: University of Chicago Press.

Becker, G. S. (1993). *Human capital: A theoretical and empirical analysis, with special reference to education* (3rd ed.). Chicago: The University of Chicago Press.

Belk, R. (1985). Materialism: Trait aspects of living in the material world. *Journal of Consumer Research, 12*(3), 265–280.

Belk, R. (1988). Possessions and the extended self. *Journal of Consumer Research, 15*(2), 139–168.

Benoit, H. (1999). In search of the Lost Aura: The object in the age of marketing romanticism. In S. Brown, A-M. Doherty, & B. Clarke (Eds.), *Romancing the market* (s. 187–201). London, New York: Routledge.

Berg, M. (2004). In pursuit of luxury: Global history and British consumer goods in the eighteenth century. *Past & Present, 182*, 85–142.

Berger, P., & Luckmann, T. (1967). *The social construction of reality: A treatise in the sociology of knowledge* (pp. 52–54). Garden City, NY: Doubleday.

Berger, P. D., & Nasr, N. I. (1998). Customer lifetime value: Marketing models and applications. *Journal of Interactive Marketing, 12*(1), 17–30.

Berry, C. (1994). *The idea of luxury: A conceptual and historical investigation*. Cambridge, UK: Cambridge University Press.

Berthon, P., Pitt, L., Parent, M., & Berthon, J. P. (2009). Aesthetics and ephemerality: Observing and preserving the luxury brand. *California Management Review, 52*(1), 45–66.

Bettman, J. R. (1979). Memory factors in consumer choice: A review. *The Journal of Marketing, 43*, 37–53.

Bettman, J. R., Luce, M. F., & Payne, J. W. (1998). Constructive consumer choice processes. *Journal of Consumer Research, 25*(3), 187–217.

Beutel, A. M., & Marini, M. M. (1995). Gender and values. *American Sociological Review, 60*, 436–448.

Beverland, M., & Lockshin, L. (2003). A longitudinal study of customers' desired value change in business-to-business markets. *Industrial Marketing Management, 32*(8), 653–666.

Białynicka-Birula, J. (2003). Wartość dzieła sztuki w kontekście teorii estetycznych & ekonomicznych. *Zeszyty Naukowe Akademii Ekonomicznej w Krakowie, 640*, 63–75.

Bian, Q., & Forsythe, S. (2012). Purchase intention for luxury brands: A cross cultural comparison. *Journal of Business Research, 65*(10), 1443–1451.

Blackwell, R. D., Miniard, P. W., & Engel, J. F. (2001). *Consumer behavior 9th.* Mason, OH: South-Western Thomas Learning.

Bless, H., Bohner, G., Schwarz, N., & Strack, F. (1990). Mood and persuasion: A cognitive response analysis. *Personality and Social Psychology Bulletin, 16*(2), 331–345.

Bless, H., Clore, G. L., Schwarz, N., Golisano, V., Rabe, C., & Wölk, M. (1996). Mood and the use of scripts: Does a happy mood really lead to mindlessness? *Journal of Personality and Social Psychology, 71*(4), 665–679.

Block, J. (1977). Advancing the psychology of personality: Paradigmatic shift or improving the quality of research. *Personality at the crossroads: Current issues in interactional psychology*, 2.

BMW Group. (2017). *Supplier management*. Pobrane z. https://www.bmw group.com.

Bochańczyk-Kupka, D. (2014). Luksus i dobra luksusowe. *Studia Ekonomiczne, 176*, 97–108.

Bośkowska, A. (2017). *Księżyc z Pewexu.* Wydawnictwo Czarne: O luksusie w PRL-u.

Bodenhausen, G. V. (1993). Emotions, arousal, and stereotypic judgments: A heuristic model of affect and stereotyping. In D. M. Mackie & D. L. Hamilton (Eds.), *Affect, cognition and stereotyping* (s. 13–37). San Diego, CA: Academic Press.

Bodenhausen, G. V., Sheppard, L. A., & Kramer, G. P. (1994). Negative affect and social judgment: The differential impact of anger and sadness. *European Journal of Social Psychology, 24*(1), 45–62.

Bolton, L. E., Warlop, L., & Alba, J. W. (2003). Consumer perceptions of price (un) fairness. *Journal of Consumer Research, 29*(4), 474–491.

Bombol, M. (2012). *Kształtująca się polska klasa wyższa: Szkice ekonomiczno-społeczne*. Warszawa: Oficyna Wydawnicza Szkoła Główna Handlowa w Warszawie.

Bond, M. H. (2002). Reclaiming the individual from Hofstede's ecological analysis—A 20-year odyssey. *Psychological Bulletin, 128*(1), 73–77.

Borys, T. (1980). *Elementy teorii jakości.* Warszawa: PWN.

Bothwell, C. (2005). *Burberry versus the Chavs: BBC news*, 28. From z. http://news.bbc.co.uk/2/hi/business/4381140.stm.

Bourdieu, P. (1977). *Outline of a theory of practice* (Vol. 16). Cambridge University Press.

Bourdieu, P. (1984). *Distinction: A social critique of the judgement of taste*. Cambridge, MA: Harvard University.

Bourdieu, P. (2013). The forms of capital by Pierre Bourdieu 1986. *Marxists Internet Archive. Np.*

Bourdieu, P., & Wacquant, L. (2013). Symbolic capital and social classes. *Journal of Classical Sociology, 13*(2), 292–302.

Braund, D. (1994). The luxuries of Athenian democracy. *Greece & Rome, 41*(1), 41–48.

Brewer, M. B. (1991). The social self: On being the same and different at the same time. *Personality and Social Psychology Bulletin, 17*(5), 475–482.

Brewer, M. B., & Gardner, W. (1996). Who is this "we"? Levels of collective identity and self-representations. *Journal of Personality and Social Psychology, 71*(1), 83–93.

Brewer, M. B., & Lui, L. N. (1989). The primacy of age and sex in the structure of person categories. *Social Cognition, 7*(3), 262–274.

Brickman, P., & Bulman, R. J. (1977). Pleasure and pain in social comparison. *Social Comparison Processes: Theoretical and Empirical Perspectives, 149*, 186.

Brodie, R. J., Löbler, H., & Fehrer, J. A. (2019). Evolution of service-dominant logic: Towards a paradigm and metatheory of the market and value cocreation? *Industrial Marketing Management, 79*, 3–12.

Brooke, S. (2004, 4 stycznia). Luxuries ain't what they used to be: Now the high street is full of designers labels and glittering prices, does anything count as exclusive. *The Daily Telegraph*, s. 4.

Brun, A., & Castelli, C. (2013). The nature of luxury: A consumer perspective. *International Journal of Retail & Distribution Management, 41*(11/12), 823–847.

Brun, A., & Moretto, A. (2012). Contract design and supply chain management in the luxury jewellery industry. *International Journal of Retail & Distribution Management,* 40(8), 607–628. From z. http://dx.doi.org/10.1108/09590551211245416.

Brzozowski, P. (2007). *Wzorcowa hierarchia wartości: polska, europejska czy uniwersalna? psychologiczne badania empiryczne*. Wydawnictwo Uniwersytetu Marii Curie-Skłodowskiej.

Burgiel, A. (2014). *Społeczne zjawiska w zachowaniach polskich konsumentów: Oddziaływania społeczne, naśladownictwo, ostentacja i snobizm*. Katowice: wydawnictwo Uniwersytetu Ekonomicznego w Katowicach.

Burgiel, A., & Sowa, I. (2000). Potrzeby konsumpcyjne jako przesłanki zachowań konsumentów. In E. Kieżel (red.), *Rynkowe zachowania*

konsumentów. Katowice: Wydawnictwo Akademii Ekonomicznej w Katowicach.
BusinessInsider. (2019). *The state of GenZ*. https://www.businessinsider.com/gen-z-shopping-habits-kill-brands-2019-7?IR=T.
Buss, D. M. (1989). Sex differences in human mate preferences: Evolutionary hypotheses tested in 37 cultures. *Behavioral and Brain Sciences, 12*(1), 1–14.
Butz, H. E., & Goodstein, L. D. (1996). Measuring customer value: Gaining the strategic advantage. *Organizational Dynamics, 24,* 63–77. https://doi.org/10.1016/S0090-2616(96)90006-6.
Bylok, F. (2012). Orientacja na przyjemność w zachowaniach konsumentów. *Konsumpcja i Rozwój, 1,* 48–60.
Bywalec, C. (2010). *Konsumpcja a rozwój gospodarczy i społeczny*. Warszawa: Wydawnictwo C.H. Beck.
Calori, R., Melin, L., Atamer, T., & Gustavsson, P. (2000). Innovative international strategies. *Journal of World Business, 35*(4), 333–354.
Camerer, C. (1999). Behavioral economics: Reunifying psychology and economics. *Proceedings of the National Academy of Sciences, 96*(19), 10575–10577.
Caniato, F., Caridi, M., Castelli, C., & Golini, R. (2009). A contingency approach for SC strategy in the Italian luxury industry: Do consolidated models fit? *International Journal of Production Economics, 120*(1), 176–189.
Caniato, F., Crippa, L., Pero, M., Sianesi, A., & Spina, G. (2015). Internationalisation and outsourcing of operations and product development in the fashion industry. *Production Planning & Control, 26*(9), 706–722.
Caniato, F., Caridi, M., Crippa, L., & Moretto, A. (2012). Environmental sustainability in fashion supply chains: An exploratory case based research. *International Journal of Production Economics, 135,* 659–670.
Carver, C. S., & Scheier, M. F. (2000). On the structure of behavioral self-regulation. In M. Boekaerts, P. R. Pintrich, & M. Zeidner (Eds.), *Handbook of self-regulation* (s. 41–84). New York: Cambridge University Press.
Castelli, C. M., & Sianesi, A. (2015). Supply chain strategy for companies in the luxury-fashion market: Aligning the supply chain towards the critical success factors. *International Journal of Retail & Distribution Management, 43*(10/11), 940–966.
Chadha, R., & Husband, P. (2006). *The cult of the luxury brand: Inside Asia's love affair with luxury*. London: Nicholas Brealey.
Chahal, H., & Kumari, N. (2012). Consumer perceived value: The development of a multiple item scale in hospitals in the Indian context. *International*

Journal of Pharmaceutical and Healthcare Marketing, 6(2), 167–190. https://doi.org/10.1108/17506121211243086.
Chailan, C. (2018). Art as a means to recreate luxury brands' rarity and value. *Journal of Business Research, 85,* 414–423.
Chandon, J. L., Laurent, G., & Valette-Florence, P. (2016a). Pursuing the concept of luxury: Introduction to the JBR special issue on "luxury marketing from tradition to innovation." *Journal of Business Research, 69*(1), 299–303.
Chandon, J. L., Laurent, G., & Valette-Florence, P. (2016b). Pursuing the concept of luxury: Introduction to the JBR special issue on "luxury marketing from tradition to innovation." *Journal of Business Research, 69*(1). http://doi.org/10.1016/j.jbusres.2015.08.001.
Chang, R. (Ed.). (1997). *Incommensurability, incomparability, and practical reason.* Cambridge: Harvard University Press.
Chang, T. Z., & Wildt, A. R. (1994). Price, product information, and purchase intention: An empirical study. *Journal of the Academy of Marketing Science, 22*(1), 16–27.
Chaudhuri, H. R. I., & Majumdar, S. (2006). Of diamonds and desires: Understanding conspicuous consumption from a contemporary marketing perspective. *Academy of Marketing Science Review, 2006,* 1.
Chen, Z., & Dubinsky, A. J. (2003). A conceptual model of perceived customer value in e-commerce: A preliminary investigation. *Psychology & Marketing, 20,* 323–347.
Chevalier, M., & Gutsatz, M. (2012). *Luxury retail management: How the world's top brands provide quality product and service support*. Singapore: Wiley.
Chevalier, M., & Mazzalovo, G. (2008). *Luxury brand management: A world of privilege*. Singapore: Wiley.
Christodoulides, G., Michaelidou, N., & Li, C.-H. (2009). Measuring perceived brand luxury: An evaluation of the BLI scale. *Brand Management, 16*(5/6), 395–405.
Christopher, A. N., Saliba, L., & Deadmarsh, E. J. (2009). Materialism and well-being: The mediating effect of locus of control. *Personality and Individual Differences, 46*(7), 682–686.
Christopher, M., & Towill, D. R. (2002). Developing market specific SC strategies. *The International Journal of Logistics Management, 31*(1), 1–14.
Churchill, G. A., Jr., & Surprenant, C. (1982). An investigation into the determinants of customer satisfaction. *Journal of Marketing Research, 19,* 491–504.

CIA. (2019). *The world factbook, religions*. https://www.cia.gov/library/publications/the-world-factbook/fields/401.html.

Cieciuch, J. (2013). Pomiar wartości w zmodyfikowanym modelu Shaloma Schwartza. *Psychologia Społeczna, 1*(124), 22–41.

Cieciuch, J. (2013). *Kształtowanie się systemu wartości od dzieciństwa do wczesnej dorosłości*. Warszawa: Wydawnictwo Liberi Libri.

Cisse, C. (2020). *In the new age of rentable luxury, consumers are less concerned with ownership than ever in*. https://www.luxurysociety.com/en/articles/2020/02/rise-sharing-economy/.

Cloutier, D. (2015). *The vice of luxury: Economic excess in a consumer age*. Washington, DC: Georgetown University Press.

Colander, D. (2000). The death of neoclassical economics. *Journal of the History of Economic Thought, 22*(2), 127–143.

Collier, M. J., & Thomas, M. (1988). Cultural identity: An interpretive perspective. *Theories in Intercultural Communication, 99,* 122–147.

Collins, B. (1999). Matters material and luxurious-eighteenth and early nineteenth-century Irish Linen consumption. In J. Hill & I. C. Lennon (Eds.), *Luxury and austerity* (s. 106–120). Dublin: University College Dublin Press.

Coombs, W. T., & Holladay, S. J. (2002). Helping crisis managers protect reputational assets: Initial tests of the situational crisis communication theory. *Management Communication Quarterly, 16*(2), 165–186.

Cooper, P. J., Calloway-Thomas, C., & Simonds, C. J. (2007). *Intercultural communication: A text with readings*. Boston, MA: Pearson Education.

Coreil, J., Levin, J. S., & Jaco, E. G. (1985). Life style—An emergent concept in the sociomedical sciences. *Culture, Medicine and Psychiatry, 9*(4), 423–437.

Corneo, G., & Jeanne, O. (1997). Conspicuous consumption, snobbism and conformism. *Journal of Public Economics, 66*(1), 55–71.

CPCStrategy. (2018). *The 2018 influencer marketing report, The rise of micro-influencers & how consumer trust drives sales*. https://learn.cpcstrategy.com/rs/006-GWW-889/images/2018%20Influencer%20Marketing%20v3.pdf.

Cristini, H., Kauppinen-Räisänen, H., Barthod-Prothade, M., & Woodside, A. (2017). Toward a general theory of luxury: Advancing from workbench definitions and theoretical transformations. *Journal of Business Research, 70,* 101–107. https://doi.org/10.1016/j.jbusres.2016.07.001.

Cronin, J. J., Brady, M. K., & Hult, G. T. M. (2000). Assessing the effects of quality, value, and customer satisfaction on consumer behavioral intentions in service environments. *Journal of Retailing, 76*(2), 193–218.

Croson, R., & Gneezy, U. (2009). Gender differences in preferences. *Journal of Economic Literature, 47*(2), 448–474.

Crotts, J. C., & Erdmann, R. (2000). Does national culture influence consumers' evaluation of travel services? A test of Hofstede's model of cross-cultural differences. *Managing Service Quality: An International Journal, 10*(6), 410–419.

Culham, P. (1982). The Lex Oppia. *Latomus, 41*(4), 786–793.

Curvelo, A. (2012). The disruptive presence of the Namban-jin in early modern Japan. *Journal of the Economic and Social History of the Orient, 55*(2–3), 581–602.

D'Arpizio, C., Levato, F., Kamel, M-A., & de Montgolfier, J. (2014). *Luxury goods worldwide market study fall-winter 2014: The rise of the borderless consumer*. From z. https://pl.scribd.com/document/281434830/Bain-Worldwide-Luxury-Goods-Report-2014.

D'Arpizio, C., Levato, F., Kamel, M-A., & de Montgolfier, J. (2017). *Luxury goods worldwide market study, fall–winter 2017*. From z. https://www.bain.com/insights/luxury-goods-worldwide-market-study-fall-winter-2017.

Daimler. (2018). https://media.daimler.com/marsMediaSite/en/instance/ko/China.xhtml?oid=9265718.

Dall'Olmo Riley, F., Pina, J. M., & Bravo, R. (2015). The role of perceived value in vertical brand extensions of luxury and premium brands. *Journal of Marketing Management, 31*(7–8), 881–913.

Danziger, P. (2019). *6 global consumer trends for 2019, and the brands that are out in front of them, in Forbes*. https://www.forbes.com/sites/pamdanziger/2019/01/13/6-global-consumer-trends-and-brands-that-are-out-in-front-of-them-in-2019/#4d8d21404fe4.

Davies, I. A., Lee, Z. I., & Ahonkhai, I. (2012). Do consumers care about ethical-luxury? *Journal of Business Ethics, 106*(1), 37–51.

De Block, A., & Dewitte, S. (2007). Mating games: Cultural evolution and sexual selection. *Biology & Philosophy, 22*(4), 475–491.

De Brito, M., Carbone, V., & Blanquart, C. (2008). Towards a sustainable fashion retail supply chain in Europe: Organisation and performance. *International Journal of Production Economics, 114*(2), 534–553.

De Mooij, M. (2010). *Global marketing and advertising: Understanding cultural paradoxes*. Thousand Oaks, CA: Sage.

De Pelsmacker, P., Driesen, L., & Rayp, G. (2003). *Are fair trade labels good business? Ethics and coffee buying intentions*. Ghent: Working Paper Ghent University Faculty of Economics and Business Administration.

Deaux, K. (1985). Sex and gender. *Annual Review of Psychology, 36*(1), 49–81.

Debevec, K., Schewe, C. D., Madden, T. J., & Diamond, W. D. (2013). Are today's millennials splintering into a new generational cohort? Maybe! *Journal of Consumer Behaviour, 12,* 20–31.

DeBono, K. G., & Harnish, R. J. (1988). Source expertise, source attractiveness, and the processing of persuasive information: A functional approach. *Journal of Personality and social Psychology, 55*(4), 541–546.

Deckop, J. R., Jurkiewicz, C. L., & Giacalone, R. A. (2010). Effects of materialism on work-related personal well-being. *Human Relations, 63*(7), 1007–1030.

Dekhili, S., Achabou, M. A., & Alharbi, F. (2019). Could sustainability improve the promotion of luxury products? *European Business Review, 31*(4), 488–511.

Delloite. (2018). *Global powers of luxury goods 2018.* From z. https://www2.deloitte.com/content/dam/Deloitte/at/Documents/consumer-business/deloitte-global-powers-of-luxury-goods-2018.pdf.

Delloite. (2019). *Global powers of luxury goods.* https://www2.deloitte.com/global/en/pages/consumer-business/articles/gx-cb-global-powers-of-luxury-goods.html.

Denzau, A. T., & North, D. C. (1994). Shared mental models: Ideologies and institutions. *Kyklos, 47*(1), 3–31.

Desmichel, P., Ordabayeva, N., & Kocher, B. (2020). What if diamonds did not last forever? Signaling status achievement through ephemeral versus iconic luxury goods. *Organizational Behavior and Human Decision Processes, 158,* 49–65.

Desmond, M. (2016). *Evicted: Poverty and profit in the American city.* New York, NY: Broadway Books.

Dewey, J. (1989). *The later works of John Dewey, 1949–1952: 1949–1952, essays, typescripts, and knowing and the known* (Vol. 16). SIU Press.

Dewey, J. (2005). *Art as experience.* New York: Penguin.

Diehl, M., & Hay, E. L. (2011). Self-concept differentiation and self-concept clarity across adulthood: Associations with age and psychological well-being. *International Journal of Aging and Human Development, 73*(2), 125–152.

Dion, D., & Arnould, E. (2011). Retail luxury strategy: Assembling charisma through art and magic. *Journal of Retailing, 87*(4), 502–520.

Dion, D., & Borraz, S. (2017). Managing status: How luxury brands shape class subjectivities in the service encounter. *Journal of Marketing, 81*(5), 67–85.

Dittmar, H. (1994). Material possessions as stereotypes: Material images of different socio-economic groups. *Journal of Economic Psychology, 15*(4), 561–585.

Dobiegała-Korona, B., & Doligalski, T. (red.). (2011). *Zarządzanie wartością klienta w przedsiębiorstwach w Polsce*. Warszawa: Oficyna Wydawnicza Szkoła Główna Handlowa w Warszawie.

Dodds, W. B., Monroe, K. B., & Grewal, D. (1991). The effects of price, brand and store information on buyers' product evaluations. *Journal of Marketing Research, 28*(3), 307–319.

Dodge, H. R., Edwards, E. A., & Fullerton, S. (1996). Consumer transgressions in the marketplace: Consumers' perspectives. *Psychology & Marketing, 13*(8), 821–835.

Domurat, A. (2009). *Identyfikacja wartości osobistych w badaniach psychologicznych Wartości jako cele działań i wyborów*. Warszawa: Wydawnictwo Uniwersytetu Warszawskiego.

Douglas, M., & Isherwood, B. C. (1979). *The world of goods: Towards an anthropology of consumption*. New York: Basic Books.

Drabik, L., Kubiak-Sokół, A., Sobol, E., Wiśniakowska, L., Stankiewicz, A., & Wydawnictwo Naukowe, P. W. N. (Eds.). (2018). *Słownik języka polskiego PWN*. Wydawnictwo Naukowe PWN SA.

Dubois, B., & Duquesne, P. (1993). The market for luxury goods: Income versus culture. *European Journal of Marketing*.

Dubois, B., & Laurent, G. (1993). Is there a Euro consumer for luxury goods? *ACR European Advances*.

Dubois, B., & Paternault, C. (1997). Does luxury have a home country? An investigation of country images in Europe. *Marketing & Research Today, 25*(2), 79–85.

Dubois, B., Czellar, S., & Laurent, G. (2005). Consumer segments based on attitudes toward luxury: Empirical evidence from twenty countries. *Marketing Letters, 16*(2), 115–128.

Dubois, B., Czellar, S., & Laurent, G. (2011). *How do consumers overcome ambivalence toward hedonic purchases? A typology of consumer strategies*. From z. https://www.researchgate.net/publication/4816098_How_Do_Consumers_Overcome_Ambivalence_toward_Hedonic_Purchases_A_Typology_of_Consumer_Strategies.

Dubois, B., Laurent, G., & Czellar, S. (2001). Consumer rapport to luxury: Analyzing complex and ambivalent attitudes (Consumer Research Working Paper, 736), Jouy-en-Josas, France: HEC.

Dzionek-Kozłowska, J. (2007). *System ekonomiczno-społeczny Alfreda Marshalla.* Warszawa: Wydawnictwo Naukowe PWN.

Eagly, A. H. (1995). The science and politics of comparing women and men. *American Psychologist, 50*(3), 145.

Eagly, A. H., & Wood, W. (1999). The origins of sex differences in human behavior: Evolved dispositions versus social roles. *American Psychologist, 54*(6), 408–423.

Economist. (2014). *Exclusively for everybody.* From z. https://www.economist.com/special-report/2014/12/11/exclusively-for-everybody.

Edelman's Earned Brand Report. (2020). https://www.edelman.com/research/covid-19-brand-trust-report.

Eggert, A., & Ulaga, W. (2002). Customer perceived value: A substitute for satisfaction in business markets? *Journal of Business & Industrial Marketing, 17*(2/3), 107–118.

Ekman, P., & Davidson, R. J. (Eds.). (1994). *Series in affective science. The nature of emotion: Fundamental questions.* Oxford University Press.

Ekman, P., & Davidson, R. J. (1999). *Natura emocji: Podstawowe zagadnienia.* Gdańsk: GWP.

Elam, C., Stratton, T., & Gibson, D. D. (2007). Welcoming a new generation to college: The millennial students. *Journal of College Admission, 195,* 20–25.

Engel, J. F., Kollat, D. T., & Blackwell, R. D. (1968). *A model of consumer motivation and behavior.* New York, NY: Holt, Rinehart and Winston.

Epstein, S. (1989). Values from the perspective of cognitive-experiential self-theory. In N. Eisenberg, J. Reykowski, & E. Staub (Eds.), *Social and moral values: Individual and societal perspectives* (s. 3–22). London: Routledge.

Etzioni, A. (2010). *Moral dimension: Toward a new economics.* New York: The Free Press.

Eurominitor Research. (2018). *Ranked: Top 10 countries by consumer expenditure.* From z. https://blog.euromonitor.com/2017/10/consumer-expenditure-top-10-countries.html.

Euromonitor International. (2018). *World market for luxury goods.* From z. https://www.euromonitor.com/world-market-for-luxury-goods/report.

Falkowski, A., & Tyszka, T. (2009). *Psychologia zachowań konsumenckich.* Gdańsk: Gdańskie Wydawnictwo Psychologiczne.

Feather, N. T. (1995). Values, valences, and choice: The influence of values on the perceived attractiveness and choice of alternatives. *Journal of Personality and Social Psychology, 68*(6), 1135–1151.

Featherstone, M. (2016). The object and art of luxury consumption. *Critical luxury studies: Art, design, media,* 108–127.

Feldman, J. M., & Lynch, J. G. (1988). Self-generated validity and other effects of measurement on belief, attitude, intention, and behavior. *Journal of Applied Psychology, 73*(3), 421–435.

Festinger, L. (1954). A theory of social comparison process. *Human Relations, 7*(2), 117–140.

Fionda, A. M., & Moore, C. M. (2009). The anatomy of the luxury fashion brand. *Journal of Brand Management, 16*(5–6), 347–363.

Fitzmaurice, J., & Comegys, C. (2006). Materialism and social consumption. *Journal of Marketing Theory and Practice, 14*(4), 287–299.

Fleetwood, S. (1997). Aristotle in the 21st century. *Cambridge Journal of Economics, 21*(6), 729–744.

Flint, D. J., & Woodruff, R. B. (2001). The initiators of changes in customers' desired value: Results from a theory building study. *Industrial Marketing Management, 30*(4), 321–337.

Flora, L. (2016). *What Trump's win means for the luxury industry in China.* From z. https://jingdaily.com/what-trumps-win-means-for-the-luxury-industry/.

Forbes. (2017). *Why Mercedes will retain global luxury sales crown in 2017, and likely for years to come.* From z. https://www.forbes.com/sites/neilwinton/2017/04/04/mercedes-will-retain-global-premium-sales-crown-in-2017-and-for-years-to-come/#3f8377a65f05.

Forgas, J. P., & Moylan, S. J. (1991). Affective influences on stereotype judgements. *Cognition & Emotion, 5*(5–6), 379–395.

Fox, C. (2018). Understanding the culture of consuming pre-owned luxury. In *Vintage luxury fashion* (pp. 45–61). Cham: Palgrave Macmillan.

Foxal, G. R., & Goldsmith, E. G. (1998). *Psychologia konsumenta dla menedżera marketingu.* Warszawa: Wydawnictwo Naukowe PWN.

Franchetti, C. (2013). A reconsideration of Werner Sombart's luxury and capitalism. *International Review of Social Sciences and Humanities, 5*(2), 135–139.

Franco, J. C., Hussain, D., & McColl, R. (2019). Luxury fashion and sustainability: Looking good together. *Journal of Business Strategy.* https://doi.org/10.1108/JBS-05-2019-0089.

Fromm, E. (1947). (Man for Himself, Chinese), Shanghai (Shanghai Translation Publishing House) 2013.

Frijda, N. H., Kuipers, P., & Ter Schure, E. (1989). Relations among emotion, appraisal, and emotional action readiness. *Journal of Personality and Social Psychology, 57*(2), 212.

Galarza, M. G., Saura, G. I. (2006). Value dimensions, perceived value, satisfaction and loyalty: An investigation of university students' travel behavior.

Tourism Management, 27, 437–452. Available at. http://dx.doi.org/10.1016/j.tourman.2004.12.002.

Gale, B., Gale, B. T., & Wood, R. C. (1994). *Managing customer value: Creating quality and service that customers can see*. Simon and Schuster.

Gallarza, M. G., & Gil-Saura, I. (2008). The concept of value and its dimensions: A tool for analyzing tourism experiences. *Tourism Review, 63*(3), 4–20.

Gallarza, M. G., Ruiz, M. E., & Gil, I. (2016). Stretching the value-satisfaction-loyalty chain by adding value dimensions and cognitive and affective satisfactions: A causal model for retailing. *Management Decisions, 54*(4), 981–1003.

Gallarza, M. G., Arteaga, F., Del Chiappa, G., & Gil-Saura, I. (2015). Value dimensions in consumers' experience: Combining the intra-and inter-variable approaches in the hospitality sector. *International Journal of Hospitality Management, 47*, 140–150.

Gallarza, M. G., Arteaga, F., Del Chiappa, G., Gil-Saura, I., & Holbrook, M. B. (2017). A multidimensional service-value scale based on Holbrook's typology of customer value. *Journal of Service Management*.

Gecas, V., & Seff, M. A. (1990). Families and adolescents: A review of the 1980s. *Journal of Marriage and the Family, 52*, 941–958.

Gerritsen, A., & Riello, G. (Eds.). (2015). *Writing material culture history*. London: Bloomsbury Publishing.

Gerzema, J., & D'Antonio, M. (2011). *Spend shift: How the post-crisis values revolution is changing the way we buy, sell and live*. San Francisco, CA: Jossey-Bass.

Gesteland, R. R. (2002). *Cross-cultural business behavior: Marketing, negotiating, sourcing and managing across cultures*. Copenhagen: Copenhagen Business School Press.

Gibson, J. J. (2002). A theory of direct visual perception. *Vision and mind: Selected readings in the philosophy of perception*, 77–90.

Girard, R., Oughourlian, J. M., & Lefort, G. (2003). *Things hidden since the foundation of the world*. Stanford, CA: A&C Black.

Giza, W. (2016). O ewolucji ekonomicznej teorii wartości. *Studia Ekonomiczne, 259*, 49–59.

Glanzmann, P. (1985). Anxiety, stress and performance. In B. D. Kirkcaldy (Ed.), *Individual preferences in movement*. Lancaster, England: MTP Press.

Global Web Index. (2020). *Consumer trends that will shape 2020*. https://www.globalwebindex.com/reports/trends-2020.

Gloeckler, G. (2008). Here come the millennials. *Business Week, 4109*, 46–50.

Göckeritz, F. (2017). From z. https://supplier-magazine.daimler.com/en/made-in-china-for-china/.

Godey, B., Manthiou, A., Pederzoli, D., Rokka, J., Aiello, G., Donvito, R., et al. (2016). Social media marketing efforts of luxury brands: Influence on brand equity and consumer behavior. *Journal of Business Research, 69*(12), 5833–5841.

Godey, B., Pederzoli, D., Aiello, G., Donvito, R., Wiedmann, K. P., & Hennigs, N. (2013). A cross-cultural exploratory content analysis of the perception of luxury from six countries. *Journal of Product & Brand Management, 22*(3), 229–237.

Godłów-Legiędź, J. (2010). *Współczesna ekonomia: ku nowemu paradygmatowi*. Warszawa: Wydawnictwo C.H. Beck.

Gołaszewska, M. (1985). *Zarys estetyki*. Warszawa: PWN.

Gourville, J. T., & Soman, D. (1998). Payment depreciation: The behavioral effects of temporally separating payments from consumption. *Journal of Consumer Research, 25*(2), 160–174.

Grewal, R., Mehta, R., & Kardes, F. R. (2004). The timing of repeat purchases of consumer durable goods: The role of functional bases of consumer attitudes. *Journal of Marketing Research, 41*(1), 101–115.

Griskevicius, V., Tybur, J. M., Sundie, J. M., Cialdini, R. B., Miller, G. F., & Kenrick, D. T. (2007). Blatant benevolence and conspicuous consumption: When romantic motives elicit strategic costly signals. *Journal of Personality and Social Psychology, 93*(1), 85.

Gromkowska-Melosik, A. (2011). *Edukacja i (nie) równość społeczna kobiet: studium dynamiki dostępu*. Kraków: Oficyna Wydawnicza Impuls.

Grönroos, C. (1997). Value-driven relational marketing: From products to resources and competencies. *Journal of Marketing Management, 13*(5), 407–419.

Guiot, J. M. (1978). Some comments on social comparison processes. *Journal for the Theory of Social Behaviour*.

Gurzki, H., & Woisetschläger, D. M. (2017). Mapping the luxury research landscape: A bibliometric citation analysis. *Journal of Business Research, 77*, 147–166.

Gutsatz, M., & Heine, K. (2018). *Luxury brand-building and development: New global challenges, new business models*. Springer.

Guyer, P. (2005). *Values of beauty: Historical essays in aesthetics*. Cambridge: Cambridge University Press.

Gwinner, K. P., & Stephens, N. (2001). Testing the implied mediational role of cognitive age. *Psychology & Marketing, 18*, 1031–1048.

Halkier, B. (2016). *Consumption challenged: Food in medialised everyday lives*. London: Routledge.
Hall, E. T. (1959). *The silent language*. New York: Doubleday.
Hall, E. T. (1989). *Beyond culture*. New York: Doubleday.
Hall, E. T., & Hall, M. R. (1990). *Understanding cultural differences: [Germans, French and Americans]* (Vol. 9). Yarmouth, ME: Intercultural Press.
Hampden, T., & Trompenaars, F. (2000). *Building cross-cultural competence*. London: John Willey & Sons.
Han, Y. J., Nunes, J. C., & Drèze, X. (2010). Signaling status with luxury goods: The role of brand prominence. *Journal of Marketing, 74*(4), 15–30.
Hanna, J. (2004). *Luxury isn't what it used to be*. From z. https://hbswk.hbs.edu/item/luxury-isnt-what-it-used-to-be.
Hanzaee, K. H., & Teimourpour, B. (2012). Segmenting consumers based on luxury value perceptions. *Middle-East Journal of Scientific Research, 12*(11), 1445–1453.
Haralambos, M., Holborn, M., & Heald, R. (1980). *Sociology: Themes and perspectives*. Slough: University Tutorial Press.
Harari, Y. N. (2018). *21 lessons for the 21st century*. Random House.
Hartmann, N. (1987). *Systematyczna autoprezentacja*. przeł. J. Garewicz, „Literatura na świecie" 1987, nr 4, s. 330.
Hartwell, R. M. (2017a). *The causes of the industrial revolution in England*. Abingdon, Oxon: Routledge.
Hayward, M. (2017b). *Rich apparel: Clothing and the law in Henry VIII's England*. London: Routledge.
Head, W. (1961, March). Adaptive sociology. *The British Journal of Sociology, 12*(1), 23–40.
Hechter, M. (1993). Values research in the social and behavioral sciences. In R. Michod, L. Nadel, & M. Hechter (Eds.), *The origin of values* (s. 1–28). New York: Aldine de Gruyer.
Heilbrunn, B. (2006). Brave new brands: Cultural branding between utopia and a-topia. In *Brand culture* (pp. 107–120). Routledge.
Heidegger, M. (1993). *Basic writings* (2nd ed.), D. F. Krell (Ed.). New York, NY: HarperCollins.
Helkkula, A., & Kelleher, C. (2010). Circularity of customer service experience and customer perceived value. *Journal of Customer Behaviour, 9*(1), 37–53.
Helkkula, A., Pihlström, M., & Kelleher, C. (2009). *From customer perceived value (PERVAL) to value-in-context experience (VALCONEX)*. From z. http://www.naplesforumonservice.it/uploads/files/HELKKULA_FROM%

20CUSTOMER%20PERCEIVED%20VALUE%20-PERVAL-TO%20VALUE-IN-CONTEXT%20EXPERIENCE%20-VALCONEX-.pdf.

Helkkula, A., Pihlström, M., & Kelleher, M. (2009). From customer perceived value (PERVAL) to value-in-context experience (VALCONEX). In *The 2009 Naples forum on service. Service-Dominant logic, service science and network theory, Napoli*. Napels, Italy: Giannini Editore.

Helsen, K., Jedidi, K., & DeSarbo, W. S. (1993). A new approach to country segmentation utilizing multinational diffusion patterns. *The Journal of Marketing, 57*(4), 60–71.

Henderson, P. W., & Peterson, R. A. (1992). Mental accounting and categorization. *Organizational Behavior and Human Decision Processes, 51*(1), 92–117.

Hennigs, N., Wiedmann, K. P., Klarmann, C., Strehlau, S., Godey, B., Pederzoli, D., ... & Taro, K. (2012). What is the value of luxury? A cross-cultural consumer perspective. *Psychology & Marketing, 29*(12), 1018–1034.

Hepler, L. (2015). *Tiffany & Co.'s new CSO on cleaning up the jewelry supply chain*. From z. https://www.greenbiz.com/article/tiffany-cos-new-cso-polishing-jewelry-supply-chain.

Hilton, M. (2004). The legacy of luxury: Moralities of consumption since the 18th century. *Journal of Consumer Culture, 4*(1), 101–123. https://doi.org/10.1177/1469540504040906 0167-4544).

Hitlin, S., & Piliavin, J. A. (2004). Values: Reviving a dormant concept. *Annual Review of Sociology, 30,* 359–393. https://doi.org/10.1146/annurev.soc.30.012703.110640.

Hoffmann, J., & Coste-Manière, I. (2012). *Global luxury trends: Innovative strategies for emerging markets*. London: Springer.

Hoffmann, J., & Coste-Manière, I. (2013). *Global luxury trends: Innovative strategies for emerging markets*. Basingstoke: Palgrave Macmillan.

Hofstede, G. (1991). *Organizations and cultures: Software of the mind*. New York: McGrawHill.

Hofstede, G. (2001). *Culture's consequences: Comparing values, behaviors, institutions, and organizations across nations* (2nd ed.). Thousand Oaks, CA: Sage.

Hofstede, G. (2016). Culture's consequences: Comparing values, behaviors, institutions, and organizations across nations. *Collegiate Aviation Review, 34*(2), 108.

Hofstede, G. (2019). https://www.hofstede-insights.com/country-comparison.

Hofstede, G. (2020). https://www.hofstede-insights.com/product/compare-countries/.

Hoge, D. R., Luna, C. L., & Miller, D. K. (1981). Trends in college students' values between 1952 and 1979: A return of the fifties? *Sociology of Education, 54*, 263–274.

Holbrook, M. B. (1996). Special session summary customer value C a framework for analysis and research. In K. P. Corfman & Jr. G. L. John (Eds.), *NA—Advances in consumer research volume 23* (s. 138–142). Provo, UT: Association for Consumer Research.

Holbrook, M. B. (1999). *Consumer value: A framework for analysis and research*. London: Routledge.

Holbrook, M. B. (2006). Consumption experience, customer value, and subjective personal introspection: An illustrative photographic essay. *Journal of Business Research, 59*(6), 714–725. https://doi.org/10.1016/j.jbusres.2006.01.008.

Holbrook, M. B., & Hirschman, E. C. (1982). The experiential aspects of consumption: Consumer fantasies, feelings, and fun. *Journal of Consumer Research, 9*(2), 132–140.

Horley, J. (1992). A longitudinal examination of lifestyles. *Social Indicators Research, 26*(3), 205–219.

Holt, D. B. (1995). How consumers consume: A typology of consumption practices. *Journal of Consumer Research, 22*(1), 1–16.

Howard, J. A., & Sheth, J. N. (1969). *The theory of buyer behavior*. New York: Wiley.

Howarth, Ch. (2018). *Does luxury's response to digital create meaningful connections?* From z. https://www.luxurydaily.com/does-luxurys-response-to-digital-create-meaningful-connections/.

Howe, N., Neil-Strauss, W., & William, R. J. (2000). *Millennials rising: The next great generation*. New York: Vintage Books.

Huber, F., Herrmann, A., & Henneberg, S. C. (2007). Measuring customer value and satisfaction in services transactions, scale development, validation and cross-cultural comparison. *International Journal of Consumer Studies, 31*(6), 554–564.

Hudders, L., & Pandelaere, M. (2012). The silver lining of materialism: The impact of luxury consumption on subjective well-being. *Journal of Happiness Studies, 13*(3), 411–437.

Hung, K., & David, K. T. (2020). Luxury brand consumption in emerging economies: Review and implications. In *Research handbook on luxury branding*. Northampton: Edward Elgar Publishing.

Husic, M., & Cicic, M. (2009). Luxury consumption factors. *Journal of Fashion Marketing and Management: An International Journal, 13*(2), s. 231–245. https://doi.org/10.1108/13612020910957734.

Iglesias, O., Singh, J. J., Casabayó, M., Hung, K. P., Chen, A. H., Peng, N., ... & Chou, C. L. (2011). Antecedents of luxury brand purchase intention. *Journal of Product & Brand Management*.

Ingarden, R. (1966). *Przeżycie, dzieło, wartość*. Kraków: Wydawnictwo Literackie.

Inglehart, R. (1995). Changing values, economic development and political change. *International Social Science Journal, 145*, 379–404.

Inglehart, R. (1997). *Modernization and postmodernization: Cultural, economic, and political change in 43 societies*. Princeton: Princeton University Press.

Inglehart, R. (2006). Pojawienie się wartości postmaterialistycznych. In P. Sztompka & M. Kucia (red.), *Socjologia: Lektury*. Kraków: Znak.

Inglehart, R. (2015). *The silent revolution: Changing values and political styles among Western publics*. Pronceton: Princeton University Press.

Irwin, S. (2003). Interdependencies, values and the reshaping of difference: Gender and generation at the birth of twentieth-century modernity. *British Journal of Sociology, 54*, 565–584.

Isen, A. M. (1984). Toward understanding the role of affect in cognition. In Jr. R. S. Wyer & T. K. Srull (Eds.), *Handbook of social cognition* (Vol. 3, s. 179–236). Mahwah, NJ: Lawrence Erlbaum Associates Publishers.

Isen, A. M. (1987). Positive affect, cognitive processes, and social behavior. In L. Berkowitz (Ed.), *Advances in experimental social psychology* (Vol. 20, pp. 203–253). San Diego, CA: Academic Press.

Isen, A. M. (2001). An influence of positive affect on decision making in complex situations: Theoretical issues with practical implications. *Journal of Consumer Psychology, 11*(2), 75–85.

Isen, A. M. (2003). Positive affect, systematic cognitive processing, and behavior: Toward integration of affect, cognition, and motivation. In F. Dansereau & F. J. Yammarino (Eds.), *Research in multi-level issues, vol. 2: Multi-level issues in organizational behavior and strategy* (s. 55–62). Oxford: Elsevier Science.

Isen, A. M., & Daubman, K. A. (1984). The influence of affect on categorization. *Journal of Personality and Social Psychology, 47*(6), 1206–1217.

Isen, A. M., & Labroo, A. A. (2003). Some ways in which positive affect facilitates decision making and judgment. In L. S. Schneider & J. Shanteau (Eds.), *Emerging perspectives on judgment and decision research*. Cambridge: Cambridge University Press.

Isen, A. M., & Means, B. (1983). The influence of positive affect on decision-making strategy. *Social Cognition, 2*(1), 18–31.
Jabłoński, M. M. (2013). *Kształtowanie modeli biznesu w procesie kreacji wartości przedsiębiorstw*. Warszawa: Difin.
Jain, V. (2018). Luxury: Not for consumption but developing extended digital self. *Journal of Human Values, 24*(1), 25–38.
Jain, V., & Schultz, D. E. (2019). How digital platforms influence luxury purchase behavior in India? *Journal of Marketing Communications, 25*(1), 41–64.
Jandt, F. E. (2015). *An introduction to intercultural communication: Identities in a global community*. Thousand Oaks, CA: Sage.
Jang, J. Y., Gon, K. W., & Bonn, M. (2011). Generation Y consumers' selection attributes and behavioral intentions concerning green restaurants. *International Journal of Hospitality Management, 30*, 803–811.
Janssen, C., Vanhamme, J., Lindgreen, A., & Lefebvre, C. (2013). The catch-22 of responsible luxury: Effects of luxury product characteristics on consumers' perceptions of fit with corporate social responsibility. *Journal of Business Ethics, 119*(1), 45–57.
Jaracz, M., & Borkowska, A. (2010). Podejmowanie decyzji w świetle badań neurobiologicznych i teorii psychologicznych. *Psychiatria, 7*(2), 68–74.
Jelinek, J. S. (2018). Art as strategic branding tool for luxury fashion brands. *Journal of Product & Brand Management, 27*(3), 294–307.
Jiang, L., & Shan, J. (2018). Heterogeneity of luxury value perception: A generational comparison in China. *International Marketing Review, 35*(3), 458–474.
Johal, M. (2012). The diffusion of luxury in ancient Rome: An analysis of funerary practices during the late republic and early empire. *Honors Thesis Collection*, 71.
Johar, J. S., & Sirgy, M. J. (1991). Value-expressive versus utilitarian advertising appeals: When and why to use which appeal. *Journal of Advertising, 20*(3), 23–33.
Johnson, A. R., & Stewart, D. W. (2005). A reappraisal of the role of emotion in consumer behavior. In *Review of marketing research* (pp. 3–34). Bingley: Emerald Group.
Johnson, H. M. (2013). *Sociology: A systematic introduction.* London: Routledge.
Jones, S. (2018). *Influencer marketing—Luxury memo special report*. From z. https://www.luxurydaily.com/influencer-marketing-luxury-memo-special-report-4/.

Joy, A., Sherry, J. F., Jr., Venkatesh, A., Wang, J., & Chan, R. (2012). Fast fashion, sustainability, and the ethical appeal of luxury brands. *Fashion Theory, 16*(3), 273–295.

Julius Baer. (2020). *Global wealth and lifestyle report 2020*. https://www.juliusbaer.com.

Kacprzak, A., & Dziewanowska, K. (2015). Does a global young consumer exist? A comparative study of South Korea and Poland. *Journal of Marketing and Consumer Behaviour in Emerging Markets, 1*(1), 47–61.

Kahn, B. E. (1995). Consumer variety-seeking among goods and services-an integrative review. *Journal of Retailing and Consumer Services, 3*(2), 139–148.

Kahneman, D. (2003). Maps of bounded rationality: Psychology for behavioral economics. *American Economic Review, 93*(5), 1449–1475.

Kahneman, D., Knetch, J., & Thaler, R. (1990). Experimental tests of the endowment effect and coase theorem. *Journal of Political Economy, 98*(6), 1325–1348.

Kale, S. H. (1995). Grouping euroconsumers: A culture-based clustering approach. *Journal of International Marketing, 3*(3), 35–48.

Kamakura, W. A., & Wedel, M. (1999). *Market segmentation: Conceptual and methodological foundations*. New York: Kluwer Academic Press.

Kapferer, J.-N. (1997). Managing luxury brands. *Journal of Brand Management, 4*(4), 251–260.

Kapferer, J.-N. (2008). *The new strategic brand management: Creating and sustaining brand equity long term* (4th ed.). London: Kogan Page Limited.

Kapferer, J.-N. (2010). All that glitters is not green: The challenge of sustainable luxury. *European Business Review, 2*, 40–45.

Kapferer, J.-N. (2012). Abundant rarity: The key to luxury growth. *Business Horizons, 55*(5), 453–462.

Kapferer, J.-N. (2014). The artification of luxury: From artisans to artists. *Business Horizons, 57*(3), 371–380.

Kapferer, J.-N., & Bastien, V. (2009). In the beginning there was luxury. *The Luxury Strategy*, 3–30.

Kapferer, J.-N., & Bastien, V. (2009). *Luxury strategy: Break the rules of marketing to build luxury brands*. London: Kogan Page Limited.

Kapferer, J.-N., & Bastien, V. (2012). *The luxury strategy: Break the rules of marketing to build luxury brands*. Kogan Page Publishers.

Kapferer, J.-N., & Bastien, V. (2017). The specificity of luxury management: Turning marketing upside down. In *Advances in luxury brand management* (pp. 65–84). Cham: Palgrave Macmillan.

Kapferer, J-N., & Michaut-Denizeau, A. (2013). Is luxury compatible with sustainable development: The consumer viewpoint. *Journal of Brand Management, 21*(I), 1–22. https://doi.org/10.1057/bm.2013.19.

Kapferer, J. N., & Michaut-Denizeau, A. (2019). Are millennials really more sensitive to sustainable luxury? A cross-generational international comparison of sustainability consciousness when buying luxury. *Journal of Brand Management, 8*(3), 1–13.

Kapferer, J.-N., & Valette-Florence, P. (2018). The impact of brand penetration and awareness on luxury brand desirability: A cross country analysis of the relevance of the rarity principle. *Journal of Business Research, 83,* 38–50.

Kashdan, T. B., & Breen, W. E. (2007). Materialism and diminished well-being: Experiential avoidance as a mediating mechanism. *Journal of Social and Clinical Psychology, 26,* 521–539.

Kasser, T. (2002). *The high price of materialism.* Cambridge: MIT.

Kasser, T. E., & Kanner, A. D. (2004). *Psychology and consumer culture: The struggle for a good life in a materialistic world*. Washington, DC: American Psychological Association.

Kassim, N. M., & Zain, M. M. (2016). Quality of lifestyle and luxury purchase inclinations from the perspectives of affluent Muslim consumers. *Journal of Islamic Marketing, 7*(1), 95–119.

Kastanakis, M. N., & Balabanis, G. (2012). Between the mass and the class: Antecedents of the "bandwagon" luxury consumption behavior. *Journal of Business Research, 65*(10), 1399–1407.

Kastanakis, M. N., & Balabanis, G. (2014). Explaining variation in conspicuous luxury consumption: An individual differences' perspective. *Journal of Business Research, 67*(10), 2147–2154.

Kauppinen-Räisänen, H., Björk, P., Lönnström, A., & Jauffret, M. N. (2018). How consumers' need for uniqueness, self-monitoring, and social identity affect their choices when luxury brands visually shout versus whisper. *Journal of Business Research, 84,* 72–81.

Kauppinen-Räisänen, H., Gummerus, J., von Koskull, C., & Christini, H. (2019). The new wave of luxury: The meaning and value of luxury to the contemporary consumer. *Qualitative Market Research: An International Journal*. https://doi.org/10.1108/QMR-03-2016-0025

Keller, K. L. (2001). *Building customer-based brand equity: A blueprint for creating strong brands* (s. 3–27). Cambridge, MA: Marketing Science Institute.

Kernstock, J., Brexendorf, T. O., & Powell, S. M. (2017). Introduction: Luxury brand management insights and opportunities. In *Advances in luxury brand management* (pp. 1–24). Cham: Palgrave Macmillan.

Khan, S. (2016). *The lure of luxury*. From z. http://bostonreview.net/forum/lure-luxury/shamus-khan-khan-response-lure-luxury.

Kieżel, E. (2004). *Racjonalność konsumpcji i zachowań konsumentów*. Warszawa: PWE.

Kieżel, E. (red.). (2003). Zachowania konsumpcyjne a racjonalność – ujęcie teoretyczne. In E. Kieżel (red.), *Zachowania konsumentów – determinanty, racjonalność*. Katowice: Wydawnictwo Akademii Ekonomicznej w Katowicach.

Kim, H. S., Moon, H. K., Choo, H. J., & Yoon, N. H. (2011). The effect of fashion luxury consumption values on the intention to maintain brand relationships-differences among segmented markets based on purchasing patterns. *Journal of the Korean Society of Clothing and Textiles, 35*(4), 408–420.

Kim, H. W., Chan, H. C., & Gupta, S. (2007). Value-based adoption of mobile internet: An empirical investigation. *Decision Support Systems, 43*(1), 111–126.

Kirsi, N. A., & Lotta, H. B. (2011). Emerging design strategies in sustainable production and consumption of textiles and clothing. *Journal of Cleaner Production, 19,* 1876–1883.

Kjeldgaard, D., & Askegaard, S. (2006). The glocalization of youth culture: The global youth segment as structures of common difference. *Journal of Consumer Research, 33*(2), 231–247.

Klopf, D. W. (1998). *Intercultural encounters: The fundamentals of intercultural communication*. Englewood, CO: Morton Publishing Company.

Kloska, G. (1982). *Pojęcia, teorie i badania wartości w naukach społecznych*. Warszawa: Państwowe Wydawnictwo Naukowe.

Kluckhorn, F. R., & Strodtbeck, F. L. (1961). *Values in values orientations*. Evanston, IL: Row Paterson.

Ko, E., Costello, J. P., & Taylor, C. R. (2019). What is a luxury brand? A new definition and review of the literature. *Journal of Business Research, 99,* 405–413.

Koester, J., & Lustig, M. W. (2015). Intercultural communication competence: Theory, measurement, and application. *International Journal of Intercultural Relations, 48*, 20–21.

Kohlberg, L. (1981). *Moral stages and the idea of justice: Essays on moral development*. New York: Academic Press.

Kohn, M. L., Naoi, A., Schoenbach, C., Schooler, C., & Slomczynski, K. M. (1990). Position in the class structure and psychological functioning in the United States, Japan, and Poland. *American Journal of Sociology, 95,* 964–1008.

Kollat, D. T., Engel, J. F., & Blackwell, R. D. (1970). Current problems in consumer behavior research. *Journal of Marketing Research, 7*(3), 327–332.

Komor, M. (2011). Segmentacja europejskich konsumentów według teorii stylu życia. *Marketing i Rynek, 7,* 14–19.

Kotler, P., & Gordon, M. (1983). *Principles of market*. Canada: Prentice Hall.

Kotler, P., & Lee, N. (2008). *Corporate social responsibility: Doing the most good for your company and your cause*. Hoboken, NJ: Wiley.

KPMG. (2018). *China's connected consumers, the rise of the millennials.* From z. https://assets.kpmg.com/content/dam/kpmg/cn/pdf/en/2017/12/chinas-connected-consumers-the-rise-of-the-millennials.pdf.

Krawczyk, D. (2002). Contributions of the prefrontal cortex to the neural basis of human decision making. *Neuroscience & Biobehavioral Reviews, 26,* 631–664.

Krokiewicz, A. (1961). *Hedonizm Epikura.* Warszawa: Instytut Wydawniczy „Pax".

Krugman, P. (2009). *How did economists get it so wrong?* From z. https://www.nytimes.com/2009/09/06/magazine/06Economic-t.html.

Kujala, S., Artto, K., Aaltonen, P., & Turkulainen, V. (2010). Business models in project-based firms—Towards a typology of solution-specific business models. *International Journal of Project Management, 28*(2), 96–106.

Kumar, A., Lee, H. J., & Kim, Y. K. (2009). Indian consumers' purchase intention toward a United States versus local brand. *Journal of Business Research, 62*(5), 521–527.

Lagier, J., & Godey, B. (2007). A scale for measuring aesthetic style in the field of luxury and art products. *International Journal of Arts Management, 9*(2), 39–50.

Lamming, R. C., Johnsen, T., Zheng, J., & Harland, C. M. (2000). An initial classification of supply networks. *International Journal of Operations & Production Management, 20*(6), 675–691.

Landreth, H., Szeworski, A., Godłów-Legiędź, J., Dzionek-Kozłowska, J., & Colander, D. C. (2013). *Historia myśli ekonomicznej.* Warszawa: Wydawnictwo Naukowe PWN.

Langer, D. (2019). *Luxury 2030, part 1: Gen Z goes mainstream and disrupts luxury, in luxury daily.* https://jingdaily.com/luxury-2030-part-1-gen-z-goes-mainstream-and-disrupts-luxury/.

Lawson, B. (2006). *How designers think: The design process demystified*. Routledge.

Lazarus, R. S. (1982). Thoughts on the relations between emotion and cognition. *American Psychologist, 37*(9), 1019–1024.

Lazarus, R. S. (1991). *Emotion and adaptation.* New York: Oxford University Press.

Lazarus, R. S. (1991). Progress on a cognitive-motivational-relational theory of emotion. *American Psychologist, 46*(8), 819–834.

LeDoux, J. E. (1995). Emotion: Clues from the brain. *Annual Review of Psychology, 46*(1), 209–235.

Lee, D., Rushworth, M. F., Walton, M. E., Watanabe, M., & Sakagami, M. (2007). Functional specialization of the primate frontal cortex during decision making. *The Journal of Neuroscience, 27,* 8170–8173.

Lee, J. E., & Watkins, B. (2016). YouTube vloggers' influence on consumer luxury brand perceptions and intentions. *Journal of Business Research, 69*(12), 5753–5760. http://dx.doi.org/10.1016/j.jbusres.2016.04.171.

Leibenstein, H. (1950). Bandwagon, snob, and Veblen effects in the theory of consumers' demand. *Quarterly Journal of Economics, 64,* 183–207.

Lemon, K. N., & Verhoef, P. C. (2016). Understanding customer experience throughout the customer journey. *Journal of Marketing, 80*(6), 69–96.

Leonard, T. C. (2008). Richard H. Thaler, Cass R. Sunstein, Nudge: Improving decisions about health, wealth, and happiness. *Constitutional Political Economy, 19*(4), 356–360.

Leroi-Werelds, S., Streukens, S., Brady, M. K., & Swinnen, G. (2014). Assessing the value of commonly used methods for measuring customer value: A multi-setting empirical study. *Journal of the Academy of Marketing Science, 42*(4), 430–451. https://doi.org/10.1007/s11747-013-0363-4.

Leslie, G. R., Larson, R. F., & Gorman, B. L. (1976). *Introductory sociology: Order and change in society*. New York: Oxford University Press.

Li, Y., Zhao, X., Shi, D., & Li, X. (2014). Governance of sustainable supply chains in the fast fashion industry. *European Management Journal, 32*(5), 823–836. https://doi.org/10.1016/j.emj.2014.03.001.

Liang, B., & He, Y. (2012). The effect of culture on consumer choice: The need for conformity vs. the need for uniqueness. *International Journal of Consumer Studies, 36*(3), 352–359.

Lichtenstein, S., & Slovic, P. (Eds.). (2006). *The construction of preference.* Cambridge University Press.

Lim, H., Childs, M., Cuevas, L., & Lyu, J. (2018). Chanel's invitation to backstage: The effects of visual storytelling and content ephemerality on

VIP emotions, International Textile and Apparel Association (ITAA) Annual Conference Proceedings.

Lin, C. H., Sher, P. J., & Shih, H. Y. (2005). Past progress and future directions in conceptualizing customer perceived value. *International Journal of Service Industry Management, 16,* 318–336. https://doi.org/10.1108/09564230510613988.

Lipiec, J. (1992). *W przestrzeni wartości: studia z ontologii wartości.* Kraków: Harcerska Oficyna Wydawnicza.

Lipiński, E. (1981). *Problemy, pytania, wątpliwości: z warsztatu ekonomisty.* Warszawa: Państwowe Wydawnictwo Ekonomiczne.

Liu, S., et al. (2016). The standardization-localization dilemma of brand communications for luxury fashion retailers' internationalization into China. *Journal of Business Research, 69*(1), 357–364. https://doi.org/10.1016/j.jbusres.2015.08.008.

Lusch, R. F., & Nambisan, S. (2015). Service innovation: A service-dominant logic perspective. *MIS Quarterly, 39*(1), 155–176.

Lustig, M. W., & Koester, J. (2003). *Intercultural competence: Interpersonal communication across cultures.* Boston: Pearson A and B.

LuxeDigital. (2020). *The future of luxury: Trends to stay ahead in 2020.* https://luxe.digital/business/digital-luxury-trends/luxury-future-trends/.

Luxury Daily Raport. (2018). *Armani predicts 2 more years of losses before 2020 recovery.* From z. https://www.luxurydaily.com/armani-predicts-2-more-years-of-losses-before-2020-recovery/.

Macquarie Research. (2016). *Diamonds & gemstones cautious on jewellers, bullish on miners flat prices? No problem, volume takes over.* www.macquarie.com/research.

Madden, T. J., Ellen, P. S., & Ajzen, I. (1992). A comparison of the theory of planned behavior and the theory of reasoned action. *Personality and Social Psychology Bulletin, 18*(1), 3–9.

Maignan, I., Ferrell, O. C., & Ferrell, L. (2005). A stakeholder model for implementing social responsibility in marketing. *European Journal of Marketing, 39,* 956–977.

Mandeville, B. (2005). From the fable of the bees. *Readings in the economics of the division of labor: The classical tradition*, 71–79.

Mandler, G. (1981). *The structure of value: Accounting for taste: Center for human information processing*. Department of Psychology. San Diego: University of California.

Mandler, G. (1993). Approaches to a psychology of value. In R. E. Michod, L. Nadel, & M. Hechter (Eds.), *The origin of values* (s. 228–258). New York: de Gruyter.
Marcoux, J. S., Filiatrault, P., & Cheron, E. (1997). The attitudes underlying preferences of young urban educated Polish consumers towards products made in Western countries. *Journal of International Consumer Marketing, 9*(4), 5–29.
Markus, H., & Kitayama, S. (1991). Culture and the self: Implications for cognition, emotion, and motivation. *Psychological Review, 98,* 224–253.
Marshall, M. (2000). Luxury, economic development, and work motivation: David Hume, Adam Smith, and J. R. McCulloch. *History of Political Economy, 32*(3), 631–648.
Martín-Ruiz, D., Gremler, D. D., Washburn, J. H., & Cepeda-Carrión, G. (2008). Service value revisited: Specifying a higher-order, formative measure. *Journal of Business Research, 61*(12), 1278–1291.
Maslow, A. H. (Ed.). (1959). *New knowledge in human values.* Oxford, England: Harper.
Mason, R. (1993). Cross cultural influences on the demand for status goods. In W. F.Van Raaij & G. J. Bamossy (Eds.), *European advances in consumer research, 1* (s. 46–51). Provo, UT: Association for Consumer Research.
Mathur, A., & Moschis, G. P. (2005). Antecedents of cognitive age: A replication and extension. *Psychology & Marketing, 22*(12), 969–994.
Mathwick, C., Malhotra, N., & Rigdon, E. (2001). Experiential value: Conceptualization, measurement and application in the catalog and Internet shopping environment. *Journal of Retailing, 77,* 39–56. https://doi.org/10.1016/S0022-4359(00)00045-2.
Matsumoto, D. (1999). Culture and self: An empirical assessment of Markus and Kitayama's theory of independent and interdependent self-construals. *Asian Journal of Social Psychology, 2,* 289–310.
Matter of Form. (2020). *The luxury report: The state of the industry in 2020 and beyond*. https://matterofform.com/the-luxury-report/.
Mazur, J. (2001). *Zarządzanie marketingiem usług*. Warszawa: Difin S.A.
Mazur, J., & Zaborek, P. (2014). Validating DART model. *International Journal of Management and Economics, 44*(1), 106–125.
Mazurek-Łopacińska, K. (2003). *Zachowania nabywców i ich konsekwencje marketingowe*. Warszawa: PWE.
Mazurek-Łopacińska, K. (2011). Postmodernistyczna kultura konsumpcyjna w kształtowaniu popytu i stylów życia współczesnego. *Konsumpcja i Rozwój, 1,* 47–57.

Mądrzycki, T. (2002). *Osobowość jako system tworzący i realizujący plany*. Gdańsk: Wydawnictwo Uniwersytetu Gdańskiego.

McCracken, G. (1986). Culture and consumption: A theoretical account of the structure and movement of the cultural meaning of consumer goods. *Journal of Consumer Research, 13*(1), 71–84.

McCracken, G. D. (2005). *Culture and consumption II: Markets, meaning, and brand management (Vol. 2)*. Indiana University Press.

McDougall, G. H. G., & Levesque, T. (2000). Customer satisfaction with services: Putting perceived value into the equation. *Journal of Services Marketing, 14*(5), 392–410.

McKeen, C. (2004). Swillsburg city limits (the 'city of pigs': Republic 370C–372D). *The Journal for Ancient Greek Political Thought, 21*(1–2), 70–92.

McKinsey. (2014). *A multifaceted future: The jewelry industry in 2020*. McKinsey & Company. From z. http://www.mckinsey.com/industries/retail/our-insights/a-multifaceted-future-the-jewelry-industry-in-2020.

McKinsey. (2020). *A perspective for the luxury-goods industry during—and after—coronavirus*. https://www.mckinsey.com/industries/retail/our-insights/a-perspective-for-the-luxury-goods-industry-during-and-after-coronavirus#.

McNeil, P., & Riello, G. (2017). *Historia luksusu*. Warsaw, Poland: Bellona.

Meredith, G. E., & Schewe, C. D. (2002). *Defining markets, defining moments: America's 7 generational cohorts, their shared experiences, and why businesses should care*. New York: Wiley.

Merriam Webster. (2018). *Luxury*. From z. https://www.merriam-webster.com/dictionary/luxury.

Michod, R. E. (1993). Biology and the origin of values. In M. Hechter, L. Nadel, & R. E. Michod (Eds.), *The origin of values* (s. 261–271). New York: de Gruyter.

Miller, C., McIntyre, S., & Mantrala, M. (1993). Toward formalizing fashion theory. *Journal of Marketing Research, 30*, 142–157.

Miller, D. (1998). *A theory of shopping*. Cornell University Press.

Miller, G. F., & Kenrick, D. T. (2007). Blatant benevolence and conspicuous consumption: When romantic motives elicit strategic costly signals. *Journal of Personality and Social Psychology, 93*(1), 85–102.

Miller, M. C. (2014). *Clothing the clergy: Virtue and power in medieval Europe, C. 800–1200*. Ithaca, NY: Cornell University Press.

Mineka, S., & Sutton, S. K. (1992). Cognitive biases and the emotional disorders. *Psychological Science, 3*, 65–69. https://doi.org/10.1111/j.1467-9280.1992.tb00260.x.

Mintel. (2020). *Global consumer trends, 2030*. https://www.mintel.com/global-consumer-trends.
Misztal, M. (1980). *Problematyka wartości w socjologii*. Nauk: Państwowe Wydawn.
Mittal, B., Ratchford, B., & Prabhakar, P. (1990). Functional and expressive attributes as determinants of brand-attitude. *Research in Marketing, 10*, 135–155.
Młody, M., & Stępień, B. (2020). Premises of reshoring development in luxury goods sector. *Journal of Management and Financial Sciences, 1*.
Moliner, M. A., Sánchez, J., Rodríguez, R. M., & Callarisa, L. (2007). Perceived relationship quality and post-purchase perceived value: An integrative framework. *European Journal of Marketing, 41*(11/12), 1392–1422.
Money, R. B., & Colton, D. (2008). The response of the 'new consumer' to promotion in the transition economies of the former Soviet bloc. *Journal of World Business, 35*(2), 189–205.
Moore, C. M., & Doherty, A. M. (2007). The international flagship stores of luxury fashion retailers. In *Fashion marketing* (pp. 301–320). Routledge.
Moore, C. M., Doherty, A. M., & Doyle, S. A. (2010). Flagship stores as a market entry method: The perspective of luxury fashion retailing. *European Journal of Marketing*.
Moore, C. M., Fernie, J., & Burt, S. (2000). Brands without boundaries: The internationalisation of the designer retailer's brand. *European Journal of Marketing, 34*(8), 919–937.
Mores, C. M. (2007). *From Fiorucci to the guerrilla stores: Shop displays in architecture marketing and communications*. Oxford: Windsor Books.
Morris, J. D., Woo, C., Geason, J. A., & Kim, J. (2002). The power of affect: Predicting intention. *Journal of Advertising Research, 42*(3), 7–17.
Mróz, B. (red.). (2009). *Oblicza konsumpcjonizmu*. Warszawa: Szkoła Główna Handlowa-Oficyna Wydawnicza.
Mruk, H., & Stępień, B. (2018). Wpływ rozwoju gospodarczego na konsumpcję dóbr luksusowych. *Konsumpcja i Rozwój, 1*(22), 55–65.
Nadeau, R., Cloutier, E., & Guay, J. H. (1993). New evidence about the existence of a bandwagon effect in the opinion formation process. *International Political Science Review, 14*(2), 203–213. https://doi.org/10.1177/019251219301400204.
Narver, J. C., & Slater, S. F. (1990). The effect of a market orientation on business profitability. *Journal of Marketing, 54*(4), 20–35.

Narver, J. C., Slater, S. F., & MacLachlan, D. L. (2004). Responsive and proactive market orientation and new-product success. *Journal of Product Innovation Management, 21*(5), 334–347.

Naylor, G., & Frank, K. E. (2001). The effect of price bundling on consumer perceptions of value. *Journal of Services Marketing, 15*(4), 270–281.

Ng, I. C., & Smith, L. A. (2012). An integrative framework of value [Special issue]. In *Toward a better understanding of the role of value in markets and marketing* (pp. 207–243). Bingley: Emerald Group.

Nicosia, F. M. (1966). *Consumer decision processes: Marketing and advertising implications*. Englewood Cliffs, NJ: Prentice-Hall.

Nijssen, E. J., & Douglas, S. P. (2011). Consumer world-mindedness and attitudes toward product positioning in advertising: An examination of global versus foreign versus local positioning. *Journal of International Marketing, 19*(3), 113–133.

Nobbs, K., Moore, C. M., & Sheridan, M. (2012). The flagship format within the luxury fashion market. *International Journal of Retail & Distribution Management, 40*(12), 920–934.

North, D. C. (1991). Institutions. *Journal of Economic Perspectives, 5*(1), 97–112.

Norušis, M. J. (1994). *SPSS advanced statistics 6.1*. SPSS.

NYTimes. (2017). https://www.nytimes.com/2017/08/03/business/alibaba-kering-fakes-luxury.html.

O'Cass, A., & Frost, H. (2002). Status brands: Examining the effects of non-product-related brand associations on status and conspicuous consumption. *Journal of Product & Brand Management, 11*(2), 67–88.

Obłój, K. (2010). *Pasja i dyscyplina strategii: Jak z marzeń i decyzji zbudować sukces firmy*. Warszawa: Poltext.

O'Cass, A., & McEwen, H. (2004). Exploring consumer status and conspicuous consumption. *Journal of Consumer Behaviour: An International Research Review, 4*(1), 25–39.

Oetzel, J., & Doh, J. P. (2009). MNEs and development: A review and reconceptualization. *Journal of World Business, 44*(2), 108–120.

Oh, H. (1999). Service quality, customer satisfaction, and customer value: A holistic perspective. *International Journal of Hospitality Management, 18*(1), 67–82.

Ohbuchi, K.-I., Fukushima, O., & Tedeschi, J. T. (1999). Cultural values in conflict management: Goal orientation, goal attainment, and tactical decision. *Journal of Cross-Cultural Psychology, 30*, 51–71.

Okonkwo, U. (2007). *Luxury fashion branding*. Basingstoke: Palgrave Macmillan.

Okonkwo, U. (2016). *Luxury fashion branding: Trends, tactics, techniques*. Springer.

Oleś, P. (2002). Z badań nad wartościami i wartościowaniem: niektóre kwestie metodologiczne. *Roczniki Psychologiczne, 5*, 53–75.

Orléan, A. (2014). *The empire of value: A new foundation for economics*. Cambridge, MA: MIT Press.

O'Shaughnessy, J. (1987). *Why people buy*. New York: Oxford University Press.

Osterwalder, A., & Pigneur, Y. (2010). *Business model generation: A handbook for visionaries, game changers, and challengers*. Hoboken, NJ: Wiley.

Otnes, C., Lowrey, T. M., & Shrum, L. J. (1997). Toward an understanding of consumer ambivalence. *Journal of Consumer Research, 24*(1), 80–93.

Overby, J. W., Woodruff, R. B., & Gardial, S. F. (2005). The influence of culture upon consumers' desired value perceptions: A research agenda. *Marketing Theory, 5*(2), 139–163.

Oxford Dictionary. (2018). *Luxury*. From z. https://en.oxforddictionaries.com/definition/luxury.

Oyserman, D., Coon, H. M., & Kemmelmeier, M. (2002). Rethinking individualism and collectivism: Evaluation of theoretical assumptions and meta-analyses. *Psychological Bulletin, 128*, 3–72.

Palaver, W. (2013). *René Girard's mimetic theory*. East Lansing: MSU Press.

Palmer, D. (2008). *Cracking the Gen Y culinary code*. Australian Food News.

Parisi, D. (2017). *Thredup enters luxury resale world with dedicated platform*. From z. https://www.luxurydaily.com/thredup-enters-luxury-resale-world-with-thredup-luxe/.

Parisi, D. (2018). *Donald Trump's proposed tariffs on imported cars would have major impact on luxury auto*. From z. https://www.luxurydaily.com/donald-trumps-proposed-tariffs-on-imported-cars-would-have-major-impact-on-luxury-auto/.

Parsons, T. (1935). The place of ultimate values in sociological theory. *International Journal of Ethics, 45*(3), 282–316.

Parsons, T., & Smelser, N. J. (1966). *Economy and society*. London: Routledge & Kegan Paul Ltd.

Patterson, P. G., & Spreng, R. A. (1997). Modelling the relationship between perceived value, satisfaction and repurchase intentions in a business-to-business, services context: An empirical examination. *International Journal of Service Industry Management, 8*(5), 414–434.

Paul, J. (2019). Masstige model and measure for brand management. *European Management Journal, 37*(3), 299–312.

Payne, A., & Holt, S. (2001). Diagnosing customer value: Integrating the value process and relationship marketing. *British Journal of Management, 12,* 159–182.

Payne, J. W., Bettman, J. R., & Johnson, E. J. (1992). Behavioral decision research: A constructive processing perspective. *Annual Review of Psychology, 43*(1), 87–131.

Pearlin, L. I., & Kohn, M. L. (1966). Social class, occupation, and parental values: A cross-national study. *American Sociological Review, 31,* 466–479.

Peng, F., Delamore, P., & Sweeney, D. (2012). Digital innovation in fashion—How to 'capture' the user experience in 3D body scanning. *International Journal of Industrial Engineering and Management, 3*(4), 233–240.

Petrick, J. F. (2002). Development of a multi-dimensional scale for measuring the perceived value of a service. *Journal of Leisure Research, 34*(2), 119–134.

Pew Research Center. (2010). *Millennials a portrait of generation next: Confident, connected, open to change.* From z. http://assets.pewresearch.org/wp-content/uploads/sites/3/2010/10/millennials-confident-connected-open-to-change.pdf.

Phan, M., Thomas, R., & Heine, K. (2011). Social media and luxury brand management: The case of Burberry. *Journal of Global Fashion Marketing, 2*(4), 213–222.

Phares, E. J. (1976). *Locus of control in personality* (Vol. 174). Morristown, NJ: General Learning Press.

Pil, K., & MacDuffie, J. (1999). Transferring competitive advantage across borders: A study of Japanese auto transplants in North America. In J. Liker, W. Fruin, & P. Adler (red.), *Remade in America: Transplanting & transforming Japanese management systems* (pp. 39–74). New York: Oxford University Press.

Pine, J., & Gilmore, J. (1999). *The experience economy.* Boston: Harvard Business School Press.

Pine, B. J., Pine, J., & Gilmore, J. H. (1999). *The experience economy: Work is theatre & every business a stage.* Harvard Business Press.

Pinnock, P. (2018). *No one in fashion is surprised Burberry Burnt £28 million of stock.* From z. https://www.forbes.com/sites/oliviapinnock/2018/07/20/no-one-in-fashion-is-surprised-burberry-burnt-28-million-of-stock/#7d52d4984793.

Plato, C. (2005). From the republic. In *Readings in the economics of the division of labor: The classical tradition* (pp. 43–49). London: World Scientific.

Polak, E. L., & McCullough, M. E. (2006). Is gratitude an alternative to materialism? *Journal of Happiness Studies, 7*(3), 343.

Popkin, R. H., & Stroll, A. (1993). *Philosophy made simple*. New York: Three Rivers Press.

Popper, K. (1979). *Three worlds*. Ann Arbor: University of Michigan.

Porter, M. E. (1985). Value chain. *The value chain and competitive advantage: Creating and sustaining superior performance*.

Porter, M. E. (2011). *Competitive advantage of nations: Creating and sustaining superior performance* (Vol. 2, pp. 1278–1291). New York: Simon and Schuster.

Półtawski, A. (1994). Wartości a ontologia Ingardena. *Sztuka i Filozofia, 8*, 5–18.

Prahalad, C. K., & Ramaswamy, V. (2004). Co-creation experiences: The next practice in value creation. *Journal of Interactive Marketing, 18*(3), 5–14.

Prensky, M. (2001). Digital natives, digital immigrants: Part 1. *On the Horizon, 9*, 1–6.

Prentice, C., & Loureiro, S. M. C. (2018). Consumer-based approach to customer engagement—The case of luxury brands. *Journal of Retailing and Consumer Services, 43*, 325–332.

Prince-Gibson, E., & Schwartz, S. H. (1998). Value priorities and gender. *Social Psychology Quarterly, 61*, 49–67.

Prymon, M. (2010). *Marketingowe strategie wartości na rynkach globalnych*. Wrocław: Wydawnictwo Uniwersytetu Ekonomicznego we Wrocławiu.

Pura, M. (2005). Linking perceived value and loyalty in location-based mobile services. *Managing Service Quality, 15*, 509–538.

Quach, S., & Thaichon, P. (2017). From connoisseur luxury to mass luxury: Value co-creation and co-destruction in the online environment. *Journal of Business Research, 81*, 163–172.

Rambourg, E. (2014). *The bling dynasty: Why the reign of Chinese luxury shoppers has only just begun*. Hoboken, NJ: Wiley.

Ramirez, S. (2018). *Influencer marketing shows no signs of slowing: Shareablee*. From z. https://www.luxurydaily.com/influencer-marketing-shows-no-signs-of-slowing-shareablee/.

Rand, D. G., & Nowak, M. A. (2013). Human cooperation. *Trends in Cognitive Sciences, 17*(8), 413–425.

Raport specjalny The Economist. (2014). *Exclusively for everybody*. From z. https://www.economist.com/special-report/2014/12/11/exclusively-for-everybody.

Ratajczak, M. (2014). Ekonomia i edukacja ekonomiczna w dobie finansyzacji gospodarki. *Ekonomista, 2,* 207–219.

Ratajczak, M. (red.). (2014b). *Współczesne teorie ekonomiczne.* Poznań: Wydawnictwo Uniwersytetu Ekonomicznego w Poznaniu.

Ravald, A., & Grönroos, C. (1996). The value concept and relationship marketing. *European Journal of Marketing, 30*(2), 19–30.

Reddy, M., Terblanche, N., Pitt, L., & Parent, M. (2009). How far can luxury brands travel? Avoiding the pitfalls of luxury brand extension. *Business Horizons, 52*(2), 187–197.

Reichheld, F. F. (1996). *The quest for loyalty: Creating value through partnership.* Boston, MA: Harvard Business Press.

Ribeiro, A. (2005). *Fashion and fiction: Dress in art and literature in Stuart England.* New Haven, CT: Yale University Press.

Richins, M. L. (2013). The material values scale : Measurement properties and development of a short form. *Journal of Consumer Research, 31,* 209–219.

Richins, M. L., & Dawson, S. (1992). A consumer values orientation for materialism and its measurement: Scale development and validation. *Journal of Consumer Research, 19*(3), 303–316.

Rickert, H. (1986). *The limits of concept formation in natural science: A logical introduction to the historical sciences (abridged edition).* Cambridge: Cambridge University Press.

Ridgeway, C. L. (2011). *Framed by gender: How gender inequality persists in the modern world.* New York: Oxford University Press.

Risius, A., Janssen, M., & Hamm, U. (2017). Consumer preferences for sustainable aquaculture products: Evidence from in-depth interviews, think aloud protocols and choice experiments. *Appetite, 113,* 246–254.

RJC. (2017). *Responsible jewellery council.* From z. http://www.responsiblejewellery.com/.

Robertson, R. (1992). *Globalization: Social theory and global culture* (Vol. 16). Sage.

Robins, K., & Morley, D. (2002). *Spaces of identity: Global media, electronic landscapes and cultural boundaries.* New York: Routledge.

Robinson, P. K., & Hsieh, L. (2016). Reshoring: A strategic renewal of luxury clothing supply chains. *Operations Management Research, 9*(3–4), 89–101.

Rogers, C. R. (1964). Toward a modern approach to values: The valuing process in the mature person. *The Journal of Abnormal and Social Psychology, 68*(2), 160–167.

Rogoziński, K. (2011). *Zarządzanie wartością z klientem.* Warszawa: Wolters Kluwer.

Rohan, M. J. (2000). A rose by any name? The values construct. *Personality and Social Psychology Review, 4*(3), 255–277.

Rokeach, M. (1973). *The nature of human values*. New York: Free Press.

Rokeach, M. (2008). *Understanding human values*. New York: Simon and Schuster.

Romanow, Z. B. (1999). *Historia myśli ekonomicznej w zarysie*. Poznań: Wydawnictwo Akademii Ekonomicznej w Poznnaiu.

Romejko, A. (2003). Teoria mimetyczno – ofiarniczna. Wprowadzenie do antropologii Rene Girarda. *Studia Gdańskie, XV–XVI,* 55–64.

Rosenbaum, M. S., Ramirez, G. C., Campbell, J., & Klaus, P. (2019). The product is me: Hyper-personalized consumer goods as unconventional luxury. *Journal of Business Research*. https://doi.org/10.1016/j.jbusres.2019.05.017.

Roux, E., Tafani, E., & Vigneron, F. (2017). Values associated with luxury brand consumption and the role of gender. *Journal of Business Research, 71,* 102–113.

Rudnicki, L. (2012). *Zachowania konsumentów na rynku*. Warszawa: Polskie Wydawnictwo Ekonomiczne.

Ruiza, D. M., Gremler, D. D., Washburn, J. H., & Carrióna, G. C. (2008). Service value revisited: Specifying a higher-order, formative measure. *Journal of Business Research, 61*(12), 1278–1291.

Russell, B. (2012). *Dzieje zachodniej filozofii*. Warszawa: Wydawnictwo Aletheia.

Ryan, N. (2007). Prada and the art of patronage. *Fashion Theory, 11*(1), 7–24.

Sagan, C. (2011). *The demon-haunted world: Science as a candle in the dark*. Random House, New York: Ballantine Books.

Samovar, L. A., Porter, R. E., McDaniel, E. R., & Roy, C. S. (2014). *Intercultural communication: A reader*. Boston: Cengage Learning.

Samovar, L. A., Porter, R. E., McDaniel, E. R., & Roy, C. S. (2015). *Communication between cultures*. Chicago, IL: Nelson Education.

Samuely, A. (2016). *Touchscreen fitting rooms revamp retail experiences*. Pobrno z. https://www.luxurydaily.com/oak-labs-exec-touchscreen-fitting-rooms-revamp-retail-experiences/.

Sánchez-Fernández, R., & Iniesta-Bonillo, M. Á. (2006). Consumer perception of value: Literature review and a new conceptual framework. *Journal of Consumer Satisfaction, Dissatisfaction and Complaining Behavior, 19,* 40–58.

Sánchez-Fernández, R., & Iniesta-Bonillo, M. Á. (2007). The concept of perceived value: A systematic review of the research. *Marketing Theory, 7*(4), 427–451.

Sánchez-Fernández, R., Iniesta-Bonillo, M. Á., & Holbrook, M. B. (2009). The conceptualization and measurement of consumer value in services. *International Journal of Market Research, 51*, 93–113.

Schade, M., Hegner, S., Horstmann, F., & Brinkmann, N. (2016). The impact of attitude functions on luxury brand consumption: An age-based group comparison. *Journal of Business Research, 69*(1), 314–322.

Scheler, M. (1973). *Formalism in ethics and non-formal ethics of values: A new attempt toward the foundation of an ethical personalism.* Illinois: Northwestern University Press.

Schmitt, B. H. (2010). *Customer experience management: A revolutionary approach to connecting with your customers.* John Wiley & Sons.

Schneider, S. C., & Barsoux, J. L. (2003). *Managing across cultures.* Canada, Montreal: Pearson Education.

Scholz, L. (2014). *Brand management and marketing of luxury goods.* Hamburg: Anchor Academic Publishing (aap_verlag).

Schwartz, S. H. (1992). Universals in the content and structure of values: Theoretical advances and empirical tests in 20 countries. In M. P. Zanna (Ed.), *Advances in experimental social psychology* (Vol. 25, s. 1–65). New York: Academic Press.

Schwartz, S. H. (1994). Beyond individualism/collectivism: New cultural dimensions of values. In U. Kim, H. C. Triandis, C. Kagitcibasi, S-C. Choi, & G. Yoon (Eds.), *Individualism and collectivism: Theory, method, and application.* Newbury Park, CA: Sage.

Schwartz, S. H. (2007). Universalism values and the inclusiveness of our moral universe. *Journal of Cross-Cultural Psychology, 38*(6), 711–728.

Schwartz, S. H. (2012). An overview of the Schwartz theory of basic values. *Online Readings in Psychology and Culture, 2*(1). https://doi.org/10.9707/2307-0919.1116.

Schwartz, S. H., & Bardi, A. (2001). Value hierarchies across cultures: Taking a similarities perspective. *Journal of Cross-Cultural Psychology, 32*, 268–290.

Schwartz, S. H., & Sagie, G. (2000). Value consensus and importance: A cross-national study. *Journal of Cross-Cultural Psychology, 31*, 465–497.

Schwartz, S. H., Cieciuch, J., Vecchione, M., Davidov, E., Fischer, R., Beierlein, C., et al. (2012). Refining the theory of basic individual values. *Journal of Personality and Social Psychology, 103*(4), 663.

Scott, W. R. (1995). *Institutions and organizations.* Thousand Oaks, CA: Sage.

Semaan, R. W., Lindsay, V., Williams, P., & Ashill, N. (2019). The influence of gender roles in the drivers of luxury consumption for women: Insights from the gulf region. *Journal of Retailing and Consumer Services, 51*, 165–175.

Sen, A. K. (1977). Rational fools: A critique of the behavioral foundations of economic theory. *Philosophy & Public Affairs*, 317–344.

Sen, A. K. (1999). Human rights and economic achievements. In J. R. Bauer & D. A. Bell (Eds.), *Bell the East Asian challenge for human rights*. Cambridge: CUP.

Sen, A. (2004). How does culture matter? In Rao, V. & Walton, M. (Hg.), *Culture and public action*, 37–58, Stanford.

Sen, A., & Hahn, F. H. (1996). On the foundations of welfare economics: Utility, capability and practical reason. *Ethics, Rationality and Economic Behavior*.

Seuring, S., & Goldbach, M. (2006). Managing sustainability performance in the textile chain. In S. Schaltegger & M. Wagner (Eds.), *Sustainable performance and business competitiveness* (466e77). Sheffield: Greenleaf Publishing.

Shavitt, S. (1989). Products, personalities and situations in attitude functions: Implications for consumer behavior. In T. K. Srull (Ed.), *NA—Advances in consumer research* (Vol. 16, s. 300–305). Provo, UT: Association for Consumer Research.

Shavitt, S. (1990). The role of attitude objects in attitude functions. *Journal of Experimental Social Psychology, 26*(2), 124–148.

Sherman, E., Schiffman, L. G., & Mathur, A. (2001). The influence of gender on the newage elderly's consumption orientation. *Psychology & Marketing, 18*(10), 1073–1089.

Sheth, J., Newman, B. I., & Gross, B. L. (1991). *Consumption values and market choices: Theory and application*. Cincinnati, OH, USA: South-Western Publishing Co.

Shukla, P. (2010). Status consumption in cross-national context. *International Marketing Review*.

Shukla, P. (2011). Impact of interpersonal influences, brand origin and brand image on luxury purchase intentions: Measuring interfunctional interactions and a cross-national comparison. *Journal of World Business, 46*(2), 242–252.

Shukla, P. (2012). The influence of value perceptions on luxury purchase intentions in developed and emerging markets. *International Marketing Review, 29*(6), 574–596.

Shukla, P., & Purani, K. (2012). Comparing the importance of luxury value perceptions in cross-national contexts. *Journal of Business Research, 65*(10), 1417–1424.

Sikora, T. (2012). Zachowanie nabywców produktów luksusowych. Monografie i Opracowania/Szkoła Główna Handlowa, (590).

Simon, H. A. (1956). Rational choice and the structure of the environment. *Psychological Review, 63*(2), 129.

Simon, H. A. (1957). *Models of man: Social and rational.*

Silver, C. B. (2002). Japanese and American identities: Values and their transmission in the family. *Sociological Inquiry, 72,* 195–219.

Silverstein, M. J., & Fiske, N. (2003). *Trading up: The new American luxury.* New York: Portfolio/Penguin Group.

Silverstein, M. J., & Fiske, N. (2003). Luxury for the masses. *Harvard Business Review, 81*(4), 48–57.

Silverstein, M. J., Fiske, N., & Butman, J. (2008). *Trading up: Why consumers want new luxury goods-and how companies create them.* New York: Penguin.

Simon, H. (1954). Bandwagon and underdog effects and the possibility of election predictions. *Public Opinion Quarterly, 18*(3), 245–253. https://doi.org/10.1086/266513.

Simon, H. A. (1955). A behavioral model of rational choice. *The Quarterly Journal of Economics, 69*(1), 99–118.

Simons, R. L., Whitbeck, L. B., Conger, R. D., & Melby, J. N. (1990). Husband and wife differences in determinants of parenting: A social learning and exchange model of parental behavior. *Journal of Marriage and Family, 52,* 375–392.

Sinclair, R. C., & Mark, M. M. (1992). The influence of mood state on judgment and action: Effects on persuasion, categorization, social justice, person perception, and judgmental accuracy. In L. L. Martin & A. Tesser (Eds.), *The construction of social judgments.* Hillsdale, NY: Lawrence Erlbaum.

Sinha, I., & DeSarbo, W. S. (1998). An integrated approach toward the spatial modeling of perceived customer value. *Journal of Marketing Research, 35,* 236–249.

Sirgy, M. J. (1985). Using self-congruity and ideal congruity to predict purchase motivation. *Journal of Business Research, 13*(3), 195–206.

Slater, S. F. (1997). *Consumer culture and modernity.* Oxford: Polity Press.

Slater, S. F., & Narver, J. C. (2000). Intelligence generation and superior customer value. *Journal of the Academy of Marketing Science, 28*(1), 120.

Slomczynski, K. M., Miller, J., & Kohn, M. L. (1981). Stratification, work and values: A Polish-United States comparison. *American Sociological Review, 46,* 720–744.

Słownik PWN. (2018). *Luksus.* From z. https://sjp.pwn.pl/sjp/luksus;2566427.html.

Smelser, N. J. (1962). *Theory of collective behavior.* New York: Putnam Publishers.

Smith, G. E., & Nagle, T. T. (1995). Frames of reference and buyers' perception of price and value. *California Management Review, 38*(1), 98–116.
Smith, J. B., & Colgate, M. (2007). Customer value creation: A practical framework. *The Journal of Marketing Theory and Practice, 15,* 7–23.
Smith, P. B., Dugan, S., & Trompenaars, F. (1996). National culture and the values of organizational employees: A dimensional analysis across 43 nations. *Journal of Cross-Cultural Psychology, 27*(2), 231–264.
Solca, L. (2015). *The 'made in' dilemma: To label, or not to label.* From z. https://www.businessoffashion.com/community/voices/discussions/does-made-in-matter/the-made-in-dilemma-to-label-or-not-to-label.
Solca, L., Grippo, M., Lucarelli, G., Pozzi, M., & Borgonovo, F. (2016). *Who buys where: Decrypting cross-border luxury demand flows.* Milan: Exane BNP Paribas Research & ContactLab.
Soman, D., & Gourville, J. T. (2001). Transaction decoupling: How price bundling affects the decision to consume. *Journal of Marketing Research, 38*(1), 30–44.
Sombart, W. (1967). *Luxury and capitalism.* Ann Arbor: University of Michigan Press.
Søndergaard, M. (1994). Research note: Hofstede's consequences: A study of reviews, citations and replications. *Organization Studies, 15*(3), 447–456.
Soopramanien, D., & Robertson, A. (2007). Adoption and usage of online shopping: An empirical analysis of the characteristics of 'buyers', 'browsers', and 'non-Internet shoppers.' *Journal of Retailing and Consumer Services, 14*(1), 73–82.
Sotirovic, M., & Holbert, R. L. (1998). Values as sociotropic judgements influencing communication patterns. *Communication Research, 25,* 453–480.
SP12 Global Insight. From z. https://ihsmarkit.com/archive-list.html.
Spreng, R. A., MacKenzie, S. B., & Olshavsky, R. W. (1996). A reexamination of the determinants of consumer satisfaction. *The Journal of Marketing, 60,* 15–32.
Stankiewicz, W. (2000). *Historia myśli ekonomicznej.* Warszawa: Polskie Wydawnictwo Ekonomiczne.
Stearns, P. N. (2006). *Consumerism in world history: The global transformation of desire.* London: Routledge.
Steele, V. (1996). *Fetish: Fashion, sex and power.* New York: Oxford University Press.
Stewart, M. S., Bond, M., & Chung, S. F. (1999). Intergenerational patterns of values and autonomy expectations in cultures of relatedness and separateness. *Journal of Cross-Cultural Psychology, 30,* 575–593.

Stępień, B. (2001). *Procesy przystosowawcze przedsiębiorstw postsocjalistycznych do warunków rynkowych*. Poznań: Akademia Ekonomiczna w Poznaniu.

Stępień, B. (2009). *Instytucjonalne uwarunkowania działalności przedsiębiorstw międzynarodowych*. Poznań: Wydawnictwo Uniwersytetu Ekonomicznego w Poznaniu.

Stępień, B. (2016). Oblicza pluralizmu metodologicznego w naukach o zarządzaniu–z perspektywy instytucjonalnej. *Studia Oeconomica Posnaniensia, 4*(1), 48–62.

Stępień, B. (2017a). In search of apprehending customers' value perception. *International Journal of Management and Economics, 53*(1), 99–117.

Stępień, B. (2017b). The "Day-After" gleam: Reverse logistics in the luxury fashion sector and its impact on consumer value perception. In *Advanced fashion technology and operations management* (pp. 92–114). IGI Global.

Stępień, B. (2018). Pomiędzy snobizmem a pogonią za tłumem-anomalie zachowań konsumenckich w sektorze dóbr luksusowych. *Marketing i Rynek, 7,* 2–10.

Stępień, B., & Hinner, M. (2018). From love to rebuff: How culture shapes the perception of luxury goods among consumers. In S. Sarma (Ed.), *Global observations of the influence of culture on consumer buying behavior* (s. 24–47). Hershey: IGI Global.

Stępień, B., Lima, A. P., Sagbansua, L., & Hinner, M. B. (2016). Comparing consumers' value perception of luxury goods: Is national culture a sufficiently explanatory factor? *Economics and Business Review, 2*(16), 74–93.

Stępień, B., & Młody, M. (2018). Premises of reshoring development in luxury goods sector. *Journal of Management and Financial Sciences,* w druku.

Stocker, M. (1990). *Plural and conflicting values.* Oxford: Clarendon Press.

Stokburger-Sauer, N., & Teichmann, K. (2013). Is luxury just a female thing? The role of gender in luxury brand consumption. *Journal of Business Research, 66*(7), 889–896.

Strizhakova, Y., Coulter, R. A., & Price, L. R. (2008). Branded products as a passport to global citizenship: Perspectives from developed and developing countries. *Journal of International Marketing, 16*(4), 57–85.

Strizhakova, Y., Coulter, R. A., & Price, L. L. (2011). Branding in a global marketplace: The mediating effects of quality and self-identity brand signals. *International Journal of Research in Marketing, 28*(4), 342–351.

Struch, N., Schwartz, S. H., & van der Kloot, W. A. (2002). Meanings of basic values for women and men: A cross-cutural analysis. *Personality and Social Psychology Bulletin, 28,* 16–28.

Sullivan, P., & Heitmeyer, J. (2008). Looking at Gen Y shopping preferences and intentions: Exploring the role of experience and apparel involvement. *International Journal of Consumer Studies, 32,* 285–295.

Sundie, J. M., Kenrick, D. T., Griskevicius, V., Tybur, J. M., Vohs, K. D., & Beal, D. J. (2011). Peacocks, Porsches, and Thorstein Veblen: Conspicuous consumption as a sexual signaling system. *Journal of Personality and Social Psychology, 100*(4), 664–680.

Sunstein, C., & Thaler, R. (2008). *Nudge: The politics of libertarian paternalism.* New Haven: Yale University Press.

Swarovski Sustainability Report. (2015). *Supply chain collaborating with suppliers for continuous improvement.* From z. https://www.swarovskigroup.com/S/aboutus/CSR-Responsible-Supply-Chain.pdf.

Sweeney, J. C., & Soutar, G. N. (2001). Consumer perceived value: The development of a multiple item scale. *Journal of Retailing, 77,* 203–220.

Szczepański, J. (1981). *Konsumpcja a rozwój człowieka: wstęp do antropologicznej teorii konsumpcji.* Warszawa: Państwowe Wydawnictwo Ekonomiczne.

Szmigin, I., & Carrigan, M. (2000). The older consumer as innovator: Does cognitive age hold the key? *Journal of Marketing Management, 16*(5), 505–527.

Sztompka, P. (1983). Zmiana strukturalna społeczeństwa: szkic teorii. *Studia Socjologiczne, 2*(39), 128–129.

Szymura-Tyc, M. (2006). Marketing we współczesnych procesach tworzenia wartości dla klienta i przedsiębiorstwa. *Prace Naukowe/Akademia Ekonomiczna w Katowicach.* Katowice: Wydawnictwo Akademii Ekonomicznej w Katowicach.

Światowy, G. (2006). *Zachowania konsumentów: Determinanty oraz metody poznania i kształtowania.* Warszawa: Polskie Wydawnictwo Ekonomiczne.

Takano, Y., & Osaka, E. (1999). An unsupported common view: Comparing Japan and the U.S. on individualism/collectivism. *Asian Journal of Social Psychology, 2*(3), 311–341.

Tallontire, A., & Rentsendorj, E. (2001). *Blowfield, ethical consumers and ethical trade: A review of current literature, policy series 12.* Kent: Natural Resources Institute.

Tapscott, D. (2008). *Grown up digital: How the net generation is changing your world.* New York: McGraw-Hill.

Tatarkiewicz, W. (1975). *Dzieje sześciu pojęć: sztuka, piękno, forma, twórczość, odtwórczość, przeżycie estetyczne.* Warszawa: Państwowe Wydawn. Naukowe.

Tatarkiewicz, W. (1988). *Historia filozofii. Tom trzeci.* Warszawa: PWN.

Tatarkiewicz, W., & Krajewski, J. (1990). *Historia filozofii* (Vol. 1). Warszawa: PWN.

Teece, D. J. (2010). Business models, business strategy and innovation. *Long Range Planning, 43*(2–3), 172–194.

Thach, E. C., & Olsen, J. (2006). The role of service quality in influencing brand attachments at winery visitor centers. *Journal of Quality Assurance in Hospitality & Tourism, 7*(3), 59–77.

Thach, L., & Olsen, J. (2015). Profiling the high frequency wine consumer by price segmentation in the US market. *Wine Economics and Policy, 4*(1), 53–59.

Thaler, R. (1985). Mental accounting and consumer choice. *Marketing Science, 4*(3), 199–214.

Thaler, R. (2018). *Zachowania niepoprawne: Tworzenie ekonomii behawioralnej.* Poznań: Wydawnictwo Media Rodzina.

Thaler, R. H. (1999). Mental accounting matters. *Journal of Behavioral Decision Making, 12*(3), 183–206.

Thaler, R. H. (Ed.). (2005). *Advances in behavioral finance, Volume II* (Vol. 2). Princeton University Press.

The China Report: Innovation in Luxury. (2018). From z. https://www.luxurydaily.com/the-china-report-innovation-in-luxury-101/.

Thompson, K. S. (1981). Changes in the values and life-style preferences of university students. *The Journal of Higher Education, 52,* 506–518.

Tischner, J. (1993). *Myślenie według wartości.* Kraków: Znak.

Tian, K. T., Bearden, W. O., & Hunter, G. L. (2001). Consumers' need for uniqueness: Scale development and validation. *Journal of Consumer Research, 28*(1), 50–66.

Titkow, A. (2007). *Tożsamość polskich kobiet: Ciągłość, zmiana, konteksty.* Warszawa: Wydawnictwo Instytutu Filozofii i Socjologii PAN.

Tjahjono, H. K. (2011). The configuration among social capital, distributive and procedural justice and its consequences to individual satisfaction. *International Journal of Information and Management Sciences, 22*(1), 87–103.

Tolbert, P. S., & Zucker, L. G. (1996). The institutionalization of institutional theory. In S. Clegg, C. Hardy, & W. Nord (Eds.), *Handbook of organization studies* (s. 182). London: Sage.

Trend Watching. (2016). *The future of luxury*. From z. https://www2.deloitte.com/content/dam/Deloitte/at/Documents/consumer-business/deloitte-global-powers-of-luxury-goods-2018.pdf.

Trend Watching. (2018). *The future of luxury*. https://www2.deloitte.com/content/dam/Deloitte/at/Documents/consumer-business/deloitte-global-powers-of-luxury-goods-2018.pdf.

Triandis, H. C. (1989). The self and social behavior in differing cultural contexts. *Psychological Review, 96*(3), 506–520.

Triandis, H. C. (1995). *Individualism and collectivism*. Boulder: Westview.

Trochimska-Kubacka, B. (1999). *Absolutyzm aksjologiczny: Rekonstrukcja oparta na aksjologii Rickerta, Schelera i Hartmanna*. Wrocław: Wydawnictwo Uniwersytetu Wrocławskiego.

Trompenaars, F., & Hampden-Turner, C. (2004). *Managing people across cultures*. Chichester: Capstone.

Trompenaars, F., & Hampden-Turner, C. (2011). *Riding the waves of culture: Understanding diversity in global business*. New York: Nicholas Brealey International.

Truong, Y., McColl, R., & Kitchen, P. J. (2009). New luxury brand positioning and the emergence of masstige brands. *Journal of Brand Management, 16*(5–6), 375–382.

Tsai, S. P. (2005). Impact of personal orientation on luxury-brand purchase value: An international investigation. *International Journal of Market Research, 47*, 429–454.

Tsai, W. S., Yang, Q., & Liu, Y. (2013). Young Chinese consumers' snob and bandwagon luxury consumption preferences. *Journal of International Consumer Marketing, 25*(5), 290–304.

Tversky, A. (1972). Elimination by aspects: A theory of choice. *Psychological Review, 79*(4), 281.

Tversky, A., & Kahneman, D. (1981). The framing of decisions and the psychology of choice. *Science, New Series, 211*(4481), 453–458.

Tversky, A., & Kahneman, D. (1991). Loss aversion in riskless choice: A reference-dependent model. *The Quarterly Journal of Economics, 106*(4), 1039–1061.

Tversky, A., Sattath, S., & Slovic, P. (1988). Contingent weighting in judgment and choice. *Psychological Review, 95*(3), 371–384.

Twitchell, J. B. (2001). *Living it up: Our love affair with luxury*. New York: Columbia University Press.

Tynan, C., McKechnie, S., & Chhuon, C. (2010). Co-creating value for luxury brands. *Journal of Business Research, 63*(11), 1156–1163.

Unity Marketing. (2020a). https://unitymarketingonline.com/prospects-for-home-brands-in-post-pandemic-world/.

Unity Marketing. (2020b). *The state of luxury*. https://unitymarketingonline.com/shop/luxury/luxury-reports/state-of-luxury-2020-the-insider-view-report/.

Urbańska, A. (1997). Koncepcja mimesis Rene Girarda. *Etnografia Polska, 41*(1–2), 21–46.

US Census Bureau. (2015). *Millennials outnumber baby boomers and are far more diverse*. From z. https://www.census.gov/newsroom/press-releases/2015/cb15-113.html.

Vågan, A. (2011). Towards a sociocultural perspective on identity formation in education. *Mind, Culture, and Activity, 18*(1), 43–57.

Van Auken, S., Barry, T. E., & Anderson, R. L. (1993). Observations: Toward the internal validation of cognitive age measures in advertising research. *Journal of Advertising Research, 33*(3), 82–85.

Vandermerwe, S. (1993). Jumping into the customer's activity cycle: A new role for customer services in the 1990s. *Columbia Journal of World Business, 28*(2), 46–66.

Van de Ven, B. (2008). An ethical framework for the marketing of corporate social responsibility. *Journal of Business Ethics, 82*(2), 339–352.

Vargo, S. L., & Lusch, R. F. (2004). Evolving to a new dominant logic for marketing. *The Journal of Marketing, 68*, 1–17.

Vargo, S. L., & Lusch, R. F. (2008). Service-dominant logic: Continuing the evolution. *Journal of the Academy of Marketing Science, 36*(1), 1–10.

Veblen, T. (2005). *The theory of the leisure class: An economic study of institutions*. Aakar Books.

Veblen, T. (2008). *Teoria klasy próżniaczej*. wydanie III. Warszawa: Wydawnictwo Literackie Muza.

Vecchi, A., Peng, F., & Al-Sayegh, M. (2014). Assessing the applicability of a sizing framework into online fashion retail. *International Journal of Advanced Information Science and Technology, 29*(29), 102–110.

Venkatesan, R., & Kumar, V. (2004). A customer lifetime value framework for customer selection and resource allocation strategy. *Journal of Marketing, 68*(4), 106–125.

Vermeir, I., & Verbeke, W. (2006). Sustainable food consumption: Exploring the consumer 'attitude—behavioral intention'. *Journal of Agricultural and Environmental Ethics, 19*, 169–194. https://doi.org/10.1007/s10806-005-5485-3.

Vigneron, F., & Johnson, L. W. (1999). A review and a conceptual framework of prestige-seeking consumer behavior. *Academy of Marketing Science Review, 1*, 1–15.

Vigneron, F., & Johnson, L. W. (2004). Measuring perceptions of brand luxury. *Journal of Brand Management, 11*(6), 484–506.

Von Mises, L. (2007). *Ludzkie działanie: Traktat o ekonomii*. tłum. W. Falkowski, Wrocław: Fundacja Instytut Ludwiga von Misesa.

von Wallpach, S., Hemetsberger, A., Thomsen, T. U., & Belk, R. W. (2019). Moments of luxury—A qualitative account of the experiential essence of luxury. *Journal of Business Research, 116*, 491–502.

Voyer, B. G., & Beckham, D. (2014). Can sustainability be luxurious? A mixed-method investigation of implicit and explicit attitudes towards sustainable luxury consumption. *Advances in Consumer Research, 42*, 245–250.

Wahba, P. (2018). *Ralph Lauren is discovering how hard it is to fix a brand*. From z. http://fortune.com/2018/02/01/ralph-lauren-earnings/.

Walter, A., Ritter, T., & Gemünden, H. G. (2001). Value creation in buyer—Seller relationships: Theoretical considerations and empirical results from a supplier's perspective. *Industrial Marketing Management, 30*(4), 365–377.

Waters, M. C. (1990). *Ethnic options choosing identities in America*. Berkeley: University of California Press.

Wealth, X. (2015). State of ultra high net worth value market, luxury insight summit, prepared by L. Raynault.

Weierter, S. J. (2001). The organization of charisma: Promoting, creating, and idealizing self. *Organization Studies, 22*(1), 91–115.

Weinstein, A. (1987). *Market segmentation: Using demographics, psychographics, and other segmentation techniques to uncover and exploit new markets*. Irwin Professional Publishing.

West, C., & Zimmerman, D. H. (1987). Doing gender. *Gender and Society, 1*(2), 125–151.

Wheeler, L. (1966). Motivation as a determinant of upward comparison. *Journal of Experimental Social Psychology, 1*, 27–31.

Whitehead, A. N. (1978). *Process and reality* (Corrected ed.). New York, NY: The Free Press.

Wiedmann, K. P., Hennigs, N., & Siebels, A. (2009). Value-based segmentation of luxury consumption behavior. *Psychology & Marketing, 26*(7), 625–651.

Wiggins, D. (1998). Weakness of will, commensurability, and the objects of deliberation and desire. In *Needs, values, truth: Essays in the philosophy of value* (3rd ed.). Oxford: Oxford University Press.

Wiktor, J. W. (2013). *Komunikacja marketingowa: Modele, struktury, formy przekazu*. Warszawa: PWN.

Wilcox, K., Kim, H. M., & Sen, S. (2009). Why do consumers buy counterfeit luxury brands? *Journal of Marketing Research, 46*(2), 247–259.

Willems, K., Janssens, W., Swinnen, G., Brengman, M., Streukens, S., & Vancauteren, M. (2012). From Armani to Zara: Impression formation based on fashion store patronage. *Journal of Business Research, 65*(10), 1487–1494.

Williams, R. (2005). *Culture and materialism: Selected essays (No. 11).* London, New York: Verso.

Wills, T. A. (1981). Downward comparison principles in social psychology. *Psychological Bulletin, 90,* 245–271.

Wind, Y. J., & Green, P. E. (2011). In William D. Wells (Ed.), *Some conceptual, measurement, and analytical problems in life style research.* Chicago: American Marketing Association.

Wong, A. C. Y., & Zaichkowsky, J. L. (1999). Understanding luxury brands in Hong Kong. *ACR European Advances.*

Wojtyna, A. (2008). Współczesna ekonomia-kontynuacja czy poszukiwanie paradygmatu? *Ekonomista, 1,* 9–32.

Wong, A., Chung, Y., & Zaichkowsky, J. L. (1999). Understanding luxury brands in Hong Kong. *European Advances in Consumer Research, 4,* 310–316.

Wong, N. Y., & Ahuvia, A. C. (1998). Personal taste and family face: Luxury consumption in Confucian and Western societies. *Psychology & Marketing, 15*(5), 423–441.

Wood, J. V. (1989). Theory and research concerning social comparisons of personal attributes. *Psychological Bulletin, 106*(2), 231–248. https://doi.org/10.1037/0033-2909.106.2.231.

Woodall, T. (2003). Conceptualising "value for the customer": An attributional, structural and dispositional analysis. *Academy of Marketing Science Review, 12,* 1–42.

Wooding, C. (2016, June 27). *Cannes Lions: Virtual reality is the new luxury game-changer*. Retrieved from https://www.luxurydaily.com/cannes-lions-virtual-reality-is-the-new-luxury-game-changer/.

Woodruff, R. B. (1997). Customer value: The next source for competitive advantage. *Journal of the Academy of Marketing Science, 25,* 139–153.

Woodruff, R. B., & Gardial, F. S. (1996). *Know your customer: New approaches to understanding customer value and satisfaction.* Cambridge, MA: Blackwell.

Workman, J. E., & Lee, S. H. (2011). Vanity and public self-consciousness: A comparison of fashion consumer groups and gender. *International Journal of Consumer Studies, 35*(3), 307–315.

Worsley, P. (1984). *The three worlds: Culture and world development*. Chicago: University of Chicago Press.
Wu, M. S. S., Chaney, I., Chen, C. H. S., Nguyen, B., & Melewar, T. C. (2015). Luxury fashion brands: Factors influencing young female consumers' luxury fashion purchasing in Taiwan. *Qualitative Market Research: An International Journal, 18*(3), 298–319.
Xiao, H. (2000). Class, gender, and parental values in the 1990s. *Gender & Society, 14,* 785–803.
Yang, K. S. (1998). Chinese responses to modernization: A psychological analysis. *Asian Journal of Social Psychology, 1,* 75–97.
Yang, Y., Han, H., & Lee, P. (2017). An exploratory study of the mechanism of sustainable value creation in the luxury fashion industry. *Sustainability, 9*(4), 483. https://doi.org/10.3390/su9040483.
Yang, Z., & Peterson, R. T. (2004). Customer perceived value, satisfaction, and loyalty: The role of switching costs. *Psychology & Marketing, 21*(10), 799–822.
Yeoman, I., & McMahon-Beattie, U. (2006). Luxury markets and premium pricing. *Journal of Revenue & Pricing Management, 4,* 319–328.
Yep, G. A. (1998). My three cultures: Navigating the multicultural identity landscape. In J. Martin, T. Nakayama, & L. Flores (Eds.), *Readings in cultural contexts* (s. 79–85). Mayfield: Mountain View.
Yi, Y., & Gong, T. (2013). Customer value co-creation behavior: Scale development and validation. *Journal of Business Research, 66*(9), 1279–1284.
Young, K., & Mack, R. W. (1959). *Sociology and social life*. New York: American Book Company.
Zajonc, R. B. (1980). Feeling and thinking: Preferences need no inferences. *American Psychologist, 35*(2), 151.
Zajonc, R. B., & Markus, H. (1982). Affective and cognitive factors in preferences. *Journal of Consumer Research, 9*(2), 123–131.
Zalega, T. (2013). Nowe trendy i makrotrendy w zachowaniach konsumenckich gospodarstw domowych w XXI. *Konsumpcja i rozwój, 2,* 3–21.
Zauner, A., Koller, M., & Hatak, I. (2015). Customer perceived value—Conceptualization and avenues for future research. *Cogent Psychology, 2*(1), 1–17.
Zboroń, H. (2009). *Teorie ekonomiczne w perspektywie poznawczej konstruktywizmu społecznego*. Poznań: Wydawnictwo Uniwersytetu Ekonomicznego w Poznaniu.

Zeithaml, V. A. (1988). Consumer perceptions of price, quality, and value: A means-end model and synthesis of evidence. *The Journal of Marketing, 52,* 2–22.

Zhan, L., & He, Y. (2012). Understanding luxury consumption in China: Consumer perceptions of best-known brands. *Journal of Business Research, 65*(10), 1452–1460.

Zimbardo, P. G., & Ruch, F. L. (1999). *Psychologia i życie*. Warszawa: PWN.

Znaniecki, F. (1910). *Zagadnienie wartości w filozofii*. Wydawnictwo Przeglądu Filozoficznego.

Zubac, A., Hubbard, G., & Johnson, L. W. (2009). The RBV and value creation: A managerial perspective. *European Business Review, 22*(5), 515–538.

Zucker, L. G. (1977). The role of institutionalization in cultural persistence. *American Sociological Review, 42,* 726–743.

Web Sites

http://www.economist.com/sites/default/files/20141213_sr_luxury.pdf.

http://kisses.burberry.com.

http://www.galleryintell.com/wp-content/uploads/2014/04/arnolfini-portrait-e1397099128643.jpg.

http://www.kering.com/en/sustainability.

https://data.worldbank.org/indicator/SI.POV.GINI.

https://matterofform.com/the-luxury-report/.

https://plato.stanford.edu/cite.html.

https://www.britannica.com/biographies/philosophy-religion.

https://www.ancient.eu/Tyrian_Purple/.

https://www.auto-motor-i-sport.pl/wydarzenia/Najdrozsze-opcje-wyposazenia-w-samochodach,19946,1.

https://www.bain.com/insights/eight-themes-that-are-rewriting-the-future-of-luxury-goods/.

https://www.businessinsider.com/how-herms-bags-are-made-2012-7?IR=T#many-of-the-leathers-like-this-blue-crocodile-skin-are-dyed-4.

https://www.forbes.com/sites/bernardmarr/2016/06/30/are-we-headed-for-automated-luxury-communism/#48489fec37e3.

https://www.heritage.org/international-economies/report/2017-index-economic-freedom-trade-and-prosperity-risk.

https://www.luxurydaily.com/influencer-marketing-shows-no-signs-of-slowing-shareablee/.
https://www.lvmh.com/group/lvmh-commitments/environment/.
https://www.nytimes.com/2017/08/03/business/alibaba-kering-fakes-luxury.html.
https://www.rolex.com/science-and-exploration.html.

Index

B. Stępień, *The Value of Luxury*, Palgrave Advances in Luxury,
https://doi.org/10.1007/978-3-030-51218-7

I

J

L

The manufacturer's authorised representative in the EU is Springer Nature Customer Service Centre GmbH, Europaplatz 3, 69115 Heidelberg, Germany. If you have any concerns regarding our products, please contact ProductSafety@springernature.com

Printed and bound by CPI Group (UK) Ltd, Croydon, CR0 4YY

30/09/2026

02225456-0014